Twin Star Exorcists

ONMYOJI

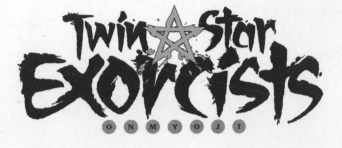

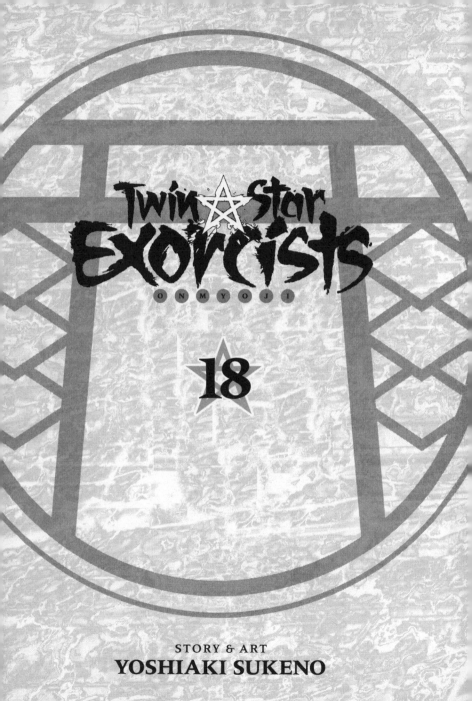

Twin★Star Exorcists
O N M Y O J I

18

STORY & ART
YOSHIAKI SUKENO

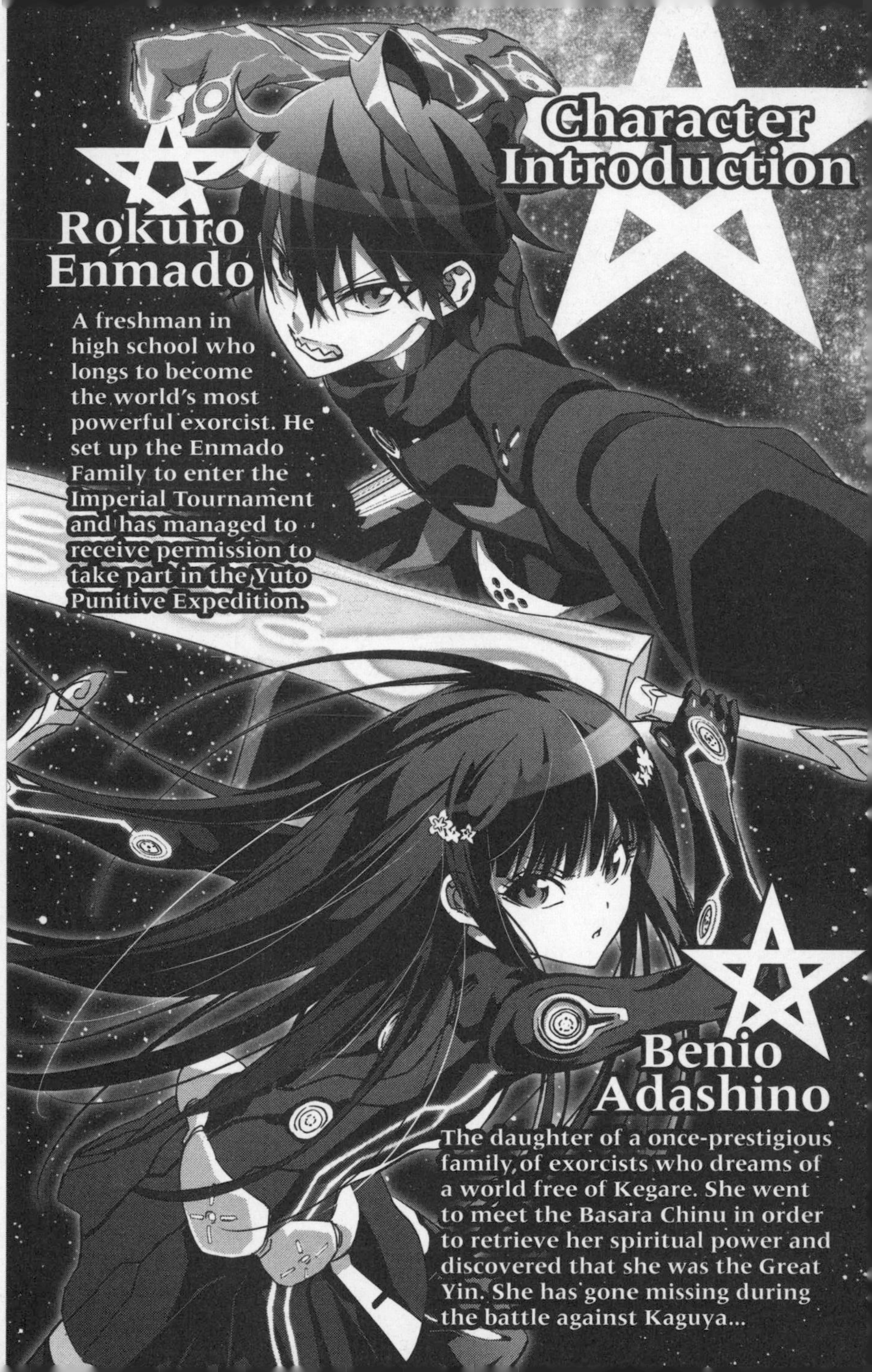
Character Introduction
Rokuro Enmado
A freshman in high school who longs to become the world's most powerful exorcist. He set up the Enmado Family to enter the Imperial Tournament and has managed to receive permission to take part in the Yuto Punitive Expedition.
Benio Adashino
The daughter of a once-prestigious family of exorcists who dreams of a world free of Kegare. She went to meet the Basara Chinu in order to retrieve her spiritual power and discovered that she was the Great Yin. She has gone missing during the battle against Kaguya...

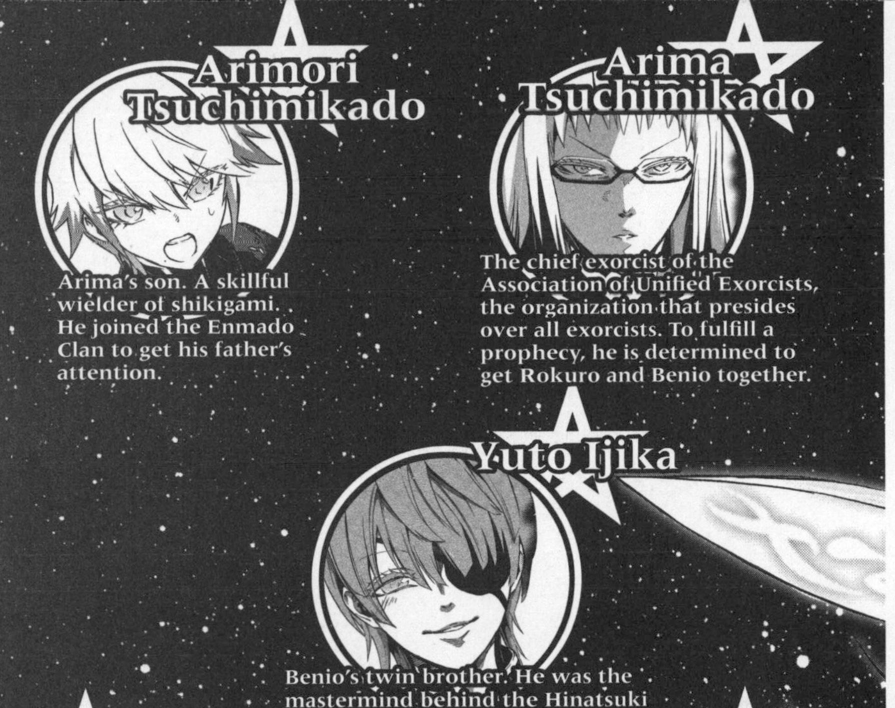
Arimori Tsuchimikado
Arima's son. A skillful wielder of shikigami. He joined the Enmado Clan to get his father's attention.
Arima Tsuchimikado
The chief exorcist of the Association of Unified Exorcists, the organization that presides over all exorcists. To fulfill a prophecy, he is determined to get Rokuro and Benio together.
Yuto Ijika
Benio's twin brother. He was the mastermind behind the Hinatsuki Tragedy and has a strong desire to fight Rokuro.
Tenma Unomiya
Twelve Guardian member God of the In-Between. Head of the Unomiya Family and said to be the most powerful exorcist. He has been under house arrest after intentionally fighting recklessly at the imperial tournament.
Sakanashi
The second-ranking Basara after Chinu. He made his appearance in this raid upon five locations at once.

Story Thus Far...

Kegare are creatures from Magano, the underworld, and it is the duty of an exorcist to hunt, exorcise and purify them. Rokuro and Benio are the Twin Star Exorcists, fated to bear the Prophesied Child who will defeat the Kegare. Their goal was to go to Tsuchimikado Island to get revenge on Yuto, the mastermind behind the Hinatsuki Tragedy and Benio's brother. After two years, Rokuro qualifies to go to the island, but Benio loses her spiritual power in battle. Rokuro heads down to the island without Benio and establishes his own Enmado Family.

Now Yuto Ijika and a gang of Basara have launched a simultaneous surprise attack in five Magano locations. It appears they are attempting to pass through into the real world and destroy Tsuchimikado Island. The exorcists who have gone to intercept them are either dead or about to be. Chief Exorcist Arima arrives to assist Rokuro and the others, but even he is struck down by Sakanashi in his Unchained form as his son, Arimori, helplessly watches... And now, the force field separating Magano from Tsuchimikado Island has dissolved...

Twin ☆ Star Exorcists

ONMYOJI

EXORCISMS

ONMYOJI have worked for the Imperial Court since the Heian era.
In addition to exorcising evil spirits, as civil servants they performed a
variety of roles, including advising nobles by foretelling the future, creating
the calendar, observing the movements of the stars, measuring time…

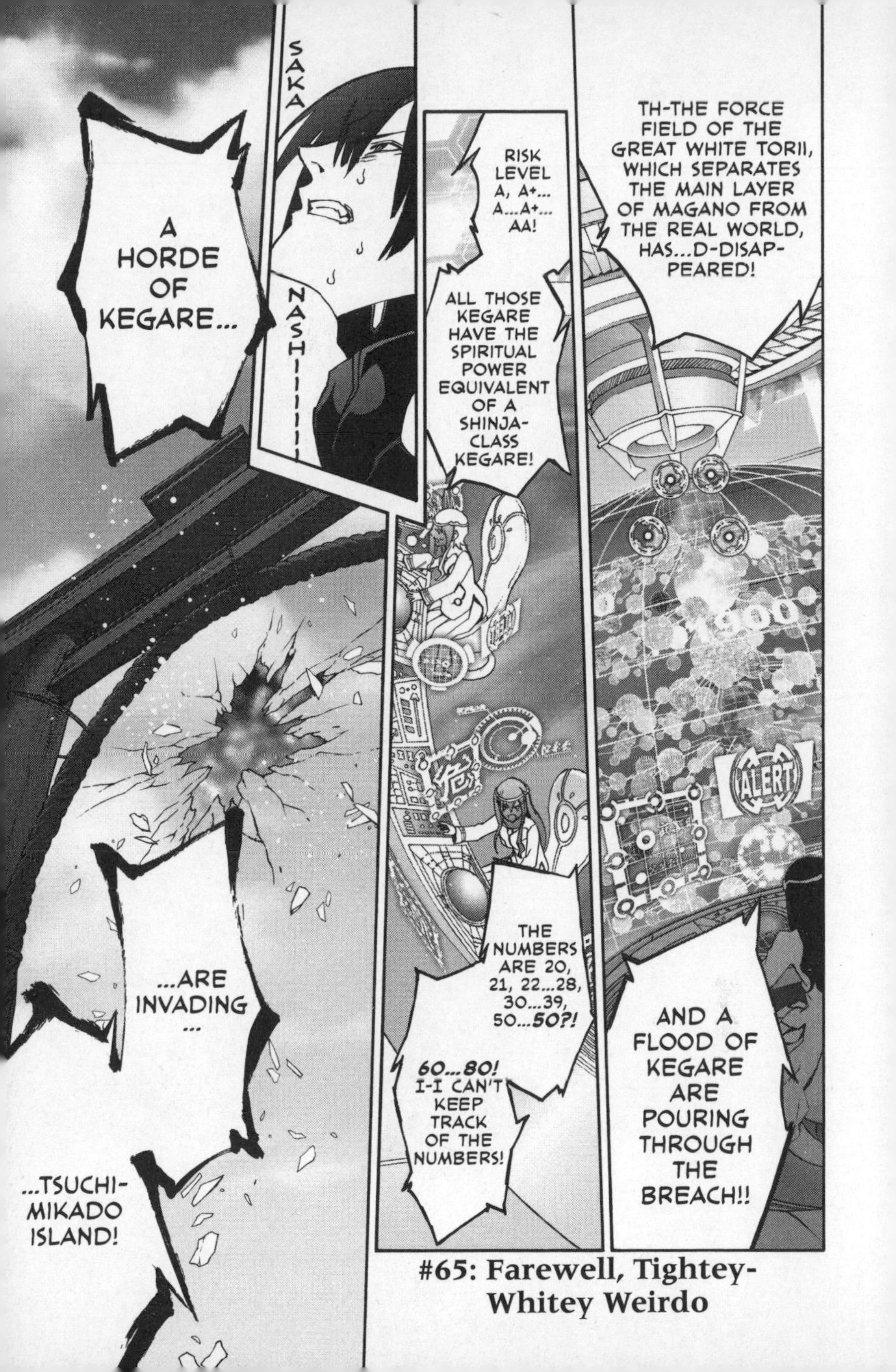
TH-THE FORCE FIELD OF THE GREAT WHITE TORII, WHICH SEPARATES THE MAIN LAYER OF MAGANO FROM THE REAL WORLD, HAS...D-DISAP-PEARED!
AND A FLOOD OF KEGARE ARE POURING THROUGH THE BREACH!!
ALERT
1900
RISK LEVEL A, A+... A...A+... AA!
ALL THOSE KEGARE HAVE THE SPIRITUAL POWER EQUIVALENT OF A SHINJA-CLASS KEGARE!
THE NUMBERS ARE 20, 21, 22...28, 30...39, 50...50?!
60...80! I-I CAN'T KEEP TRACK OF THE NUMBERS!
SAKA
NASH!!!!!!!!
A HORDE OF KEGARE...
...ARE INVADING...
...TSUCHI-MIKADO ISLAND!

#65: Farewell, Tightey-Whitey Weirdo

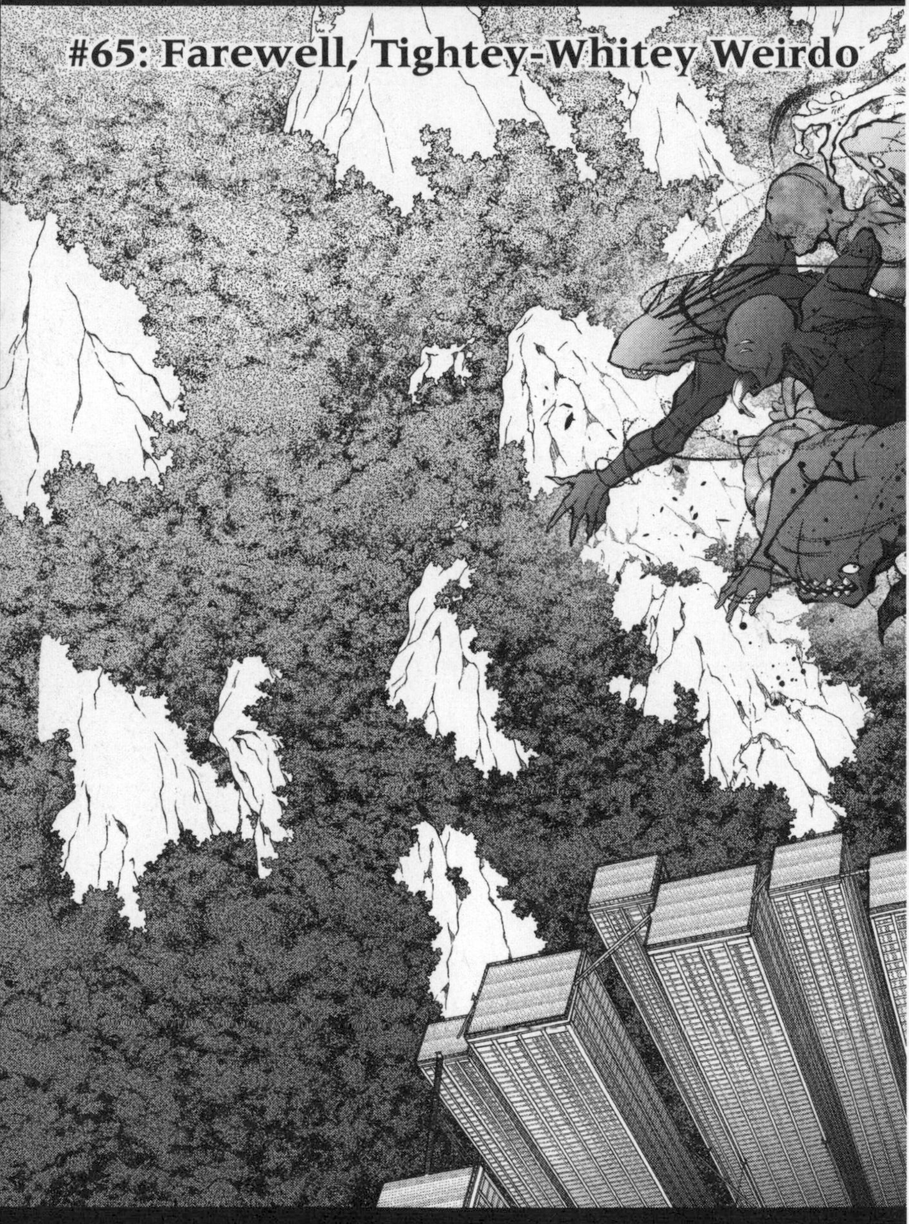
#65: Farewell, Tightey-Whitey Weirdo

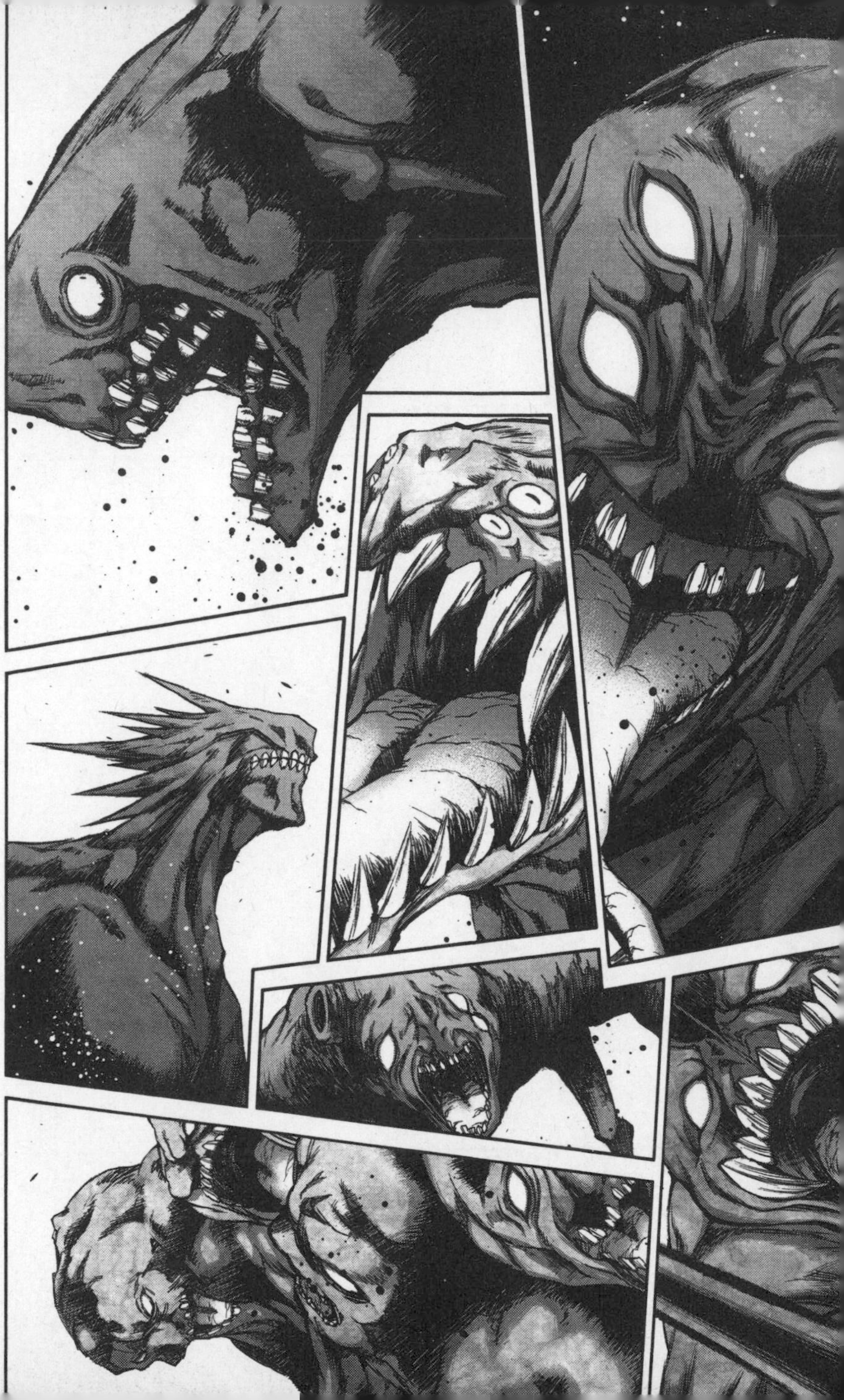

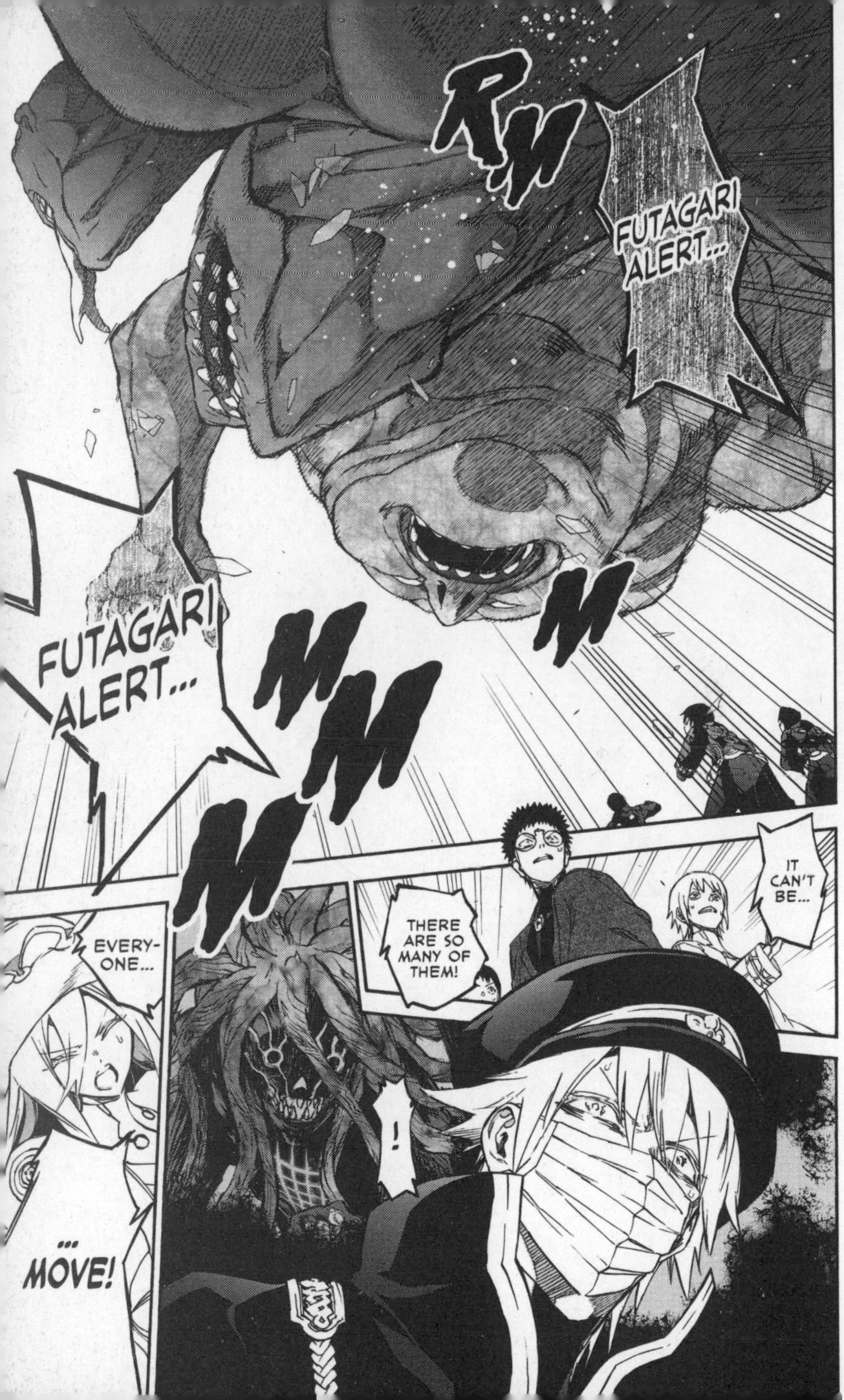
FUTAGARI ALERT...
RMMMMMM
FUTAGARI ALERT...
IT CAN'T BE...
THERE ARE SO MANY OF THEM!
EVERY-ONE...
!
...MOVE!

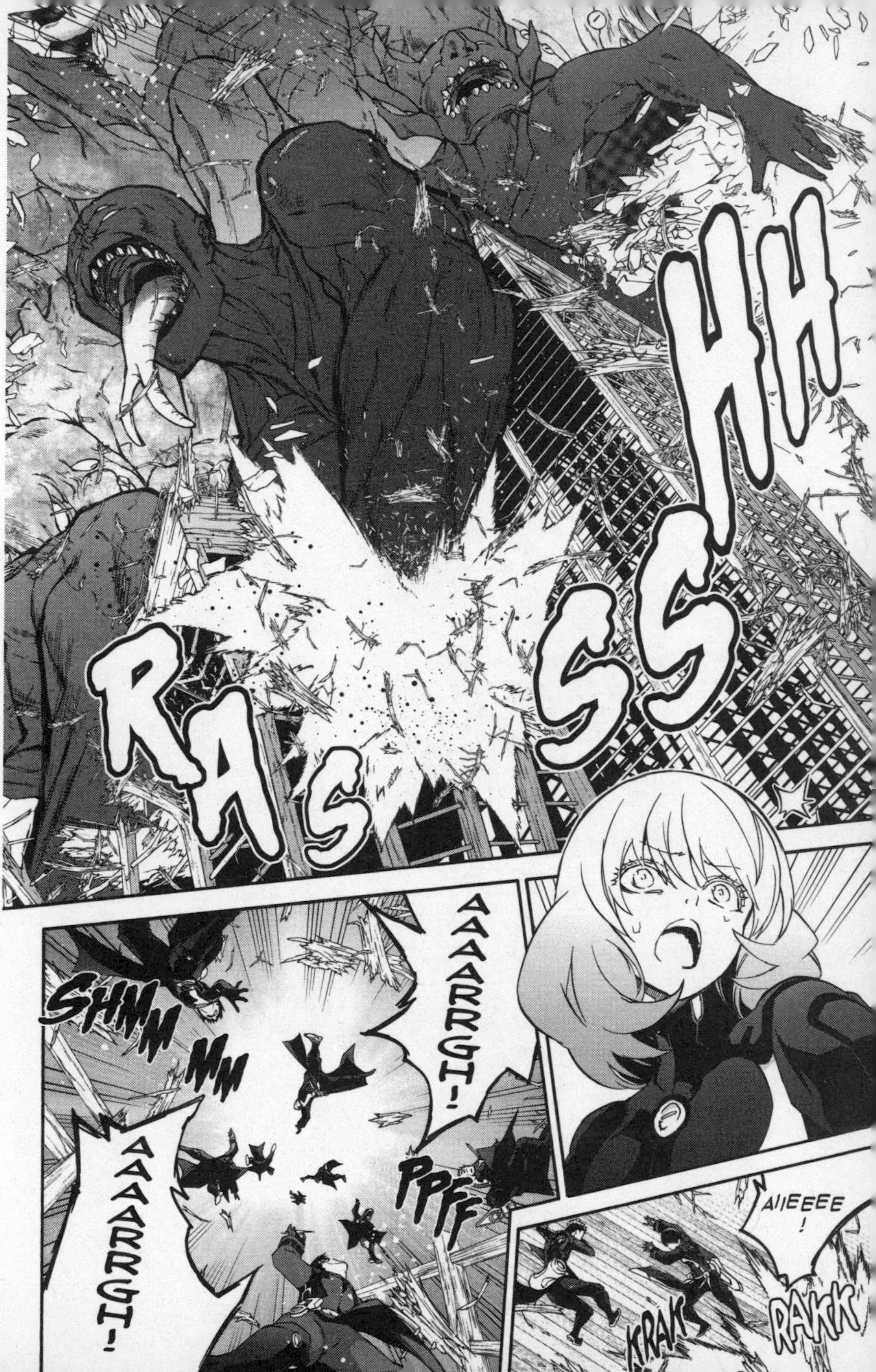
RASSSHH
AIIEEEE!
RAKK
KRAK
AAAARRGH!
PPFF
SHMMMMM
AAAARRGH!

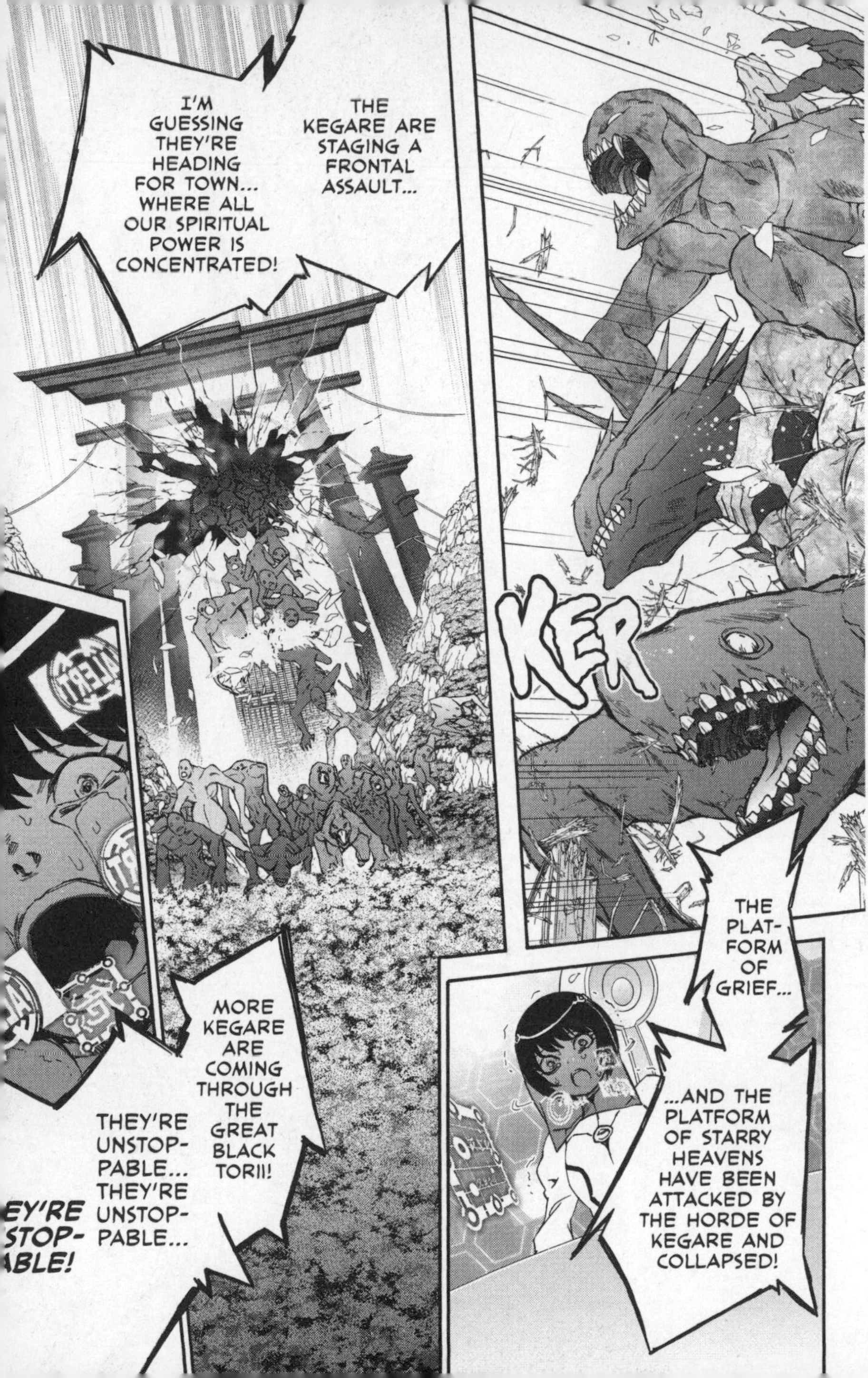
KER
THE PLATFORM OF GRIEF...
...AND THE PLATFORM OF STARRY HEAVENS HAVE BEEN ATTACKED BY THE HORDE OF KEGARE AND COLLAPSED!
THE KEGARE ARE STAGING A FRONTAL ASSAULT...
I'M GUESSING THEY'RE HEADING FOR TOWN... WHERE ALL OUR SPIRITUAL POWER IS CONCENTRATED!
MORE KEGARE ARE COMING THROUGH THE GREAT BLACK TORII!
THEY'RE UNSTOPPABLE... THEY'RE UNSTOPPABLE...
EY'RE STOP- ABLE!

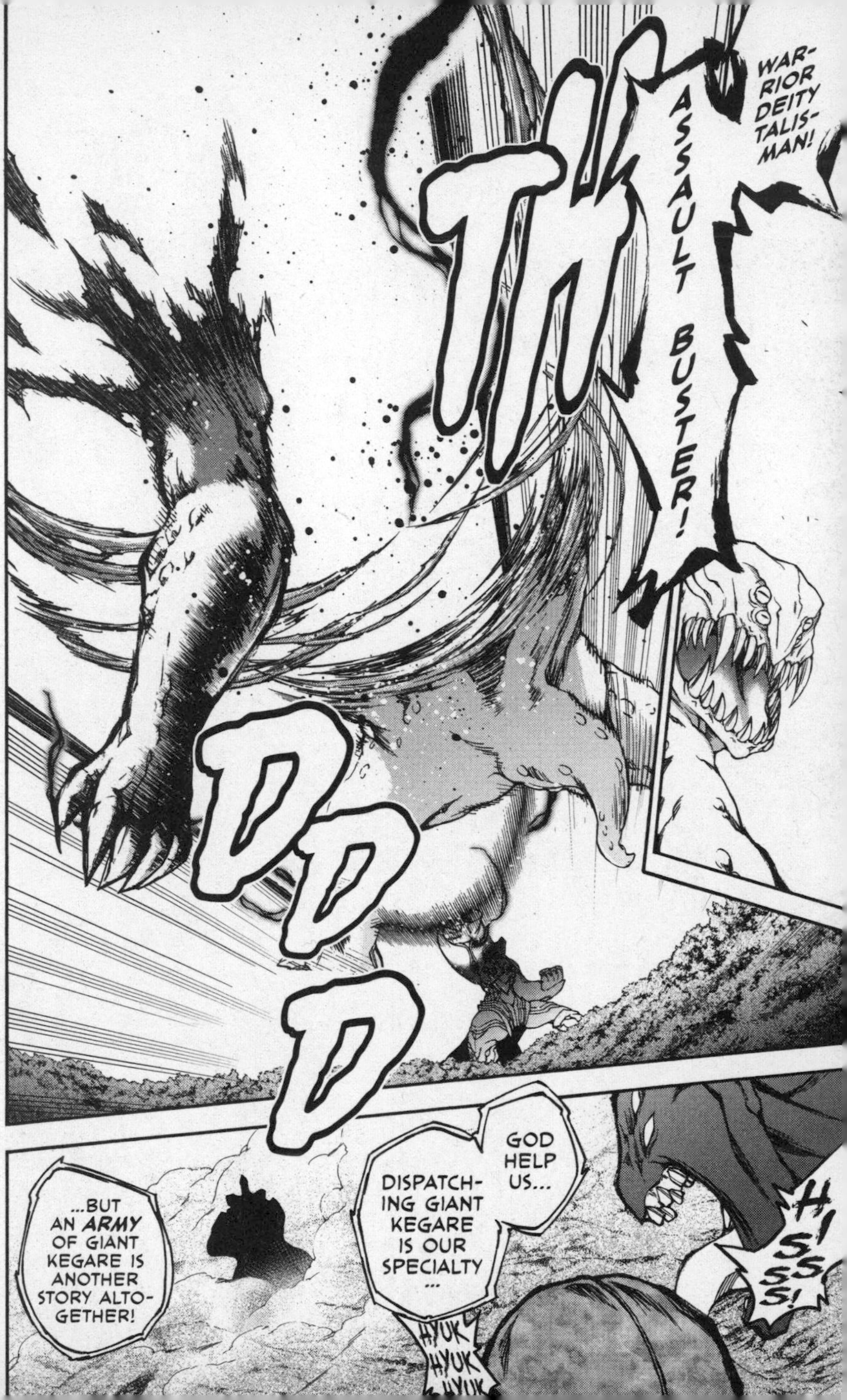
WAR-RIOR DEITY TALIS-MAN!
ASSAULT BUSTER!
DDD
HISSS!
GOD HELP US...
DISPATCH-ING GIANT KEGARE IS OUR SPECIALTY...
...BUT AN ARMY OF GIANT KEGARE IS ANOTHER STORY ALTO-GETHER!
HYUK HYUK HYUK

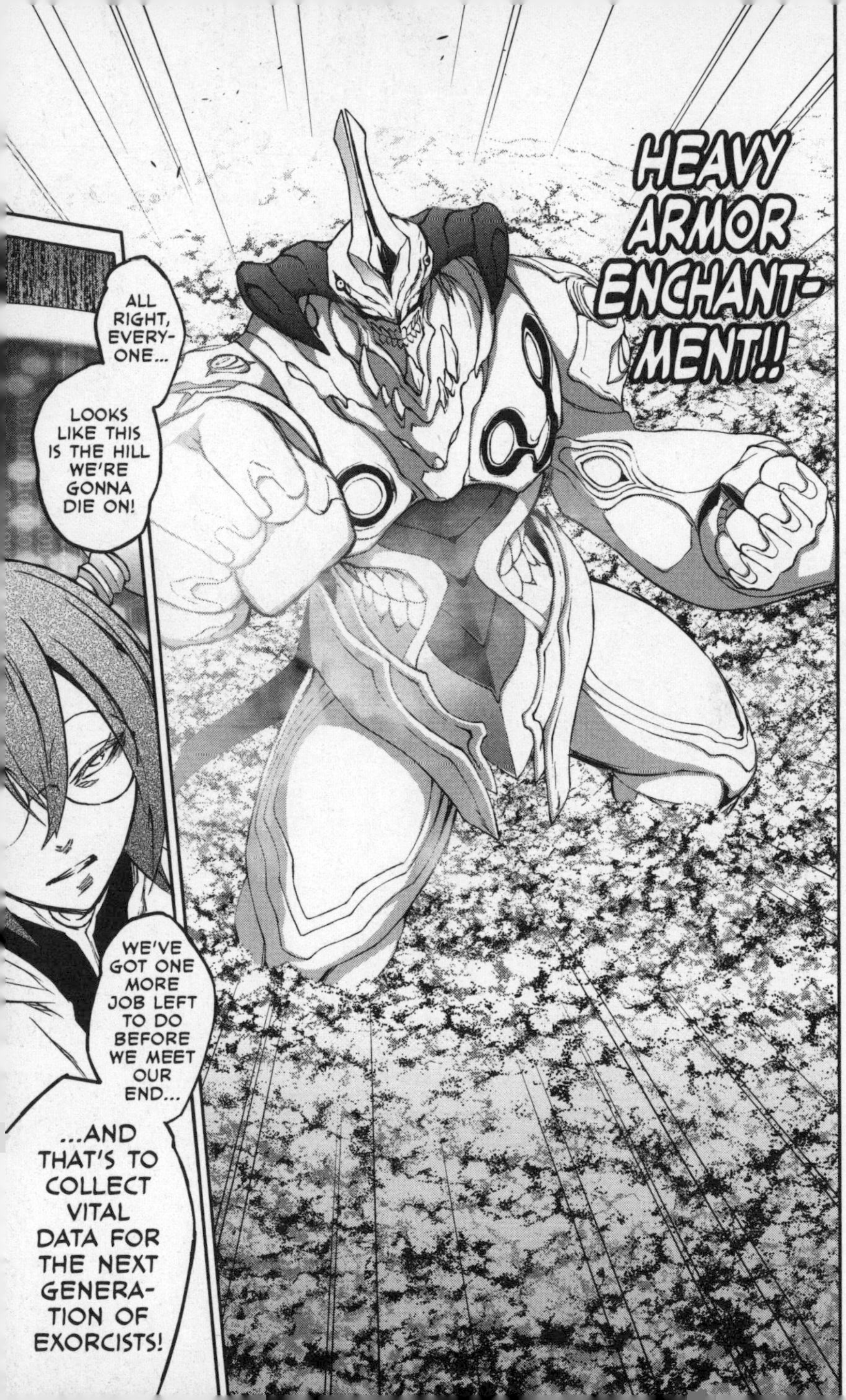
HEAVY ARMOR ENCHANT-MENT!!
ALL RIGHT, EVERY-ONE...
LOOKS LIKE THIS IS THE HILL WE'RE GONNA DIE ON!
WE'VE GOT ONE MORE JOB LEFT TO DO BEFORE WE MEET OUR END...
...AND THAT'S TO COLLECT VITAL DATA FOR THE NEXT GENERA-TION OF EXORCISTS!

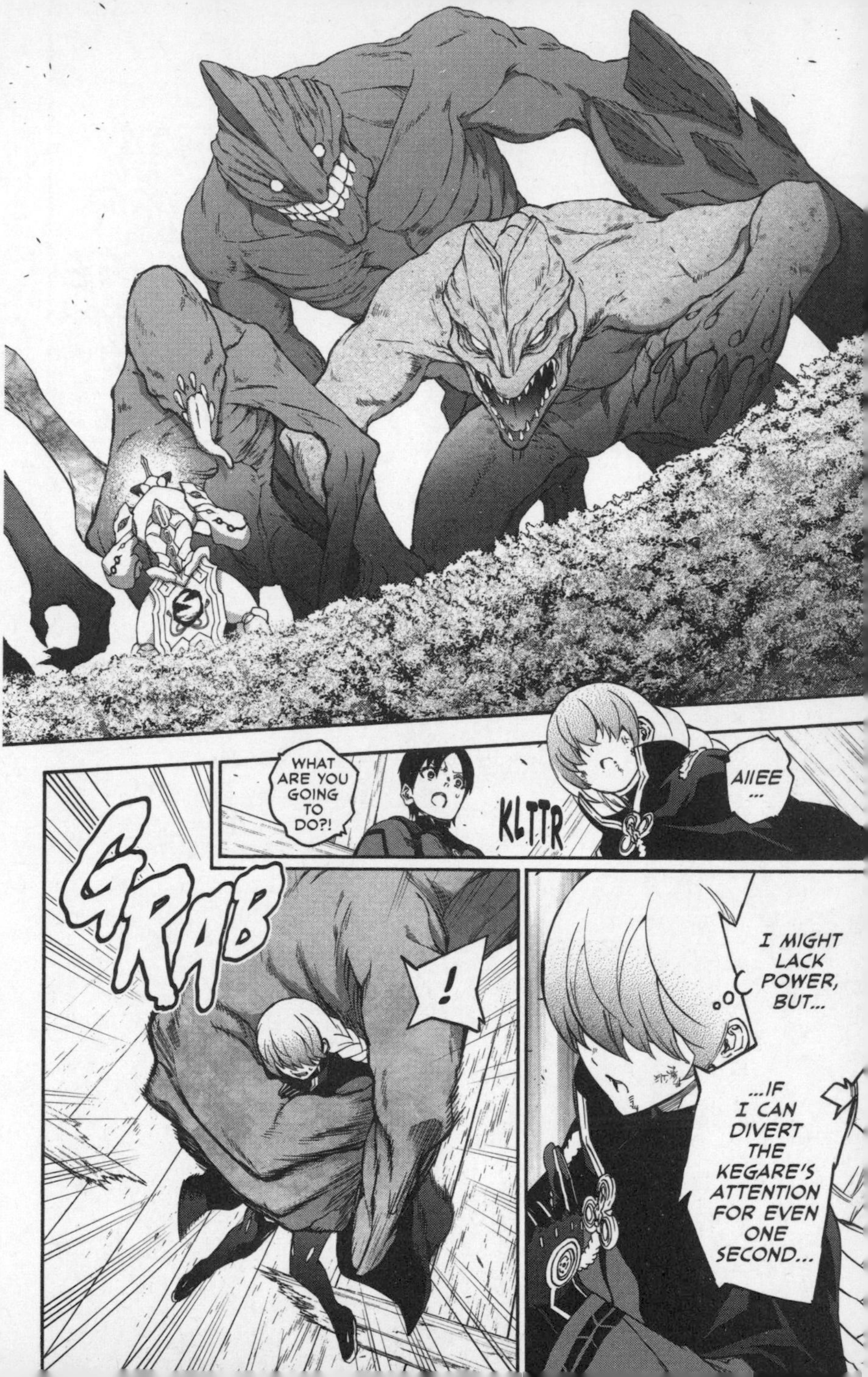
AIIEE ...
KLTTR
WHAT ARE YOU GOING TO DO?!
I MIGHT LACK POWER, BUT...
...IF I CAN DIVERT THE KEGARE'S ATTENTION FOR EVEN ONE SECOND...
GRAB
!

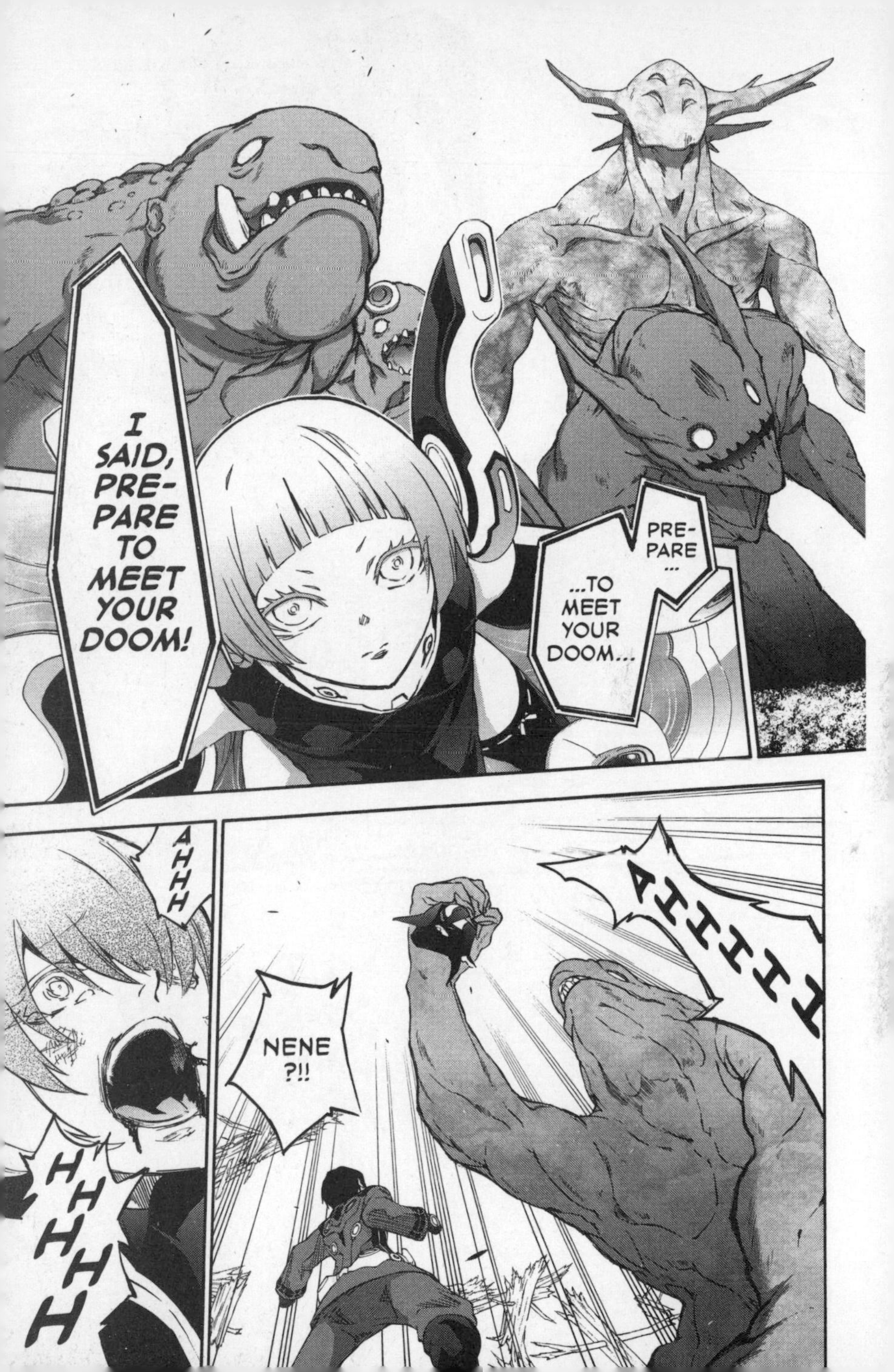
PRE-PARE...
...TO MEET YOUR DOOM...
I SAID, PRE-PARE TO MEET YOUR DOOM!
AIIIII
NENE ?!!
AHHH
HHHHHH

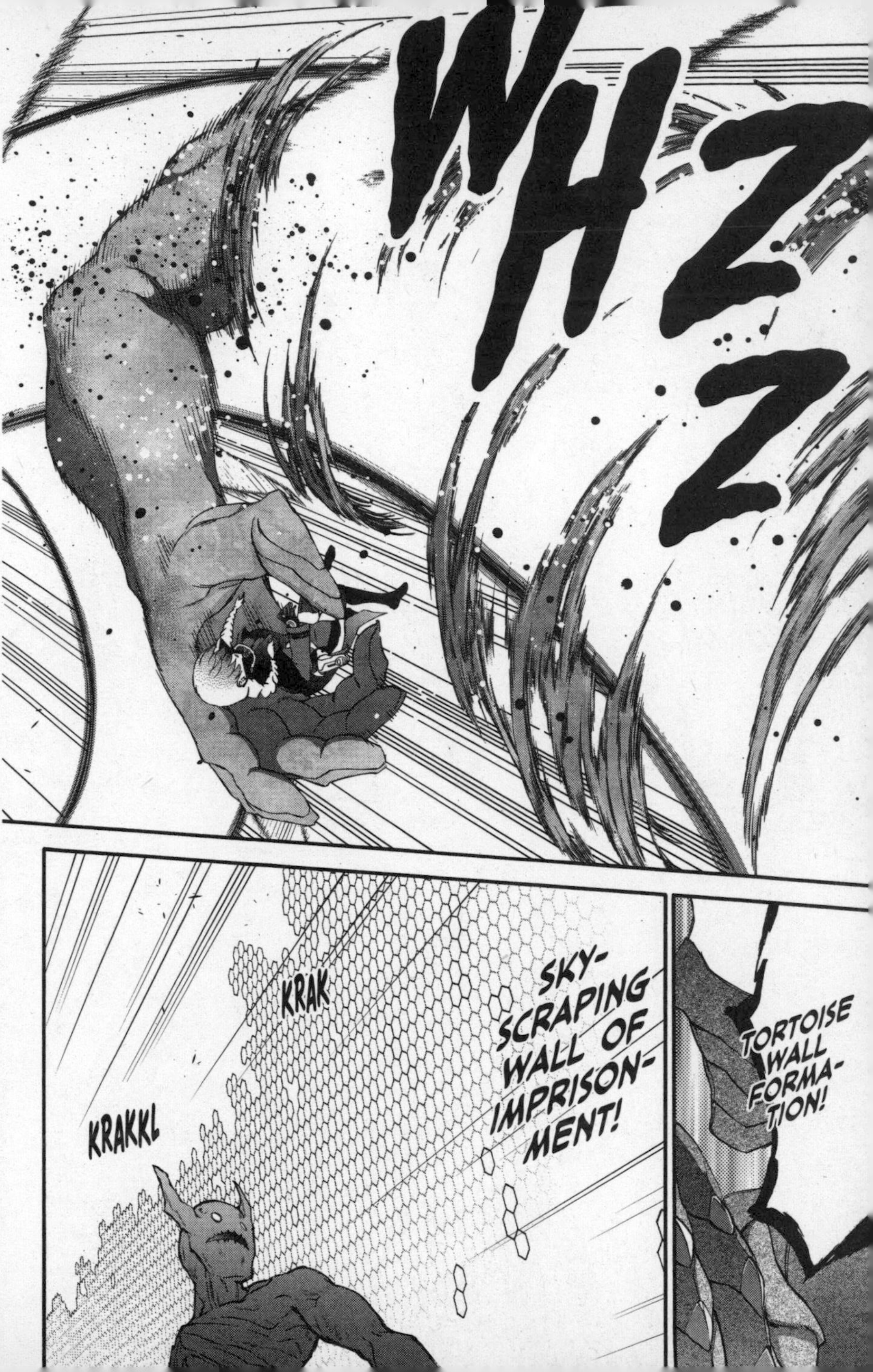
WHZZ
TORTOISE WALL FORMATION!
SKY-SCRAPING WALL OF IMPRISONMENT!
KRAK
KRAKKL

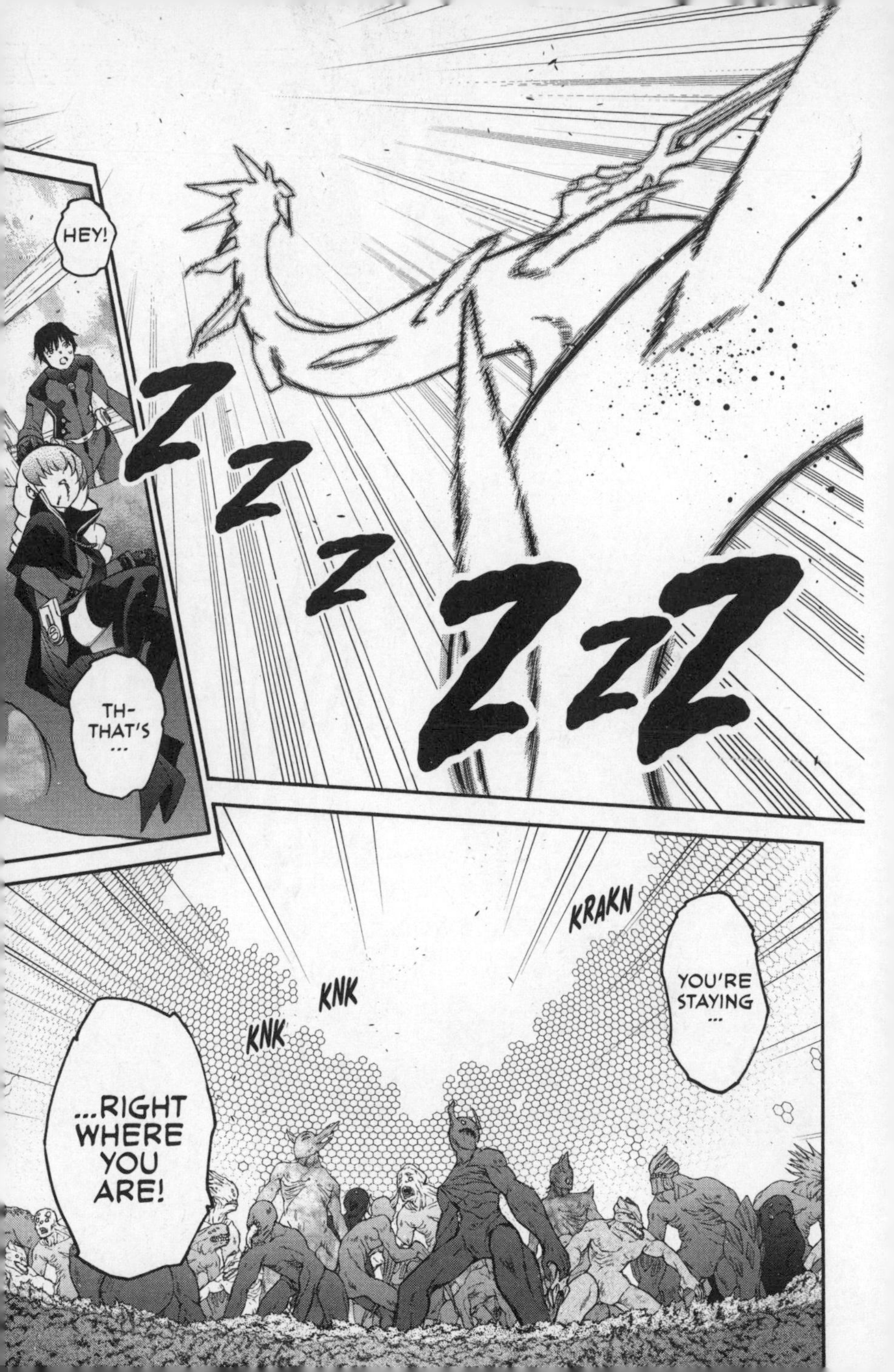
ZZZZZZ
HEY!
TH-THAT'S...
KRAKN
YOU'RE STAYING...
KNK
KNK
...RIGHT WHERE YOU ARE!

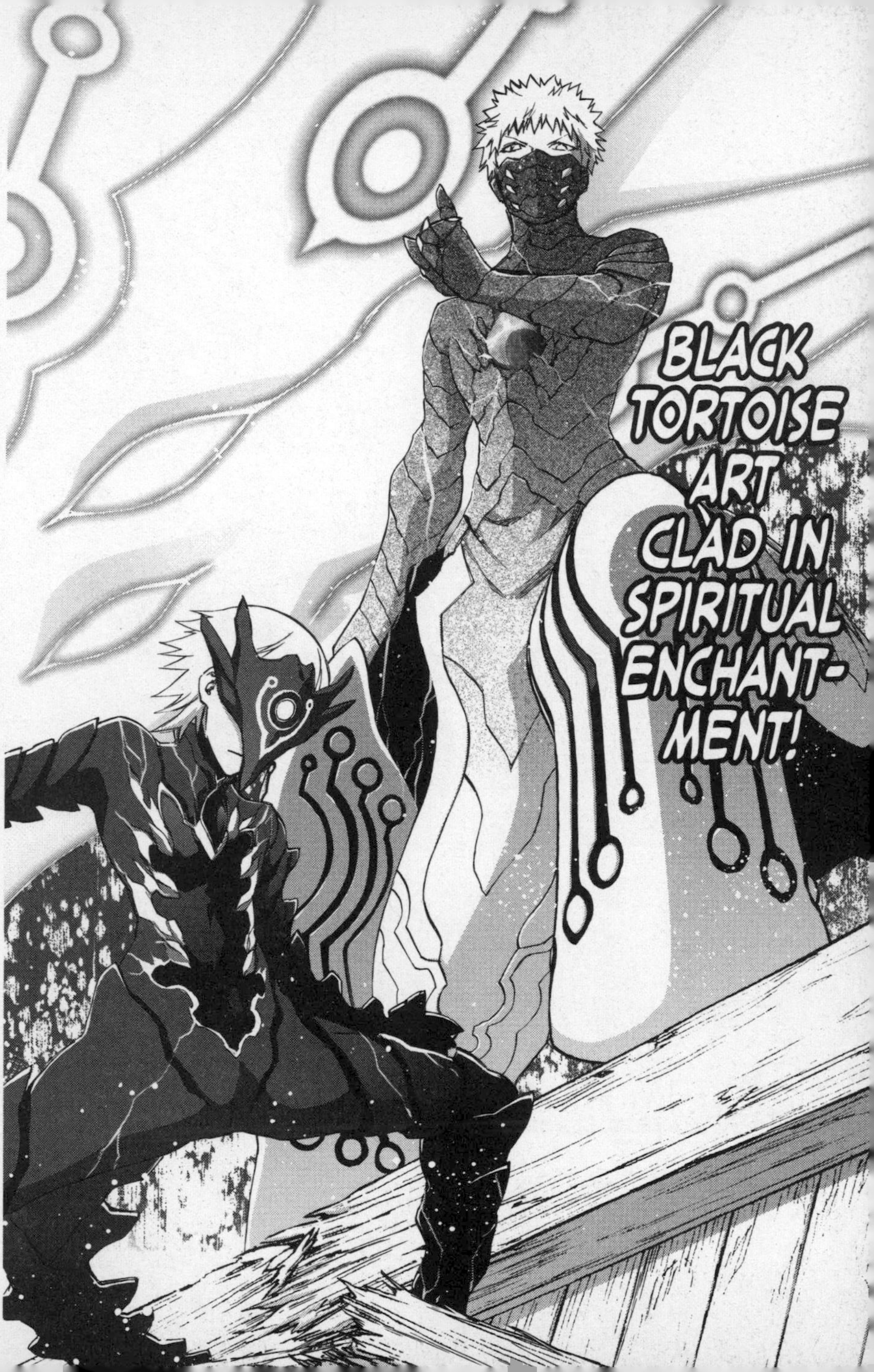
BLACK TORTOISE ART CLAD IN SPIRITUAL ENCHANT-MENT!

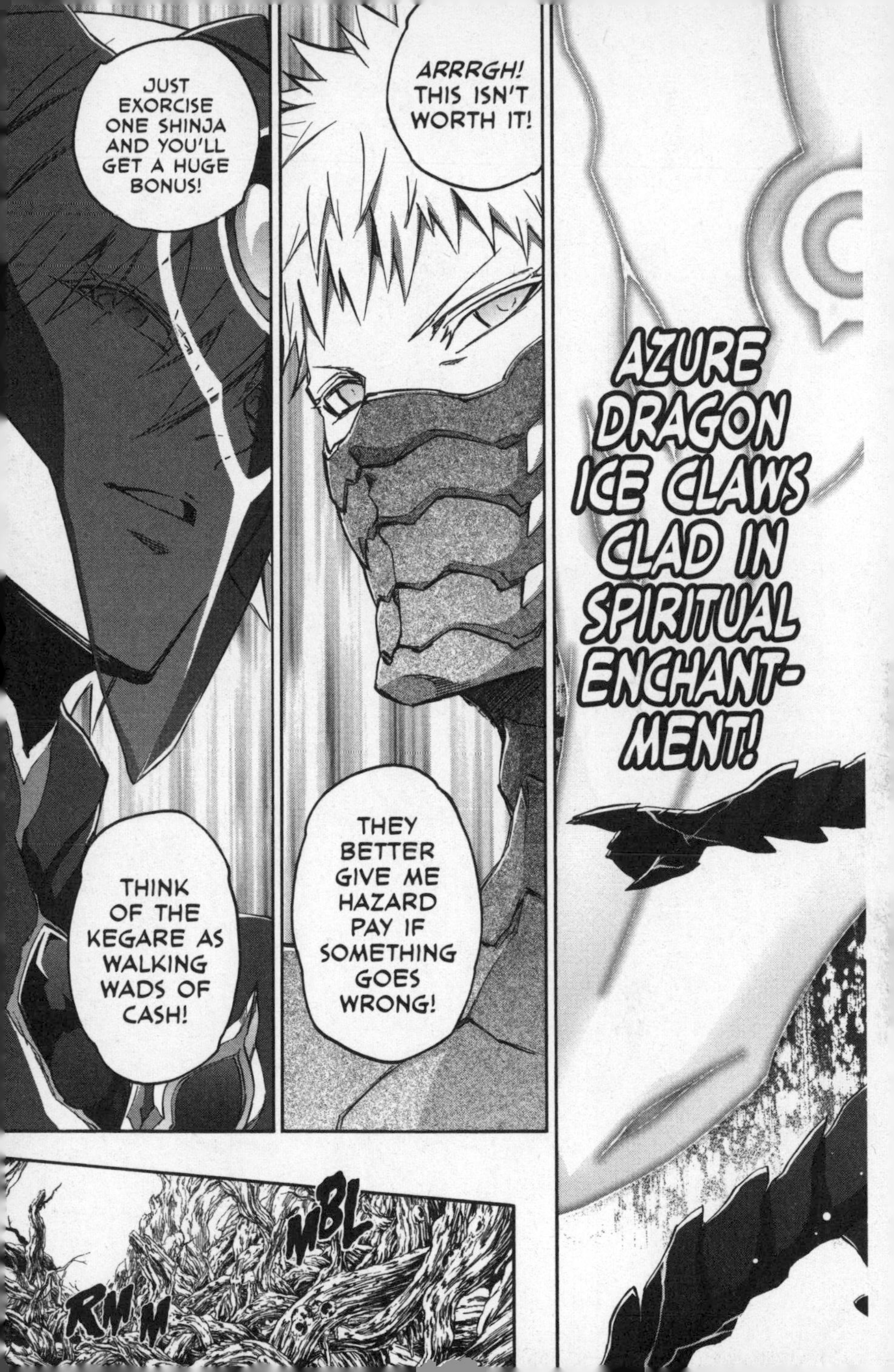
AZURE DRAGON ICE CLAWS CLAD IN SPIRITUAL ENCHANT-MENT!
ARRRGH! THIS ISN'T WORTH IT!
THEY BETTER GIVE ME HAZARD PAY IF SOMETHING GOES WRONG!
JUST EXORCISE ONE SHINJA AND YOU'LL GET A HUGE BONUS!
THINK OF THE KEGARE AS WALKING WADS OF CASH!
MBL
RMN

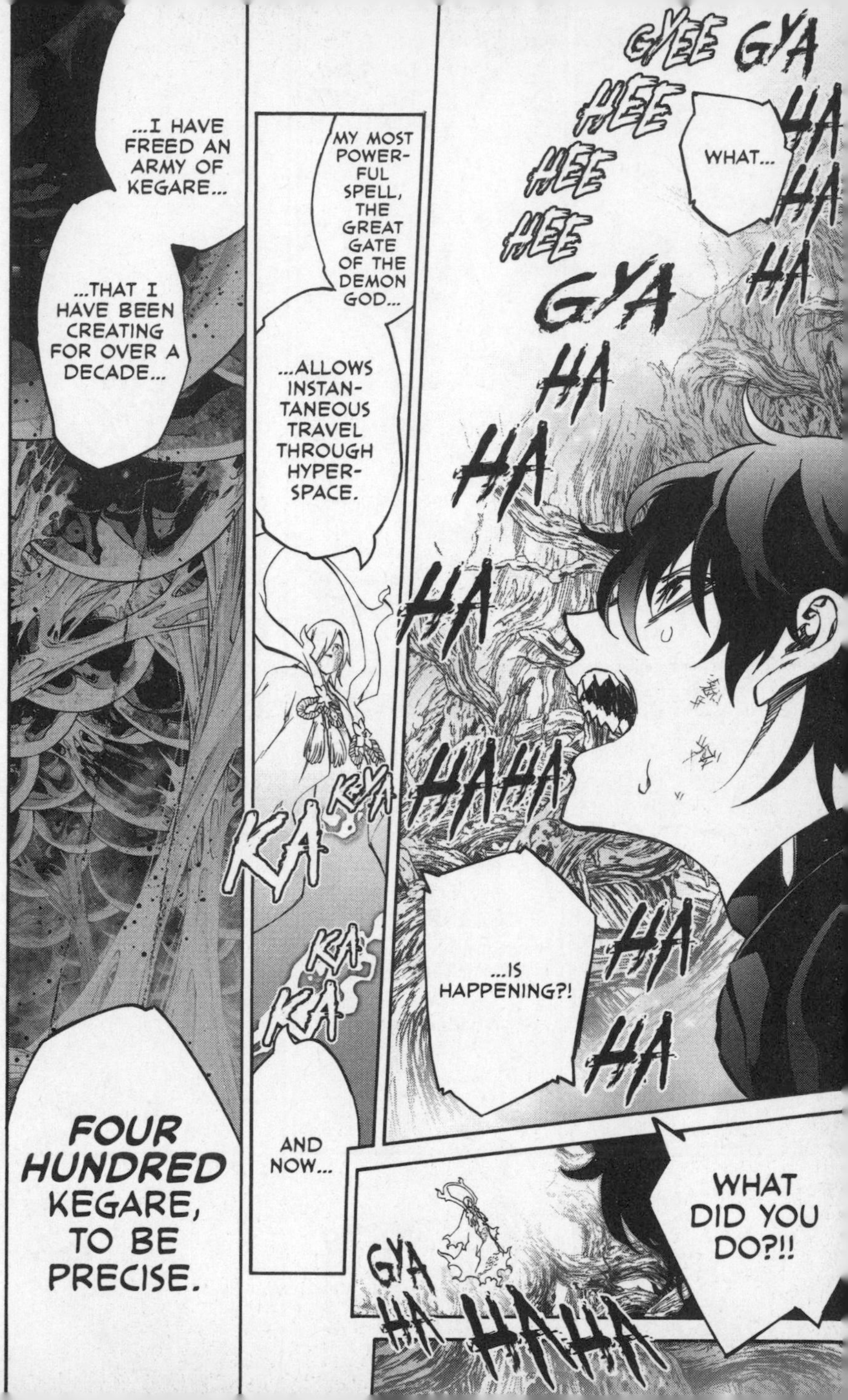
GYEE GYA
YA HA HA
HEE HEE HEE
WHAT...
GYA HA HA HA HA HAHA
...IS HAPPENING?!
HA HA
WHAT DID YOU DO?!!
GYA HA HA HAHA
MY MOST POWERFUL SPELL, THE GREAT GATE OF THE DEMON GOD...
...ALLOWS INSTANTANEOUS TRAVEL THROUGH HYPERSPACE.
KA KYA
KA KA KA
AND NOW...
...I HAVE FREED AN ARMY OF KEGARE...
...THAT I HAVE BEEN CREATING FOR OVER A DECADE...
FOUR HUNDRED KEGARE, TO BE PRECISE.

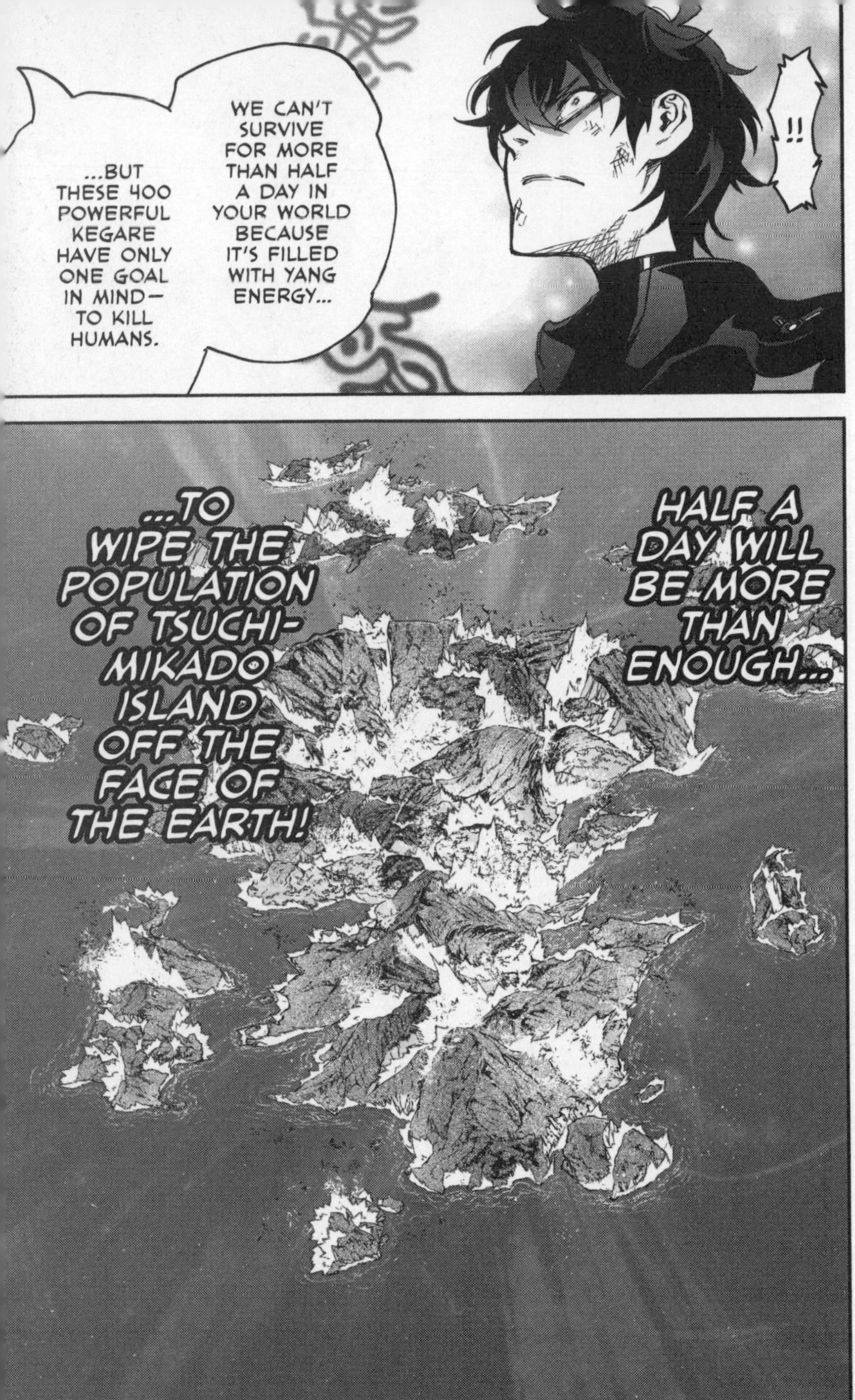
!!
WE CAN'T SURVIVE FOR MORE THAN HALF A DAY IN YOUR WORLD BECAUSE IT'S FILLED WITH YANG ENERGY...
...BUT THESE 400 POWERFUL KEGARE HAVE ONLY ONE GOAL IN MIND— TO KILL HUMANS.
HALF A DAY WILL BE MORE THAN ENOUGH...
...TO WIPE THE POPULATION OF TSUCHI-MIKADO ISLAND OFF THE FACE OF THE EARTH!

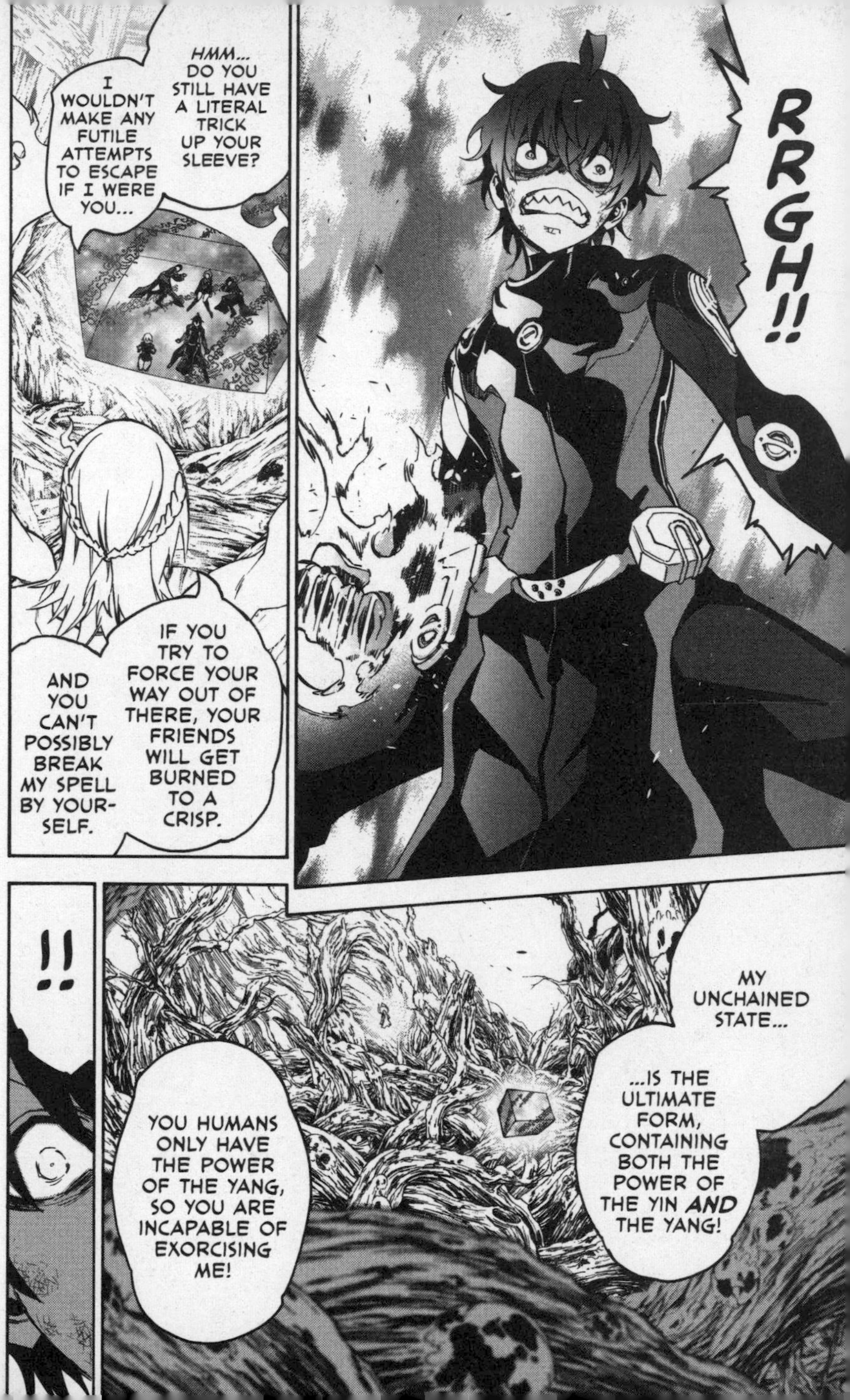
RRGH!!
HMM... DO YOU STILL HAVE A LITERAL TRICK UP YOUR SLEEVE?
I WOULDN'T MAKE ANY FUTILE ATTEMPTS TO ESCAPE IF I WERE YOU...
IF YOU TRY TO FORCE YOUR WAY OUT OF THERE, YOUR FRIENDS WILL GET BURNED TO A CRISP.
AND YOU CAN'T POSSIBLY BREAK MY SPELL BY YOUR-SELF.
MY UNCHAINED STATE...
...IS THE ULTIMATE FORM, CONTAINING BOTH THE POWER OF THE YIN *AND* THE YANG!
YOU HUMANS ONLY HAVE THE POWER OF THE YANG, SO YOU ARE INCAPABLE OF EXORCISING ME!
!!

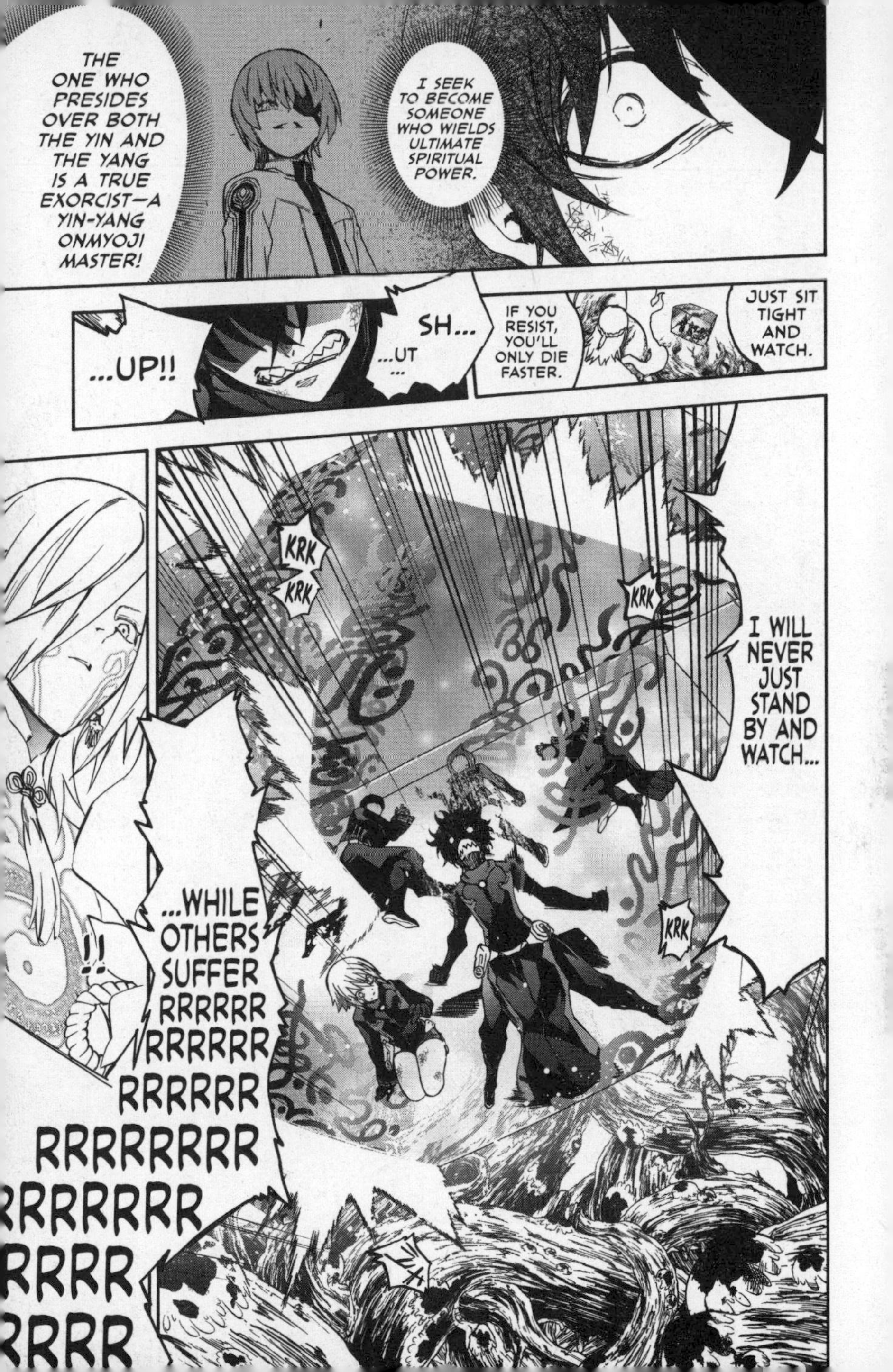
I SEEK TO BECOME SOMEONE WHO WIELDS ULTIMATE SPIRITUAL POWER.
THE ONE WHO PRESIDES OVER BOTH THE YIN AND THE YANG IS A TRUE EXORCIST—A YIN-YANG ONMYOJI MASTER!
JUST SIT TIGHT AND WATCH.
IF YOU RESIST, YOU'LL ONLY DIE FASTER.
SH...
...UT...
...UP!!
I WILL NEVER JUST STAND BY AND WATCH...
KRK
KRK
KRK
KRK
...WHILE OTHERS SUFFER RRRRRR RRRRRR RRRRRR RRRRRRRR RRRRRRR RRRR RRRR
!!

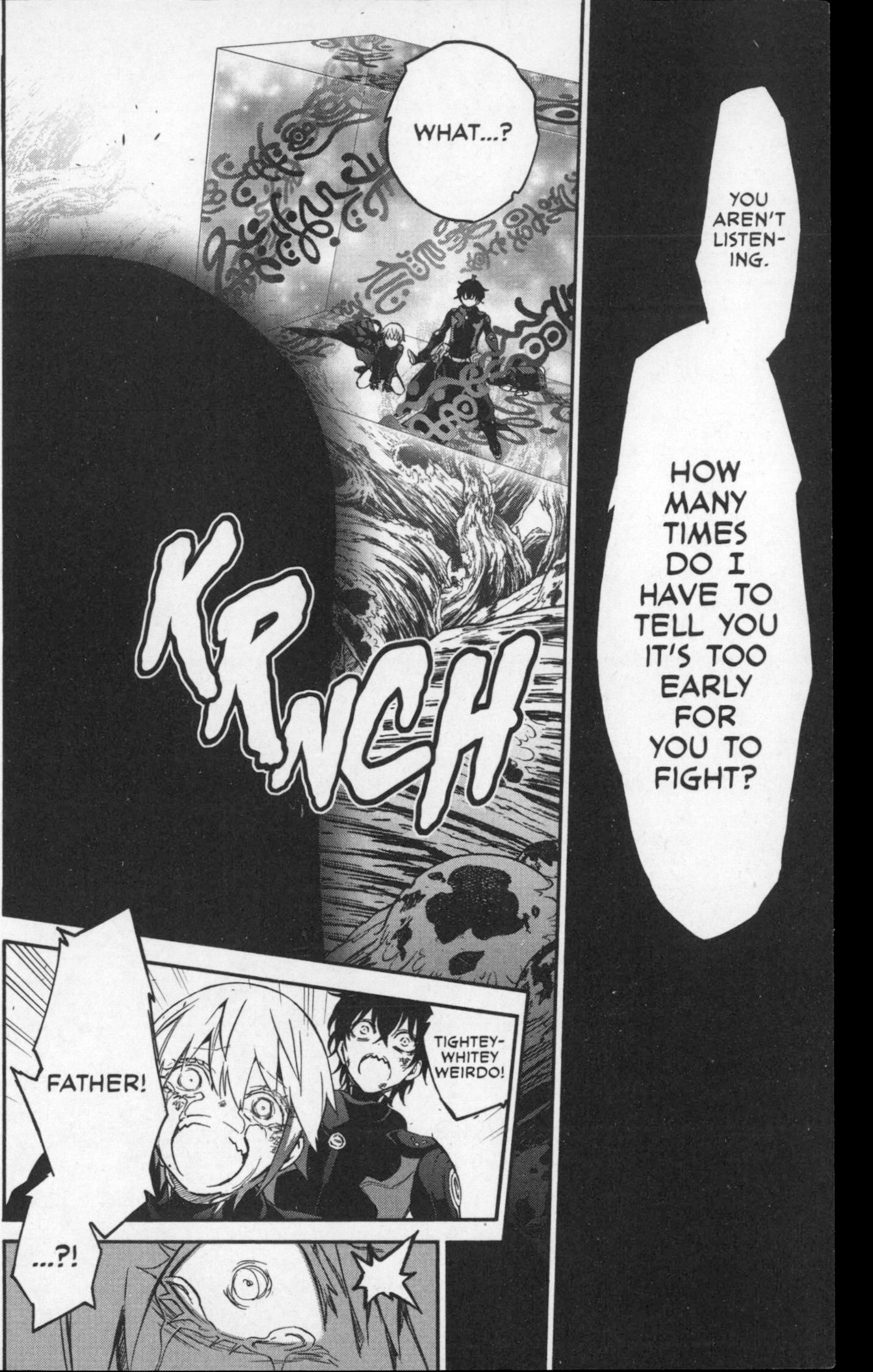
YOU AREN'T LISTENING.
HOW MANY TIMES DO I HAVE TO TELL YOU IT'S TOO EARLY FOR YOU TO FIGHT?
WHAT...?
KRNCH
TIGHTEY-WHITEY WEIRDO!
FATHER!
...?!

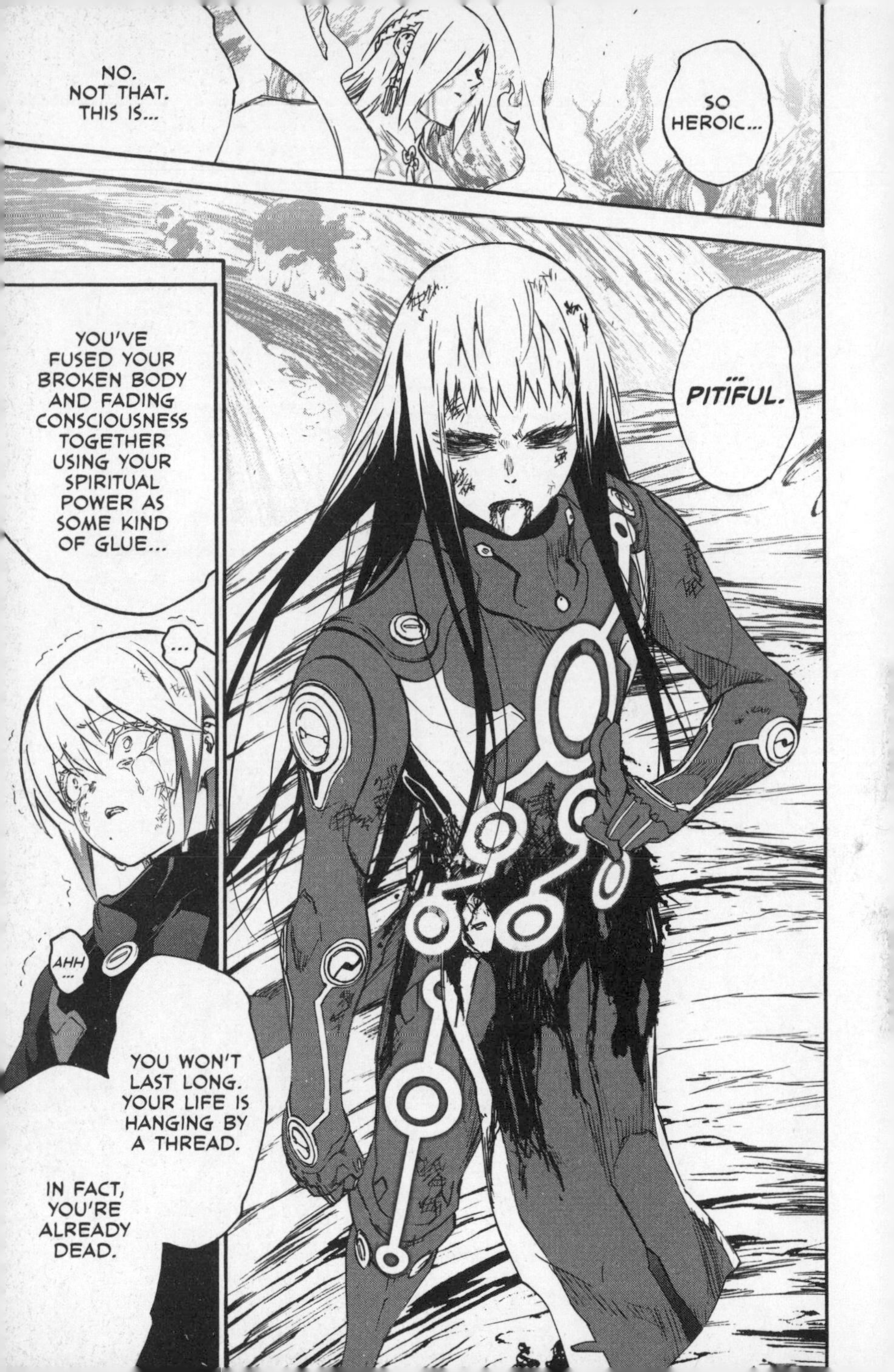
SO HEROIC...
NO. NOT THAT. THIS IS...
...PITIFUL.
YOU'VE FUSED YOUR BROKEN BODY AND FADING CONSCIOUSNESS TOGETHER USING YOUR SPIRITUAL POWER AS SOME KIND OF GLUE...
...
AHH...
YOU WON'T LAST LONG. YOUR LIFE IS HANGING BY A THREAD.
IN FACT, YOU'RE ALREADY DEAD.

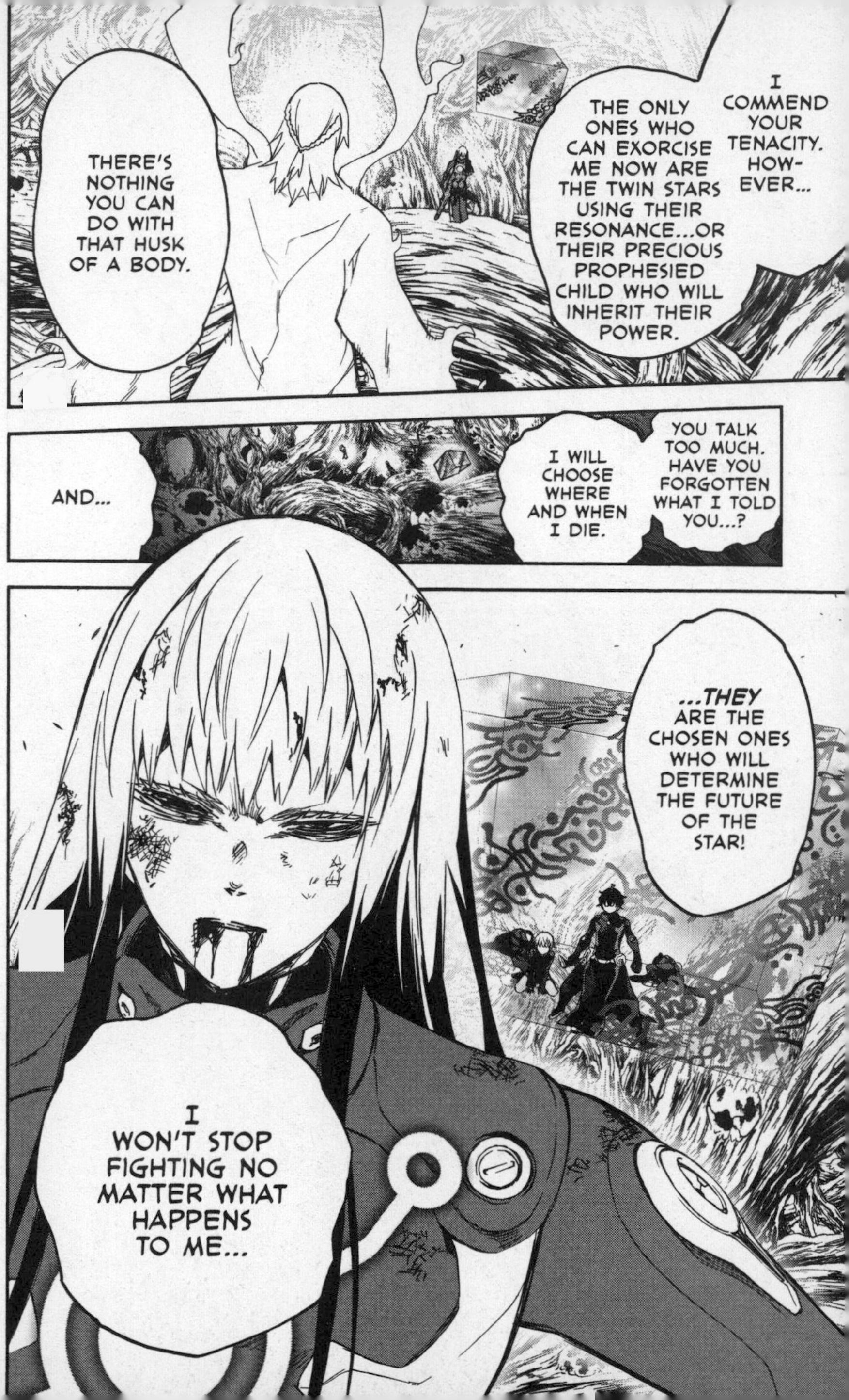
I COMMEND YOUR TENACITY. HOW-EVER...
THE ONLY ONES WHO CAN EXORCISE ME NOW ARE THE TWIN STARS USING THEIR RESONANCE...OR THEIR PRECIOUS PROPHESIED CHILD WHO WILL INHERIT THEIR POWER.
THERE'S NOTHING YOU CAN DO WITH THAT HUSK OF A BODY.
YOU TALK TOO MUCH. HAVE YOU FORGOTTEN WHAT I TOLD YOU...?
I WILL CHOOSE WHERE AND WHEN I DIE.
AND...
...*THEY* ARE THE CHOSEN ONES WHO WILL DETERMINE THE FUTURE OF THE STAR!
I WON'T STOP FIGHTING NO MATTER WHAT HAPPENS TO ME...

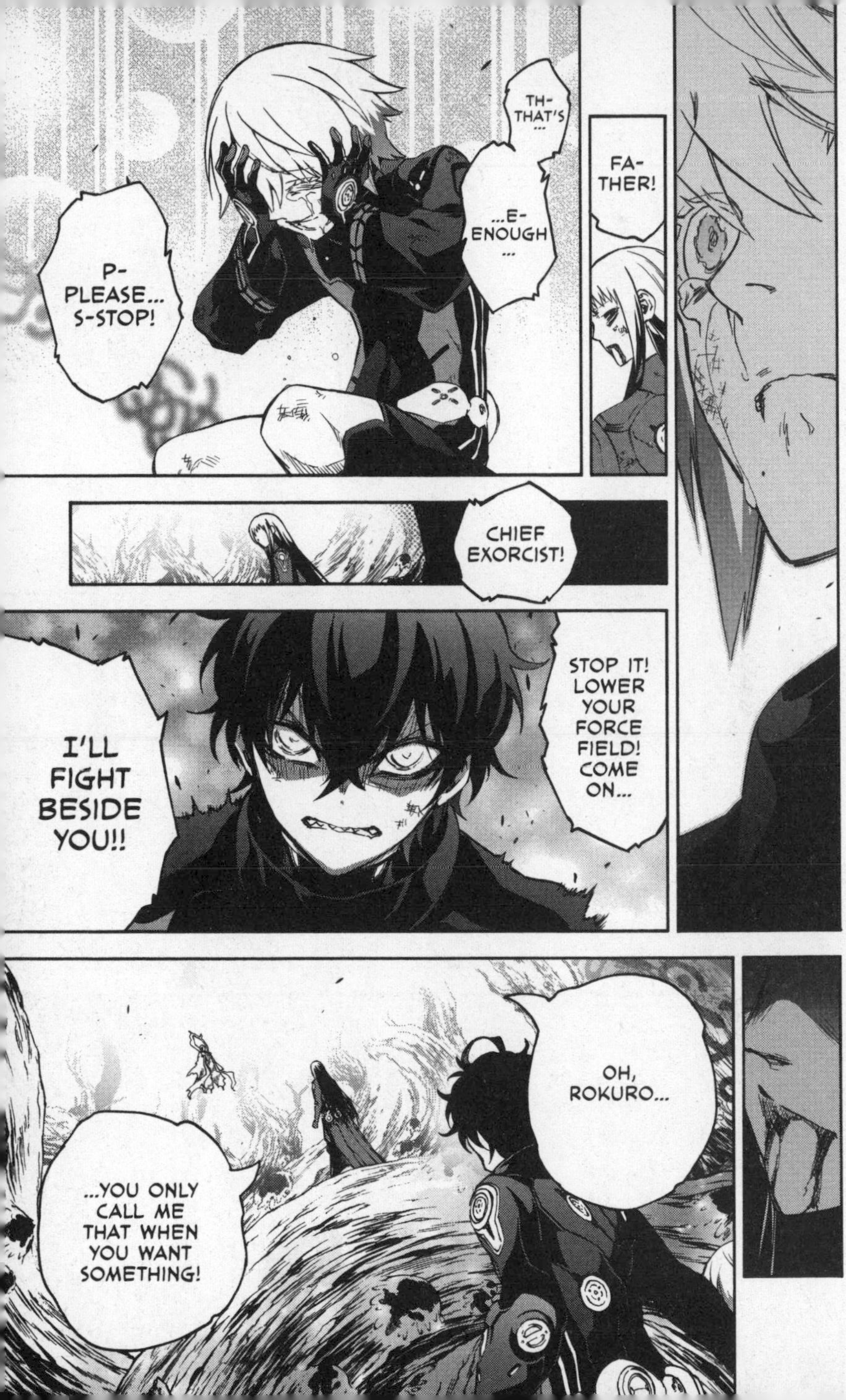

FA-THER!
TH-THAT'S...
...E-ENOUGH...
P-PLEASE... S-STOP!
CHIEF EXORCIST!
STOP IT! LOWER YOUR FORCE FIELD! COME ON...
I'LL FIGHT BESIDE YOU!!
OH, ROKURO...
...YOU ONLY CALL ME THAT WHEN YOU WANT SOMETHING!

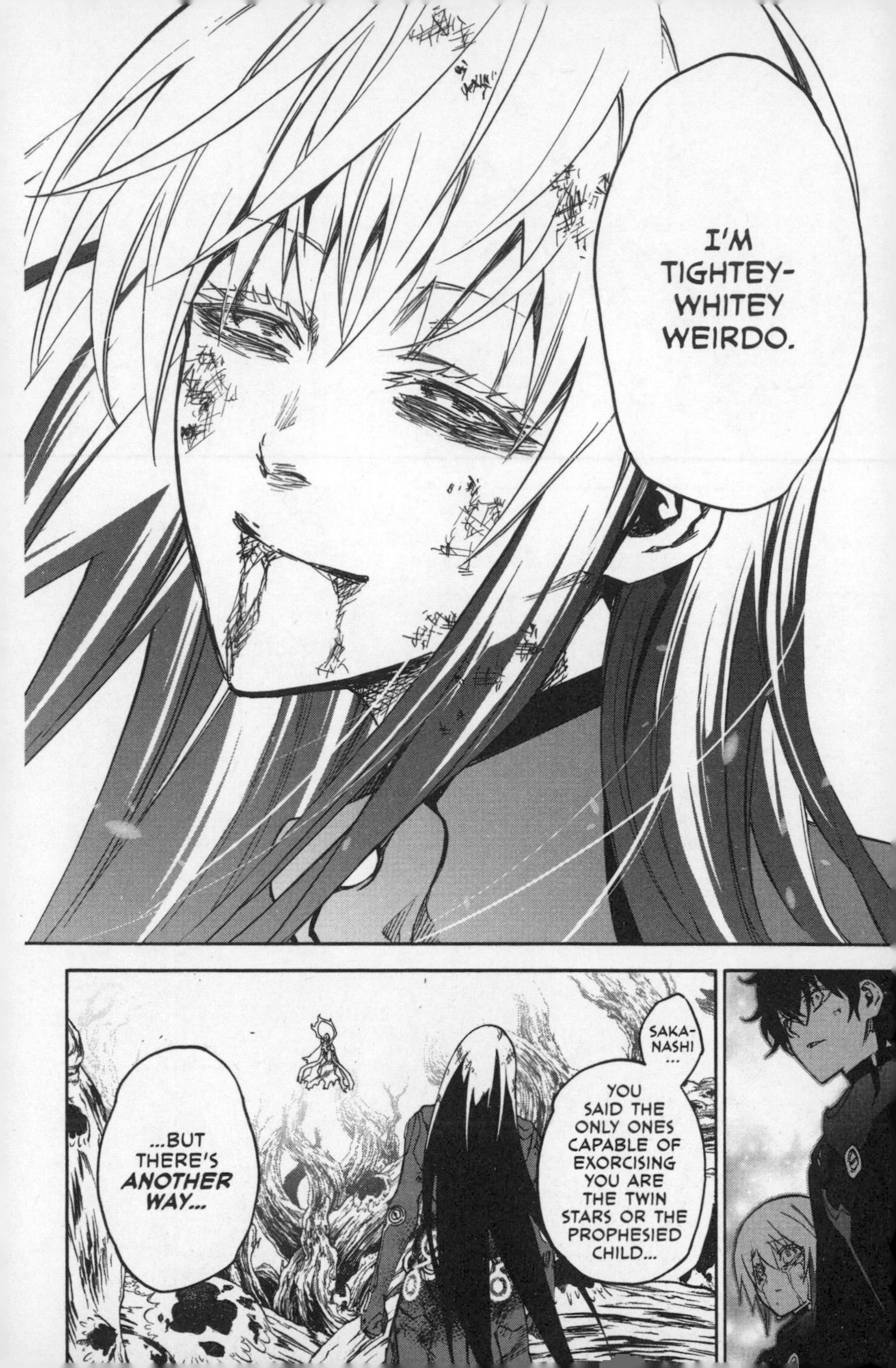
I'M TIGHTEY-WHITEY WEIRDO.
SAKA-NASHI...
YOU SAID THE ONLY ONES CAPABLE OF EXORCISING YOU ARE THE TWIN STARS OR THE PROPHESIED CHILD...
...BUT THERE'S ***ANOTHER WAY...***

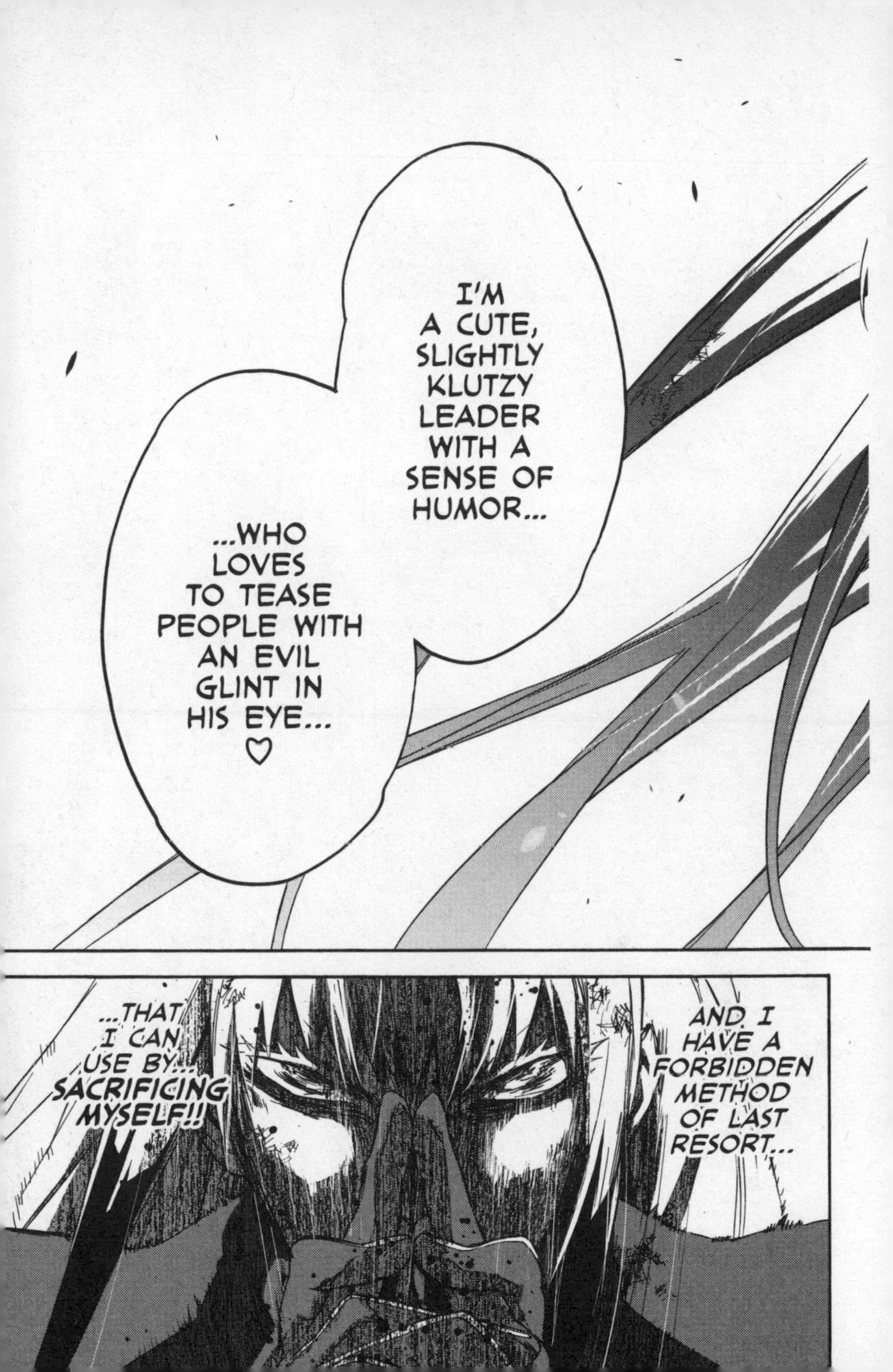
I'M A CUTE, SLIGHTLY KLUTZY LEADER WITH A SENSE OF HUMOR...
...WHO LOVES TO TEASE PEOPLE WITH AN EVIL GLINT IN HIS EYE... ♡
AND I HAVE A FORBIDDEN METHOD OF LAST RESORT...
...THAT I CAN USE BY... SACRIFICING MYSELF!!

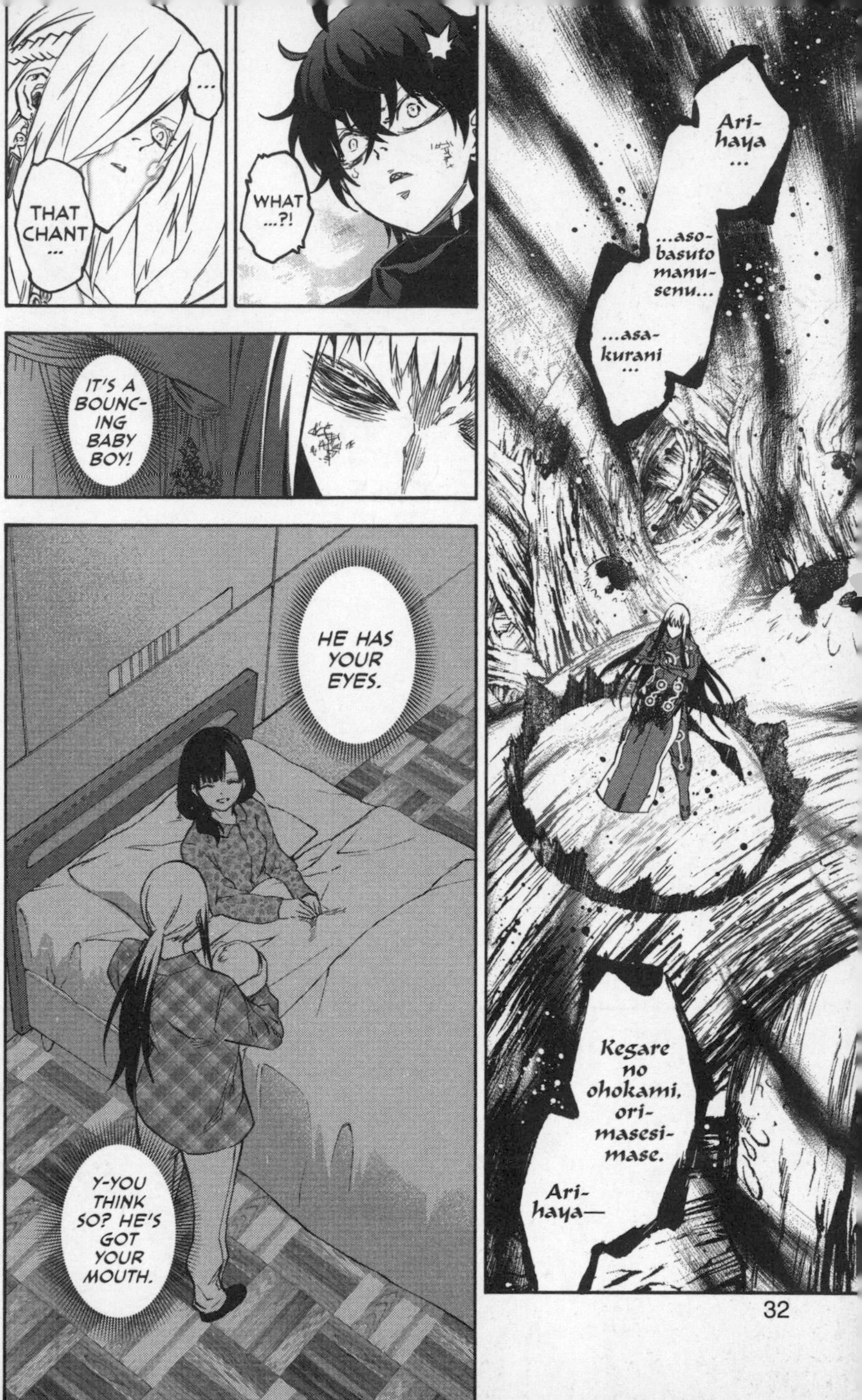
Ari-
haya
...
...aso-
basuto
manu-
senu...
...asa-
kurani
...
Kegare
no
ohokami,
ori-
masesi-
mase.
Ari-
haya—
WHAT
...?!
...
THAT
CHANT
...
IT'S A
BOUNC-
ING
BABY
BOY!
HE HAS
YOUR
EYES.
Y-YOU
THINK
SO? HE'S
GOT
YOUR
MOUTH.

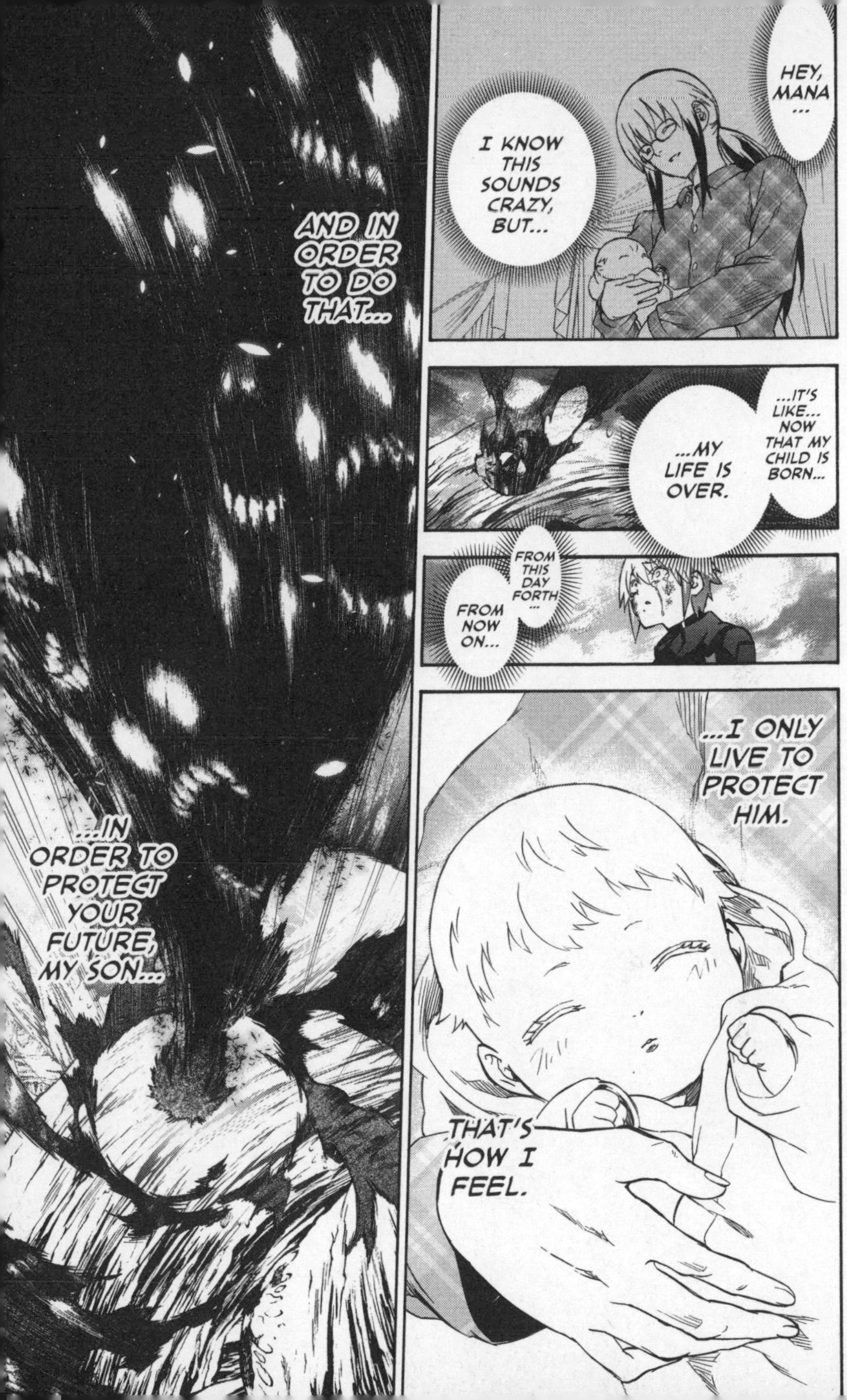
HEY, MANA...
I KNOW THIS SOUNDS CRAZY, BUT...
...IT'S LIKE... NOW THAT MY CHILD IS BORN...
...MY LIFE IS OVER.
FROM THIS DAY FORTH...
FROM NOW ON...
...I ONLY LIVE TO PROTECT HIM.
THAT'S HOW I FEEL.
AND IN ORDER TO DO THAT...
...IN ORDER TO PROTECT YOUR FUTURE, MY SON...

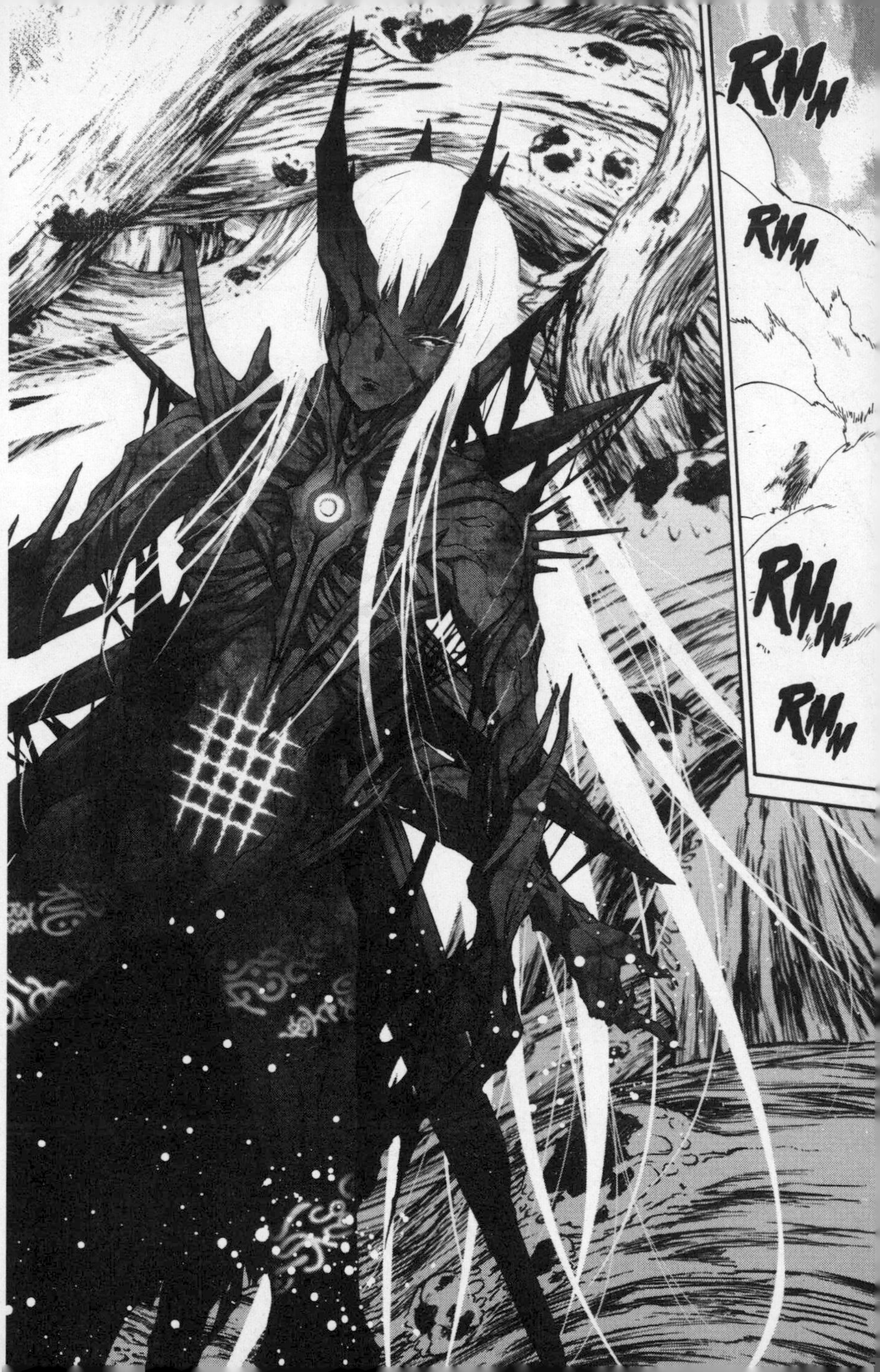
RMM
RMM
RMM
RMM

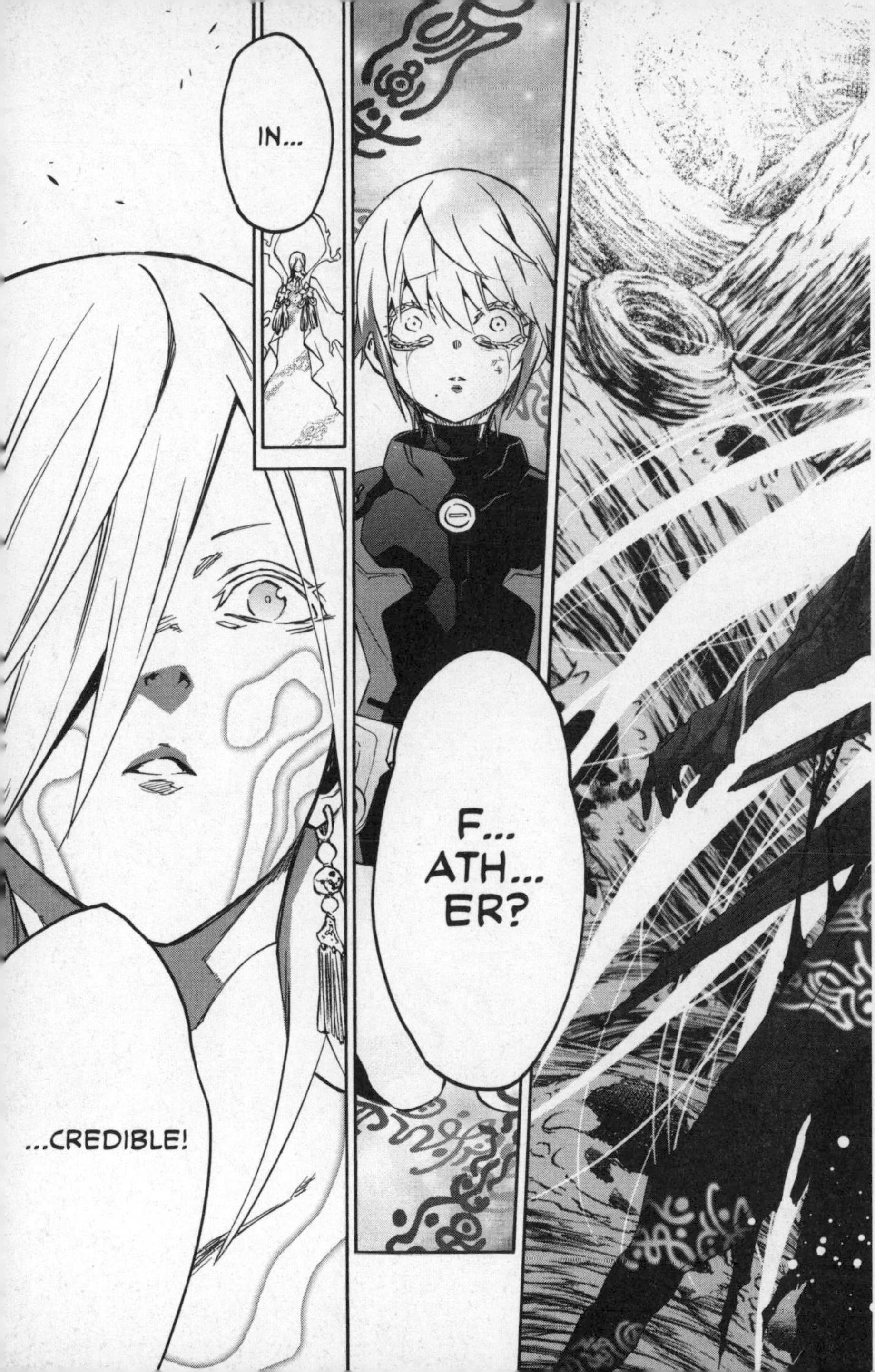
F... ATH... ER?
IN...
...CREDIBLE!

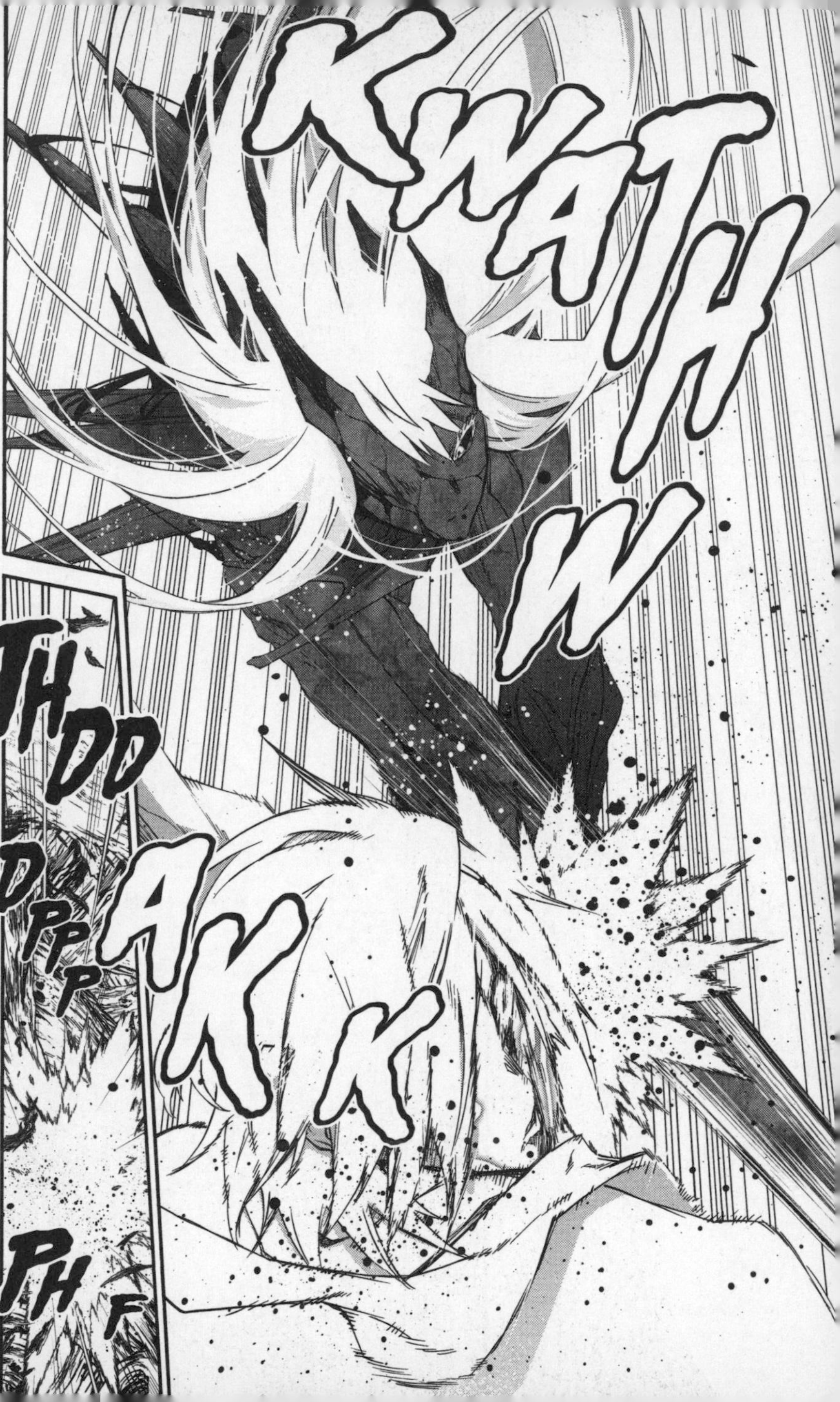
KWATHHW
THDDDPPPP
AKK
PHF

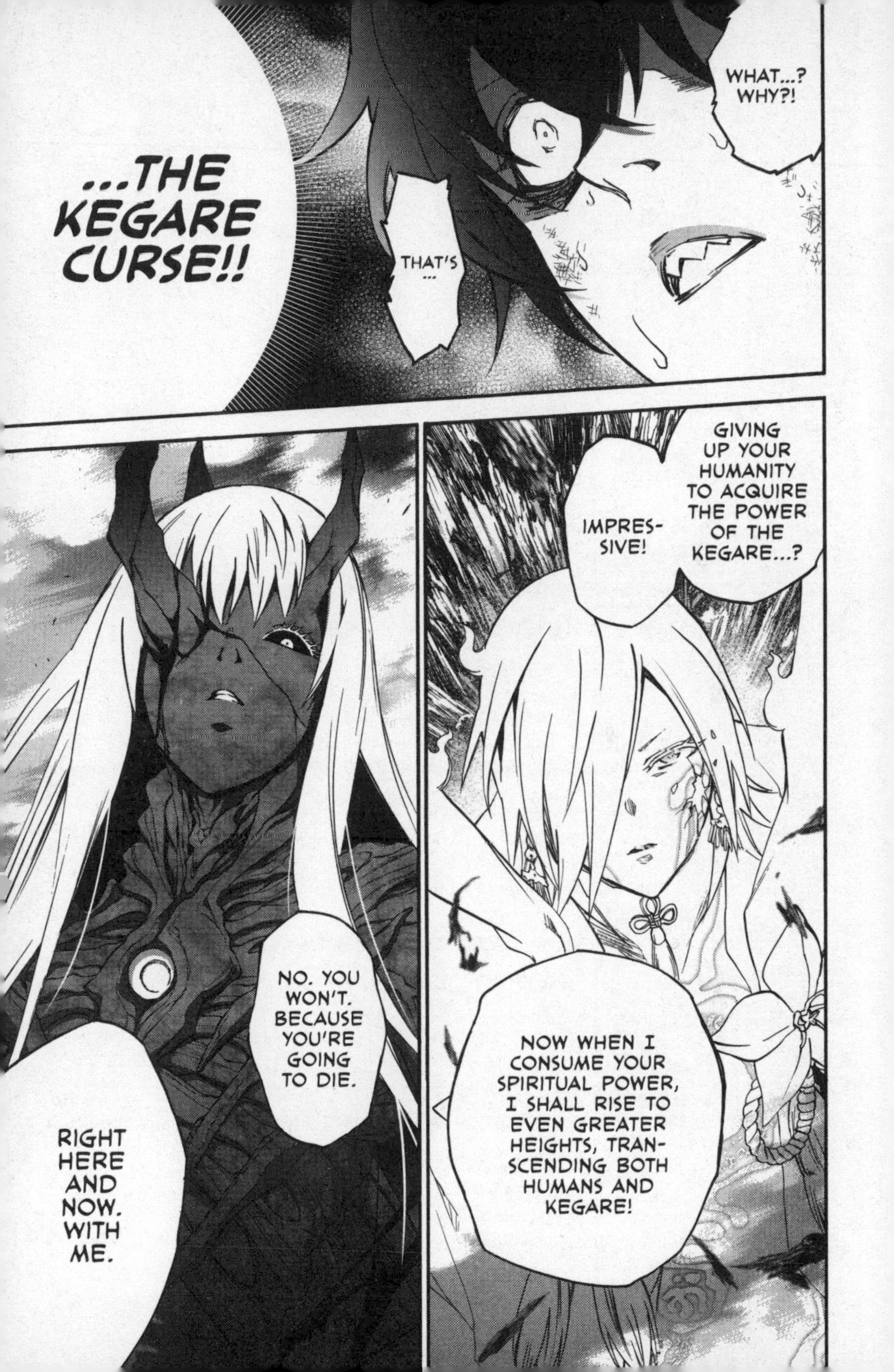
WHAT...? WHY?!
THAT'S ...
...THE KEGARE CURSE!!
GIVING UP YOUR HUMANITY TO ACQUIRE THE POWER OF THE KEGARE...?
IMPRES-SIVE!
NOW WHEN I CONSUME YOUR SPIRITUAL POWER, I SHALL RISE TO EVEN GREATER HEIGHTS, TRAN-SCENDING BOTH HUMANS AND KEGARE!
NO. YOU WON'T. BECAUSE YOU'RE GOING TO DIE.
RIGHT HERE AND NOW. WITH ME.

CHARACTER PROFILE 4

The fourth in this series, which began in vol. 10!
Introducing more characters, including Rokuro's Enmado Family!

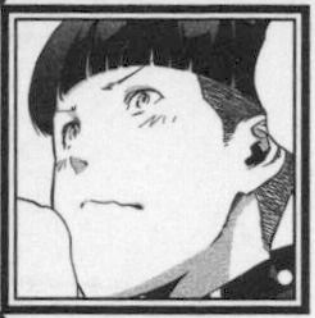

Kimihiko Shigita (16 years old)

Birthday: April 1 Blood type: A Height: 5'9" Weight: 99.2 lbs.
Likes: Drawing, Rokuro
Dislikes: Fighting, training, Kegare

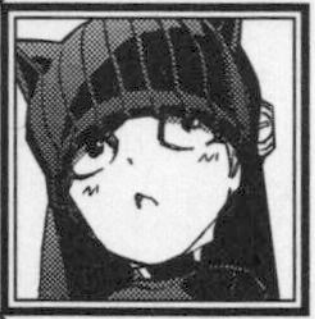

Kinta Ochikata (16 years old)

Birthday: August 15 Blood type: O Height: 5'0" Weight: 97 lbs.
Likes: Music festivals, mainland music
Dislikes: Fighting, training, Kegare

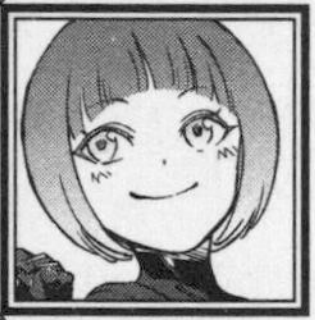

Ringo Akebihara (16 years old)

Birthday: April 7 Blood type: A Height: 5'2" Weight: 103.6 lbs.
Likes: Sweets, cats, Rokuro
Dislikes: Training, Kegare, caterpillars

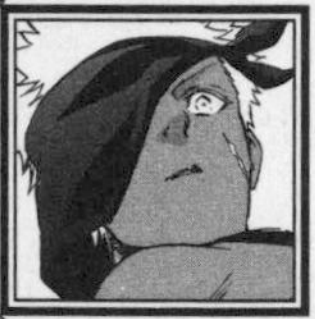

Kazuma Ioroi (20 years old)

Birthday: March 31 Blood type: B Height: 5'11" Weight: 152 lbs.
Likes: Family, sports, summer
Dislikes: Mathematics, using his brain

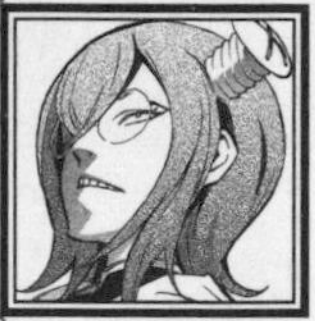

Shozan Saragi (27 years old)

Birthday: January 30 Blood type: AB Height: 5'9" Weight: 132.3 lbs.
Likes: Collecting data, refurbishing weapons, Cordelia's repair and upkeep
Dislikes: Most animals, meatheads (Ioroi Family)

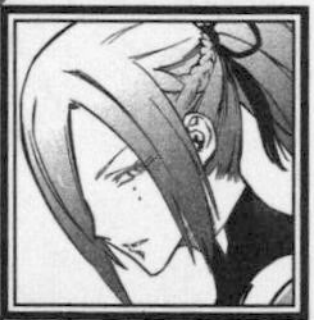

Shusuke Gein (27 years old)

Birthday: September 25 Blood type: AB Height: 5'11" Weight: 143 lbs.
Likes: Little Tenmy, natto
Dislikes: Avocado

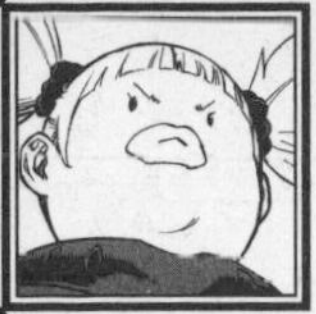

Fuguyo Mushuguchi (24 years old)

Birthday: October 28 Blood type: A Height: 9’9”/5’6”

Weight: 727.5 lbs./116.8 lbs

Likes: Tenma, eating

Dislikes: Low ceilings

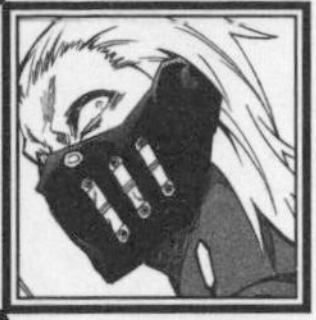

Juzo Nakiri (29 years old)

Birthday: November 10 Blood type: B Height: 6'1" Weight: 165.4 lbs.

Likes: Lady Miku, young women

Dislikes: Big boobs, men who like big boobs

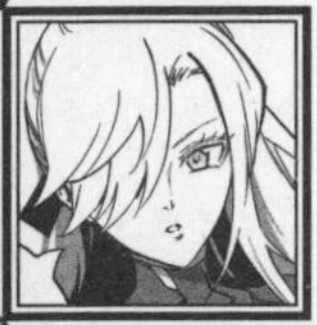

Rui Fuka (28 years old)

Birthday: July 20 Blood type: O Height: 5'7" Weight: 126 lbs.

Likes: Black coffee, monaka

Dislikes: Pervs, eel

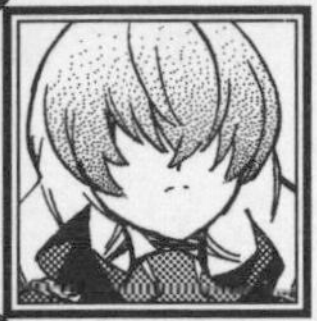

Nene Hinazuka (23 years old)

Birthday: December 15 Blood type: A Height: 5'1" Weight: 104 lbs.

Likes: Black tea, plants, Kankuro

Dislikes: People with loud voices, meat

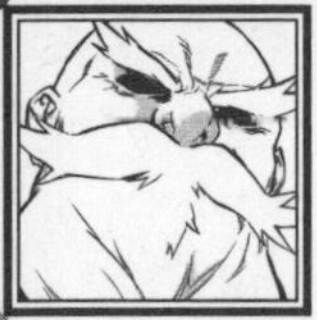

Danma Kurozu (68 years old)

Birthday: May 31 Blood type: A Height: 6'4" Weight: 278 lbs.

Likes: Practice, castella sponge cake

Dislikes: Show-offs

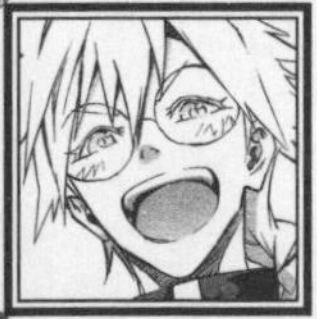

Tsubaki Sada (Deceased: 34 years old)

Birthday: March 13 Blood type: B Height: 5'11" Weight: 1165 lbs.

Likes: Sakura, practice, plushies

Dislikes: Sweets, caterpillars

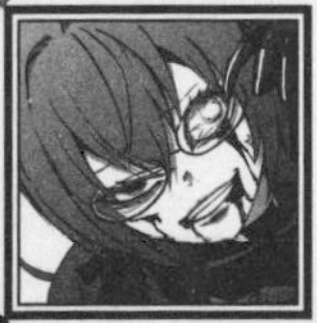

Senri Unomiya (Deceased: 12 years old)

Birthday: August 24 Blood type: AB Height: 5'0" Weight: 95 lbs.

Likes: Studying, insects

Dislikes: Dumplings

QQnyoritsuryo!

Question Corner

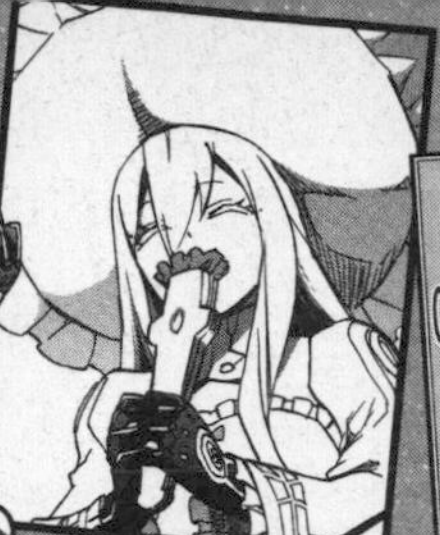

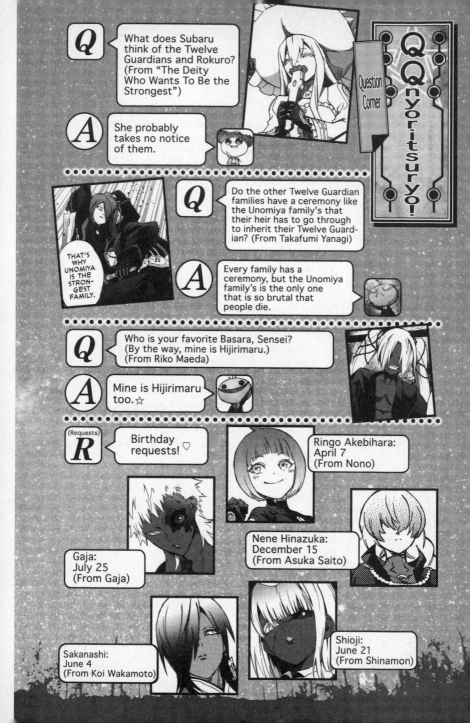

Q What does Subaru think of the Twelve Guardians and Rokuro? (From "The Deity Who Wants To Be the Strongest")

A She probably takes no notice of them.

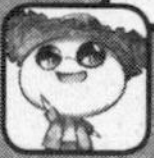

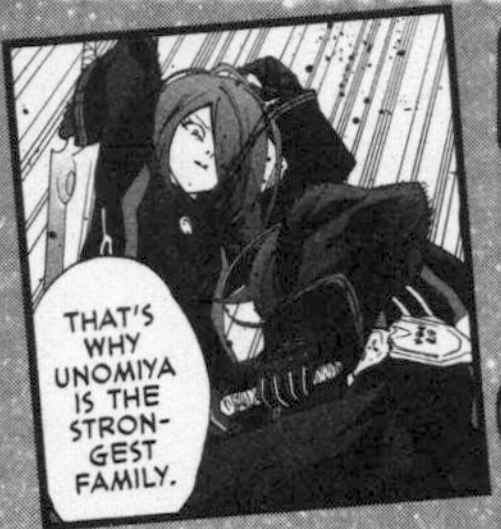
THAT'S WHY UNOMIYA IS THE STRONGEST FAMILY.

Q Do the other Twelve Guardian families have a ceremony like the Unomiya family's that their heir has to go through to inherit their Twelve Guardian? (From Takafumi Yanagi)

A Every family has a ceremony, but the Unomiya family's is the only one that is so brutal that people die.

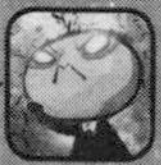

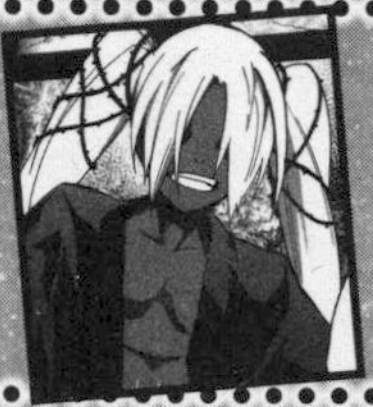

Q Who is your favorite Basara, Sensei? (By the way, mine is Hijirimaru.) (From Riko Maeda)

A Mine is Hijirimaru too.☆

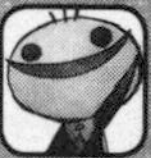

R (Requests) Birthday requests! ♡

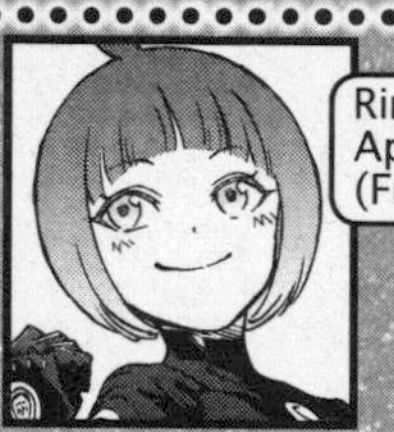

Ringo Akebihara: April 7 (From Nono)

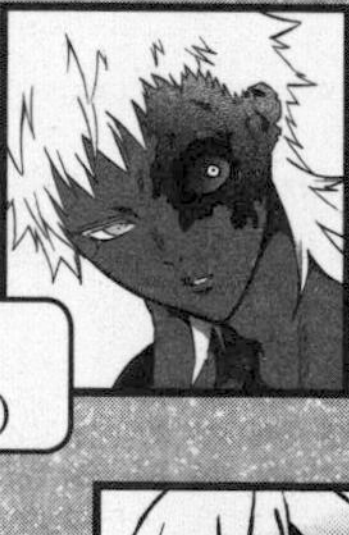

Gaja: July 25 (From Gaja)

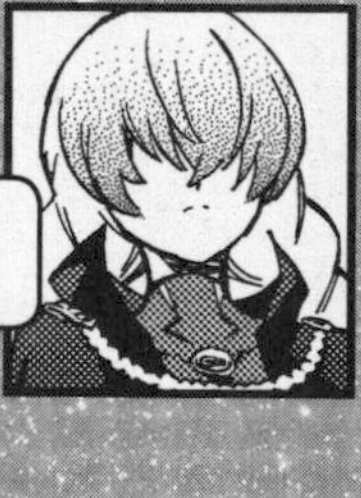

Nene Hinazuka: December 15 (From Asuka Saito)

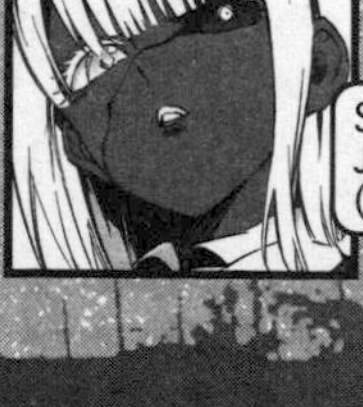

Shioji: June 21 (From Shinamon)

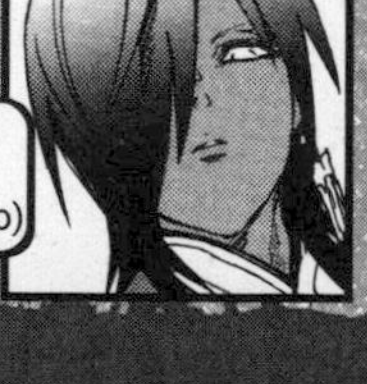

Sakanashi: June 4 (From Koi Wakamoto)

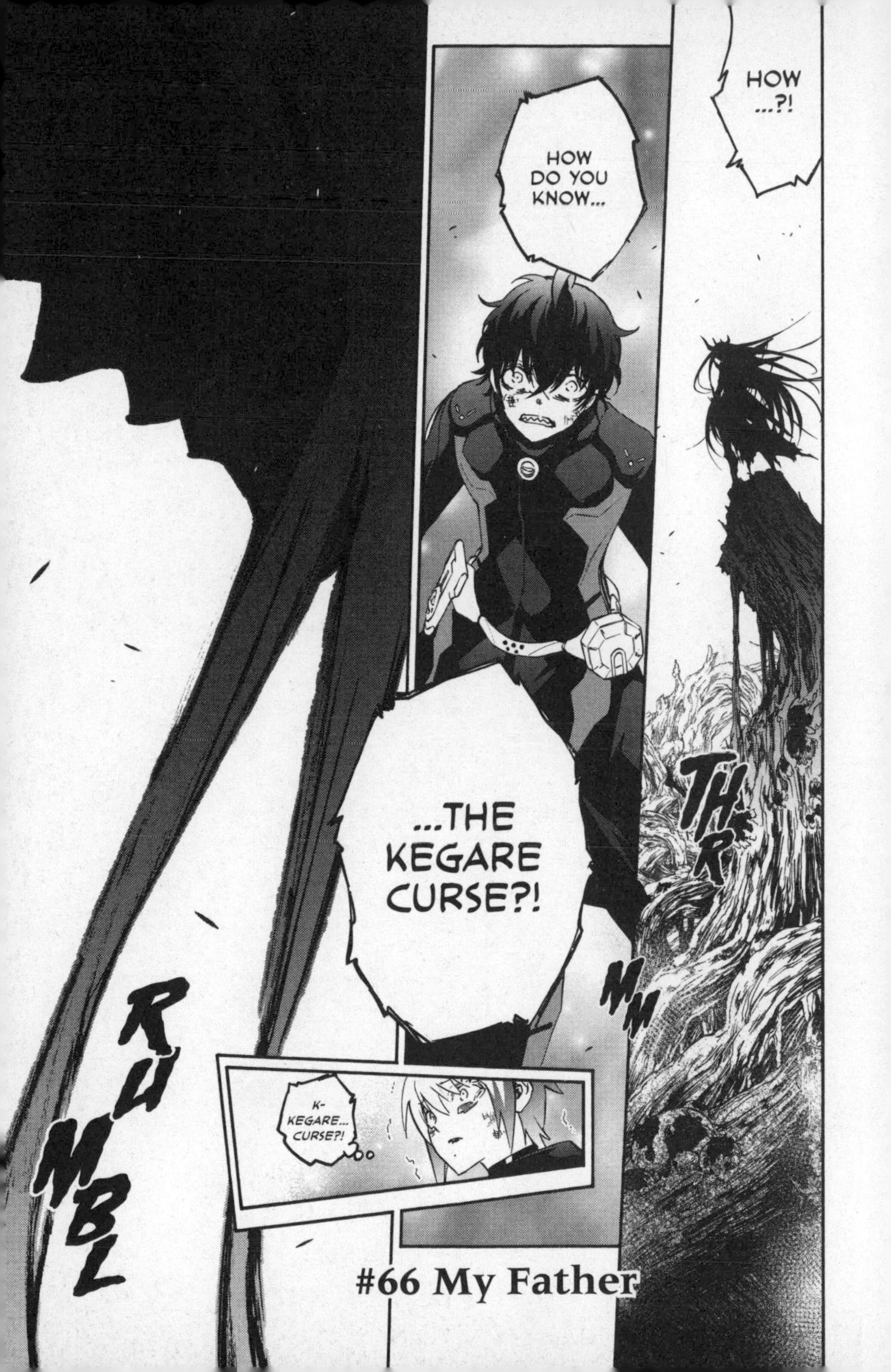
HOW ...?!
HOW DO YOU KNOW...
...THE KEGARE CURSE?!
THRMM
K-KEGARE... CURSE?!
RUMBL

#66 My Father

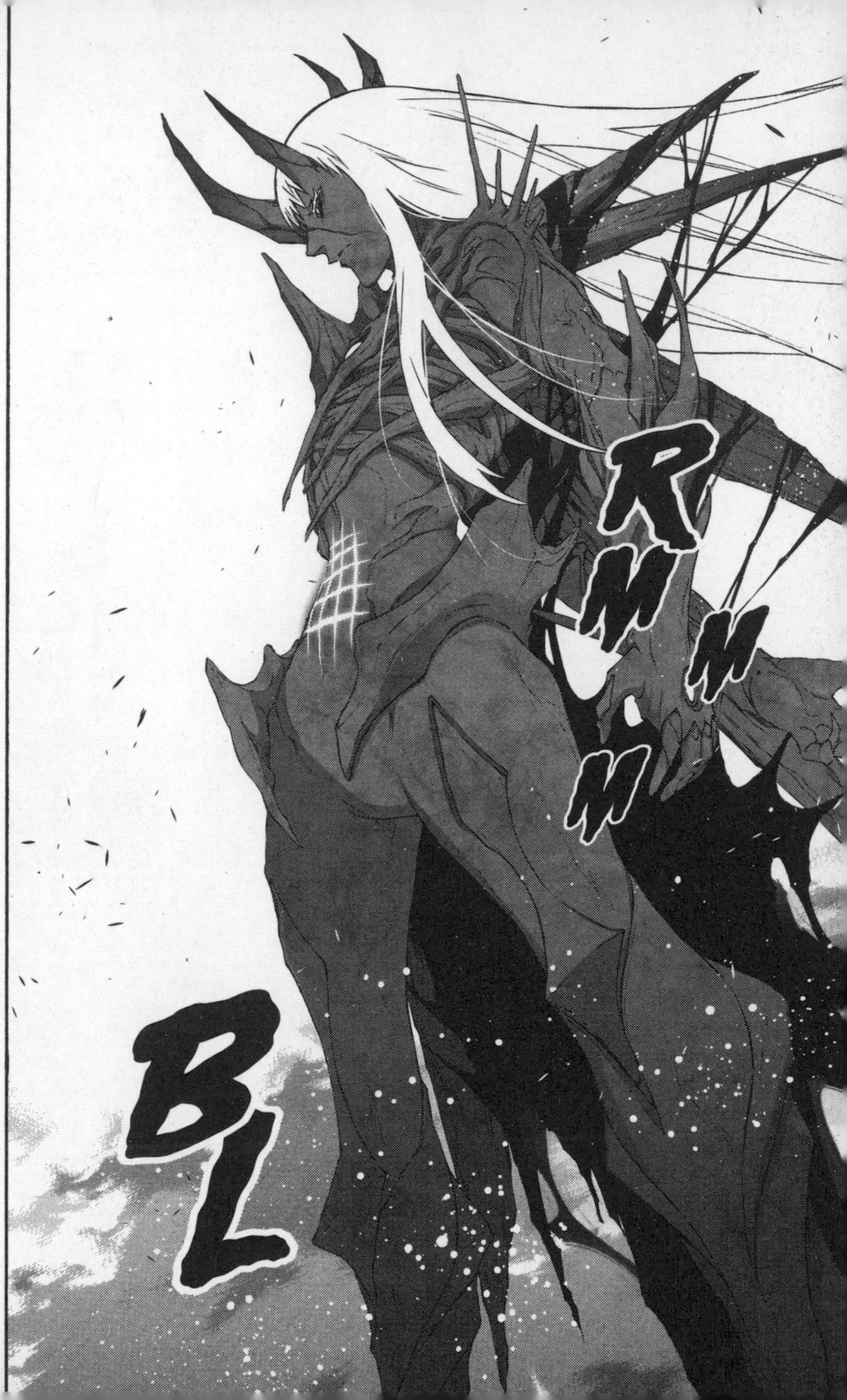
RMMMM
BL

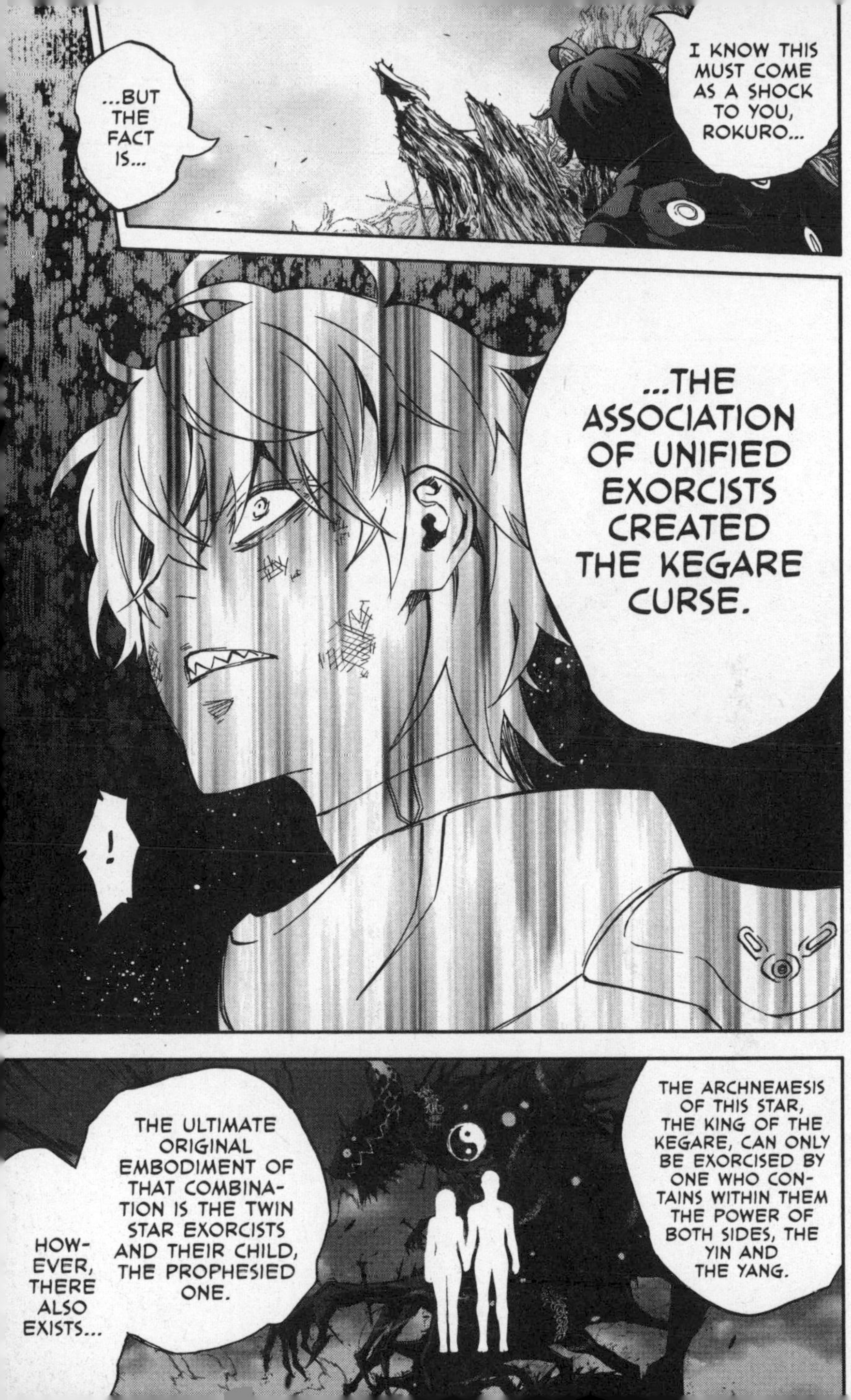
I KNOW THIS MUST COME AS A SHOCK TO YOU, ROKURO...
...BUT THE FACT IS...
...THE ASSOCIATION OF UNIFIED EXORCISTS CREATED THE KEGARE CURSE.
!
THE ARCHNEMESIS OF THIS STAR, THE KING OF THE KEGARE, CAN ONLY BE EXORCISED BY ONE WHO CON-TAINS WITHIN THEM THE POWER OF BOTH SIDES, THE YIN AND THE YANG.
THE ULTIMATE ORIGINAL EMBODIMENT OF THAT COMBINA-TION IS THE TWIN STAR EXORCISTS AND THEIR CHILD, THE PROPHESIED ONE.
HOW-EVER, THERE ALSO EXISTS...

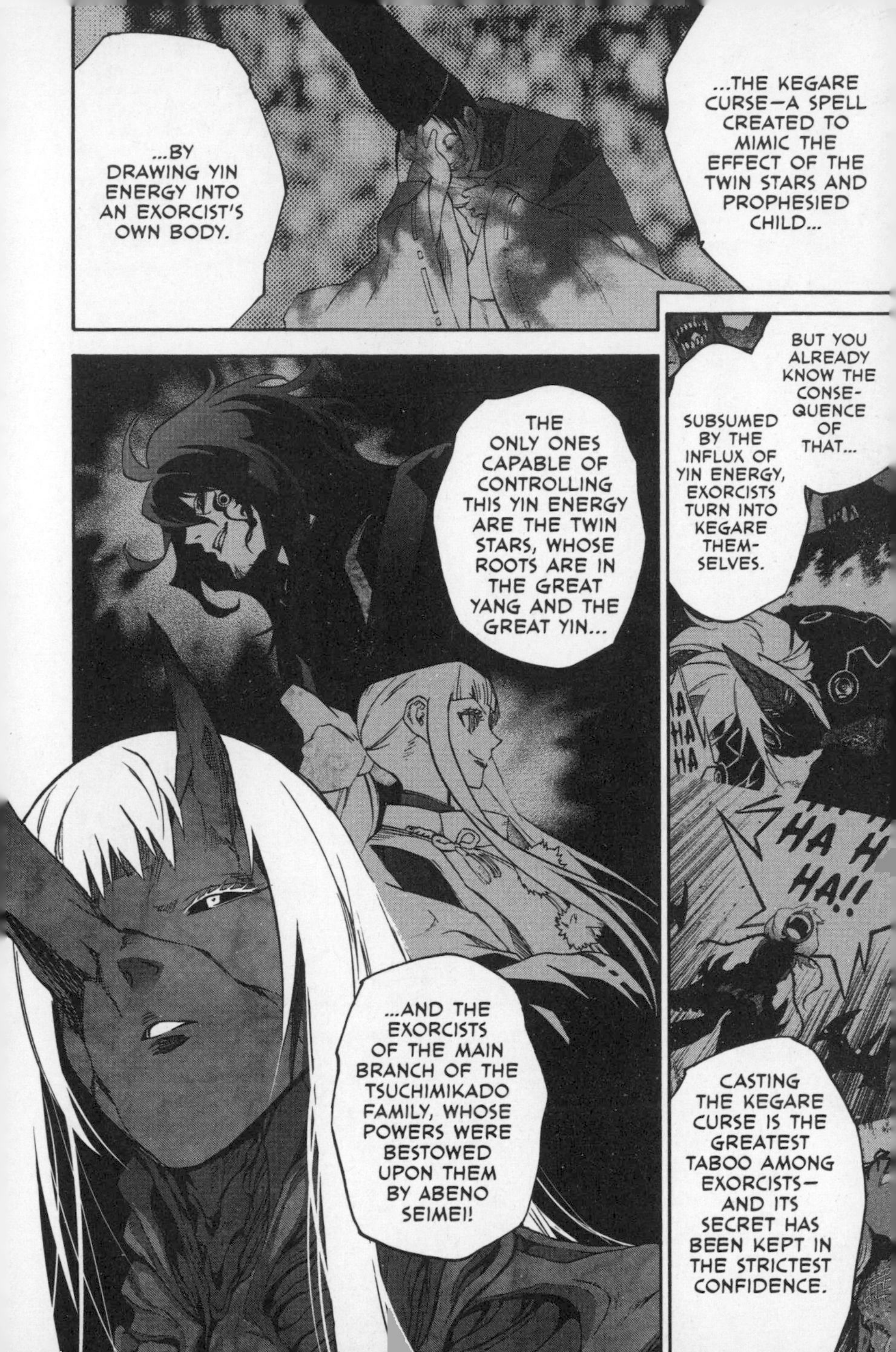
...THE KEGARE CURSE—A SPELL CREATED TO MIMIC THE EFFECT OF THE TWIN STARS AND PROPHESIED CHILD...
...BY DRAWING YIN ENERGY INTO AN EXORCIST'S OWN BODY.
BUT YOU ALREADY KNOW THE CONSE-QUENCE OF THAT...
SUBSUMED BY THE INFLUX OF YIN ENERGY, EXORCISTS TURN INTO KEGARE THEM-SELVES.
HA HA HA HA
HA HA HA!!
CASTING THE KEGARE CURSE IS THE GREATEST TABOO AMONG EXORCISTS—AND ITS SECRET HAS BEEN KEPT IN THE STRICTEST CONFIDENCE.
THE ONLY ONES CAPABLE OF CONTROLLING THIS YIN ENERGY ARE THE TWIN STARS, WHOSE ROOTS ARE IN THE GREAT YANG AND THE GREAT YIN...
...AND THE EXORCISTS OF THE MAIN BRANCH OF THE TSUCHIMIKADO FAMILY, WHOSE POWERS WERE BESTOWED UPON THEM BY ABENO SEIMEI!

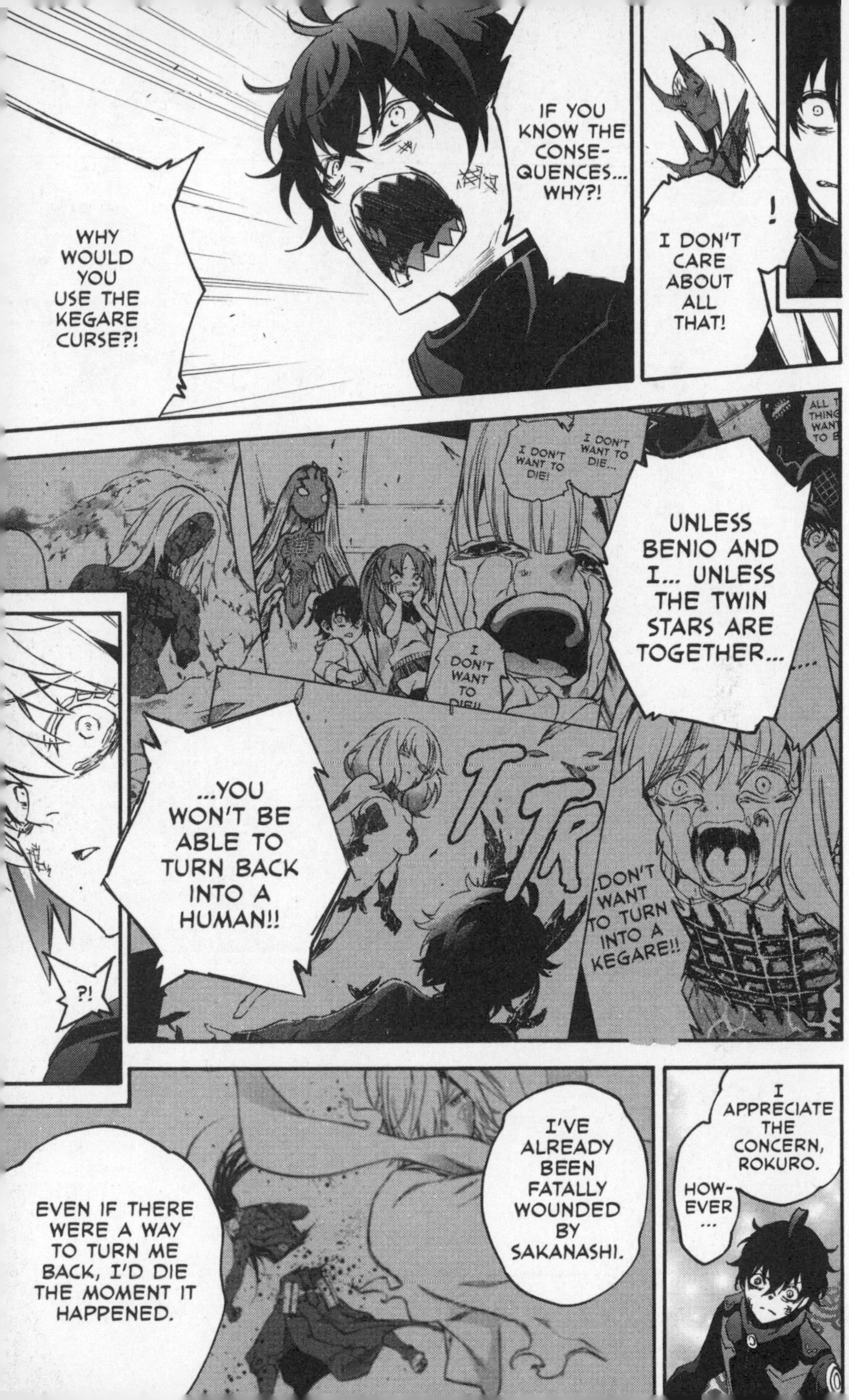
!
I DON'T CARE ABOUT ALL THAT!
IF YOU KNOW THE CONSE-QUENCES... WHY?!
WHY WOULD YOU USE THE KEGARE CURSE?!
UNLESS BENIO AND I... UNLESS THE TWIN STARS ARE TOGETHER...
I DON'T WANT TO DIE...
I DON'T WANT TO DIE!
I DON'T WANT TO DIE!!
DON'T WANT TO TURN INTO A KEGARE!!
...YOU WON'T BE ABLE TO TURN BACK INTO A HUMAN!!
?!
I APPRECIATE THE CONCERN, ROKURO.
HOW-EVER...
I'VE ALREADY BEEN FATALLY WOUNDED BY SAKANASHI.
EVEN IF THERE WERE A WAY TO TURN ME BACK, I'D DIE THE MOMENT IT HAPPENED.

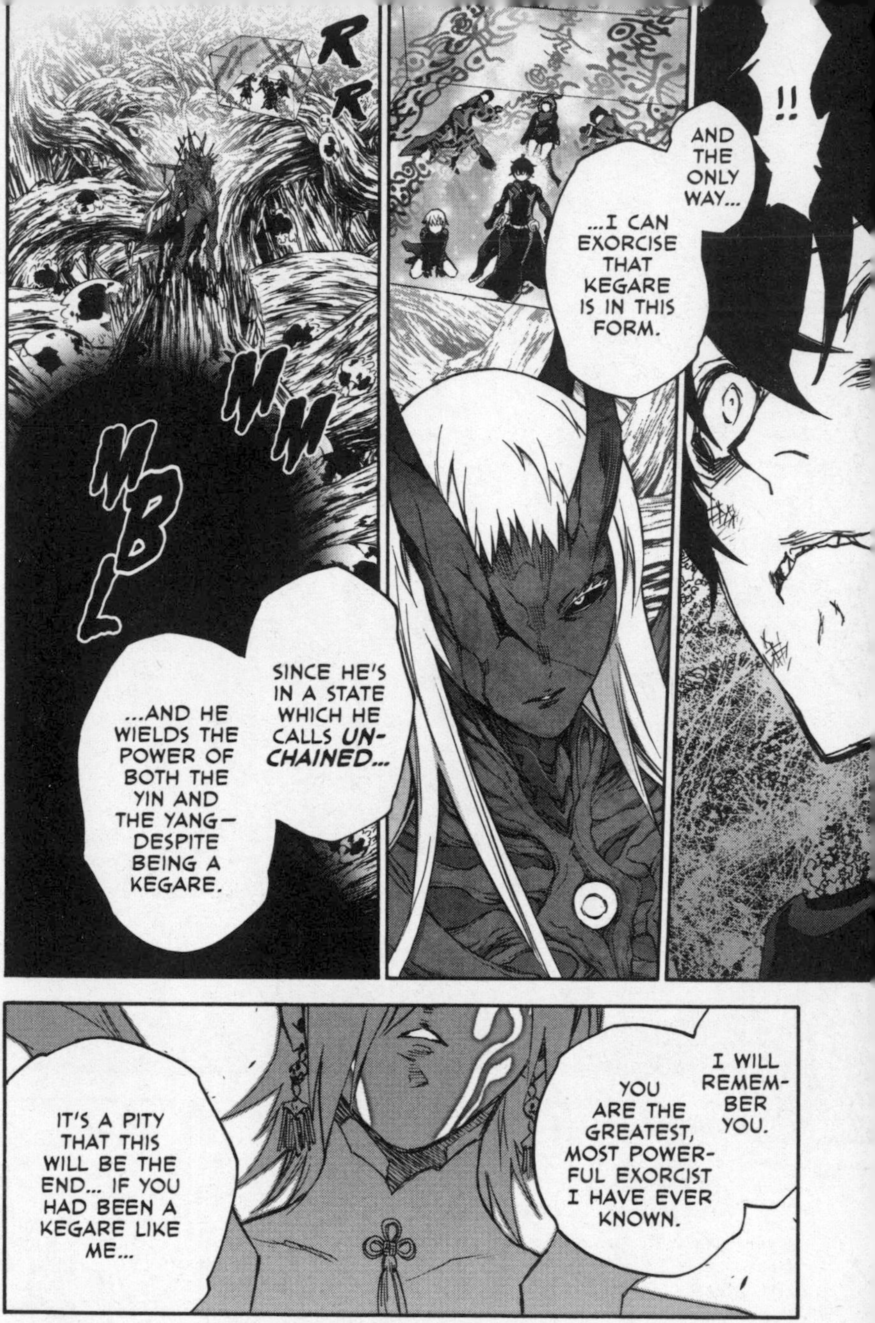
!!
AND THE ONLY WAY...
...I CAN EXORCISE THAT KEGARE IS IN THIS FORM.
RR
SINCE HE'S IN A STATE WHICH HE CALLS *UN-CHAINED*...
...AND HE WIELDS THE POWER OF BOTH THE YIN AND THE YANG—DESPITE BEING A KEGARE.
MMM
MBL
I WILL REMEMBER YOU.
YOU ARE THE GREATEST, MOST POWERFUL EXORCIST I HAVE EVER KNOWN.
IT'S A PITY THAT THIS WILL BE THE END... IF YOU HAD BEEN A KEGARE LIKE ME...

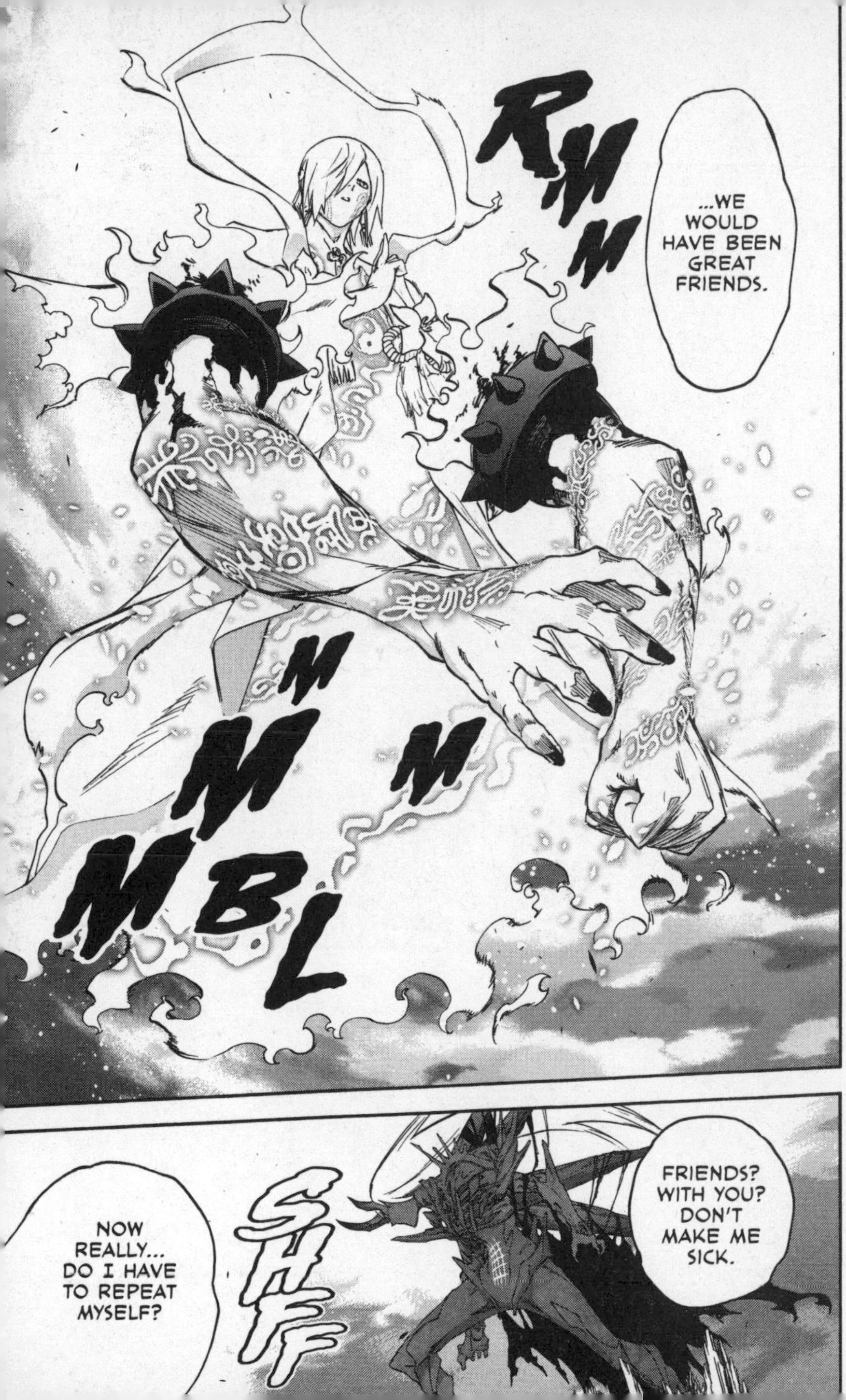

...WE WOULD HAVE BEEN GREAT FRIENDS.
RMMM
MMMMBL
FRIENDS? WITH YOU? DON'T MAKE ME SICK.
SHFF
NOW REALLY... DO I HAVE TO REPEAT MYSELF?

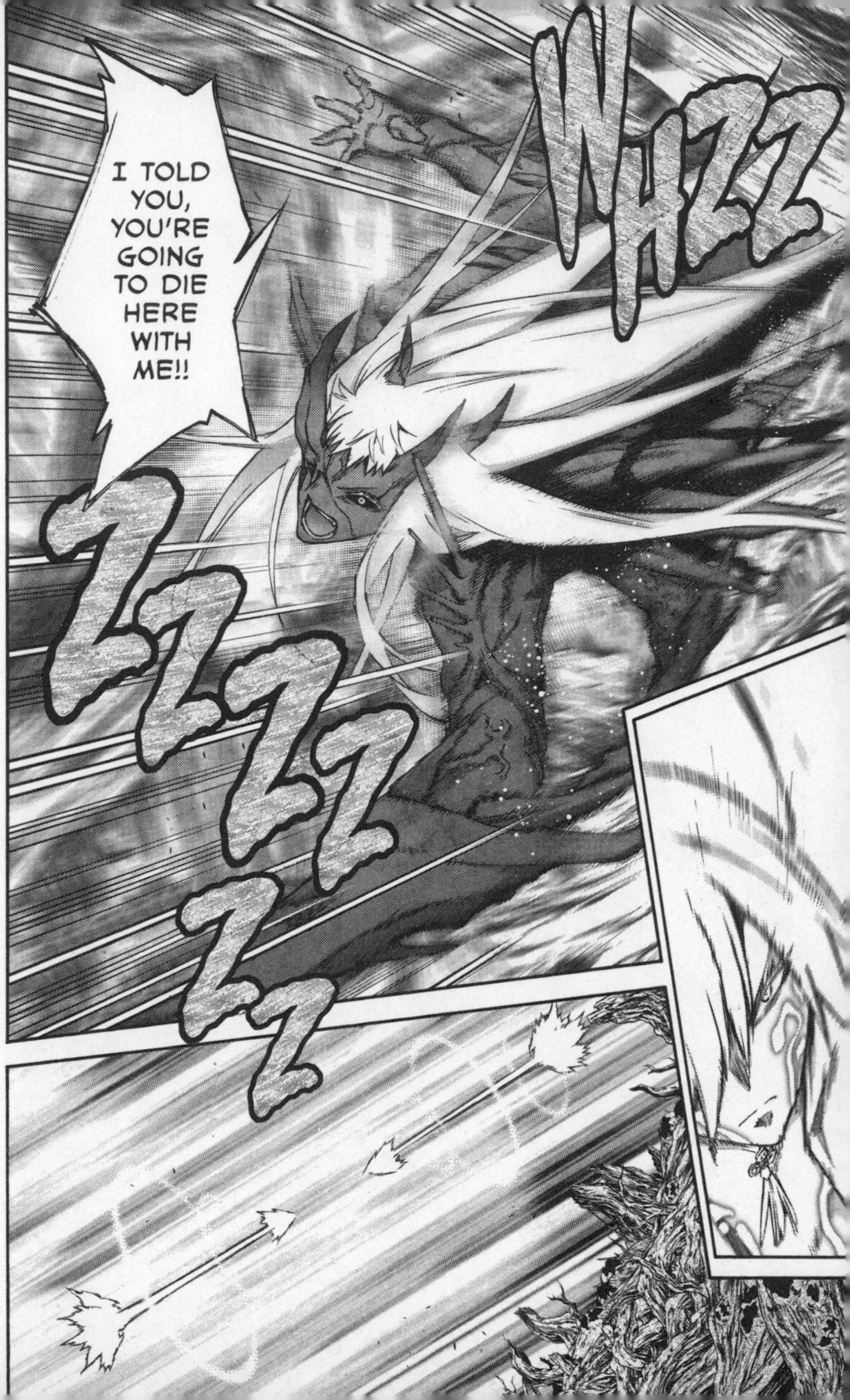
WHZZ
I TOLD YOU, YOU'RE GOING TO DIE HERE WITH ME!!
ZZZZZZ

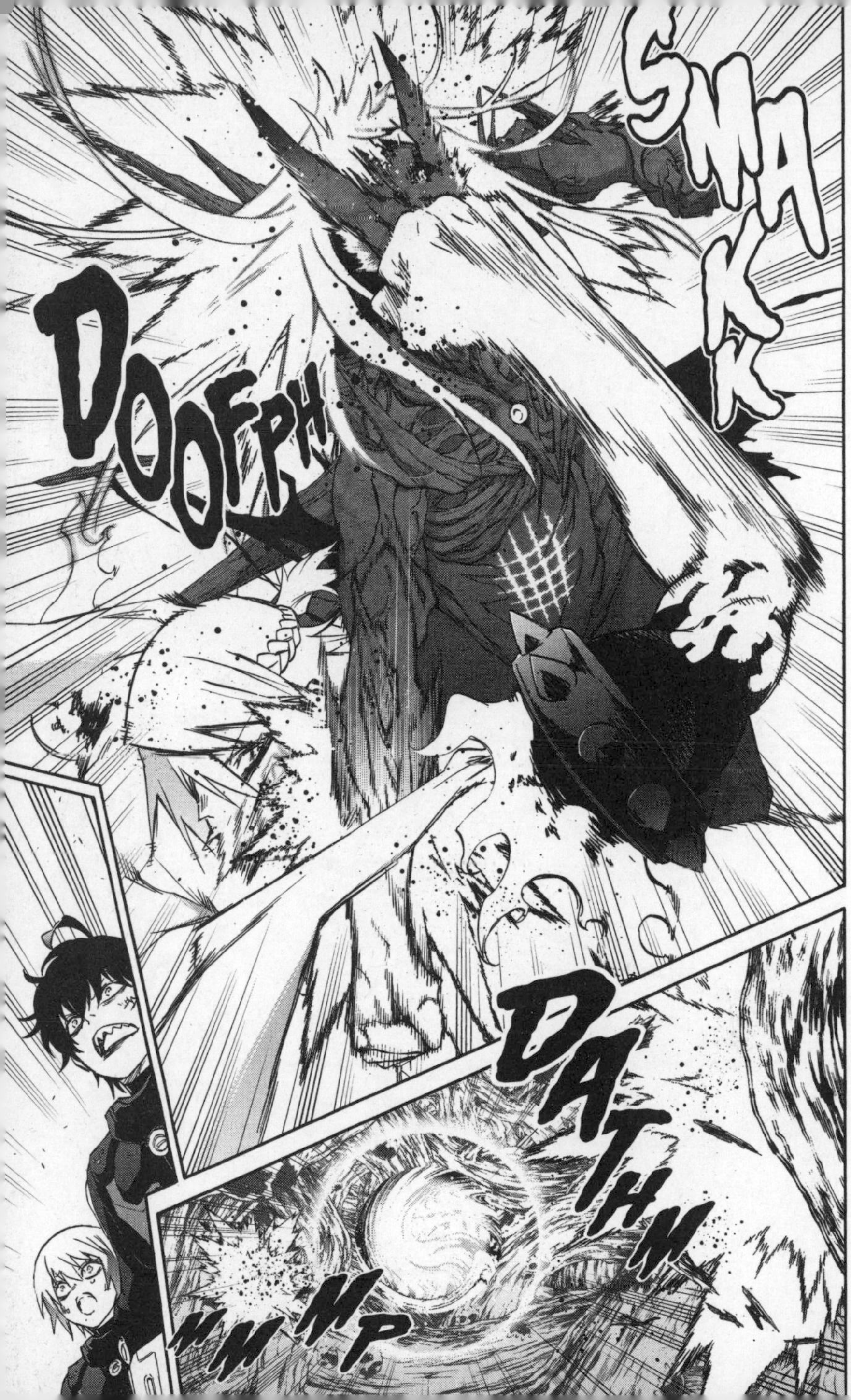
SMAKK
DOOFPH
DATHMMMMP

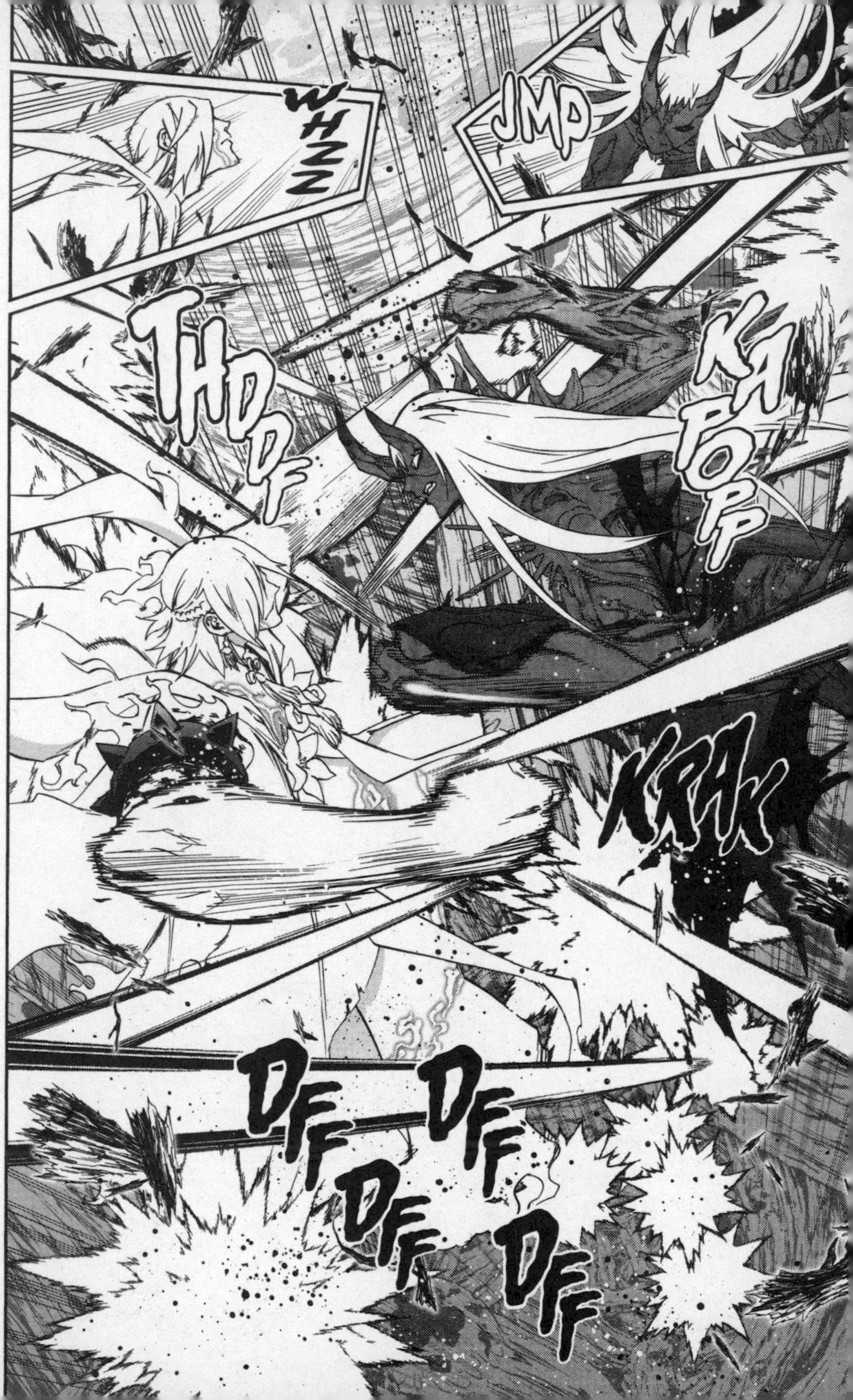
JMP
WHZZ
KAPOPP
THDDF
KRAK
DFF
DFF
DFF
DFF

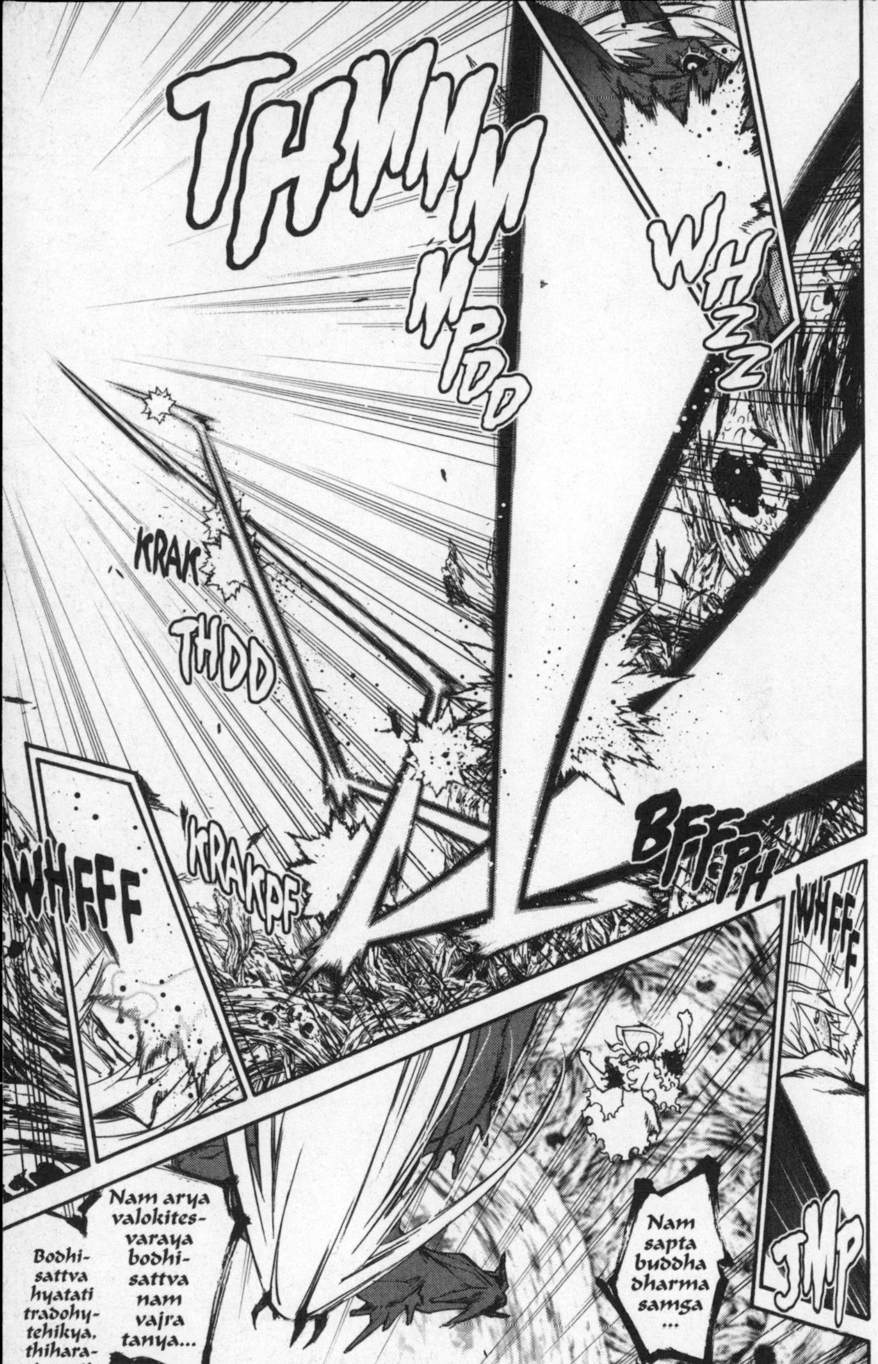
WHZZ
THMMMMPDD
KRAK
THDD
BFFPH
KRAKPF
WHFFF
WHFFF
JMP
Nam sapta buddha dharma samga ...
Nam arya valokites-varaya bodhi-sattva nam vajra tanya...
Bodhi-sattva hyatati tradohy-tehikya, thihara-javarti svaha—!

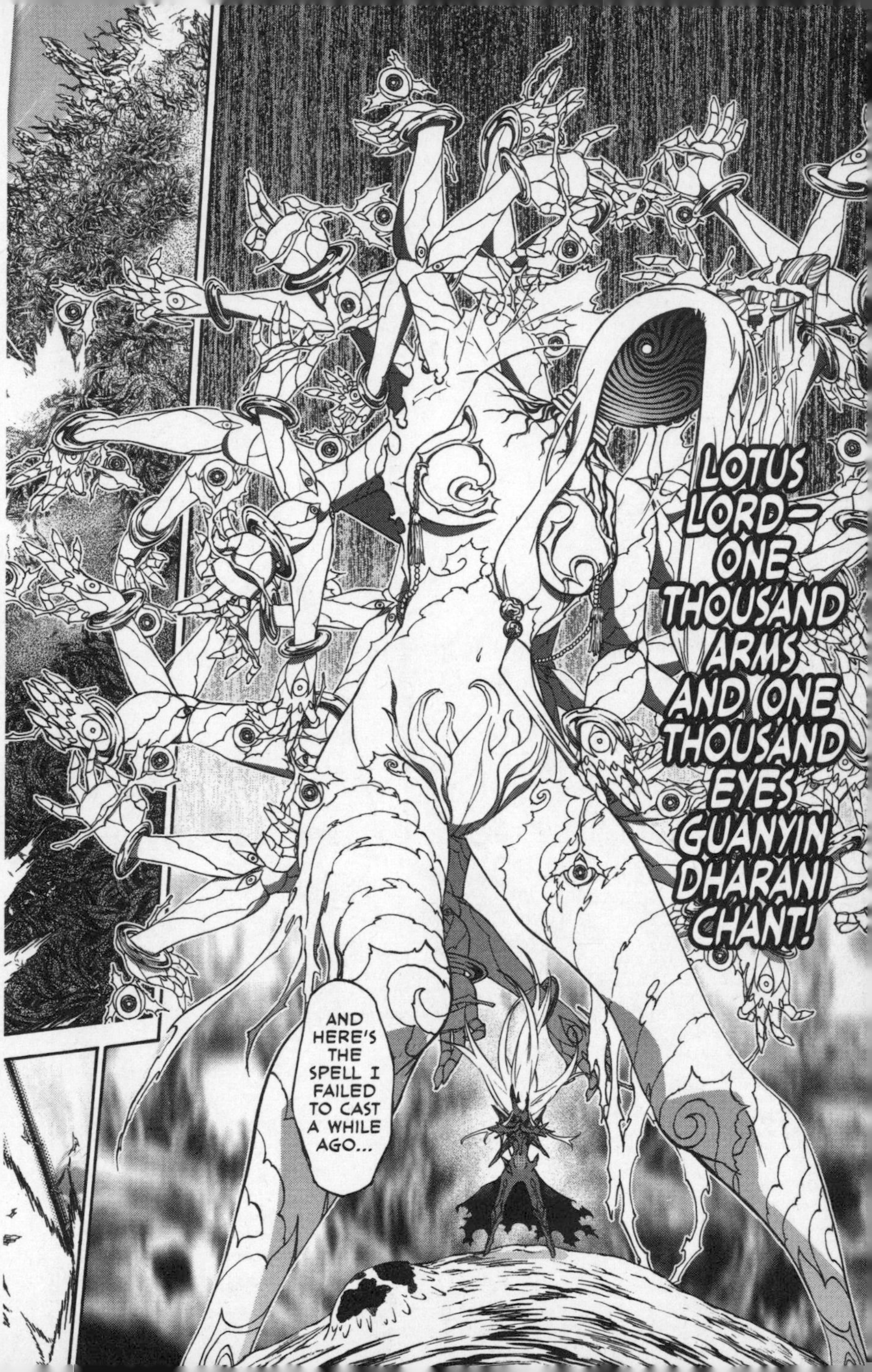
LOTUS LORD— ONE THOUSAND ARMS AND ONE THOUSAND EYES GUANYIN DHARANI CHANT!
AND HERE'S THE SPELL I FAILED TO CAST A WHILE AGO...

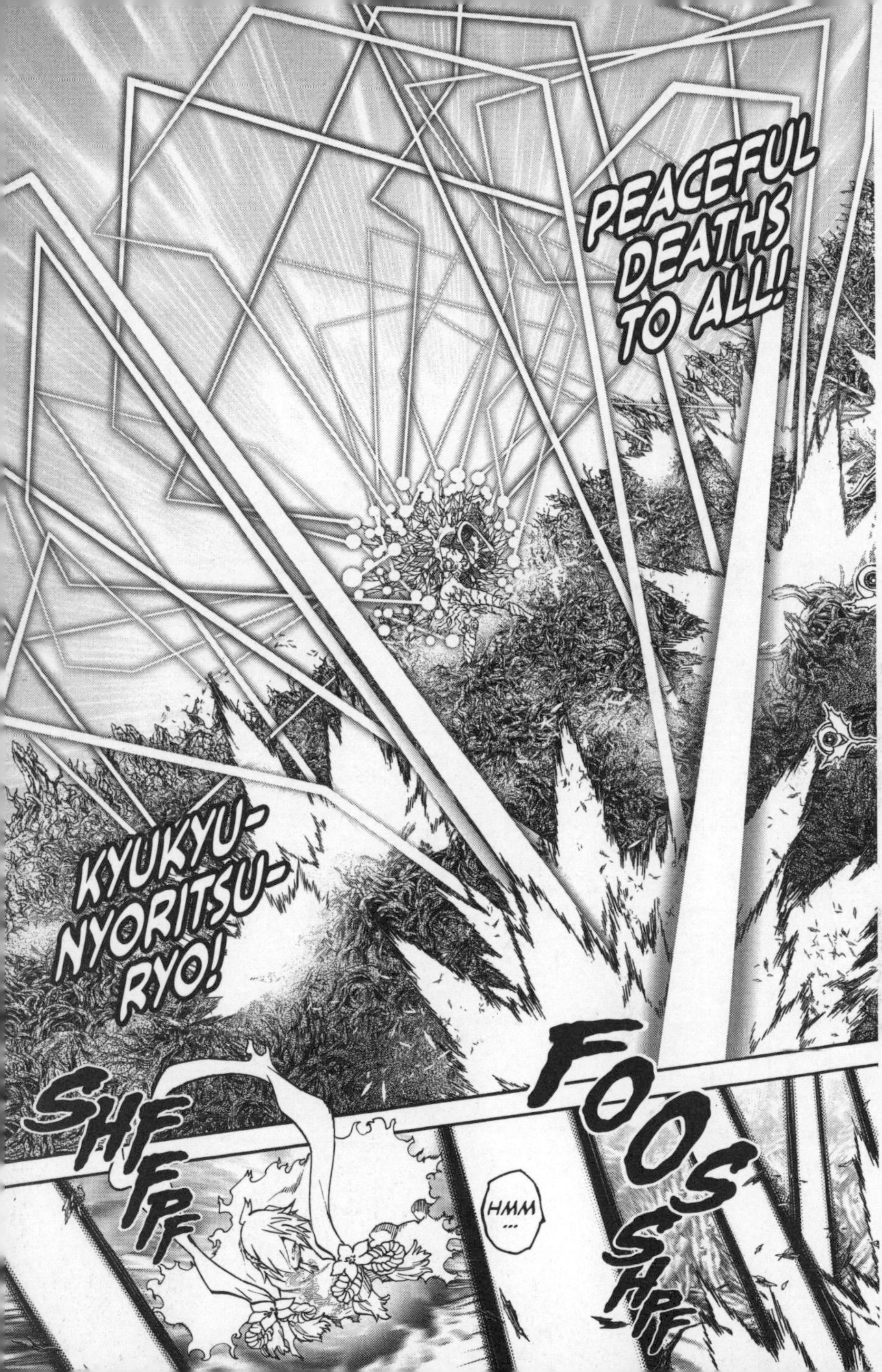
PEACEFUL DEATHS TO ALL!
KYUKYU-NYORITSU-RYO!
FOOS
SHPF
HMM...
SHFPF

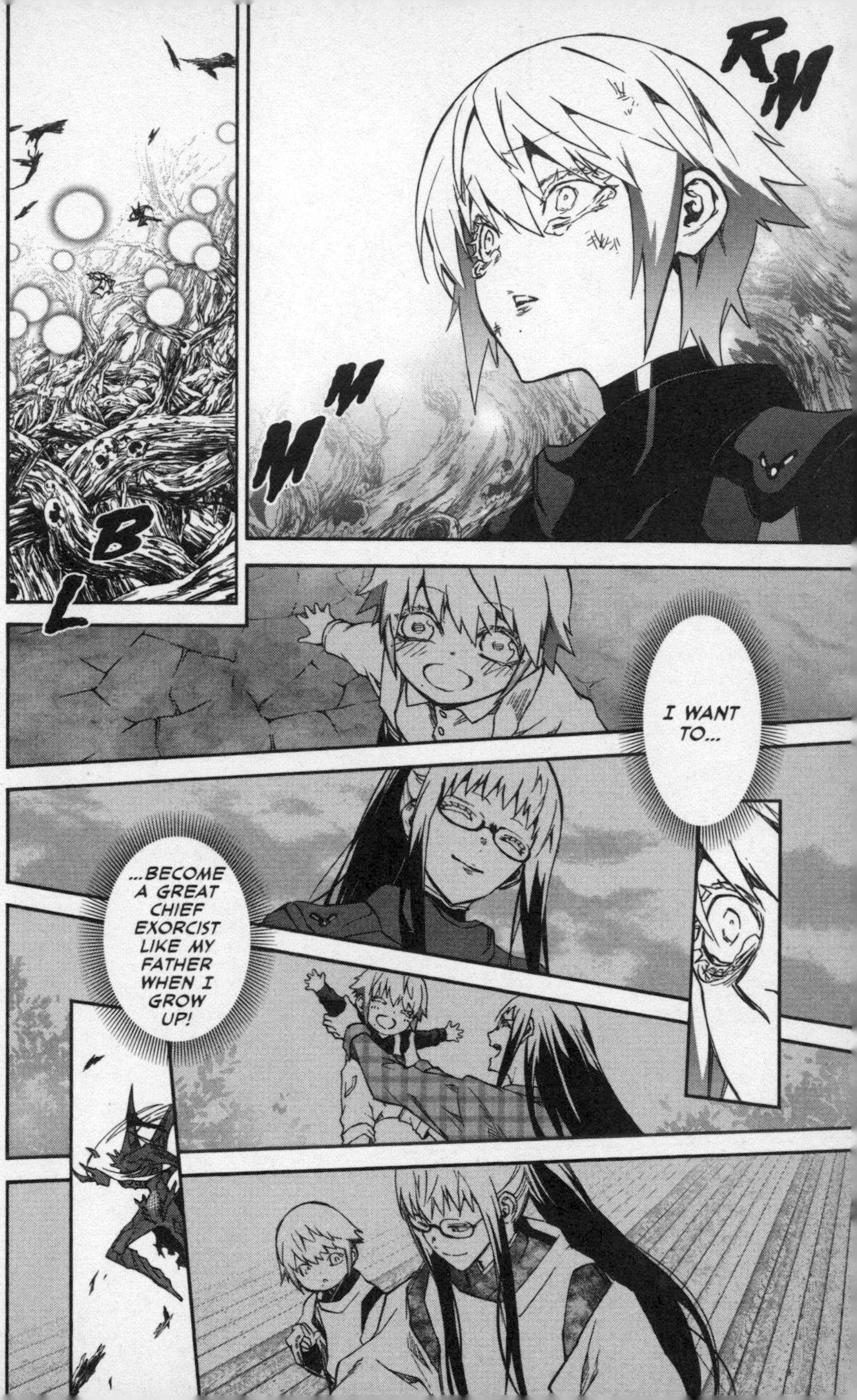
RMMMBL
I WANT TO...
...BECOME A GREAT CHIEF EXORCIST LIKE MY FATHER WHEN I GROW UP!

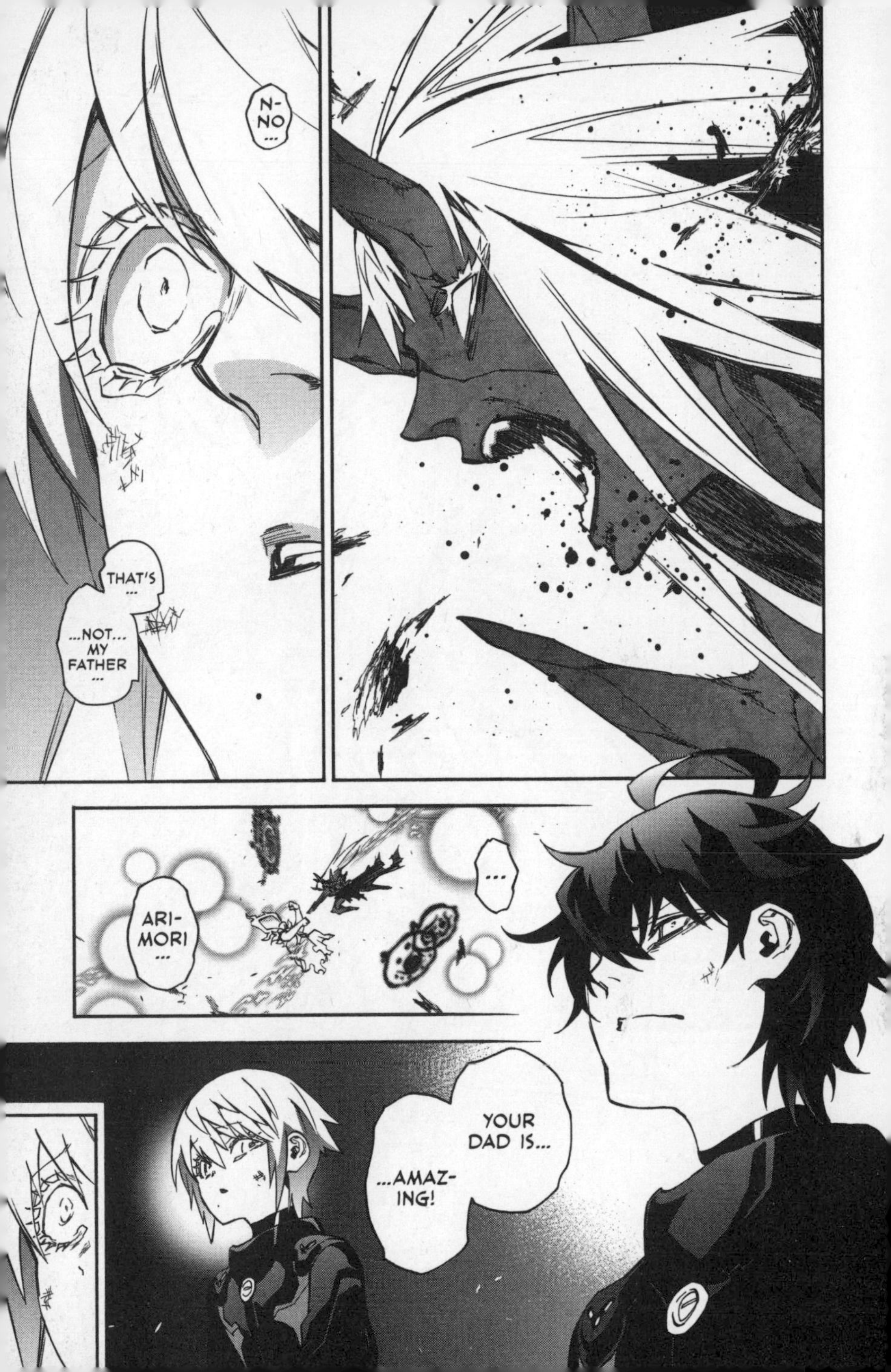
N-NO...
THAT'S...
...NOT... MY FATHER...
...
ARI-MORI...
YOUR DAD IS...
...AMAZ-ING!

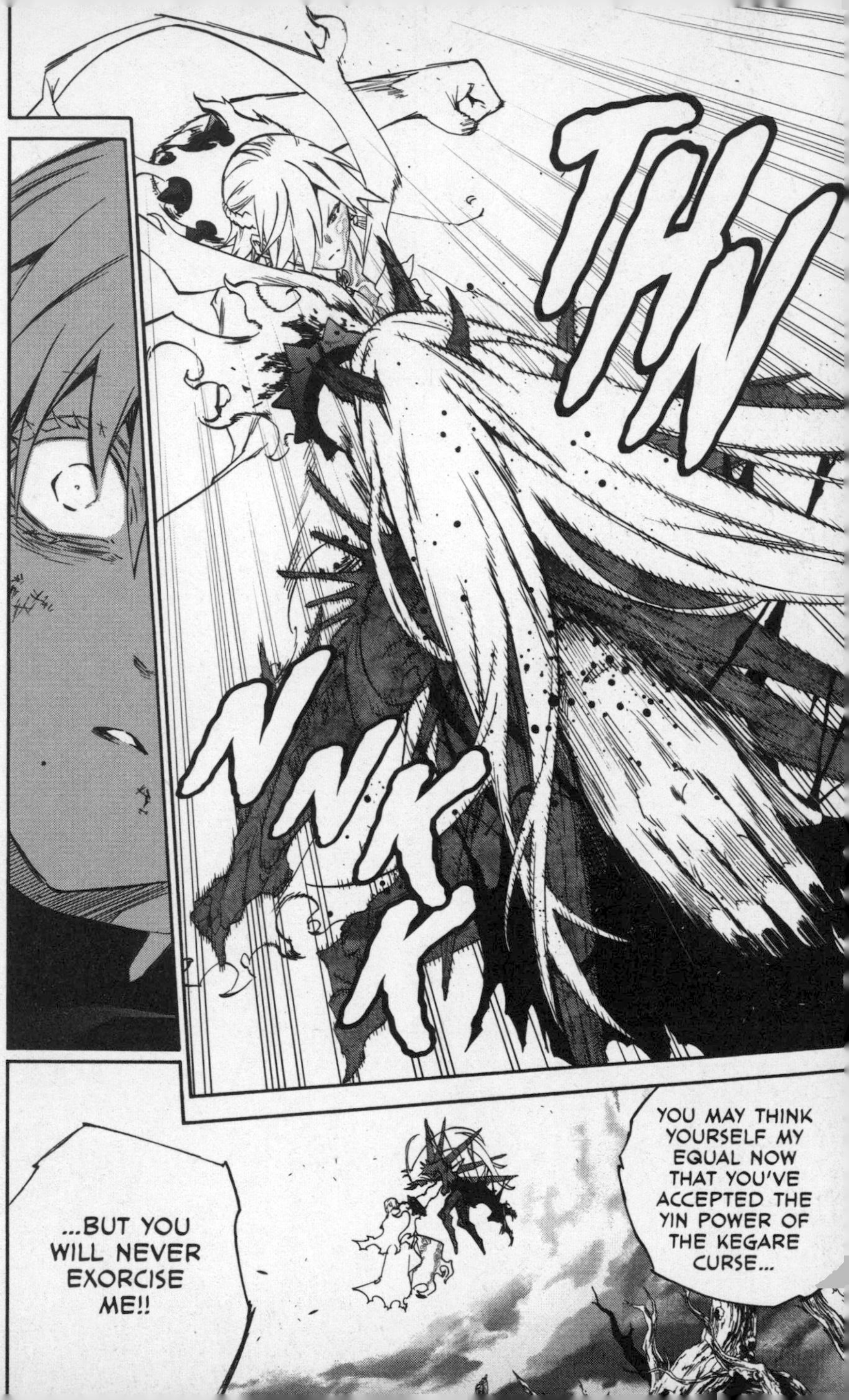
THN
NKK
YOU MAY THINK YOURSELF MY EQUAL NOW THAT YOU'VE ACCEPTED THE YIN POWER OF THE KEGARE CURSE...
...BUT YOU WILL NEVER EXORCISE ME!!

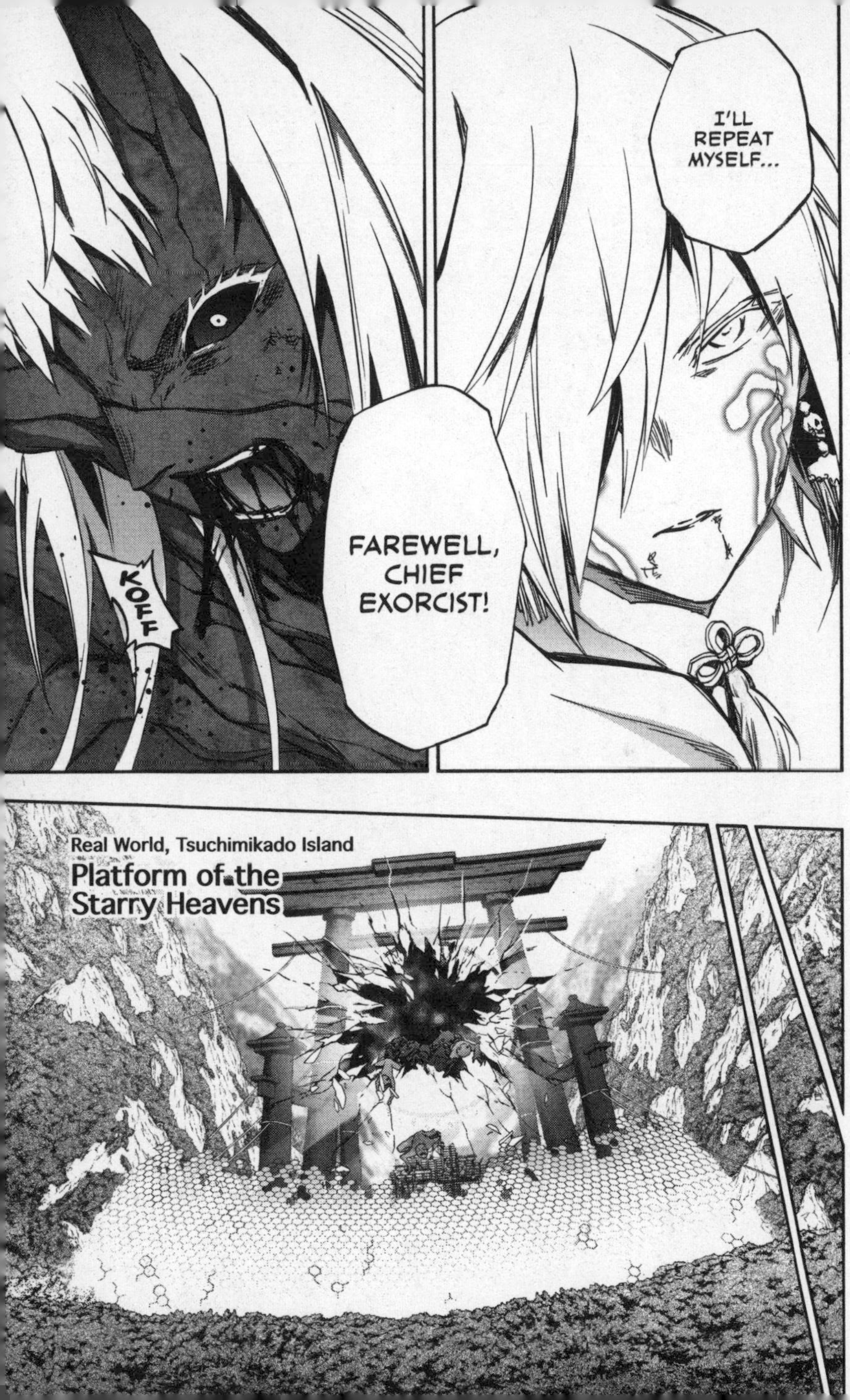
I'LL REPEAT MYSELF...
FAREWELL, CHIEF EXORCIST!
KOFF
Real World, Tsuchimikado Island
Platform of the Starry Heavens

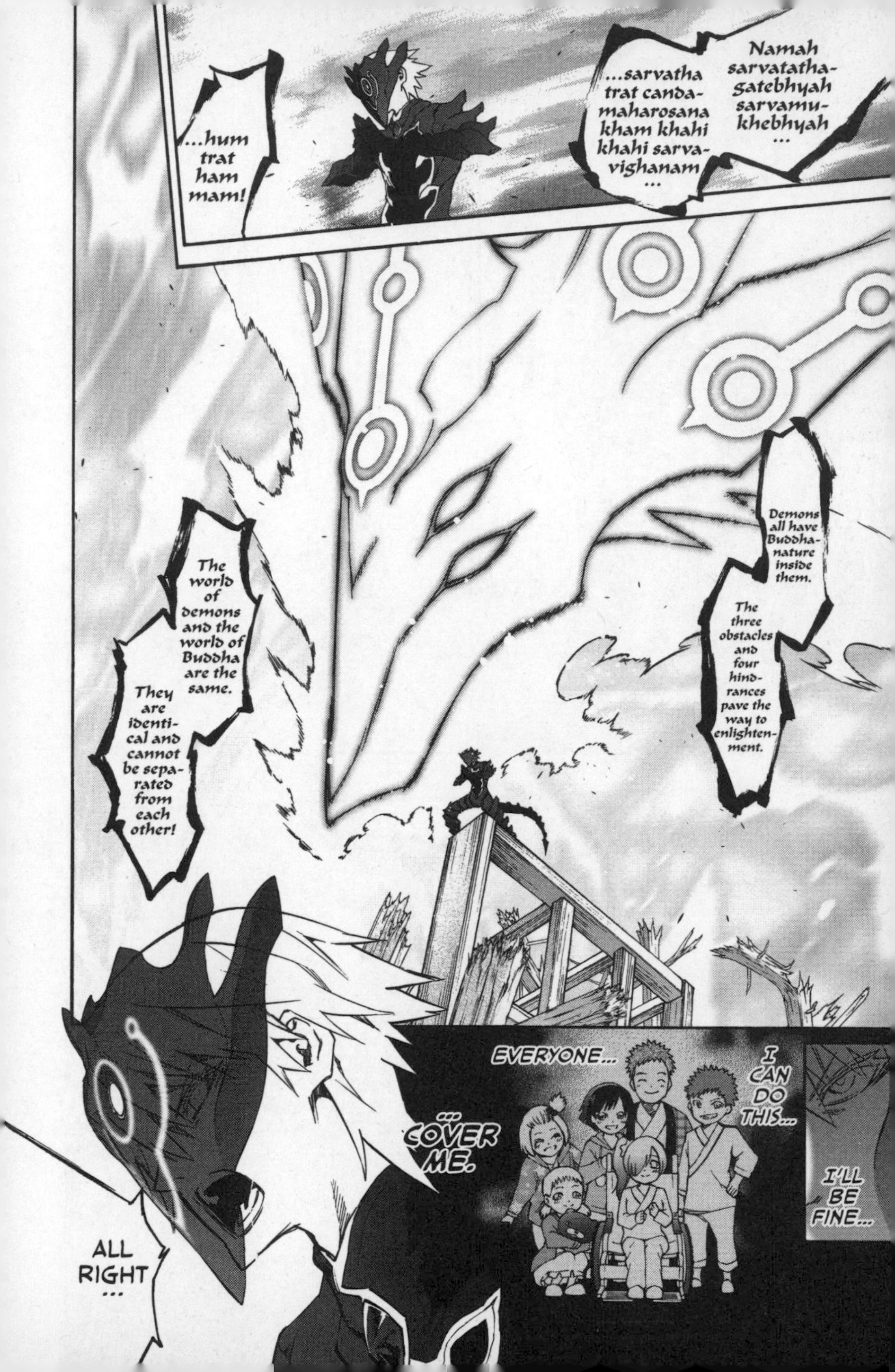
Namah sarvatatha-gatebhyah sarvamu-khebhyah ...
...sarvatha trat canda-maharosana kham khahi khahi sarva-vighanam ...
...hum trat ham mam!
Demons all have Buddha-nature inside them.
The three obstacles and four hind-rances pave the way to enlighten-ment.
The world of demons and the world of Buddha are the same.
They are identi-cal and cannot be sepa-rated from each other!
I'LL BE FINE...
I CAN DO THIS...
EVERYONE...
...COVER ME.
ALL RIGHT ...

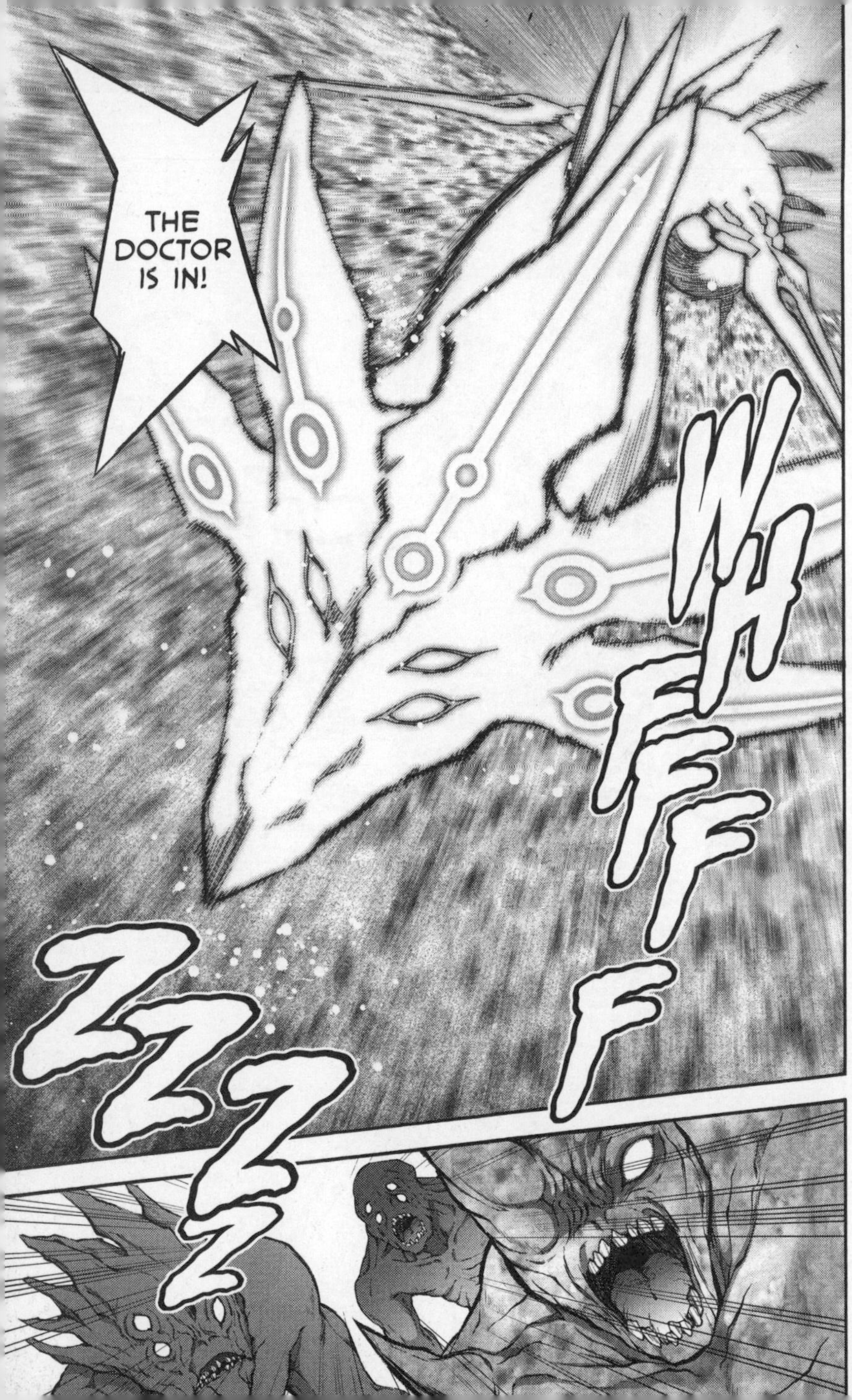
THE DOCTOR IS IN!
WHFFFF
ZZZZZ

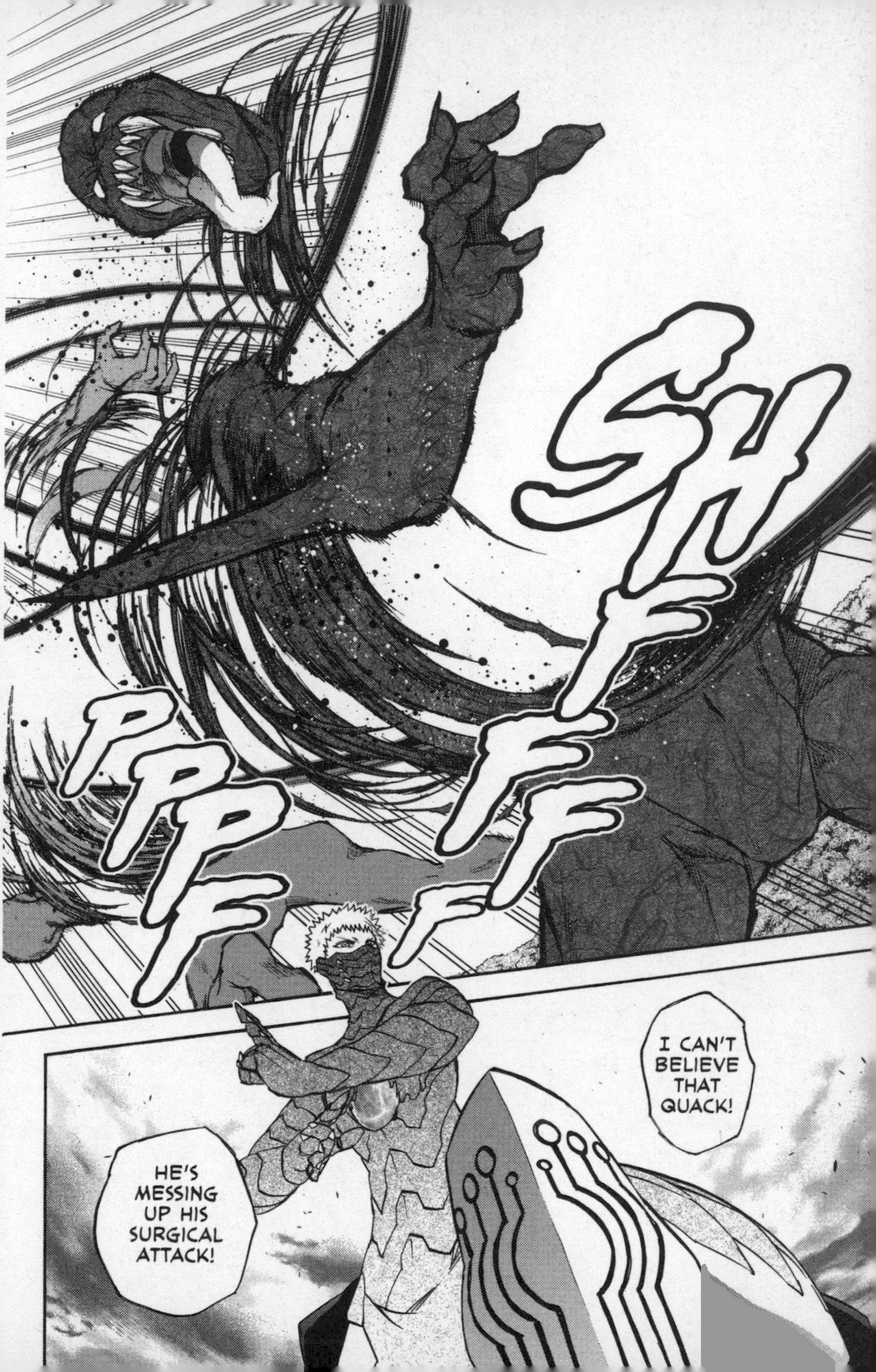
SHFFFF
PPPF
I CAN'T BELIEVE THAT QUACK!
HE'S MESSING UP HIS SURGICAL ATTACK!

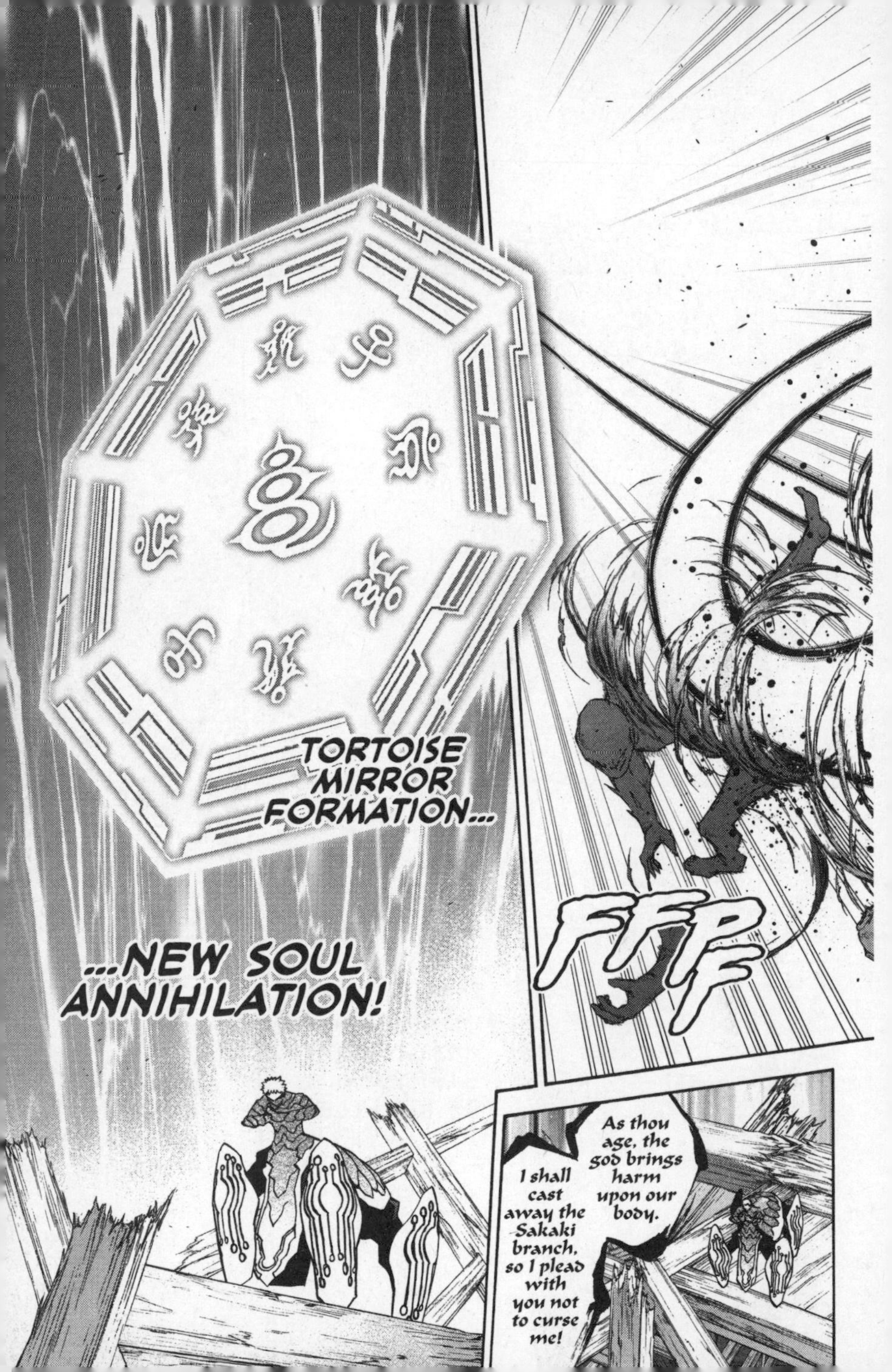
FFP
As thou age, the god brings harm upon our body.
I shall cast away the Sakaki branch, so I plead with you not to curse me!
TORTOISE MIRROR FORMATION...
...NEW SOUL ANNIHILATION!

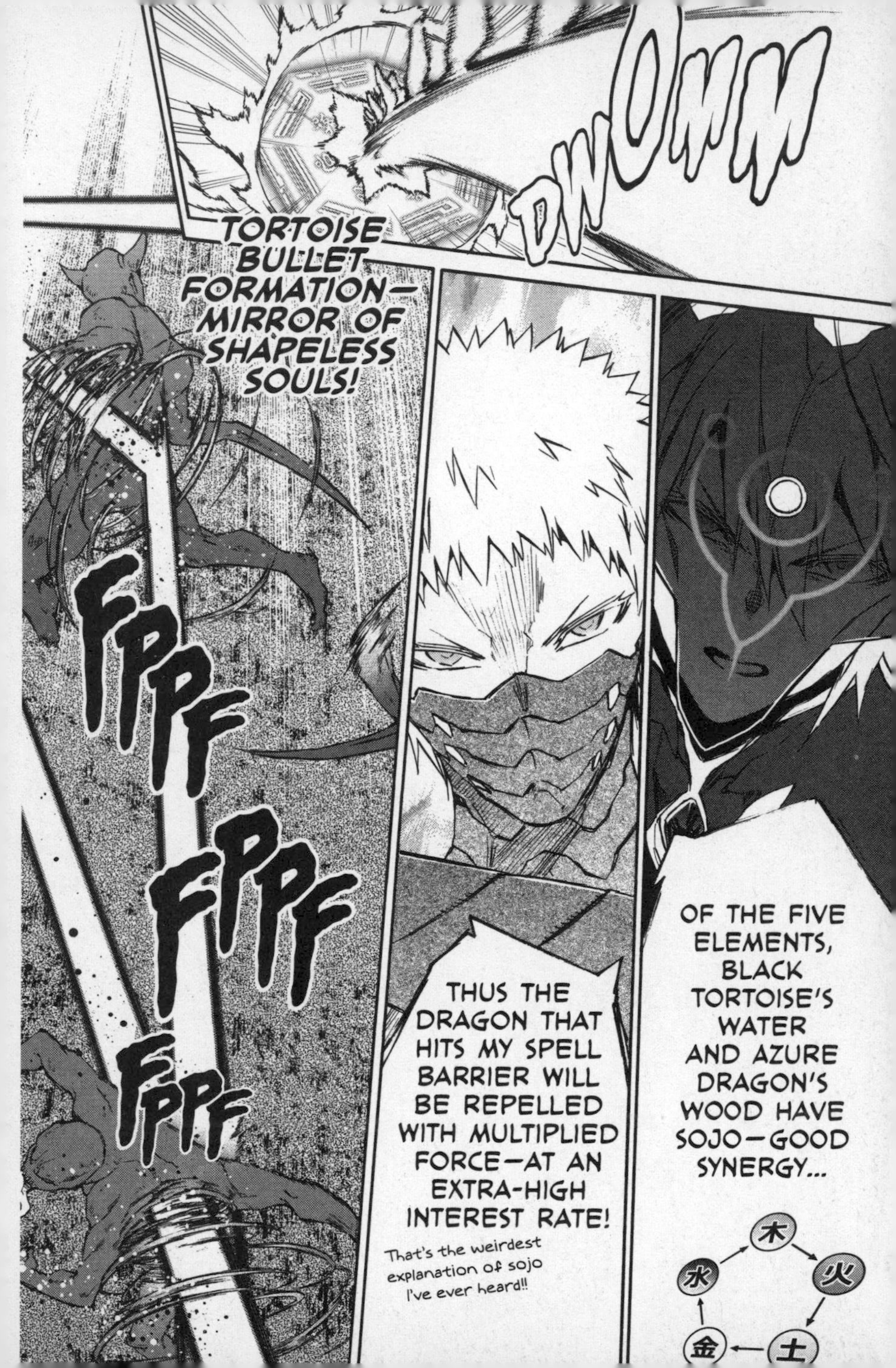
DWOMMM
TORTOISE BULLET FORMATION—MIRROR OF SHAPELESS SOULS!
OF THE FIVE ELEMENTS, BLACK TORTOISE'S WATER AND AZURE DRAGON'S WOOD HAVE SOJO—GOOD SYNERGY...
木
火
土
金
水
THUS THE DRAGON THAT HITS MY SPELL BARRIER WILL BE REPELLED WITH MULTIPLIED FORCE—AT AN EXTRA-HIGH INTEREST RATE!
That's the weirdest explanation of sojo I've ever heard!!
FPPF
FPPF
FPPF

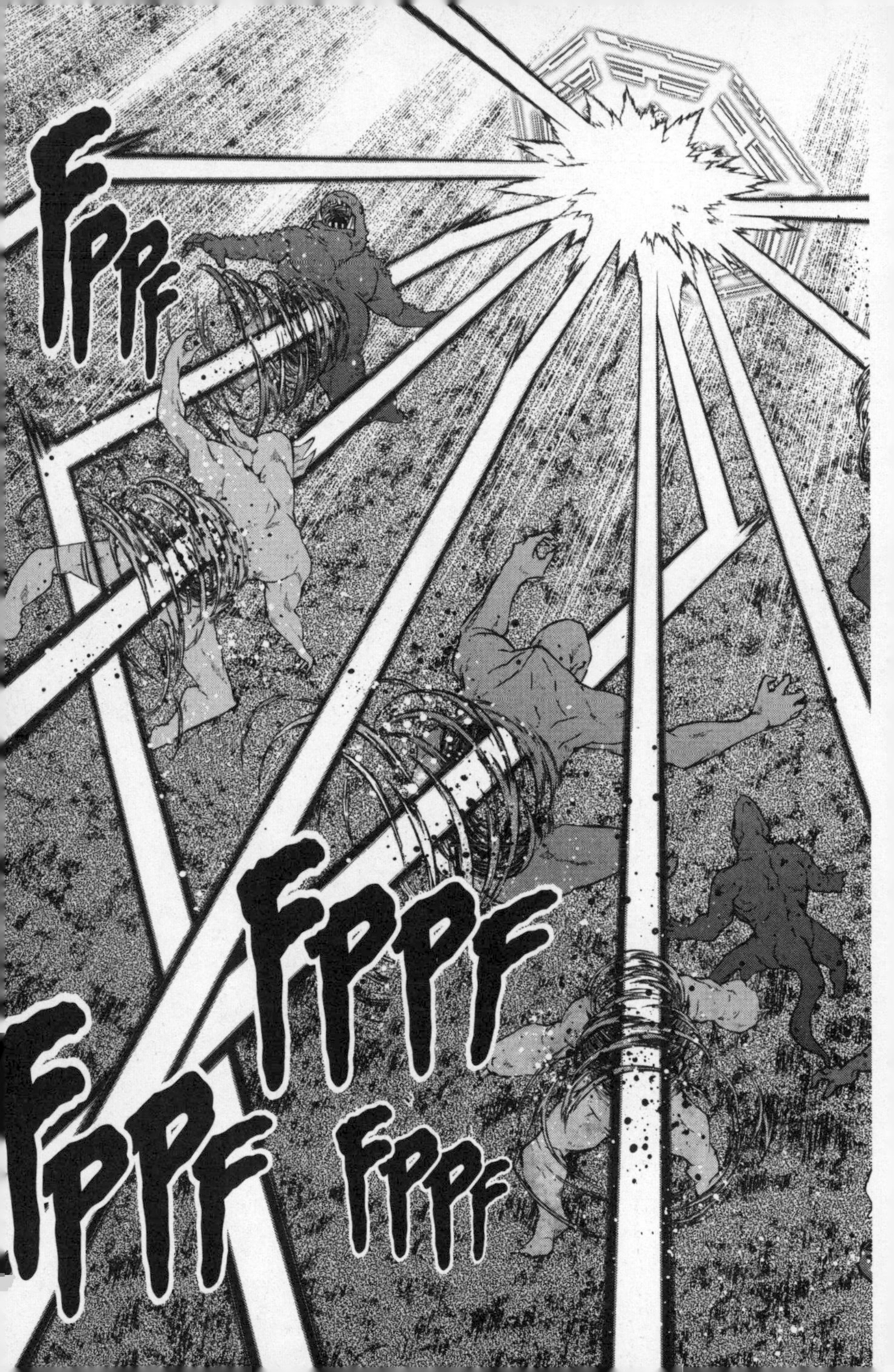
FPPF
FPPF
FPPF
FPPF

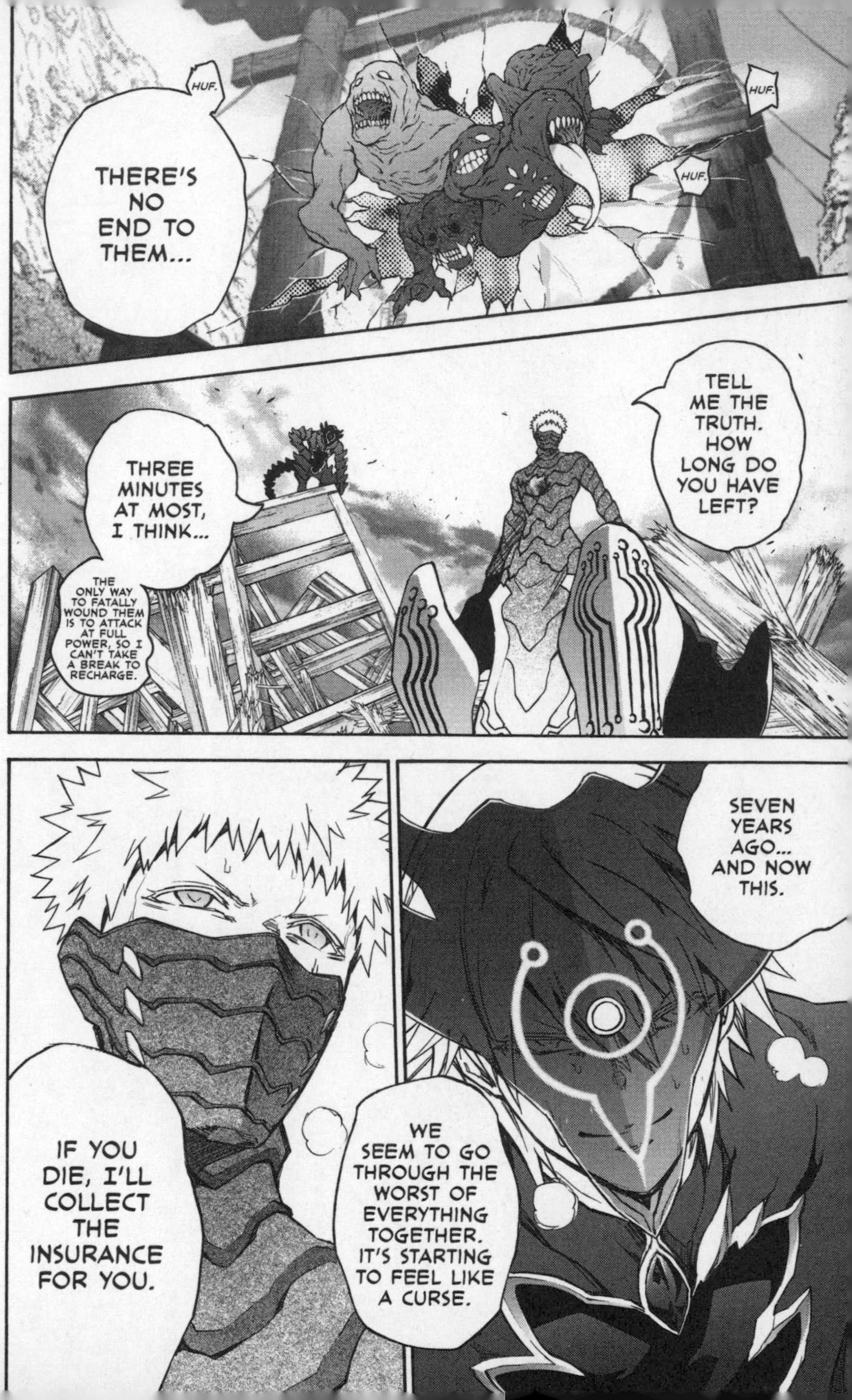
HUF.
HUF.
HUF.
THERE'S NO END TO THEM...
TELL ME THE TRUTH. HOW LONG DO YOU HAVE LEFT?
THREE MINUTES AT MOST, I THINK...
THE ONLY WAY TO FATALLY WOUND THEM IS TO ATTACK AT FULL POWER, SO I CAN'T TAKE A BREAK TO RECHARGE.
SEVEN YEARS AGO... AND NOW THIS.
WE SEEM TO GO THROUGH THE WORST OF EVERYTHING TOGETHER. IT'S STARTING TO FEEL LIKE A CURSE.
IF YOU DIE, I'LL COLLECT THE INSURANCE FOR YOU.

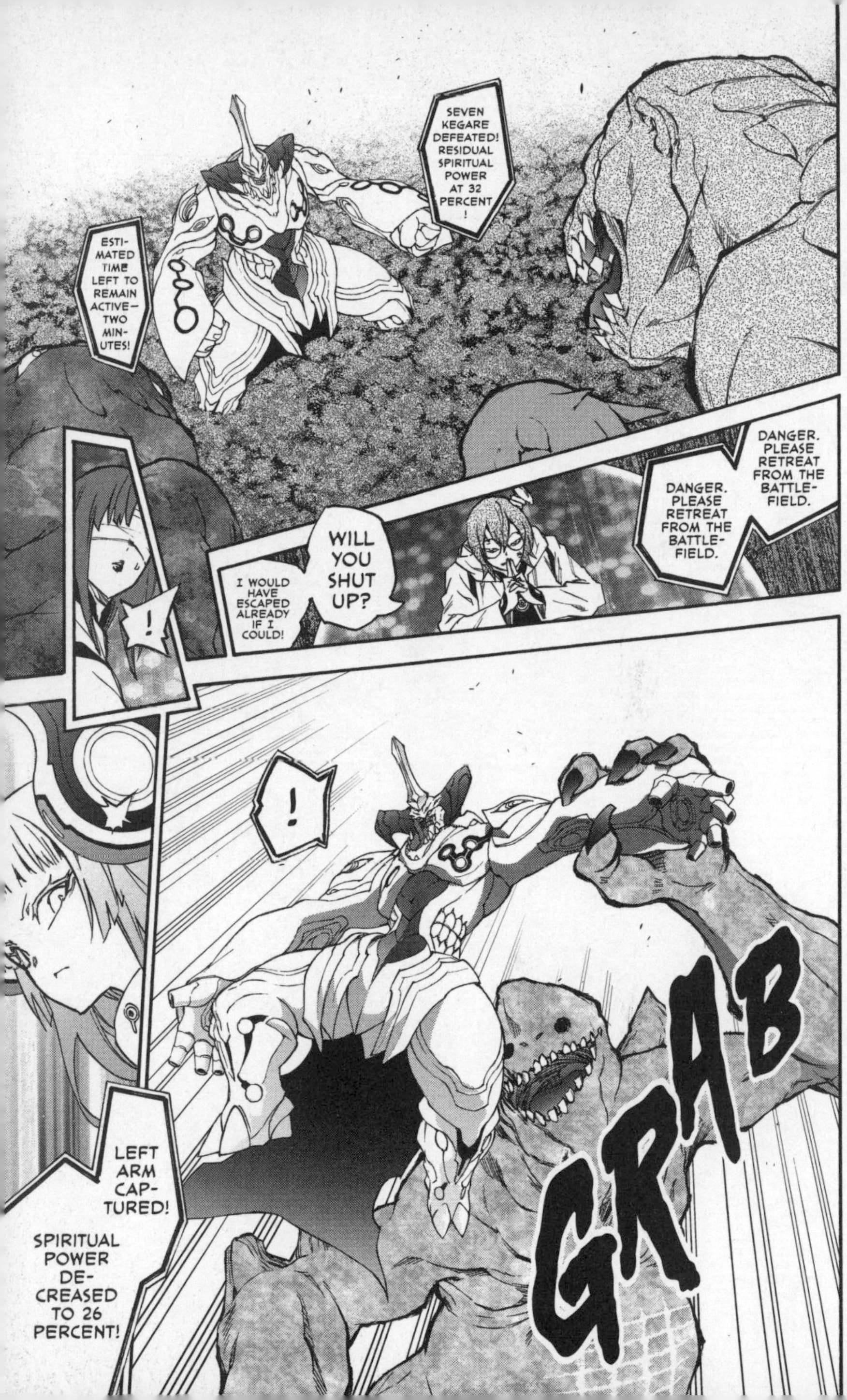
SEVEN KEGARE DEFEATED! RESIDUAL SPIRITUAL POWER AT 32 PERCENT!
ESTIMATED TIME LEFT TO REMAIN ACTIVE—TWO MINUTES!
DANGER. PLEASE RETREAT FROM THE BATTLEFIELD.
DANGER. PLEASE RETREAT FROM THE BATTLEFIELD.
WILL YOU SHUT UP?
I WOULD HAVE ESCAPED ALREADY IF I COULD!
!
!
GRAB
LEFT ARM CAPTURED!
SPIRITUAL POWER DECREASED TO 26 PERCENT!

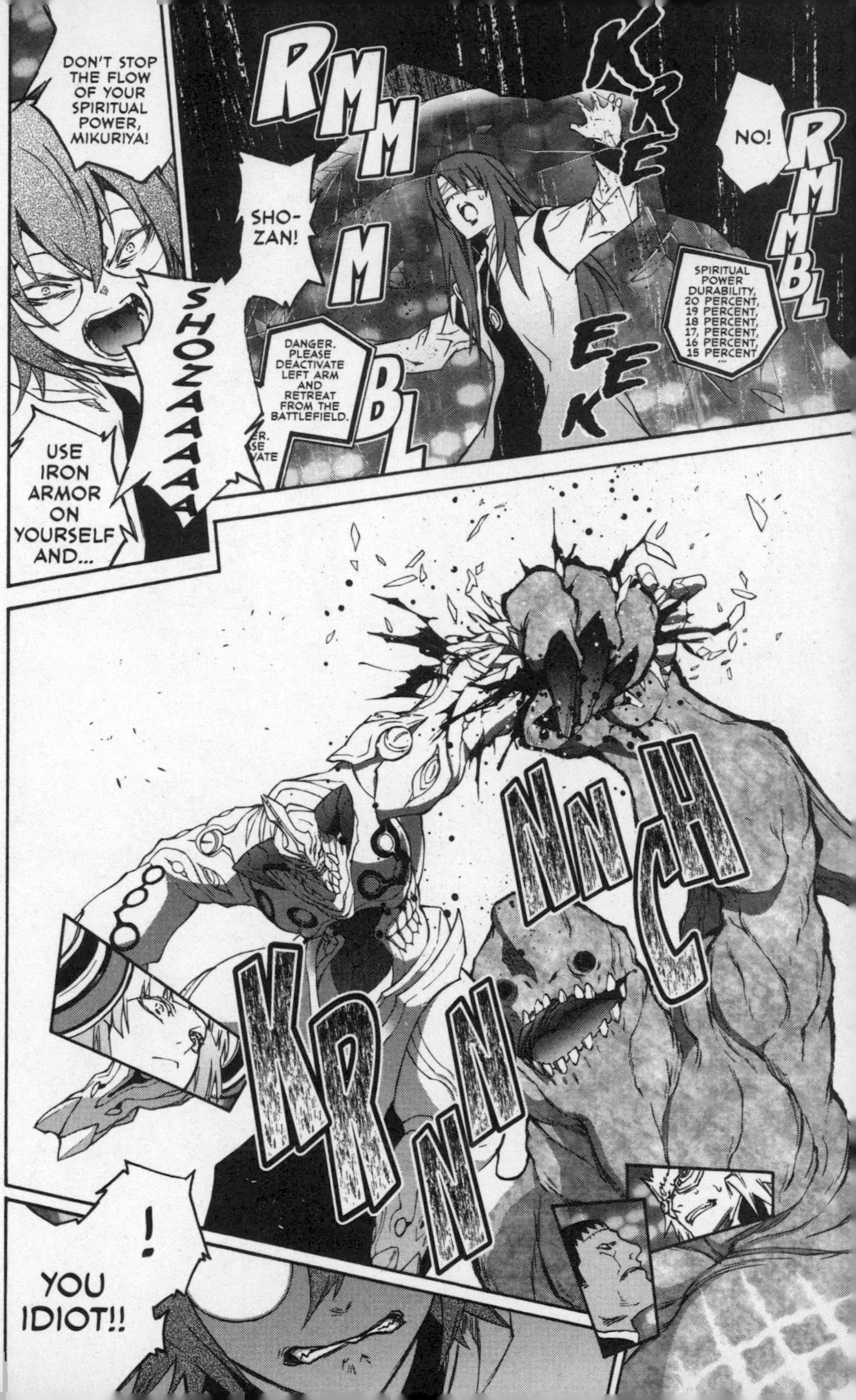
NO!
RMMBL
SPIRITUAL POWER DURABILITY, 20 PERCENT, 19 PERCENT, 18 PERCENT, 17, PERCENT, 16 PERCENT, 15 PERCENT ...
KREEEK
RMMMMBL
SHO-ZAN!
DANGER. PLEASE DEACTIVATE LEFT ARM AND RETREAT FROM THE BATTLEFIELD.
DON'T STOP THE FLOW OF YOUR SPIRITUAL POWER, MIKURIYA!
SHOZAAAAAA
USE IRON ARMOR ON YOURSELF AND...
KRNNNNCH
!
YOU IDIOT!!

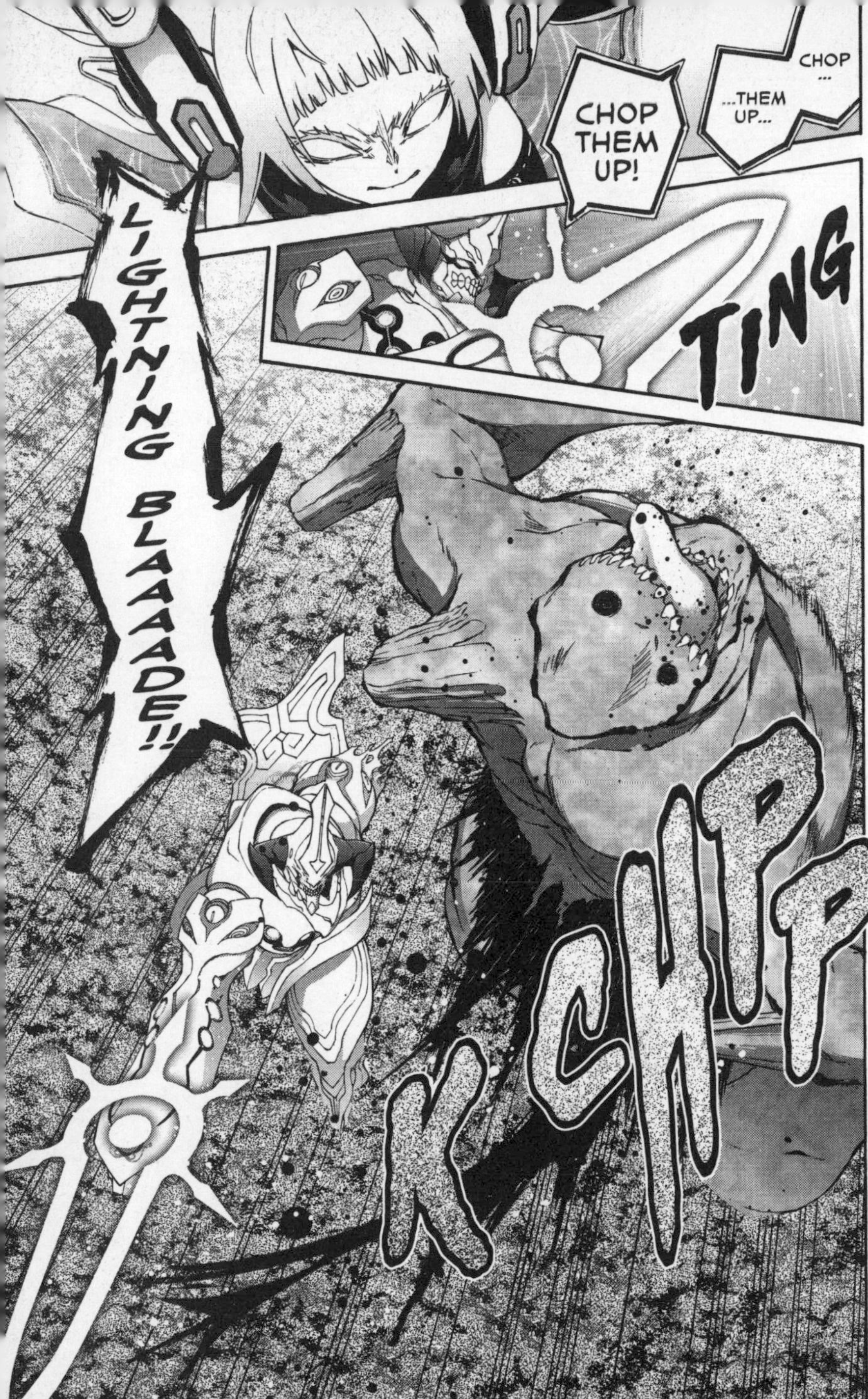
CHOP ...
...THEM UP...
CHOP THEM UP!
TING
LIGHTNING BLAAAADE!!
KCHPP

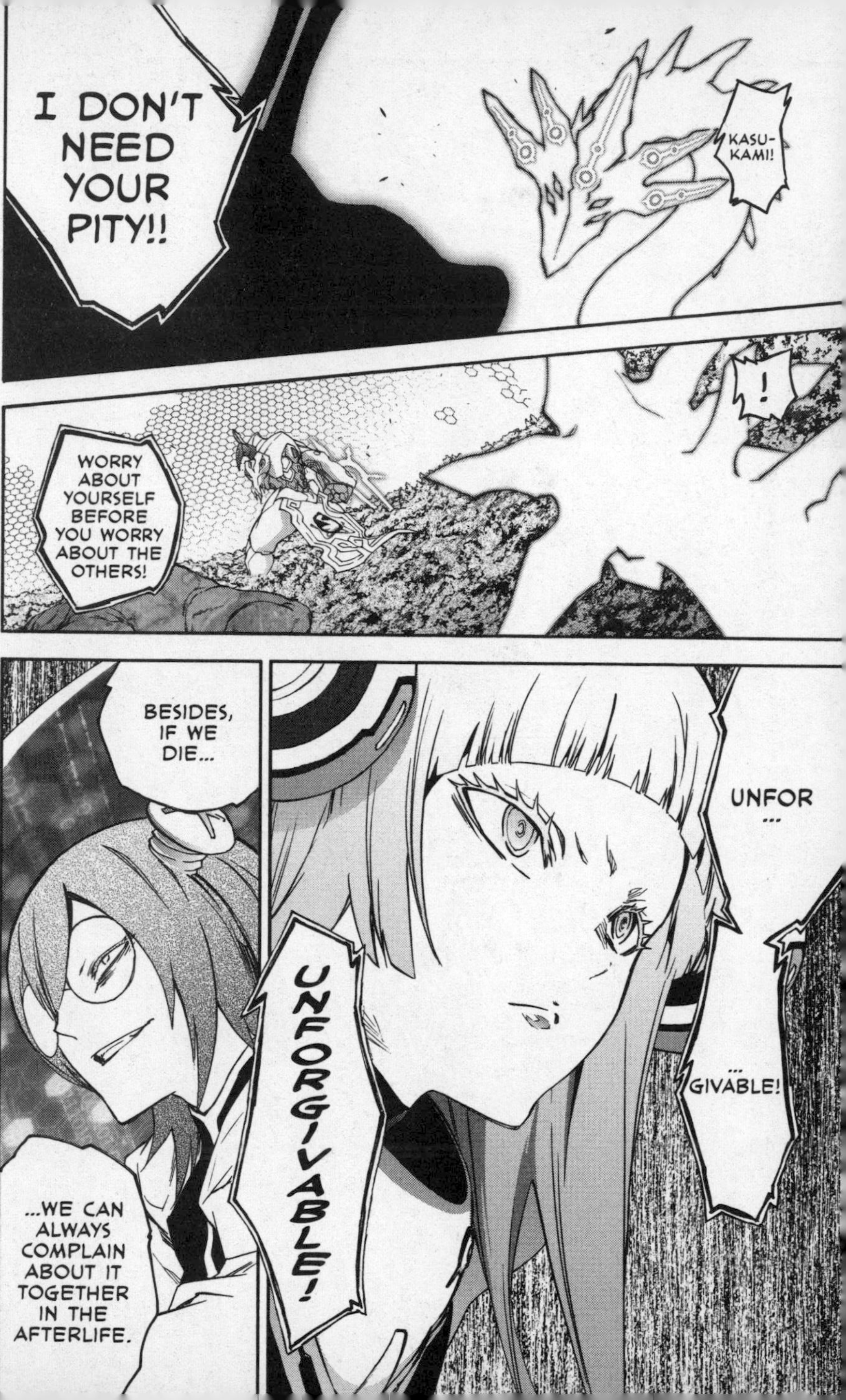
KASU-KAMI!
I DON'T NEED YOUR PITY!!
!
WORRY ABOUT YOURSELF BEFORE YOU WORRY ABOUT THE OTHERS!
UNFOR...
...GIVABLE!
UNFORGIVABLE!
BESIDES, IF WE DIE...
...WE CAN ALWAYS COMPLAIN ABOUT IT TOGETHER IN THE AFTERLIFE.

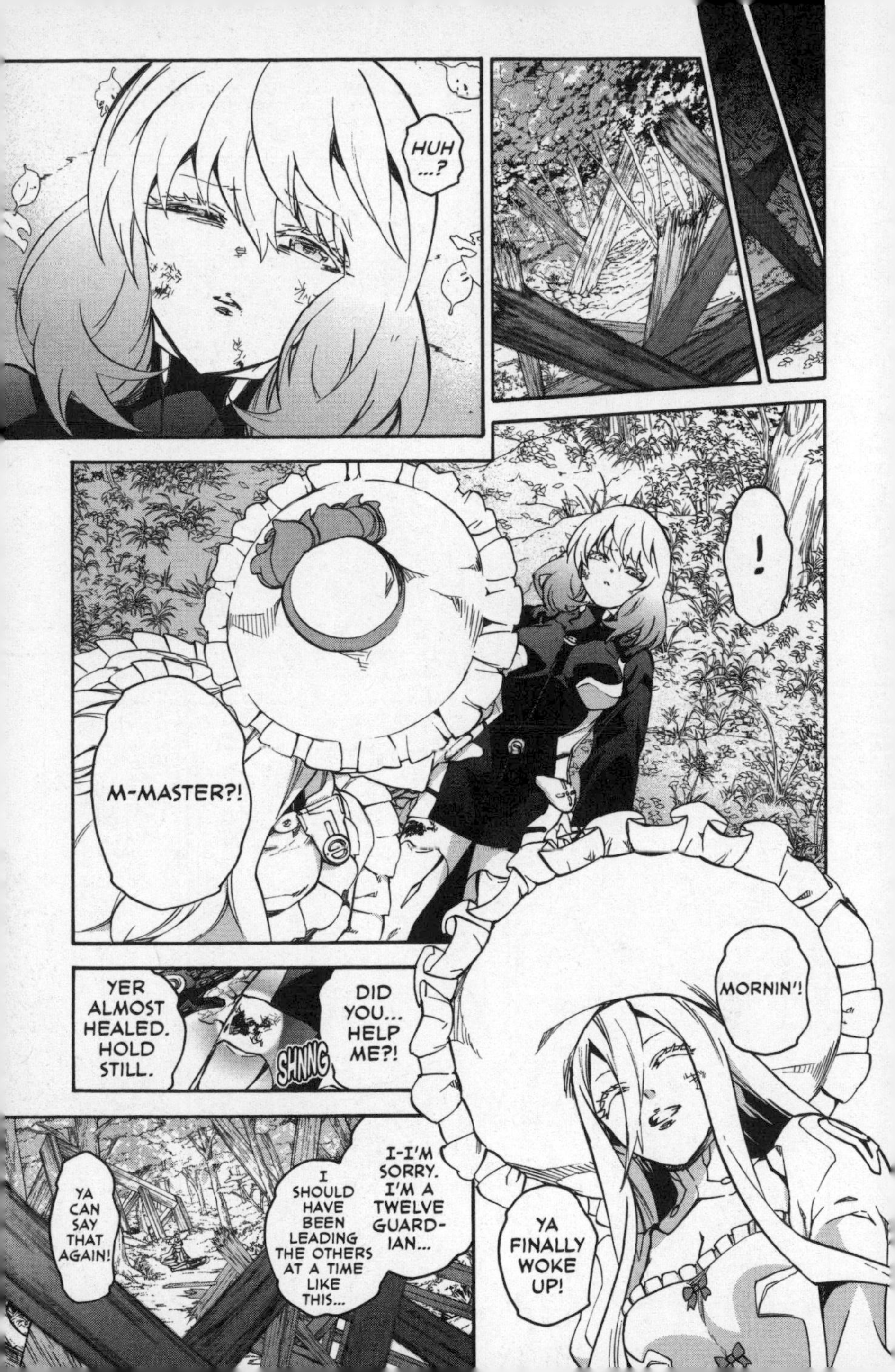
HUH ...?
!
M-MASTER?!
MORNIN'!
DID YOU... HELP ME?!
SHNNG
YER ALMOST HEALED. HOLD STILL.
YA FINALLY WOKE UP!
I-I'M SORRY. I'M A TWELVE GUARD-IAN...
I SHOULD HAVE BEEN LEADING THE OTHERS AT A TIME LIKE THIS...
YA CAN SAY THAT AGAIN!

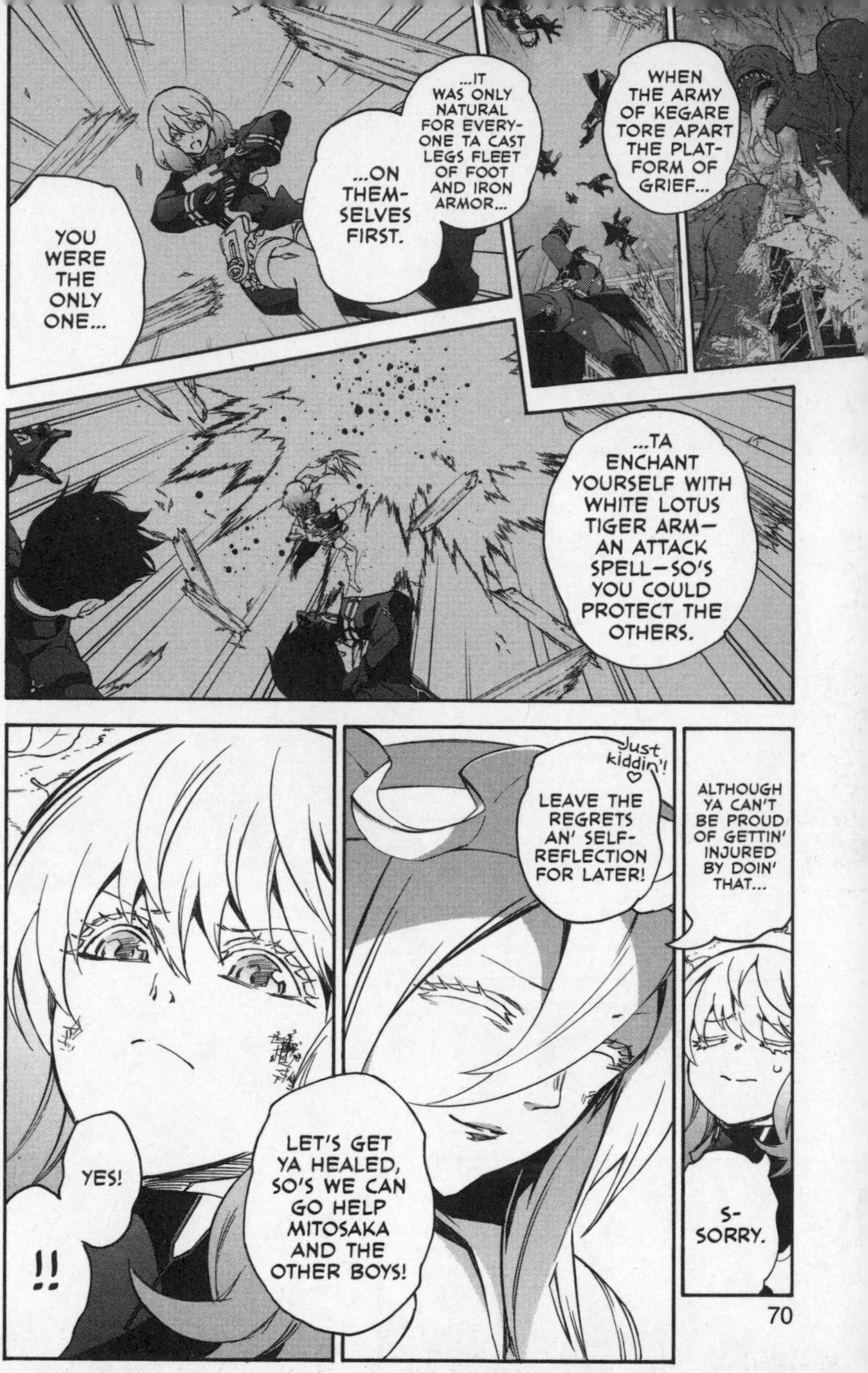
WHEN THE ARMY OF KEGARE TORE APART THE PLATFORM OF GRIEF...
...IT WAS ONLY NATURAL FOR EVERYONE TA CAST LEGS FLEET OF FOOT AND IRON ARMOR...
...ON THEMSELVES FIRST.
YOU WERE THE ONLY ONE...
...TA ENCHANT YOURSELF WITH WHITE LOTUS TIGER ARM—AN ATTACK SPELL—SO'S YOU COULD PROTECT THE OTHERS.
ALTHOUGH YA CAN'T BE PROUD OF GETTIN' INJURED BY DOIN' THAT...
S-SORRY.
Just kiddin'! ♡
LEAVE THE REGRETS AN' SELF-REFLECTION FOR LATER!
LET'S GET YA HEALED, SO'S WE CAN GO HELP MITOSAKA AND THE OTHER BOYS!
YES!
!!

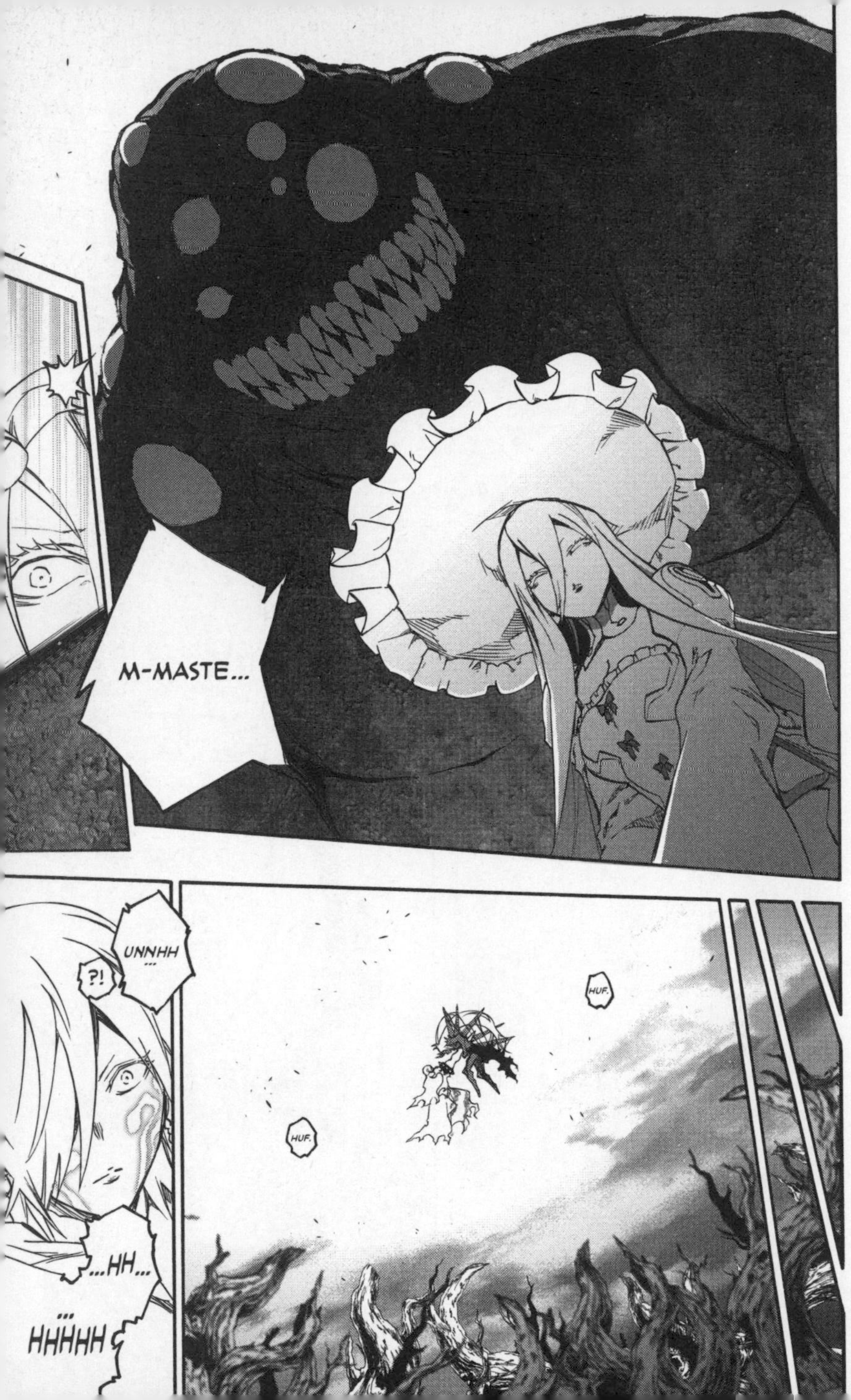
M-MASTE...
HUF.
HUF.
UNNHH...
?!
...HH...
...HHHHH

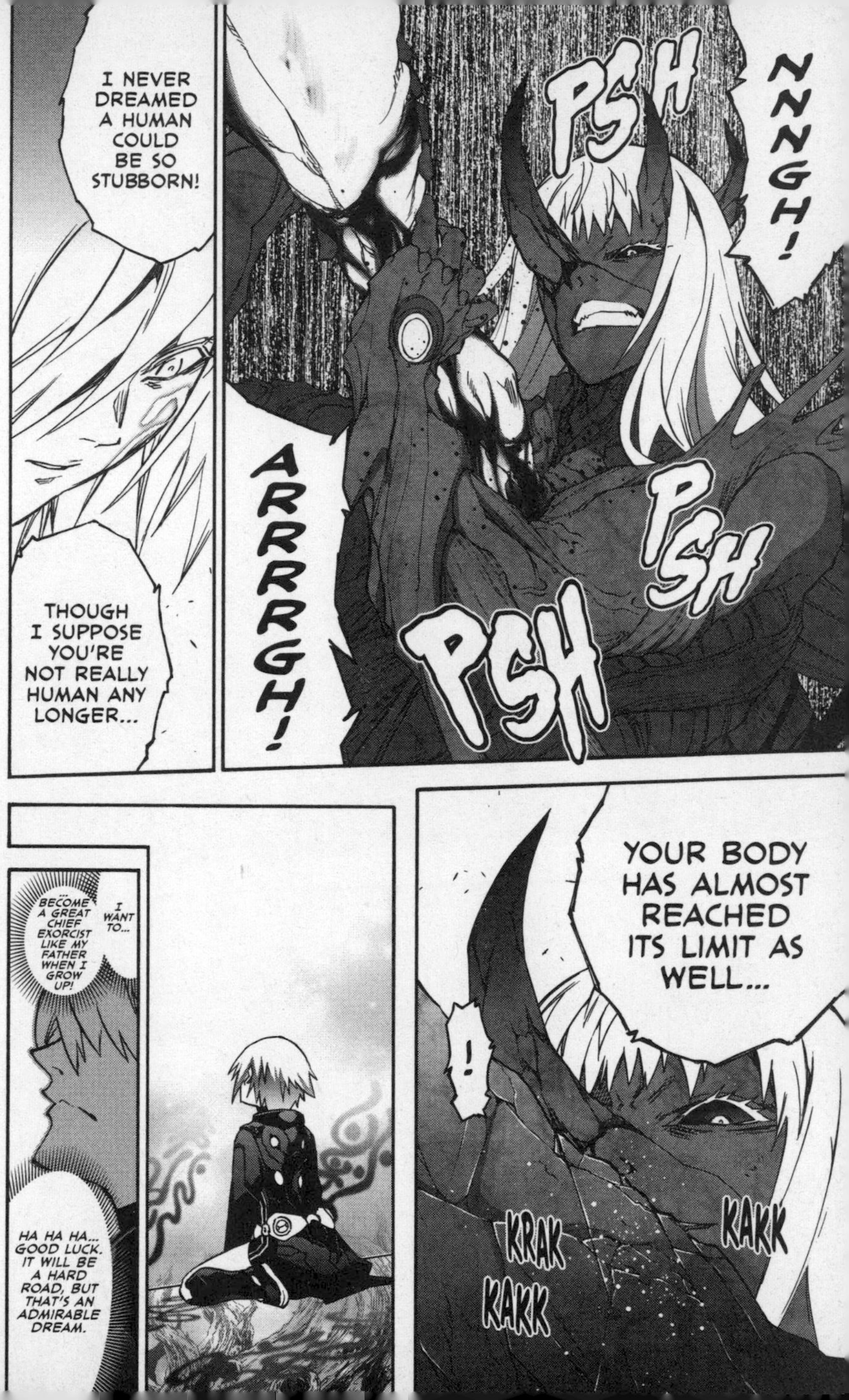
NNNGH!
PSH
PSH
PSH
ARRRRGH!
I NEVER DREAMED A HUMAN COULD BE SO STUBBORN!
THOUGH I SUPPOSE YOU'RE NOT REALLY HUMAN ANY LONGER...
YOUR BODY HAS ALMOST REACHED ITS LIMIT AS WELL...
!
KAKK
KRAK
KAKK
I WANT TO...
...BECOME A GREAT CHIEF EXORCIST LIKE MY FATHER WHEN I GROW UP!
HA HA HA... GOOD LUCK. IT WILL BE A HARD ROAD, BUT THAT'S AN ADMIRABLE DREAM.

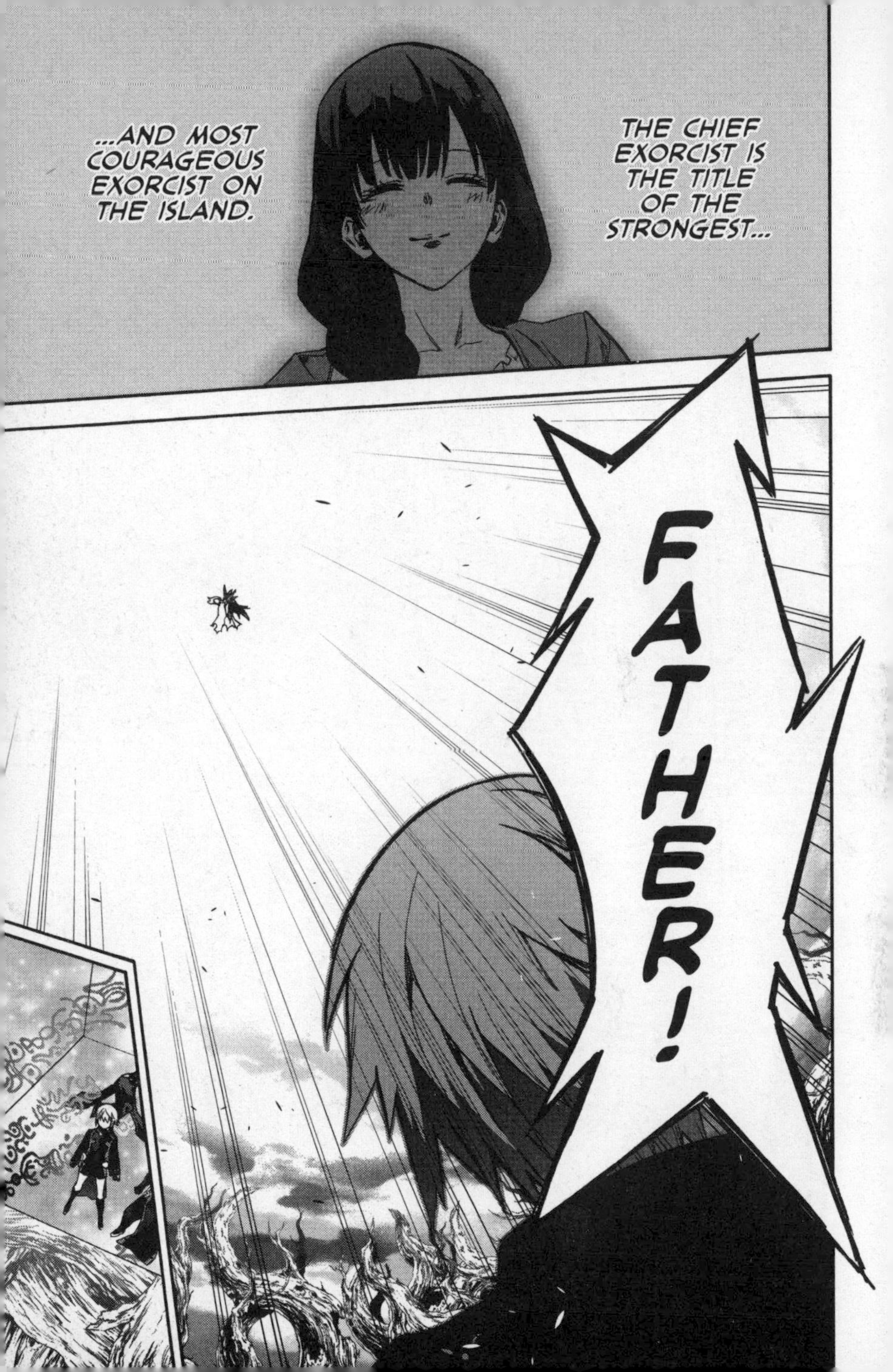
THE CHIEF EXORCIST IS THE TITLE OF THE STRONGEST...
...AND MOST COURAGEOUS EXORCIST ON THE ISLAND.
FATHER!

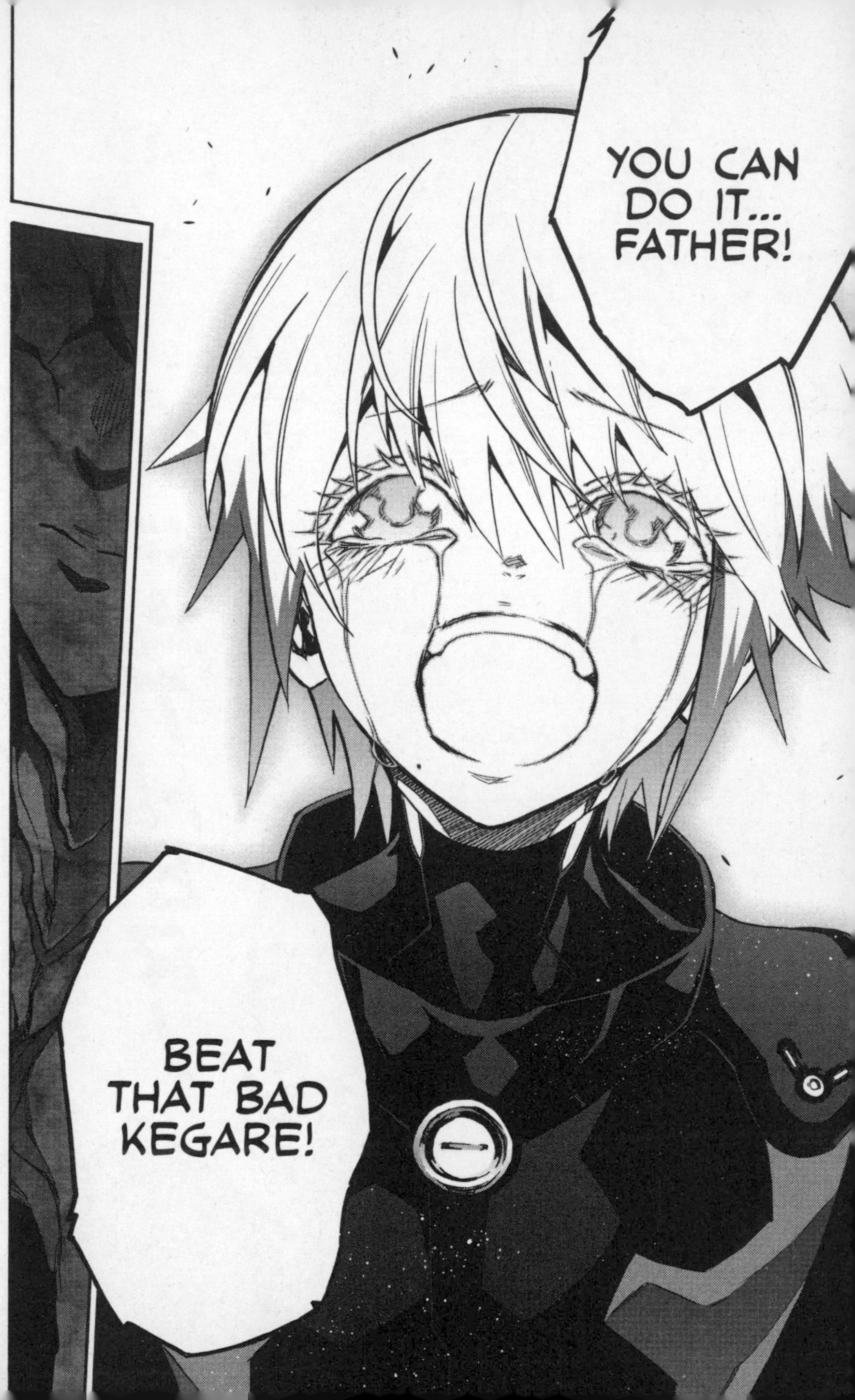
YOU CAN DO IT... FATHER!
BEAT THAT BAD KEGARE!

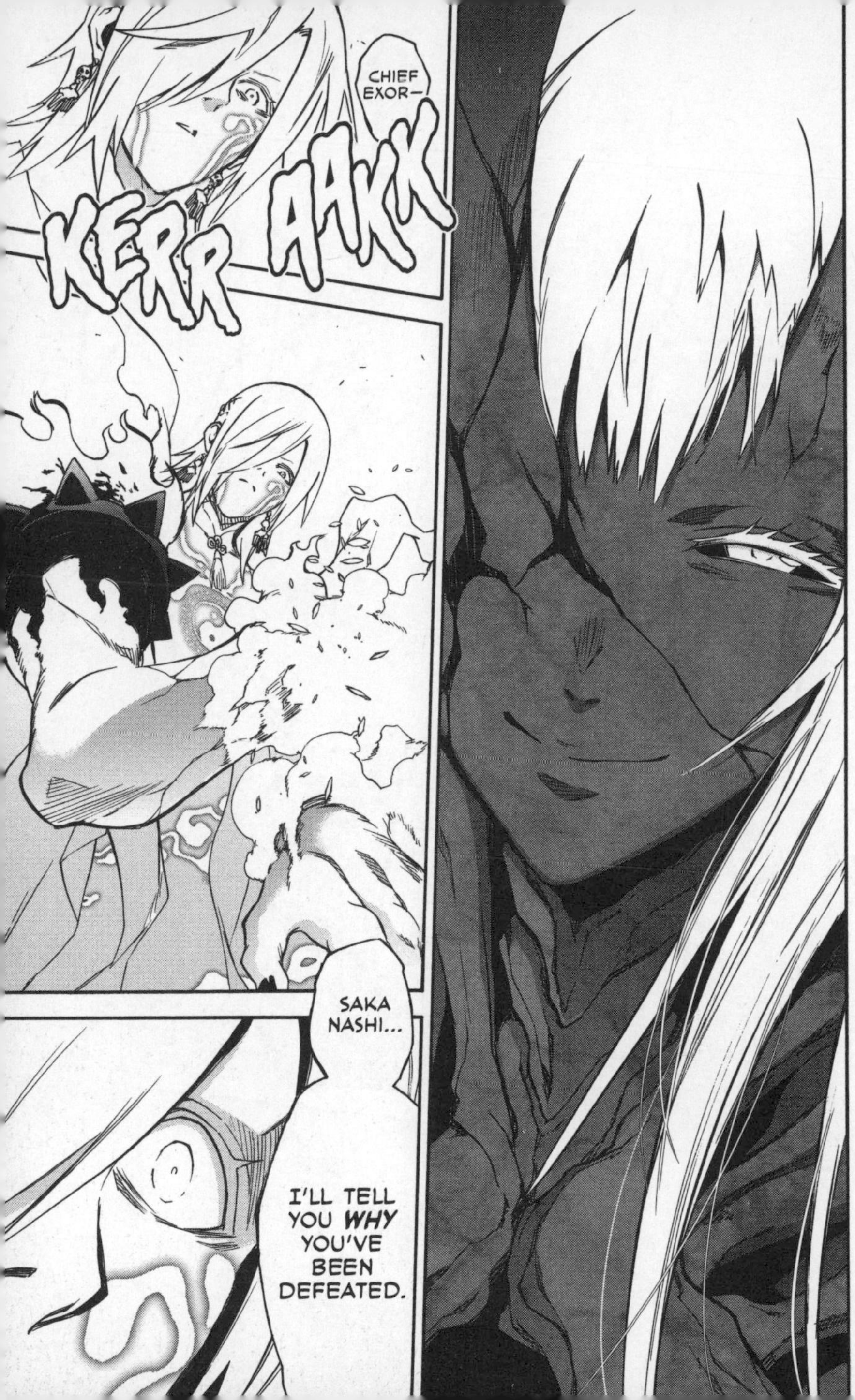
CHIEF EXOR—
KERR AAKK
SAKA NASHI...
I'LL TELL YOU *WHY* YOU'VE BEEN DEFEATED.

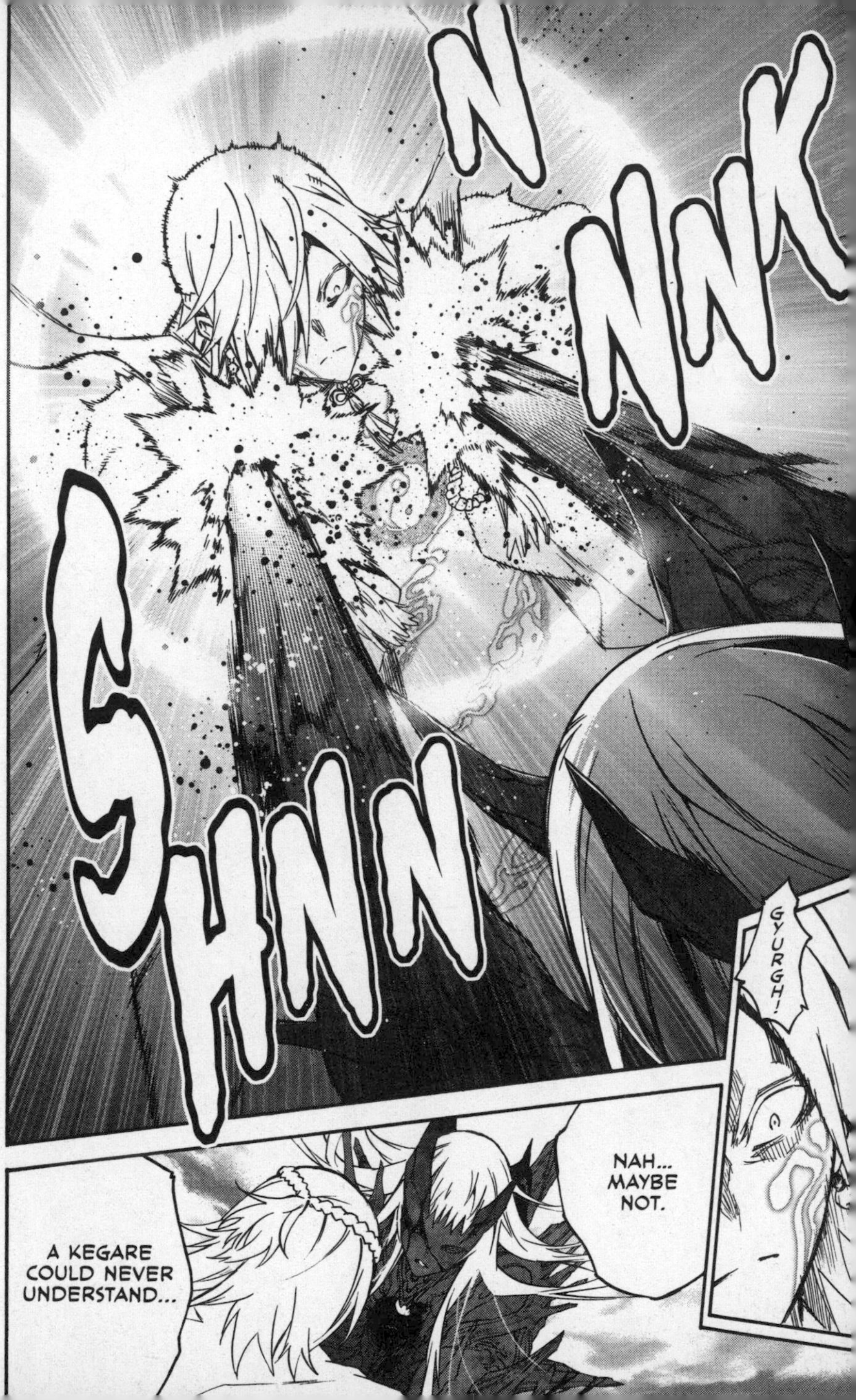
SHNNNNNK
GYURGH!
NAH... MAYBE NOT.
A KEGARE COULD NEVER UNDERSTAND...

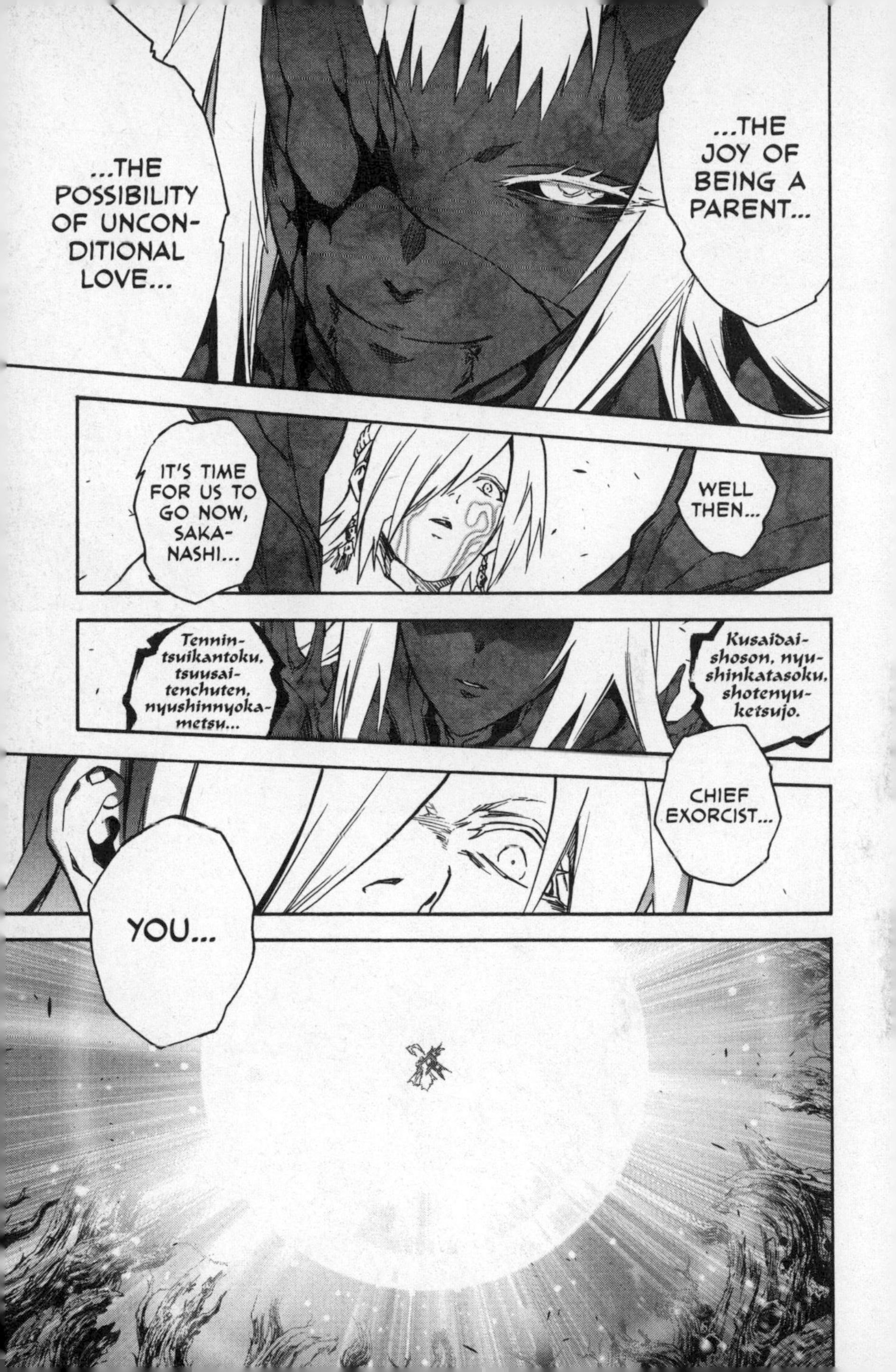
...THE JOY OF BEING A PARENT...
...THE POSSIBILITY OF UNCON-DITIONAL LOVE...
WELL THEN...
IT'S TIME FOR US TO GO NOW, SAKA-NASHI...
Kusaidai-shoson, nyu-shinkatasoku, shotenyu-ketsujo.
Tennin-tsuikantoku, tsuusai-tenchuten, nyushinnyoka-metsu...
CHIEF EXORCIST...
YOU...

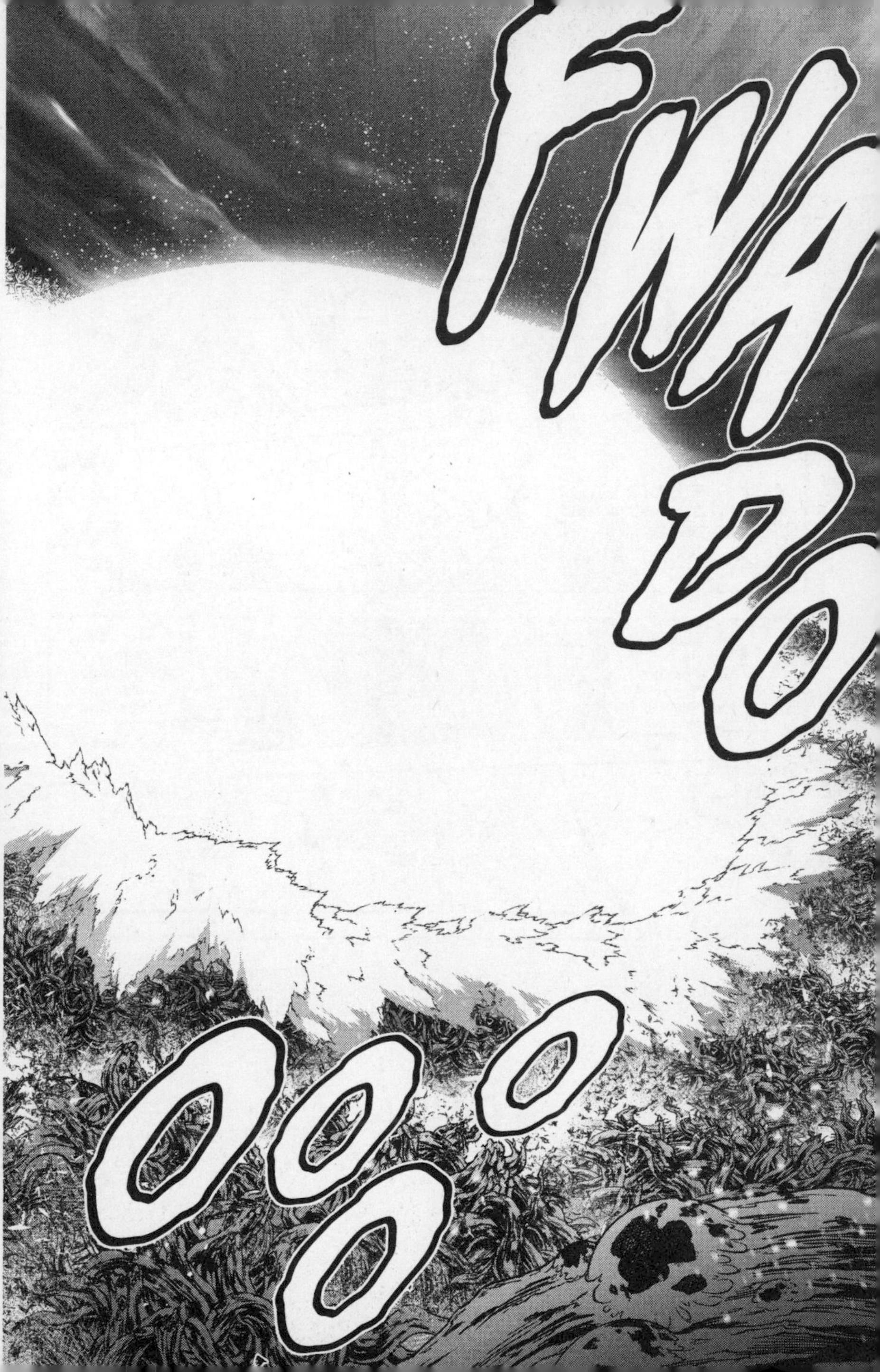
FWADOOOOO

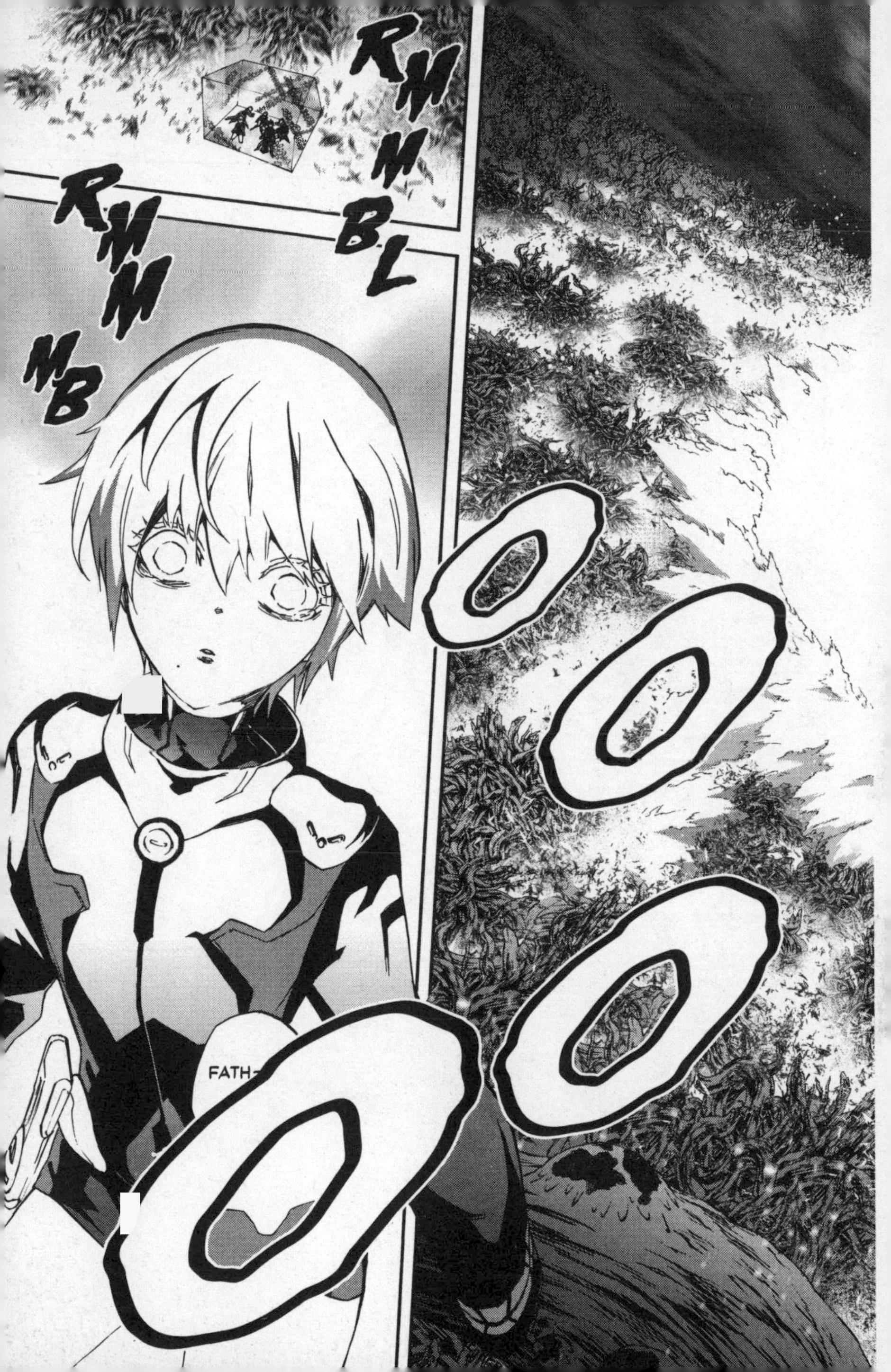
RMMMBL
RMMMB
FATH-
OOOOO

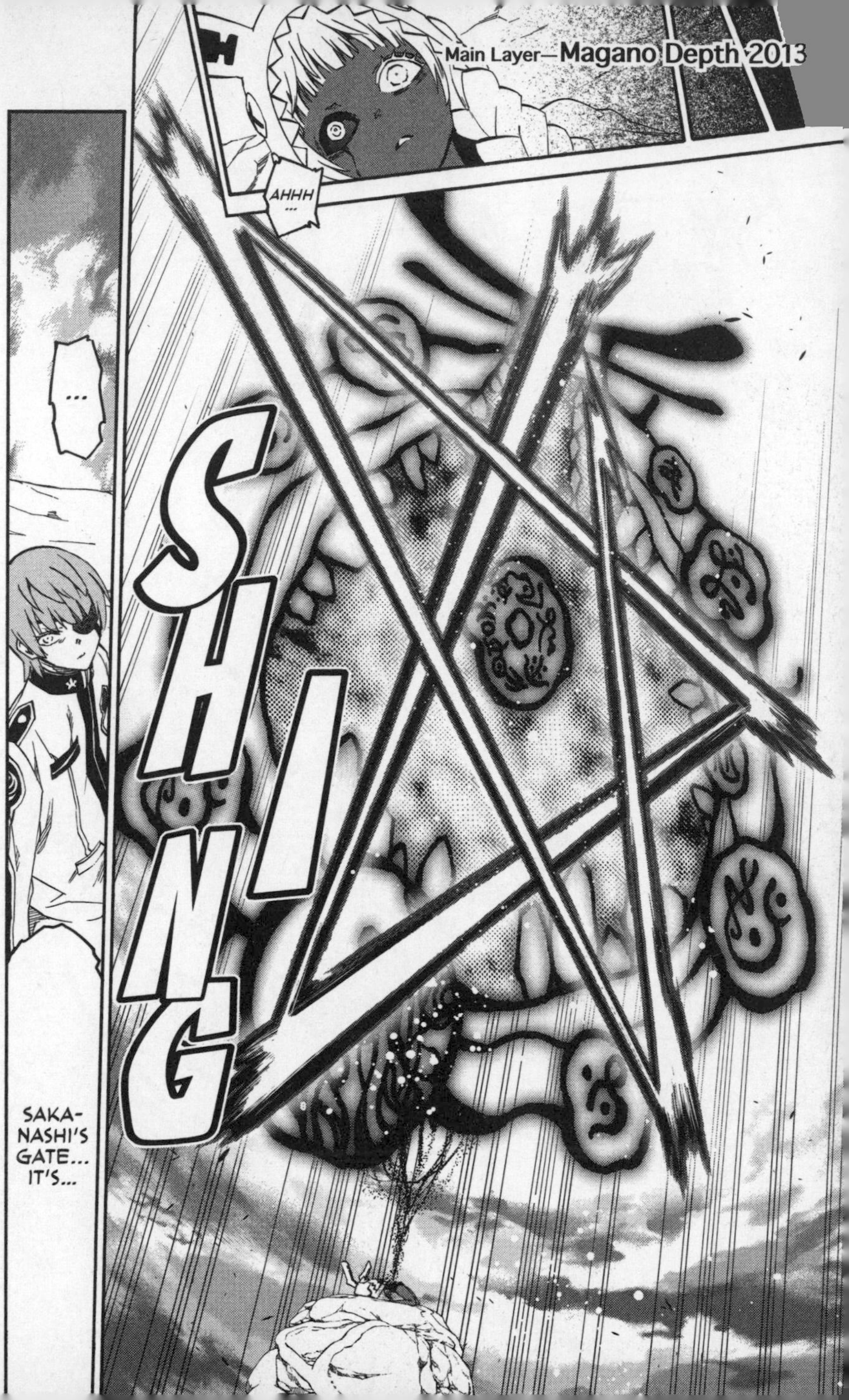
Main Layer—Magano Depth 2013
AHHH...
SHING
...
SAKA-NASHI'S GATE... IT'S...

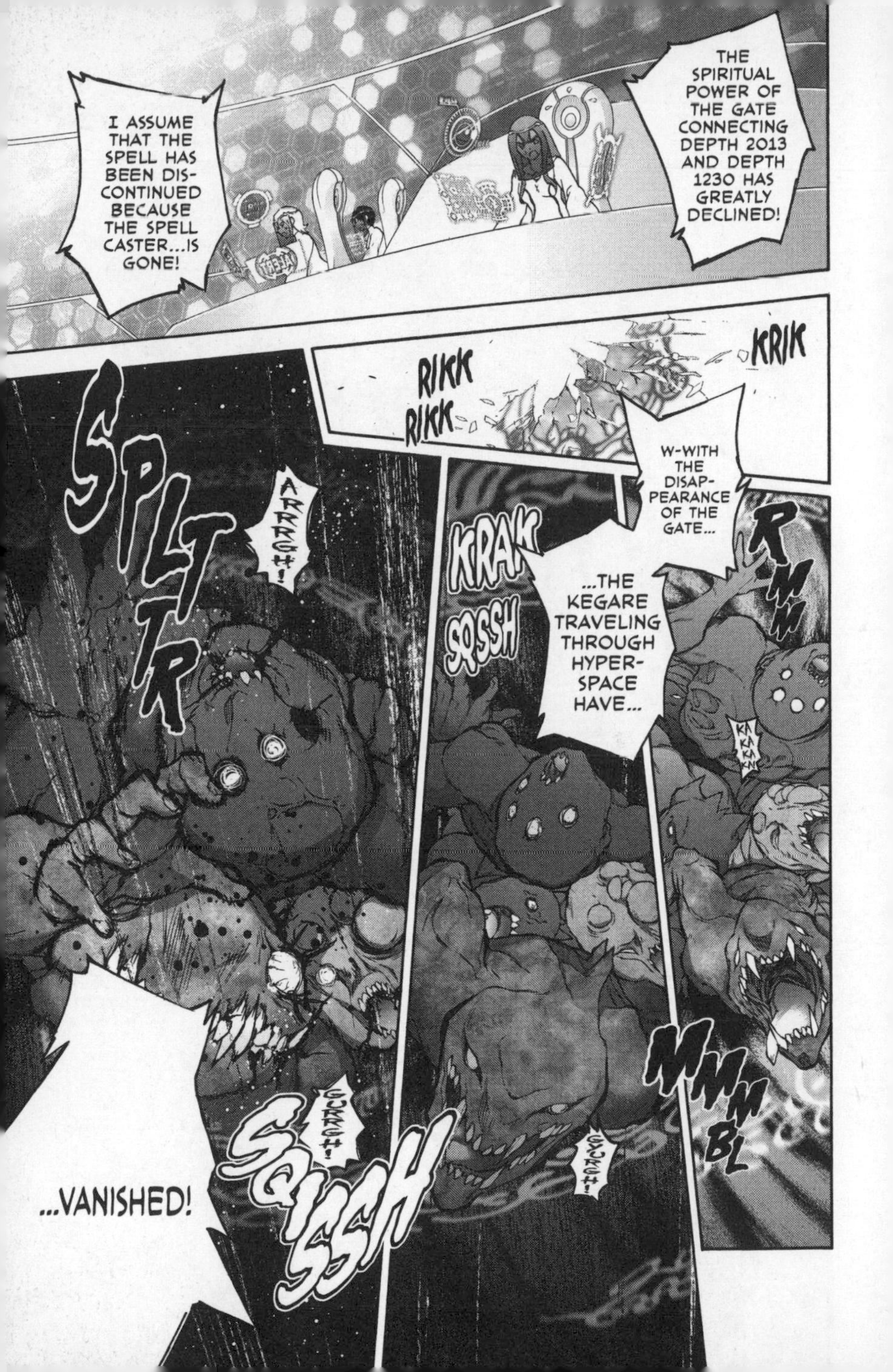
THE SPIRITUAL POWER OF THE GATE CONNECTING DEPTH 2013 AND DEPTH 1230 HAS GREATLY DECLINED!
I ASSUME THAT THE SPELL HAS BEEN DIS-CONTINUED BECAUSE THE SPELL CASTER...IS GONE!
KRIK
RIKK RIKK
W-WITH THE DISAP-PEARANCE OF THE GATE...
RMMM
KAKAKAKA
MMMMBL
KRAK
SQSSH
...THE KEGARE TRAVELING THROUGH HYPER-SPACE HAVE...
GURRGH!
SPLTTR
ARRRGH!
GURRGH!
SQSSH
...VANISHED!

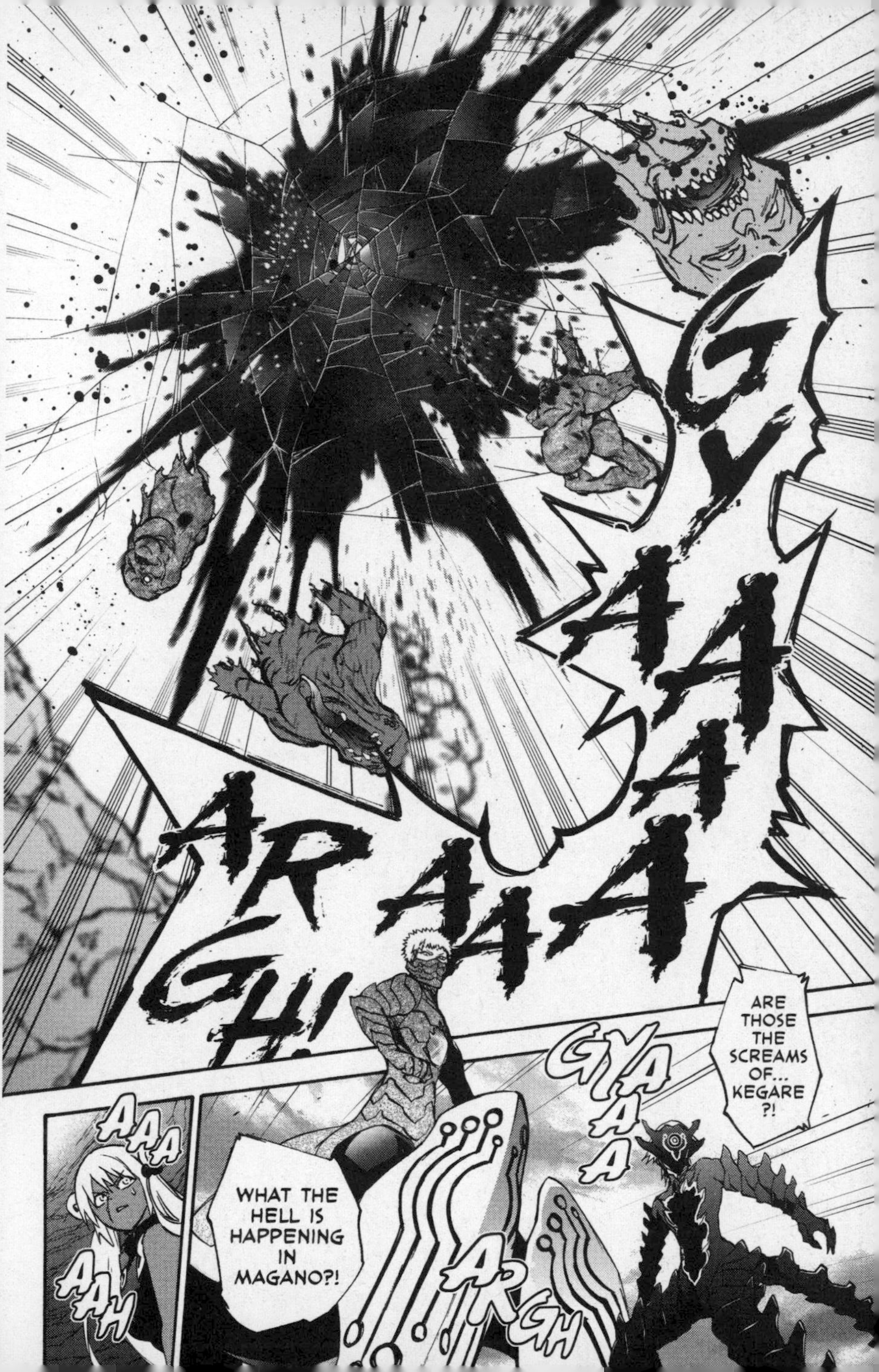
GYAAA
AAA
ARGH!
ARE THOSE THE SCREAMS OF... KEGARE?!
GYAAAA
WHAT THE HELL IS HAPPENING IN MAGANO?!
ARGH
AAA
AAH

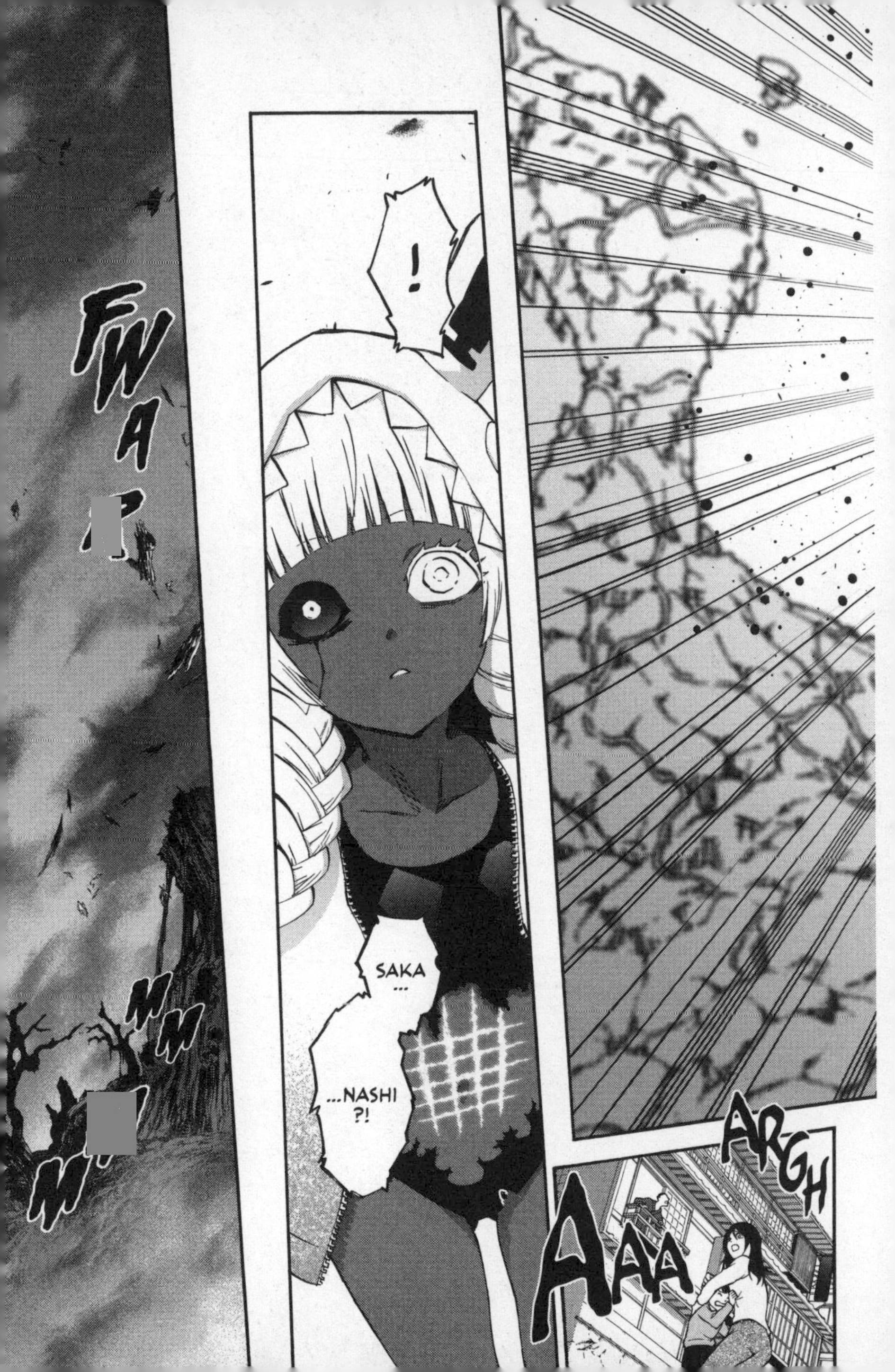
AAA ARGH
!
SAKA...
...NASHI?!
FWAP
MMMMM

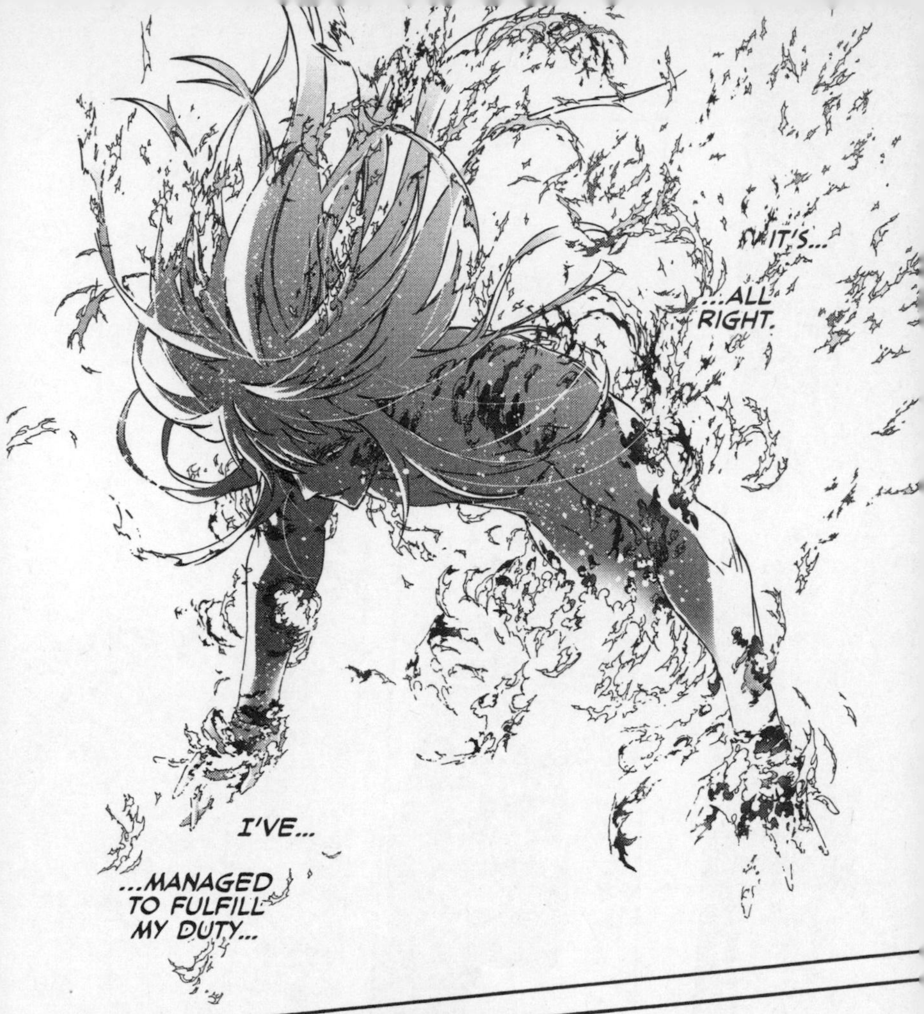
IT'S...
...ALL RIGHT.
I'VE...
...MANAGED TO FULFILL MY DUTY...
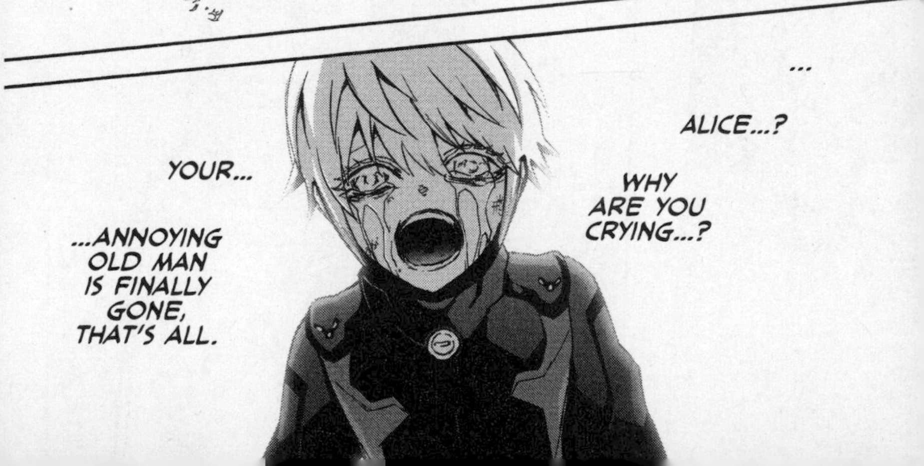
...
ALICE...?
WHY ARE YOU CRYING...?
YOUR...
...ANNOYING OLD MAN IS FINALLY GONE, THAT'S ALL.

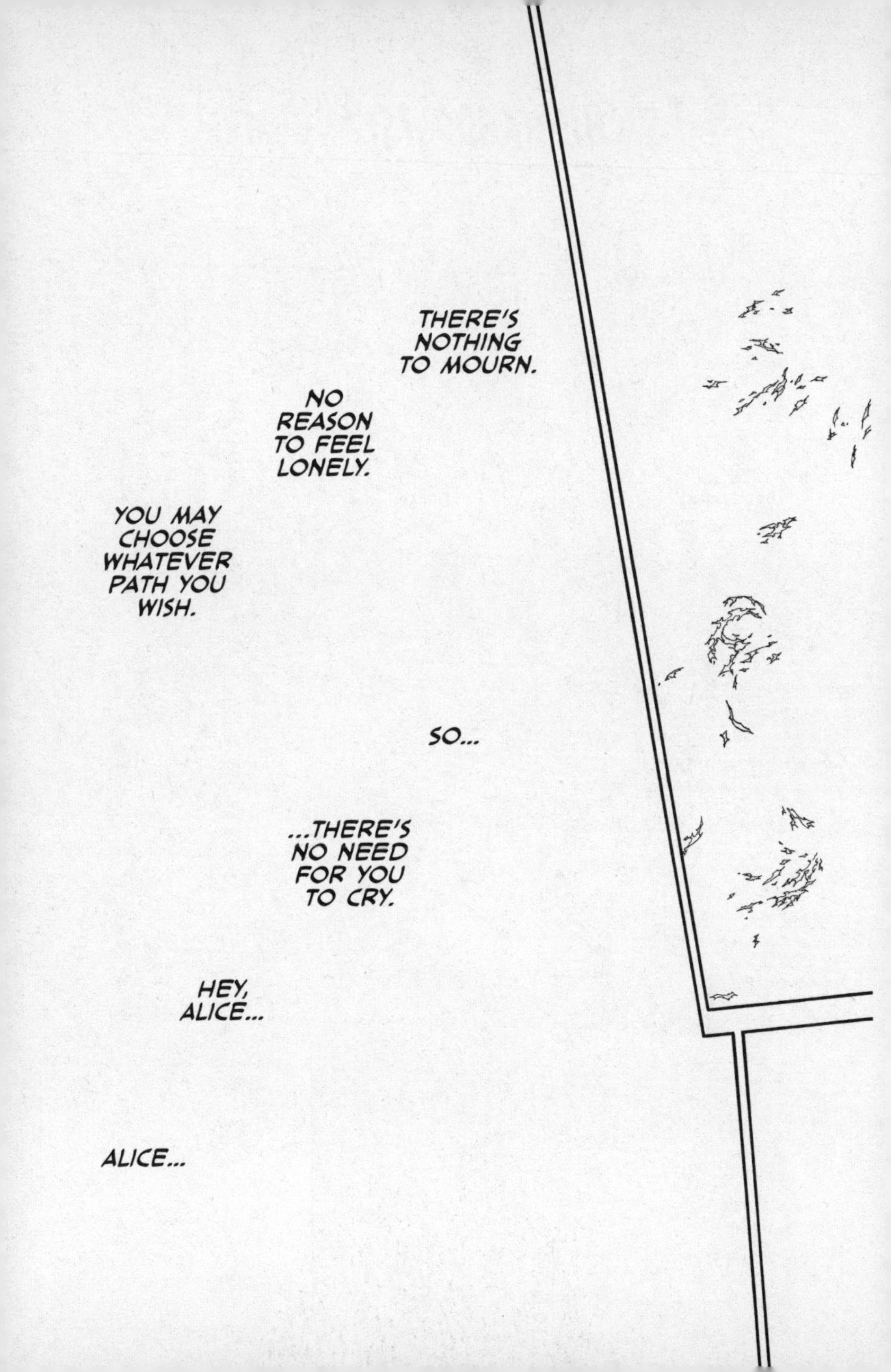
THERE'S NOTHING TO MOURN.
NO REASON TO FEEL LONELY.
YOU MAY CHOOSE WHATEVER PATH YOU WISH.
SO...
...THERE'S NO NEED FOR YOU TO CRY.
HEY, ALICE...
ALICE...

~TSUCHIMIKADO ISLAND MAP~

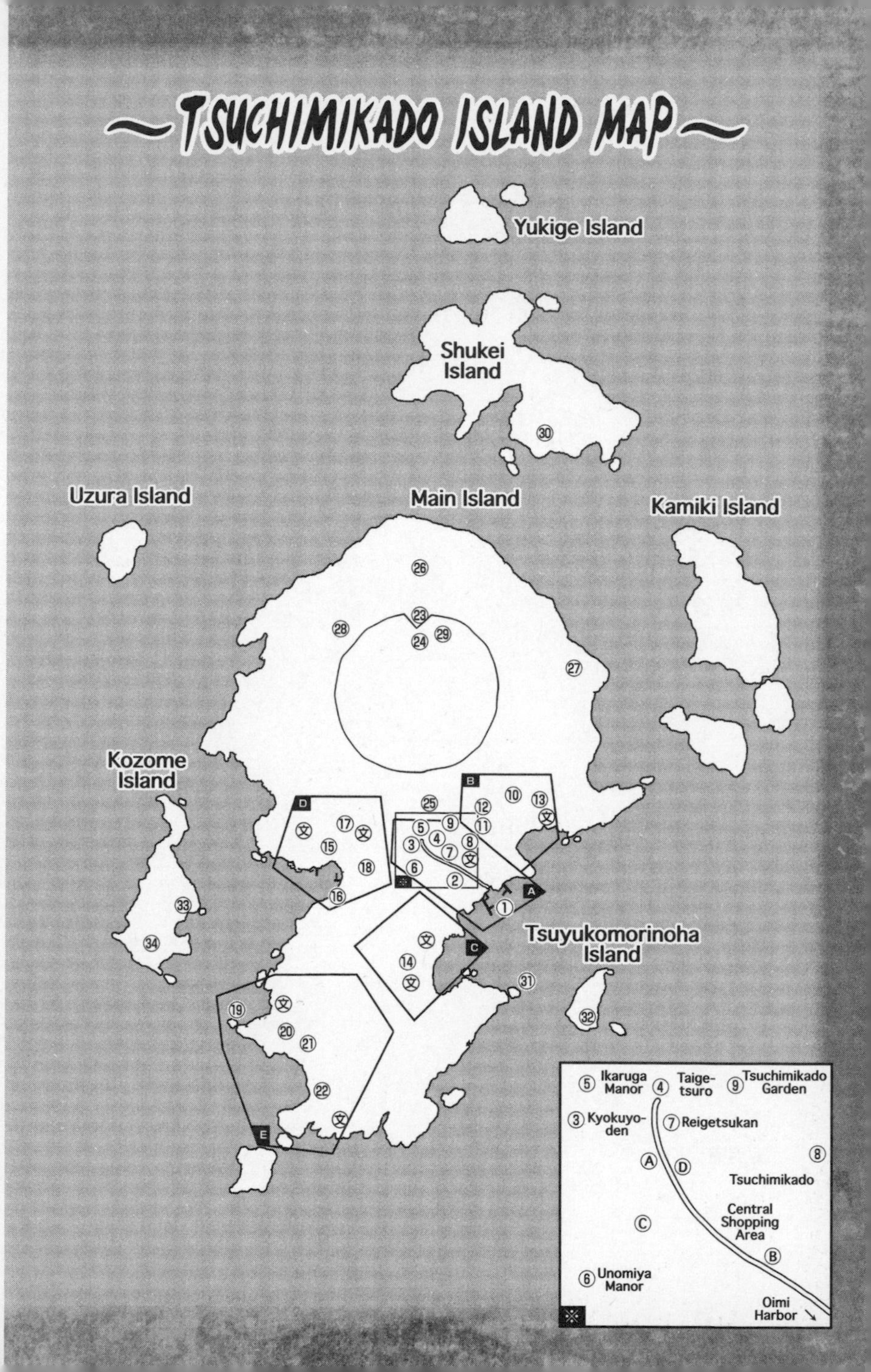

Yukige Island
Shukei Island
Uzura Island
Main Island
Kamiki Island
Kozome Island
Tsuyukomorinoha Island
A
B
C
D
E
Ikaruga Manor
Taige-tsuro
Tsuchimikado Garden
Kyokuyo-den
Reigetsukan
Tsuchimikado
Central Shopping Area
Unomiya Manor
Oimi Harbor

A: Kaminari District

① Oimi Harbor (The harbor Rokuro arrived at)

② Kisaragi City (Central Shopping Area)

③ Kyokuyoden

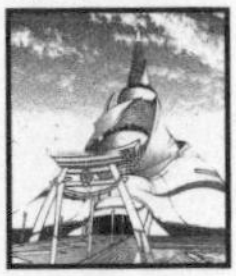

④ Taigetsuro

⑤ Ikaruga Manor

⑥ Hagusa Manor

⑦ Arima Tsuchimikado Manor Reigetsukan

⑧ Seicho Elementary School

⑨ Tsuchimikado Garden

B: Odakari District

⑩ Seiyoin

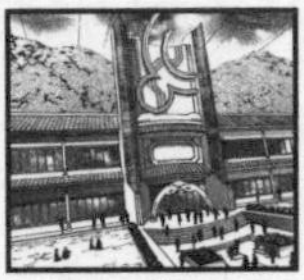

⑪ Mitosaka Private Hospital

⑫ Mitosaka Manor

⑬ Uji Manor

C: Umehatsu District

⑭ Enmado Manor (Adashino Manor)

D: Shizuosome District

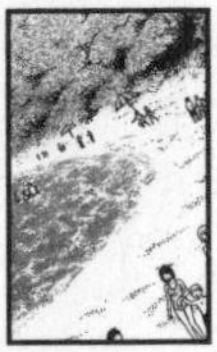

⑮ Bakery "Mameo"
(Tatara's favorite baker)

⑯ Suzukure Beach

⑰ Inanaki Manor

⑱ Ioroi Manor

E: Konohatori District

⑲ A training island owned by the Ikaruga Family
(The island Shimon and Mayura used in "The Fang Honing of Shimon and Mayura")

⑳ Sada Manor

㉑ Zeze Manor

㉒ Mitejima Manor

Other Locations: Main Island

㉓ Great Black Torii

㉔ Platform of Starry Heavens

㉕ The hill where Sayo got a view of the whole island

㉖ Tsuchimikado Cemetery

㉗ The Kogen House
(The house where Seigen lived in the novel *Heavenly Bond of the Young Tiger*)

㉘ Hagusa Manor

㉙ Village of force field technicians who are members of the Uji family's branch family

Other Islands

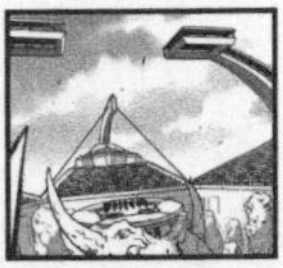

㉚ Hadarae Castle

㉛ Amawaka Manor

㉜ Kasukami Manor

㉝ Restaurant Junno
(Tamami Ioroi's parent's house)

㉞ Narumi's Training Ground

Ⓐ Weapon Shop Matasa
(Where Rokuro ordered his gauntlet)

Ⓑ Sweets Parlor Hazukitei
(The favorite place of Benio's father, Hyoga. They serve a Jumbo Anmitsu sweet for couples only.)

Ⓒ Japanese Pub Tamasu
(Where Gunki and Keiji were drinking.)

Ⓓ Yukimachitei
(The inn where Rokuro stayed.)

Yukige Island: Where the kodoku ceremony is held

Kamiki Island: An island inhabited only by Shikigami

Uzura Island: A farming island inhabited by the Gozu

Tsuyukomorinoha Island: Special weapons and equipment are made on this island

Kozome Island: Many of the exorcists with relatively weak spiritual power live here

Shukei Island: The island where Hadarae Castle is located

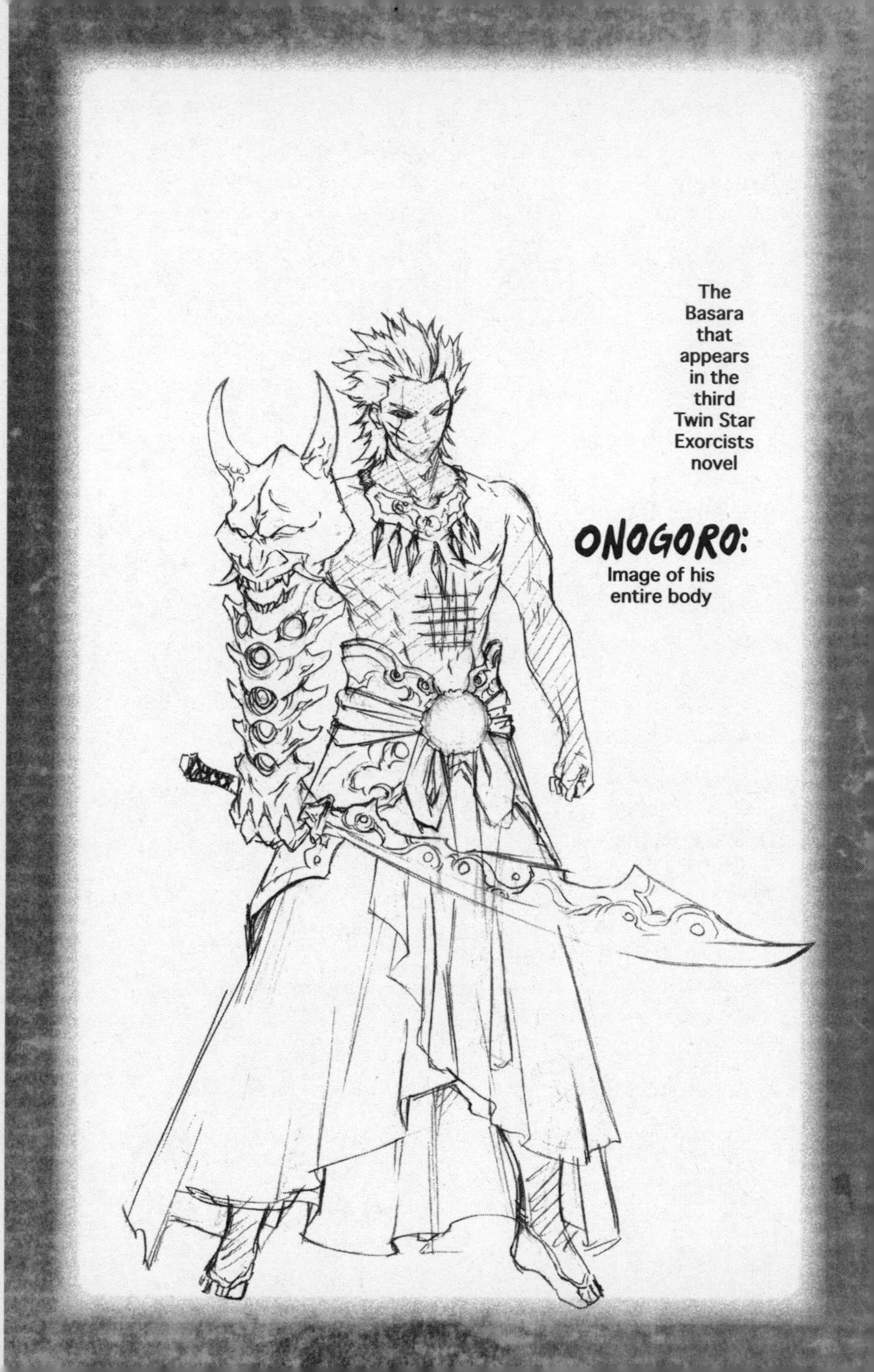
The Basara that appears in the third Twin Star Exorcists novel
ONOGORO:
Image of his entire body

#67 For Your Future

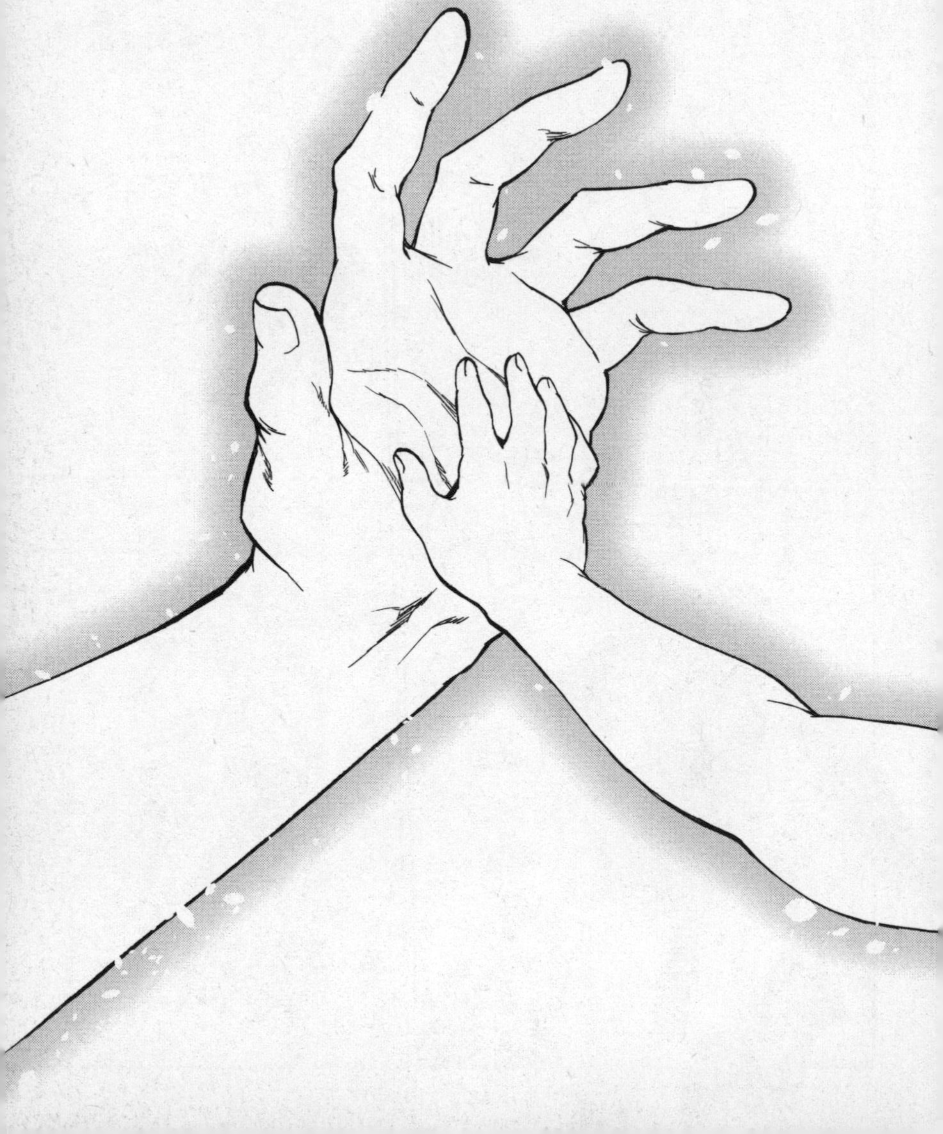

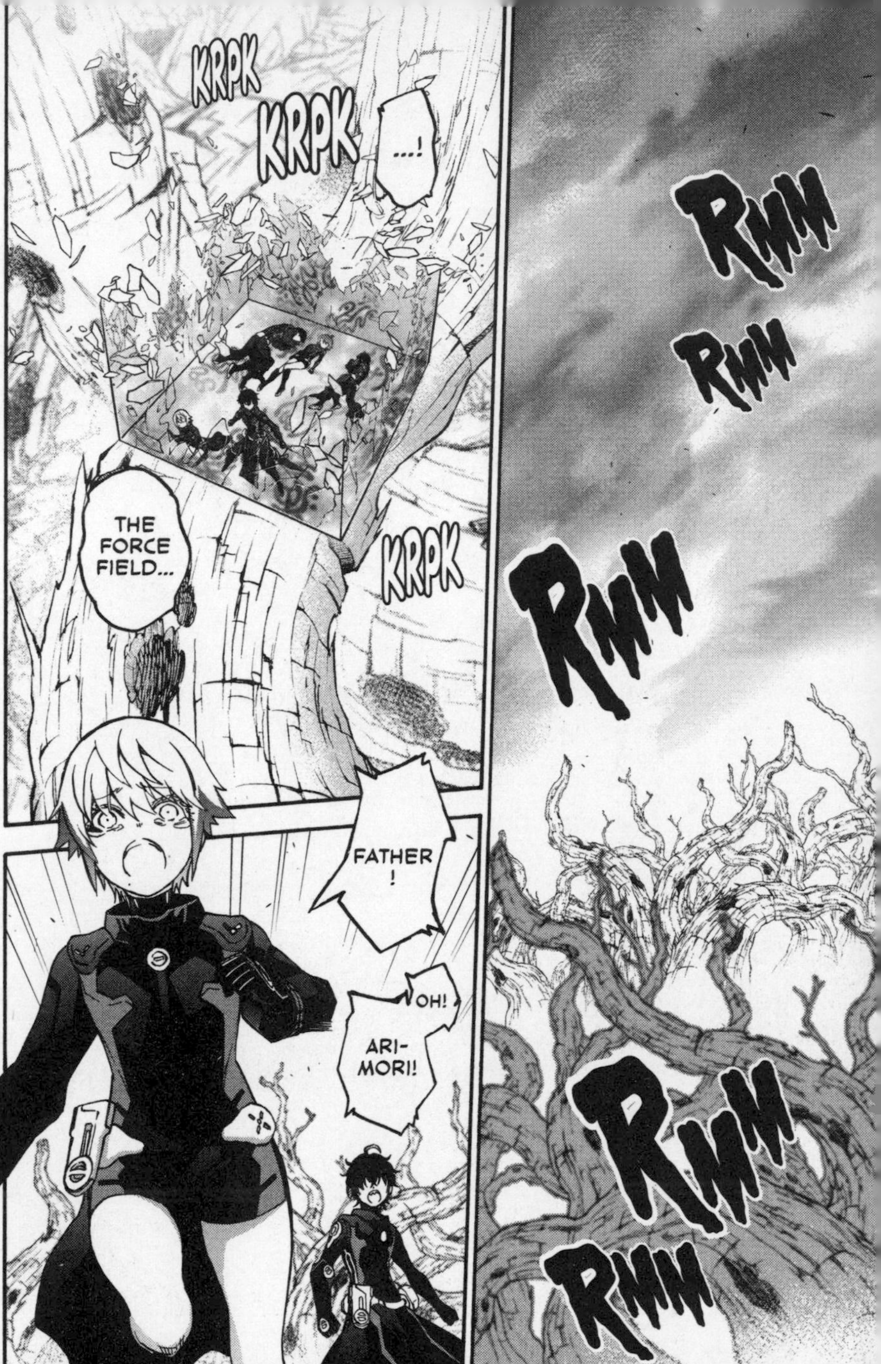
RMM
RMM
RMM
RMM
RMM
KRPK
KRPK
...!
THE FORCE FIELD...
KRPK
FATHER!
OH!
ARI-MORI!

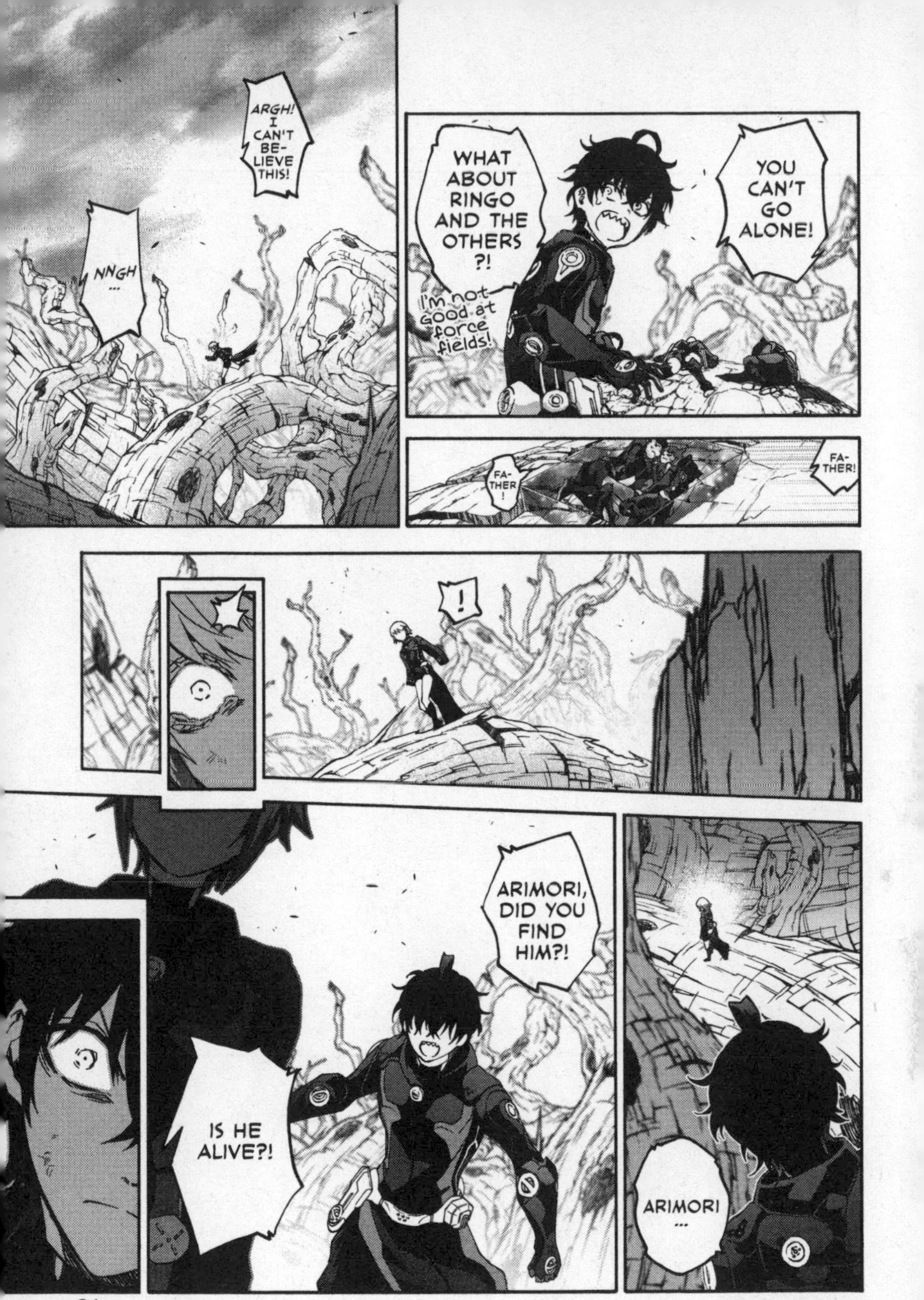

YOU CAN'T GO ALONE!
WHAT ABOUT RINGO AND THE OTHERS?!
I'm not good at force fields!
FATHER!
FATHER!
ARGH! I CAN'T BELIEVE THIS!
NNGH...
!
ARIMORI...
ARIMORI, DID YOU FIND HIM?!
IS HE ALIVE?!

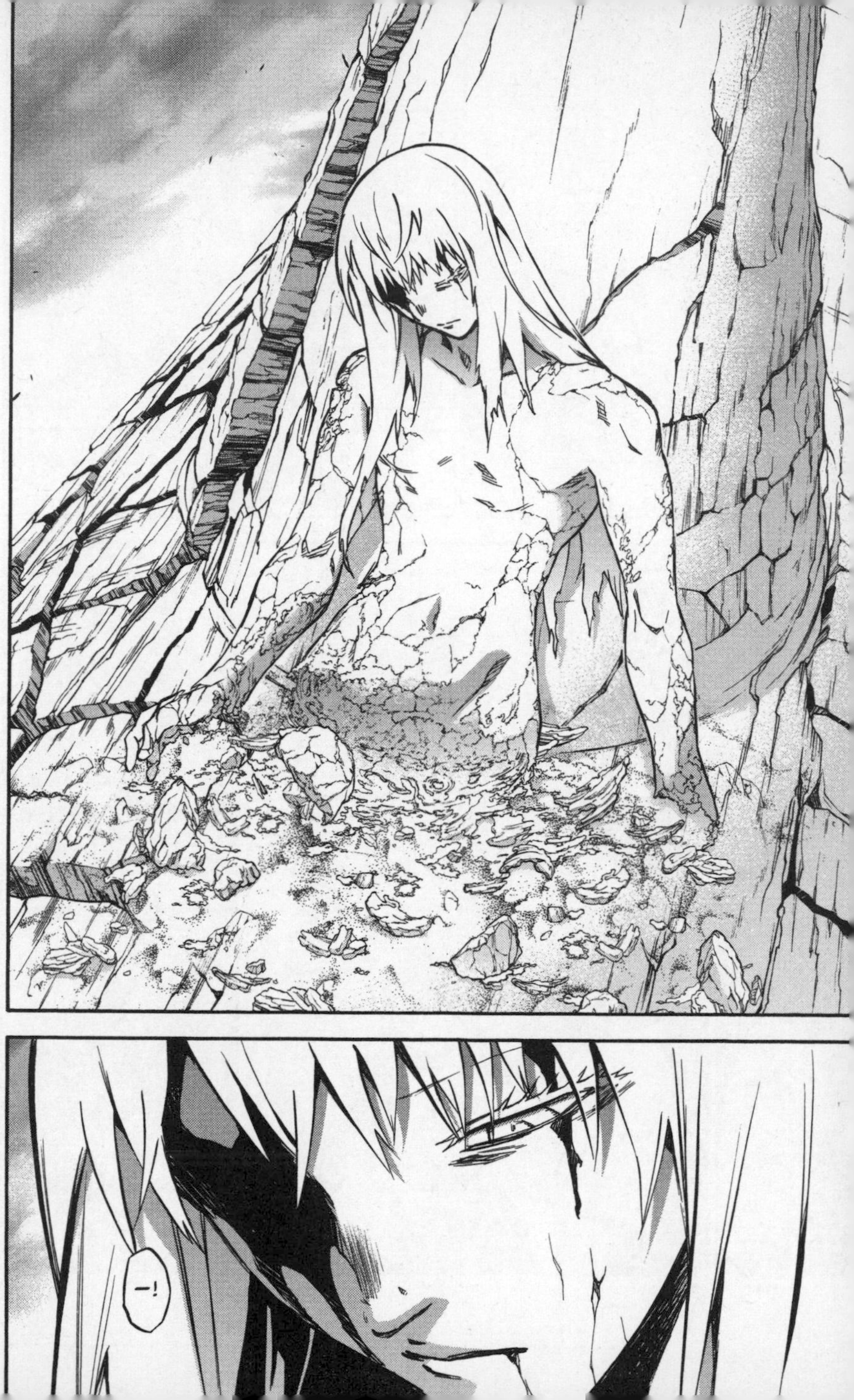
—!

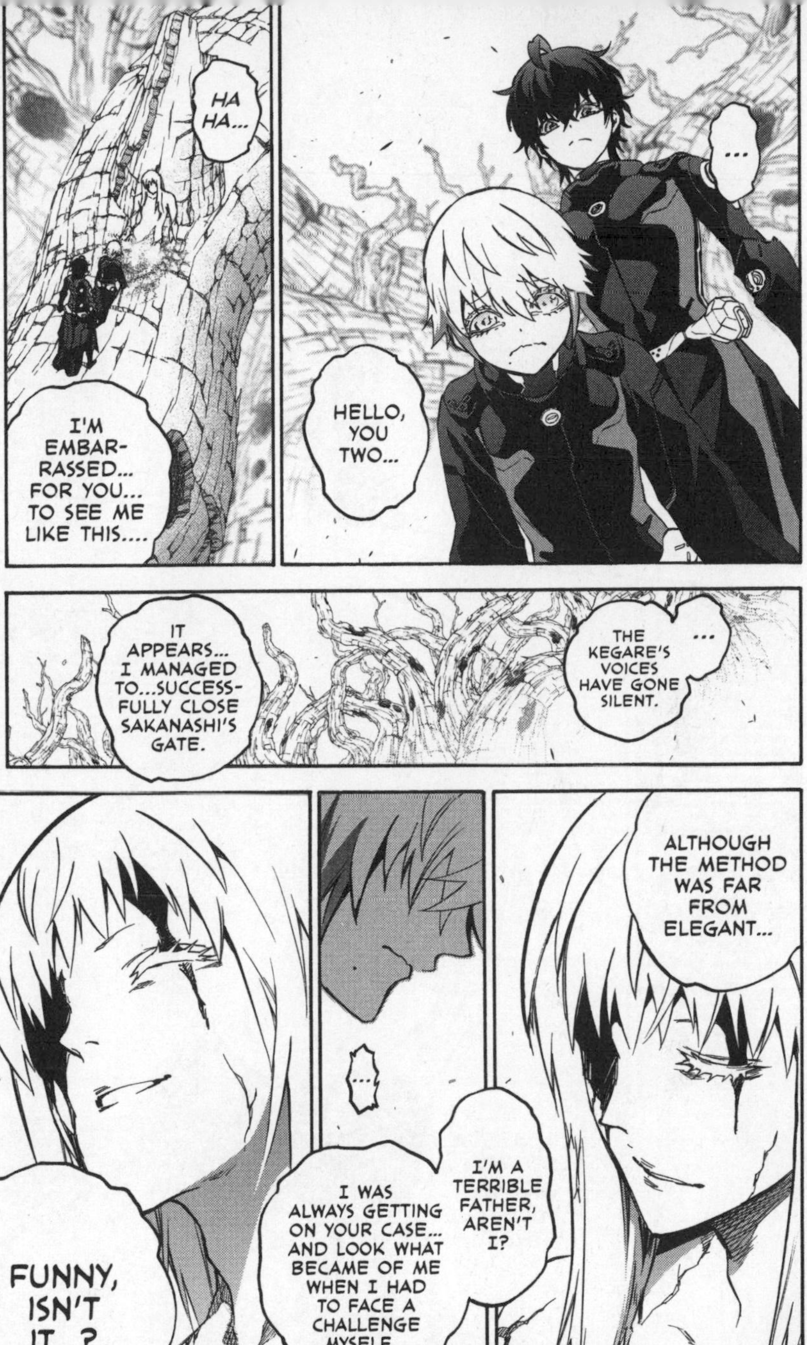
...
HELLO, YOU TWO...
HA HA...
I'M EMBARRASSED... FOR YOU... TO SEE ME LIKE THIS....
...
THE KEGARE'S VOICES HAVE GONE SILENT.
IT APPEARS... I MANAGED TO...SUCCESSFULLY CLOSE SAKANASHI'S GATE.
ALTHOUGH THE METHOD WAS FAR FROM ELEGANT...
I'M A TERRIBLE FATHER, AREN'T I?
...
I WAS ALWAYS GETTING ON YOUR CASE... AND LOOK WHAT BECAME OF ME WHEN I HAD TO FACE A CHALLENGE MYSELF...
FUNNY, ISN'T IT...?

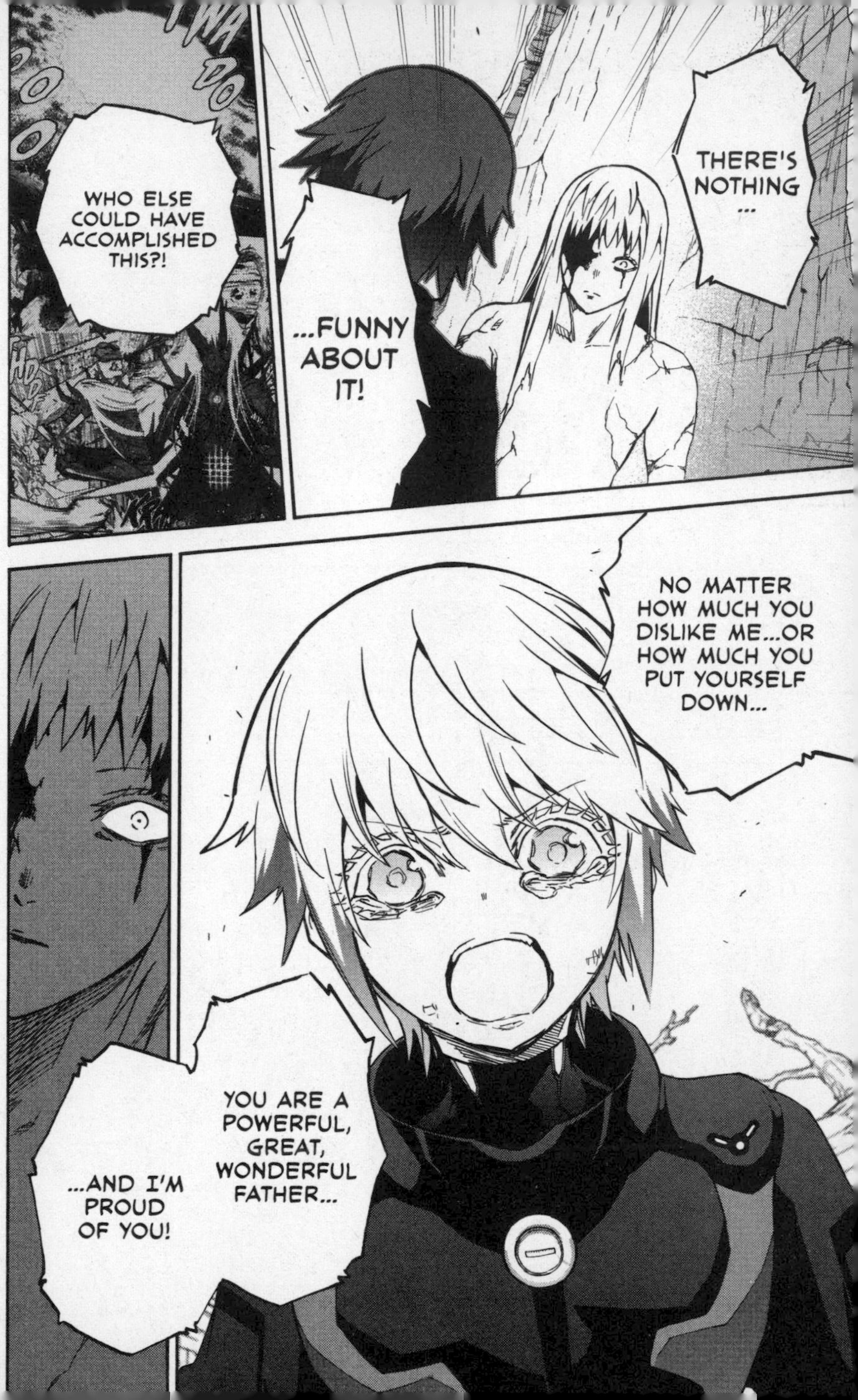

THERE'S NOTHING ...
...FUNNY ABOUT IT!
WHO ELSE COULD HAVE ACCOMPLISHED THIS?!
NO MATTER HOW MUCH YOU DISLIKE ME...OR HOW MUCH YOU PUT YOURSELF DOWN...
YOU ARE A POWERFUL, GREAT, WONDERFUL FATHER...
...AND I'M PROUD OF YOU!

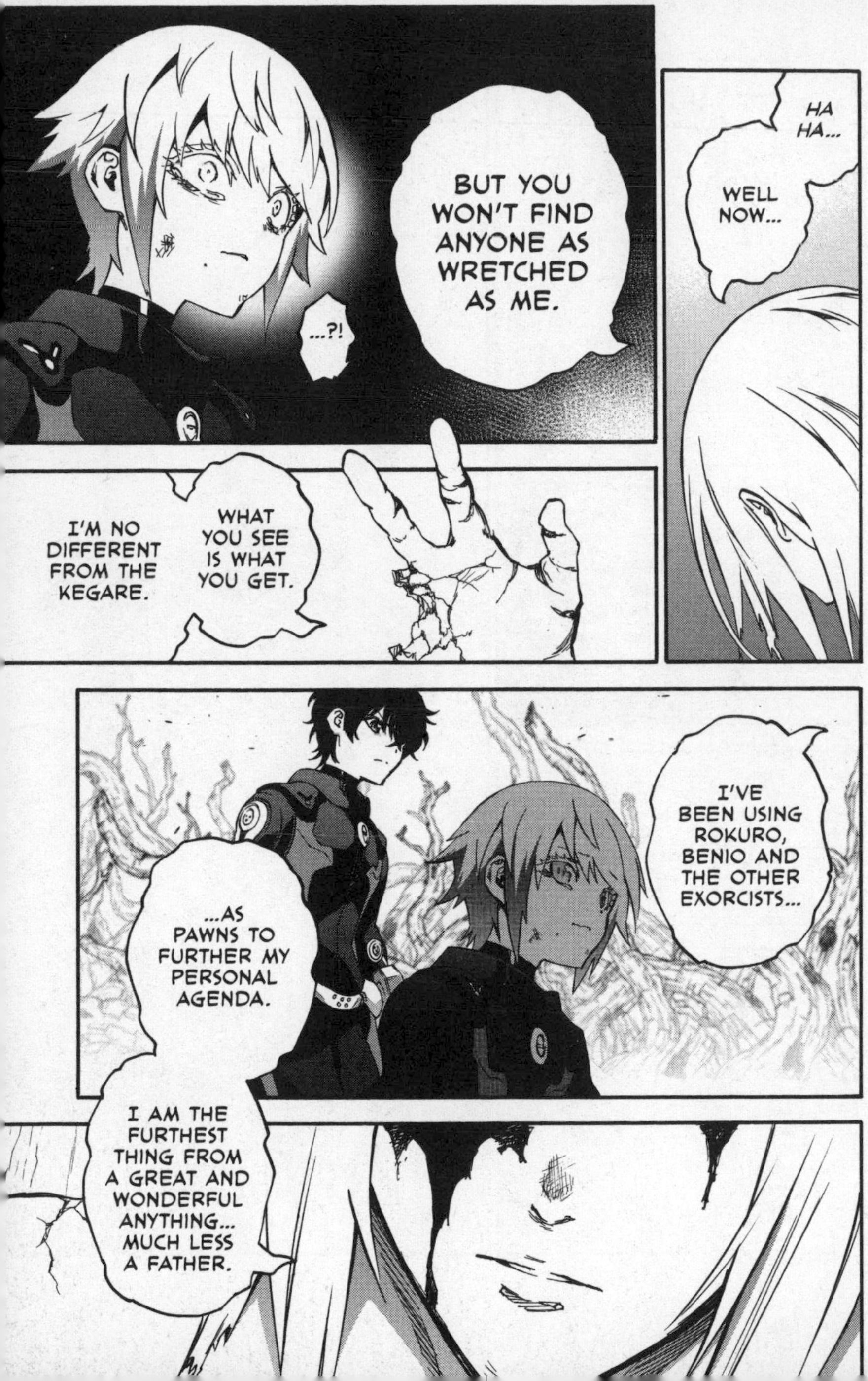
HA HA...
WELL NOW...
BUT YOU WON'T FIND ANYONE AS WRETCHED AS ME.
...?!
WHAT YOU SEE IS WHAT YOU GET.
I'M NO DIFFERENT FROM THE KEGARE.
I'VE BEEN USING ROKURO, BENIO AND THE OTHER EXORCISTS...
...AS PAWNS TO FURTHER MY PERSONAL AGENDA.
I AM THE FURTHEST THING FROM A GREAT AND WONDERFUL ANYTHING... MUCH LESS A FATHER.

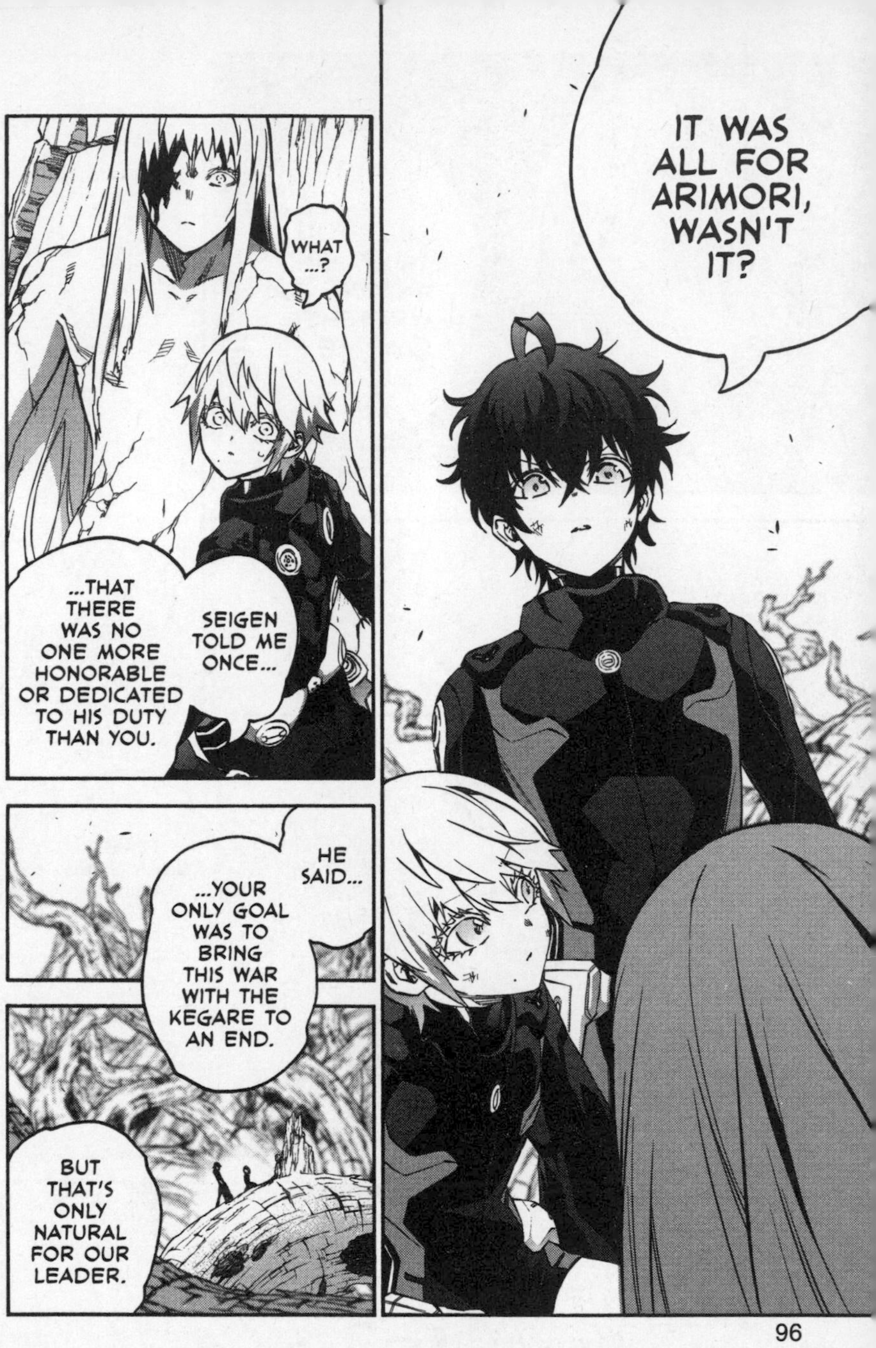
IT WAS ALL FOR ARIMORI, WASN'T IT?
WHAT ...?
SEIGEN TOLD ME ONCE...
...THAT THERE WAS NO ONE MORE HONORABLE OR DEDICATED TO HIS DUTY THAN YOU.
HE SAID...
...YOUR ONLY GOAL WAS TO BRING THIS WAR WITH THE KEGARE TO AN END.
BUT THAT'S ONLY NATURAL FOR OUR LEADER.

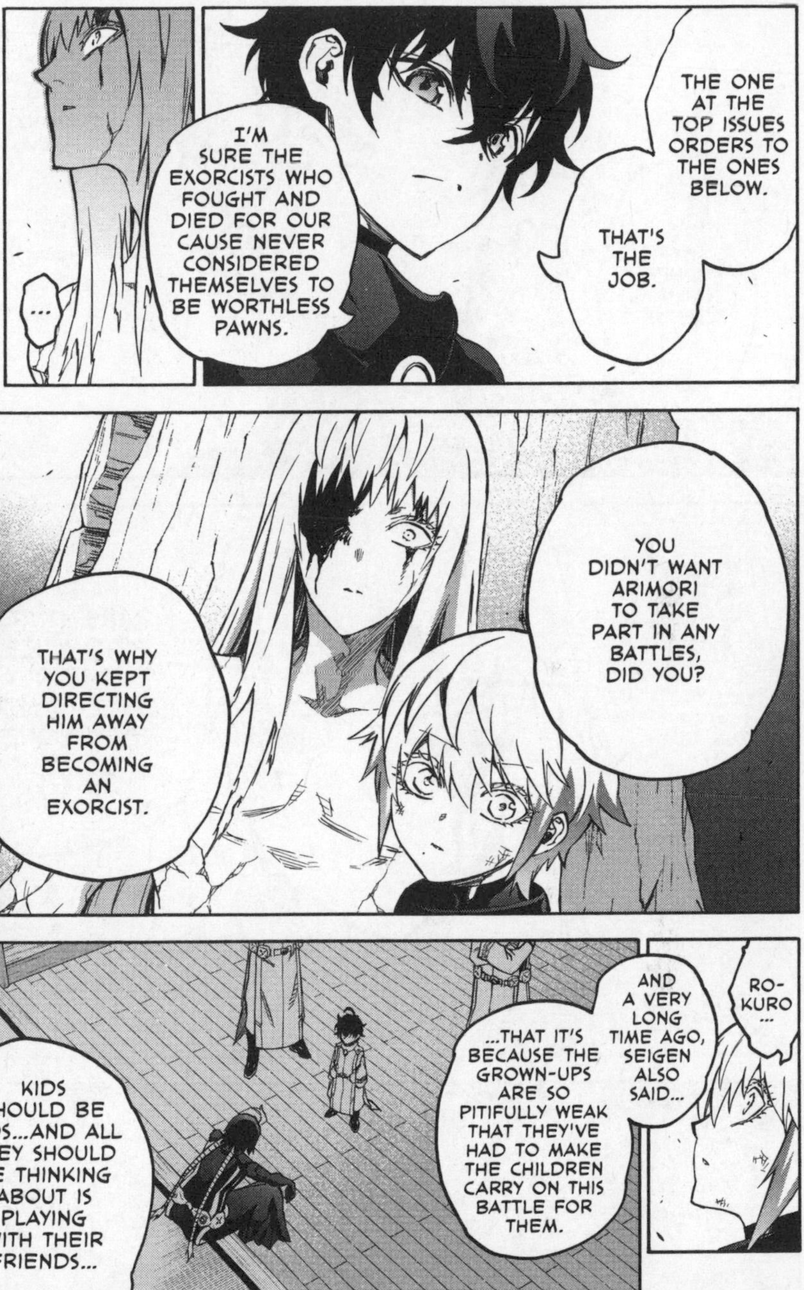
THE ONE AT THE TOP ISSUES ORDERS TO THE ONES BELOW.
THAT'S THE JOB.
I'M SURE THE EXORCISTS WHO FOUGHT AND DIED FOR OUR CAUSE NEVER CONSIDERED THEMSELVES TO BE WORTHLESS PAWNS.
...
YOU DIDN'T WANT ARIMORI TO TAKE PART IN ANY BATTLES, DID YOU?
THAT'S WHY YOU KEPT DIRECTING HIM AWAY FROM BECOMING AN EXORCIST.
RO-KURO...
AND A VERY LONG TIME AGO, SEIGEN ALSO SAID...
...THAT IT'S BECAUSE THE GROWN-UPS ARE SO PITIFULLY WEAK THAT THEY'VE HAD TO MAKE THE CHILDREN CARRY ON THIS BATTLE FOR THEM.
KIDS SHOULD BE KIDS...AND ALL THEY SHOULD BE THINKING ABOUT IS PLAYING WITH THEIR FRIENDS...

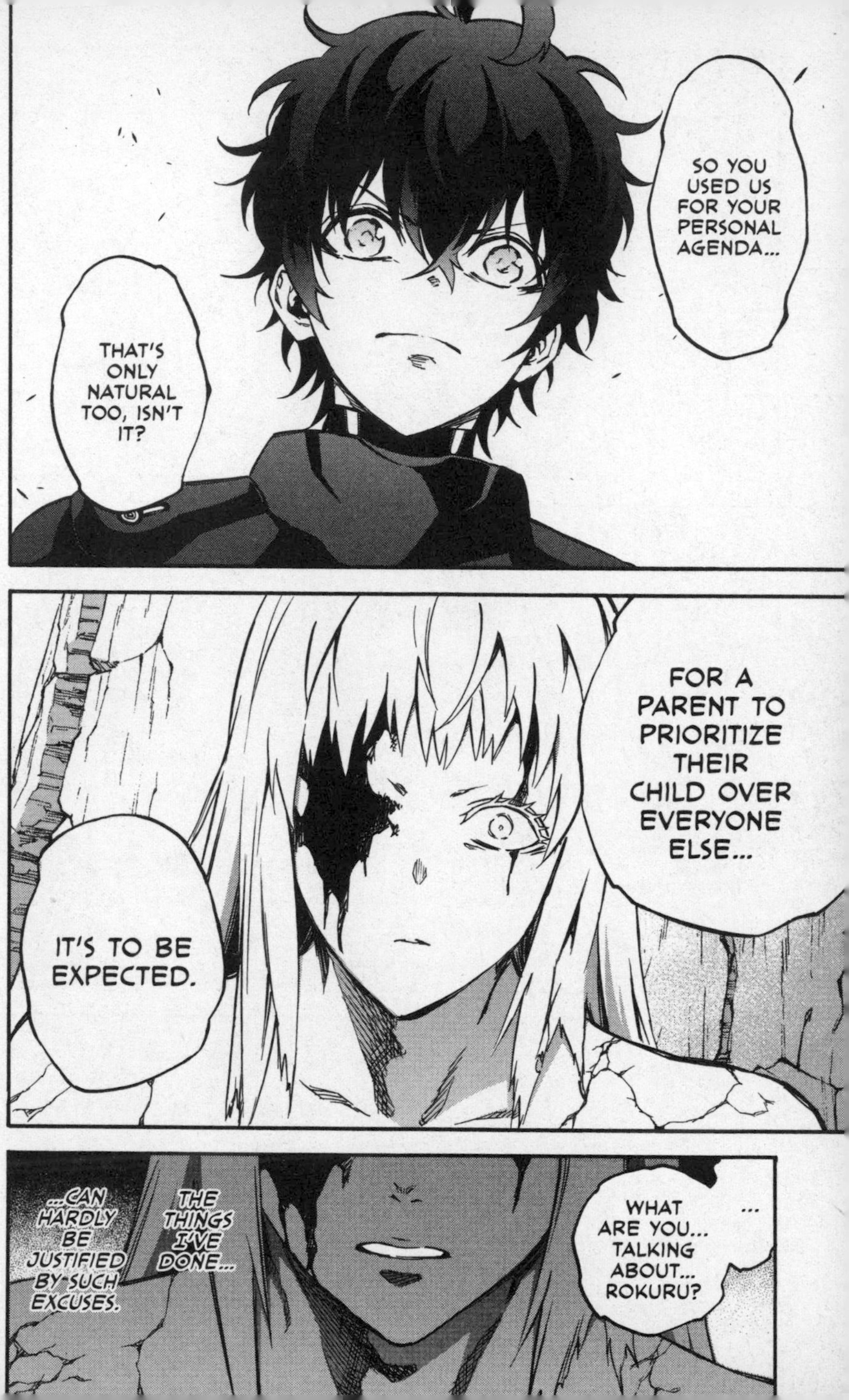
SO YOU USED US FOR YOUR PERSONAL AGENDA...
THAT'S ONLY NATURAL TOO, ISN'T IT?
FOR A PARENT TO PRIORITIZE THEIR CHILD OVER EVERYONE ELSE...
IT'S TO BE EXPECTED.
...
WHAT ARE YOU... TALKING ABOUT... ROKURU?
THE THINGS I'VE DONE...
...CAN HARDLY BE JUSTIFIED BY SUCH EXCUSES.

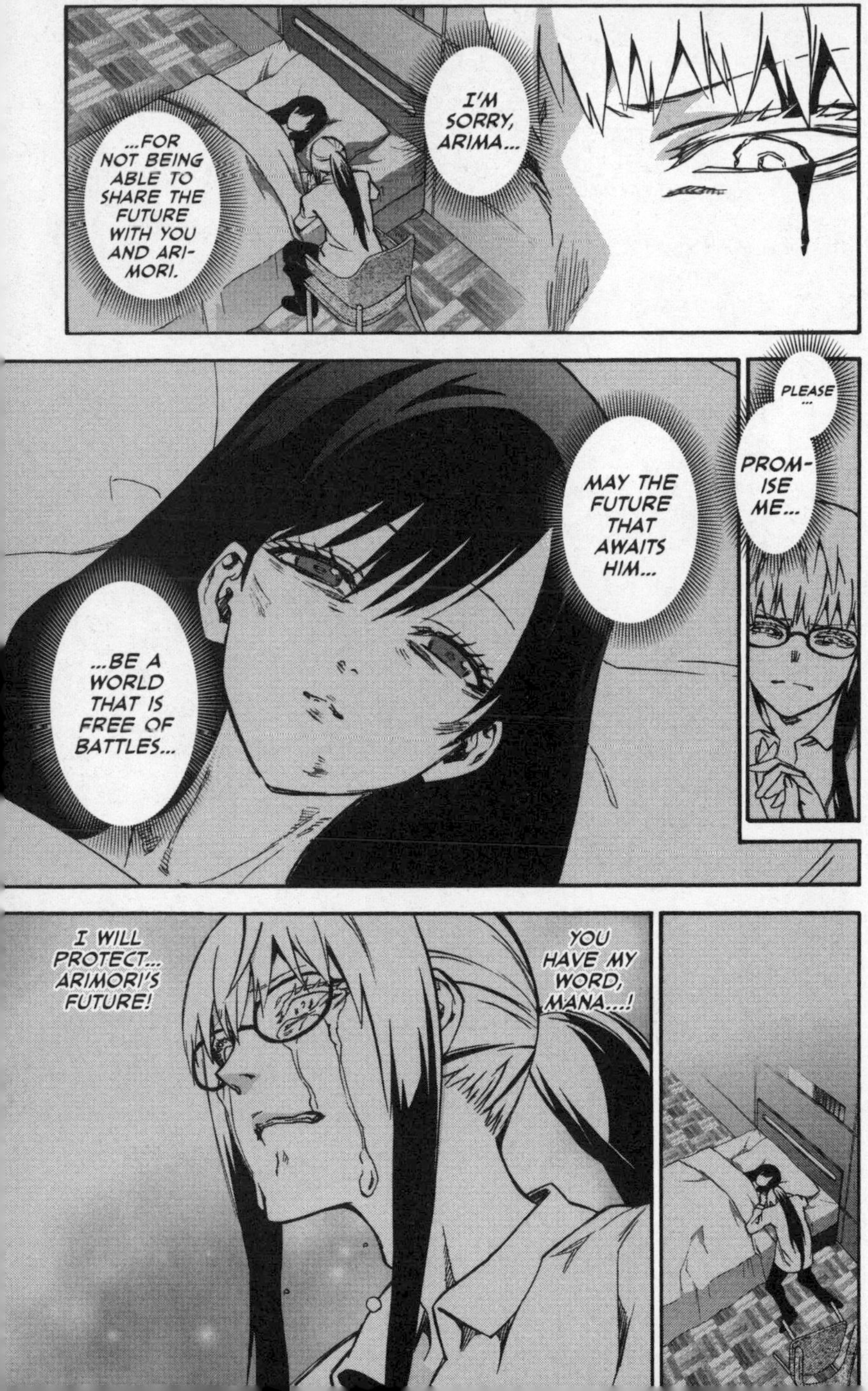
I'M SORRY, ARIMA...
...FOR NOT BEING ABLE TO SHARE THE FUTURE WITH YOU AND ARI-MORI.
PLEASE...
PROM-ISE ME...
MAY THE FUTURE THAT AWAITS HIM...
...BE A WORLD THAT IS FREE OF BATTLES...
YOU HAVE MY WORD, MANA...!
I WILL PROTECT... ARIMORI'S FUTURE!

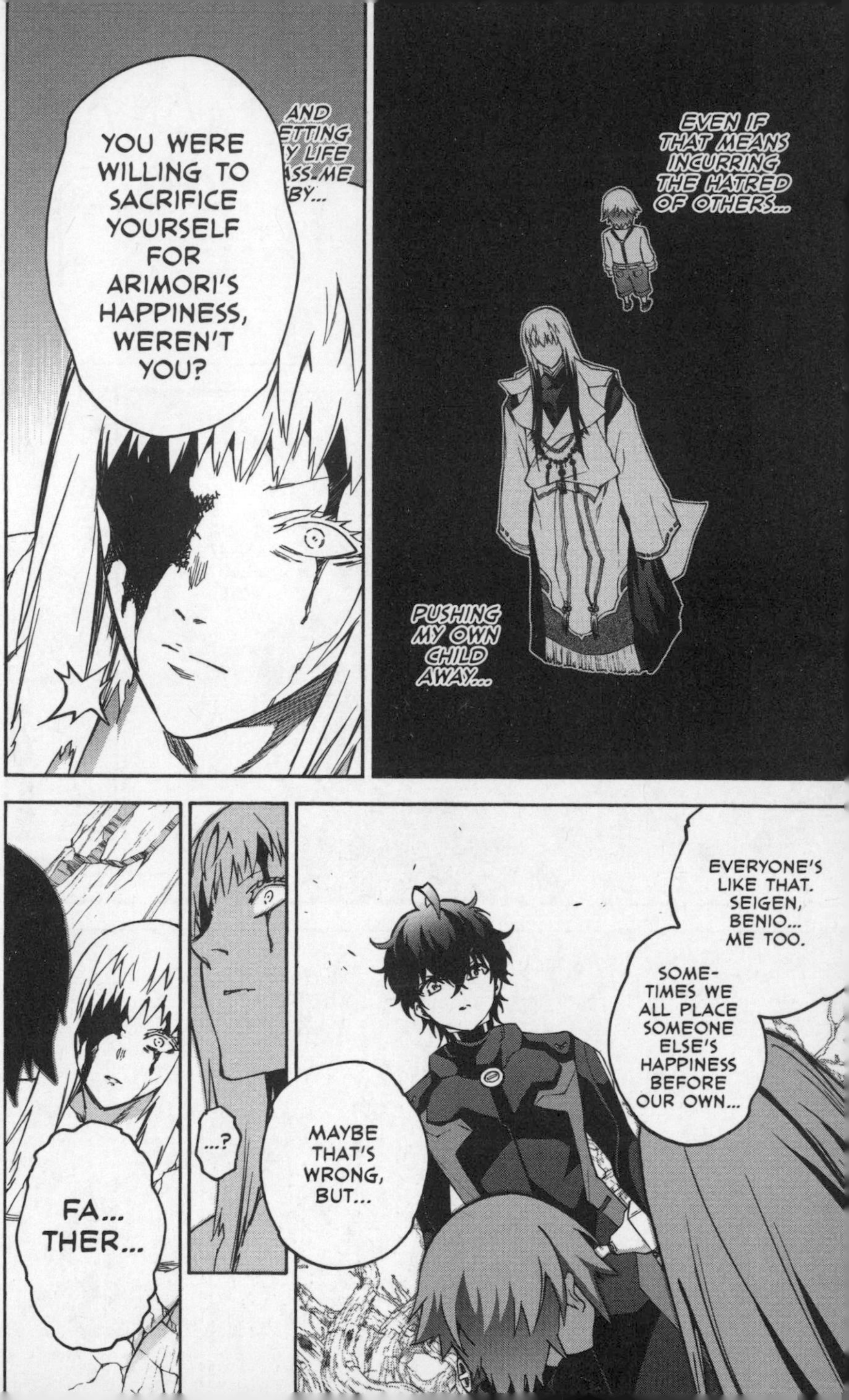
EVEN IF THAT MEANS INCURRING THE HATRED OF OTHERS...
PUSHING MY OWN CHILD AWAY...
YOU WERE WILLING TO SACRIFICE YOURSELF FOR ARIMORI'S HAPPINESS, WEREN'T YOU?
EVERYONE'S LIKE THAT. SEIGEN, BENIO... ME TOO.
SOME-TIMES WE ALL PLACE SOMEONE ELSE'S HAPPINESS BEFORE OUR OWN...
MAYBE THAT'S WRONG, BUT...
...?
FA... THER...

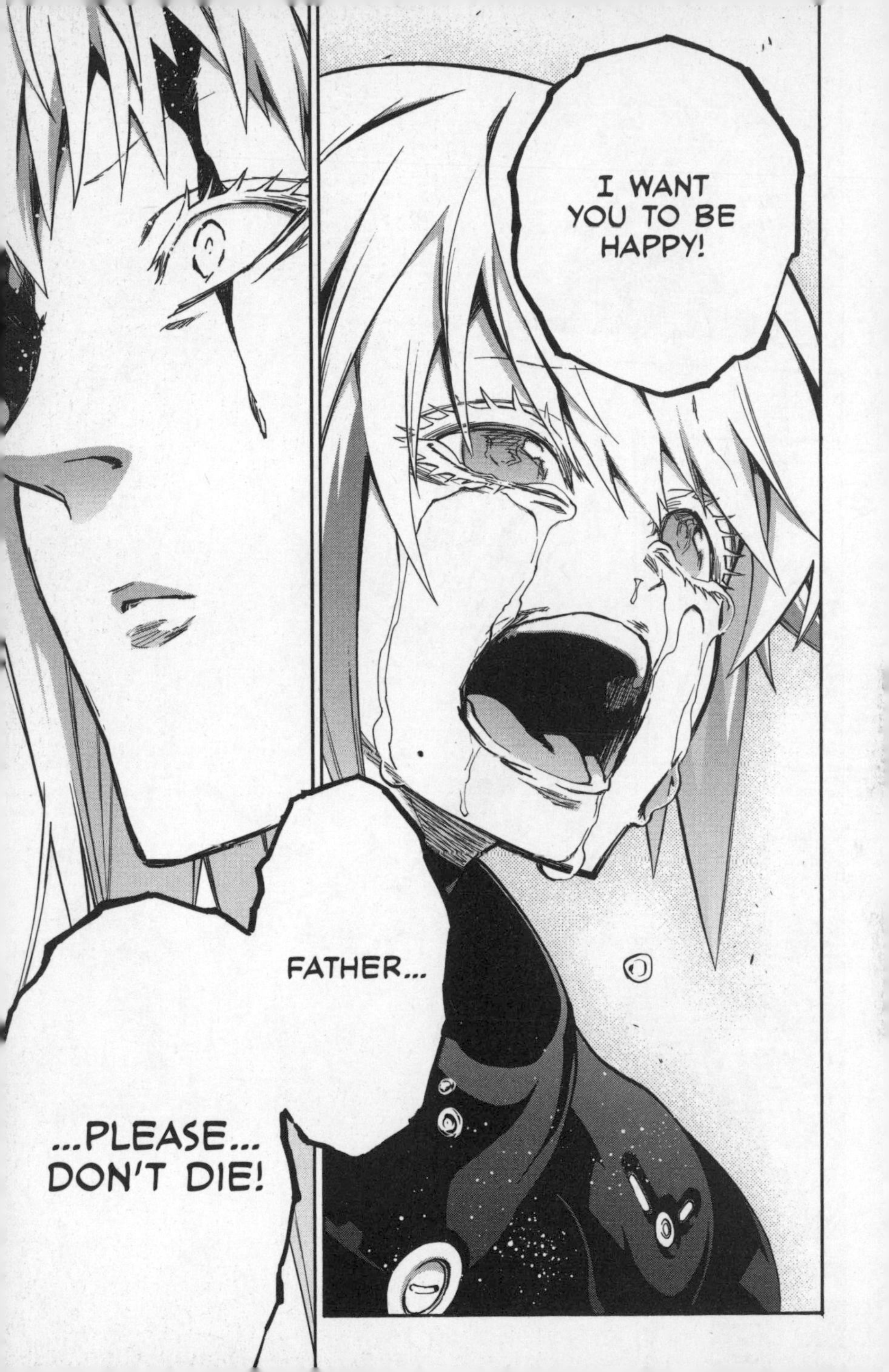
I WANT YOU TO BE HAPPY!
FATHER...
...PLEASE... DON'T DIE!

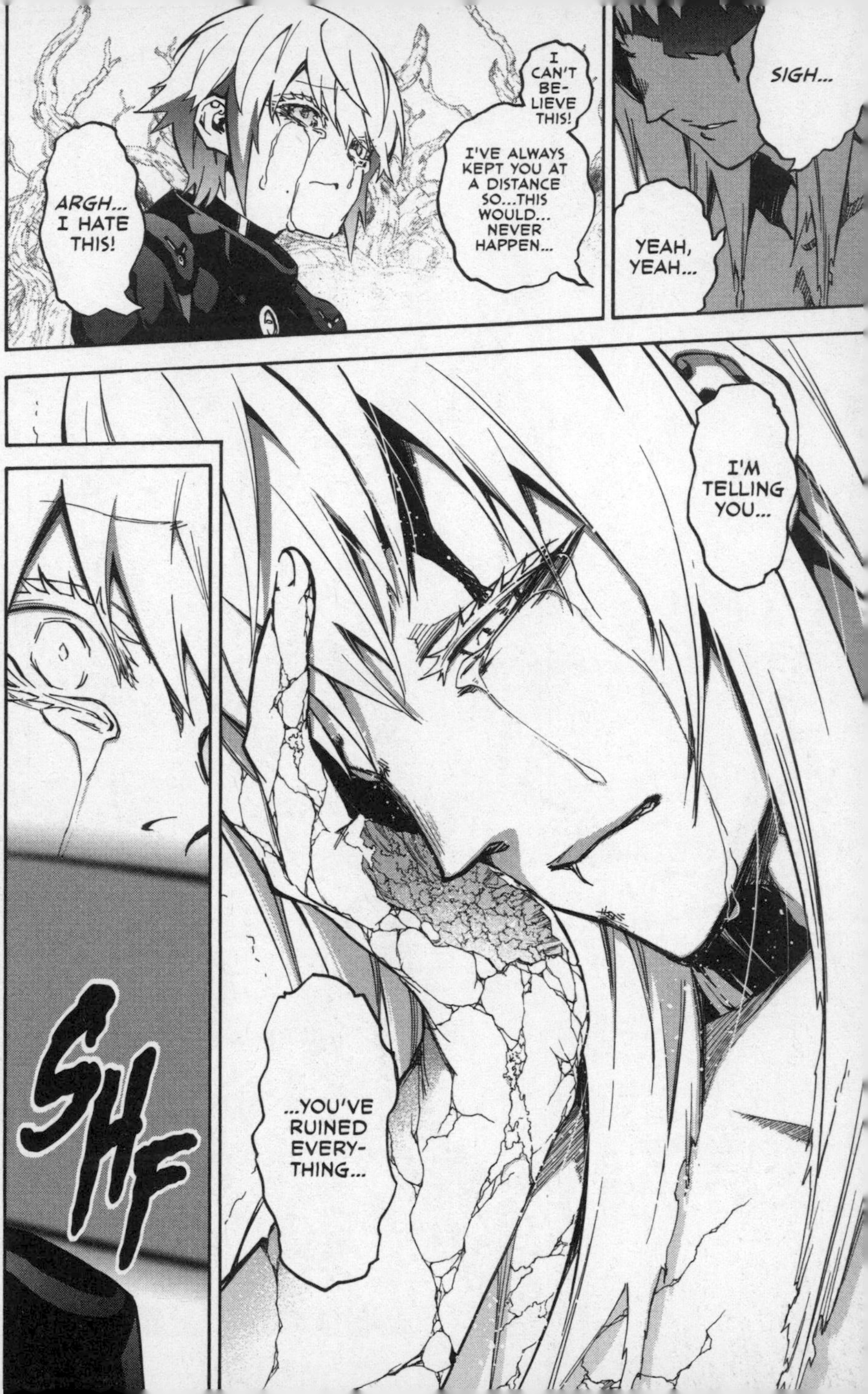
SIGH...
YEAH, YEAH...
I CAN'T BE-LIEVE THIS!
I'VE ALWAYS KEPT YOU AT A DISTANCE SO...THIS WOULD... NEVER HAPPEN...
ARGH... I HATE THIS!
I'M TELLING YOU...
...YOU'VE RUINED EVERY-THING...
SHF

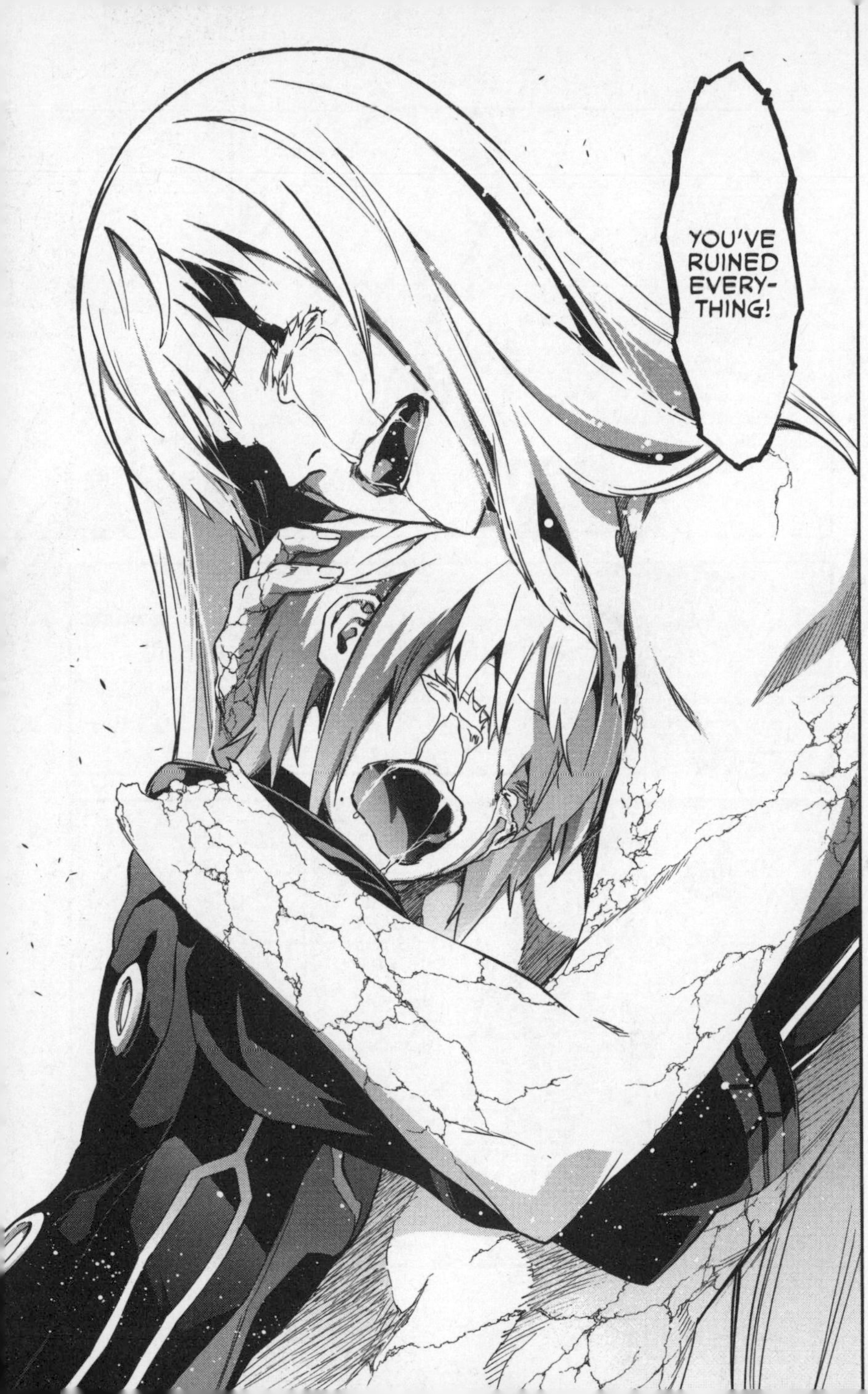
YOU'VE RUINED EVERY-THING!

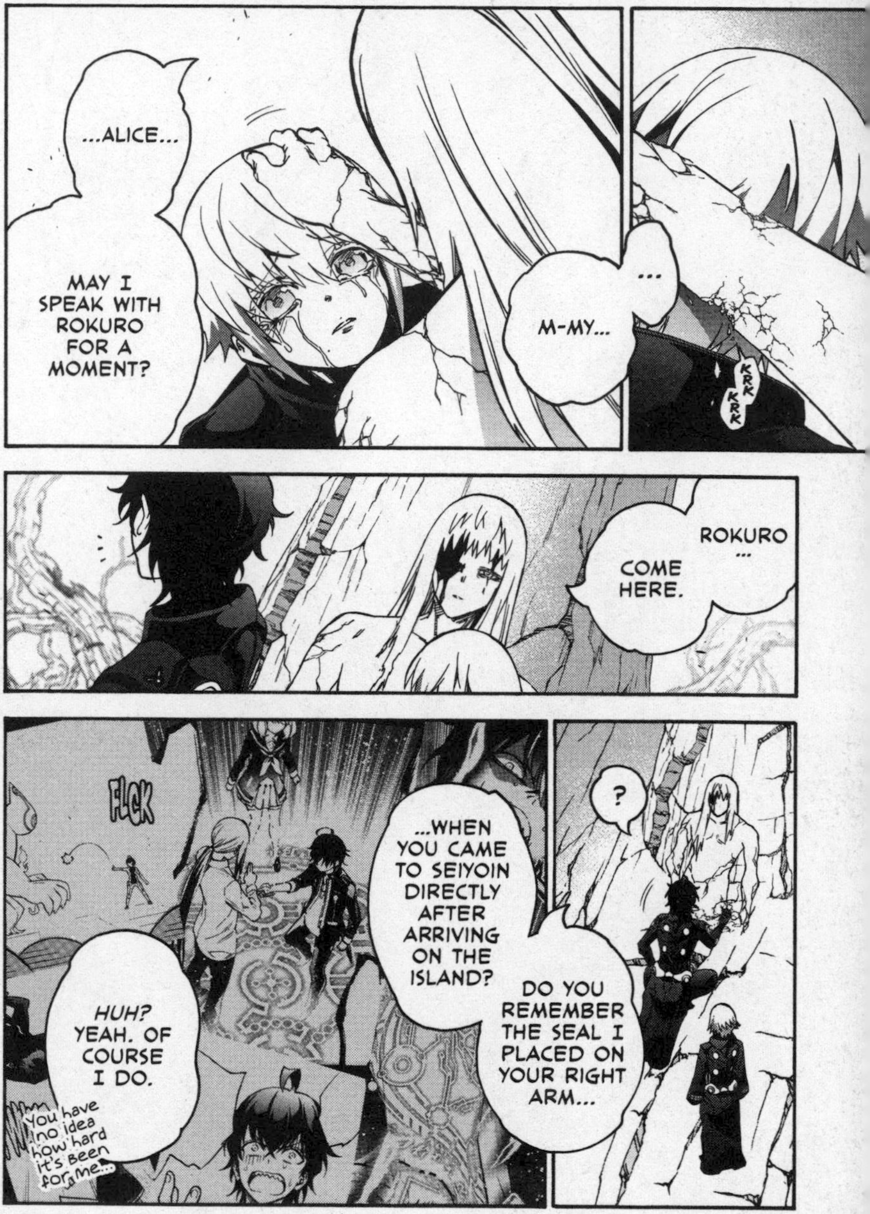
...
M-MY...
KRK KRK
...ALICE...
MAY I SPEAK WITH ROKURO FOR A MOMENT?
ROKURO ...
COME HERE.
?
DO YOU REMEMBER THE SEAL I PLACED ON YOUR RIGHT ARM...
FLCK
...WHEN YOU CAME TO SEIYOIN DIRECTLY AFTER ARRIVING ON THE ISLAND?
HUH? YEAH. OF COURSE I DO.
You have no idea how hard it's been for me...

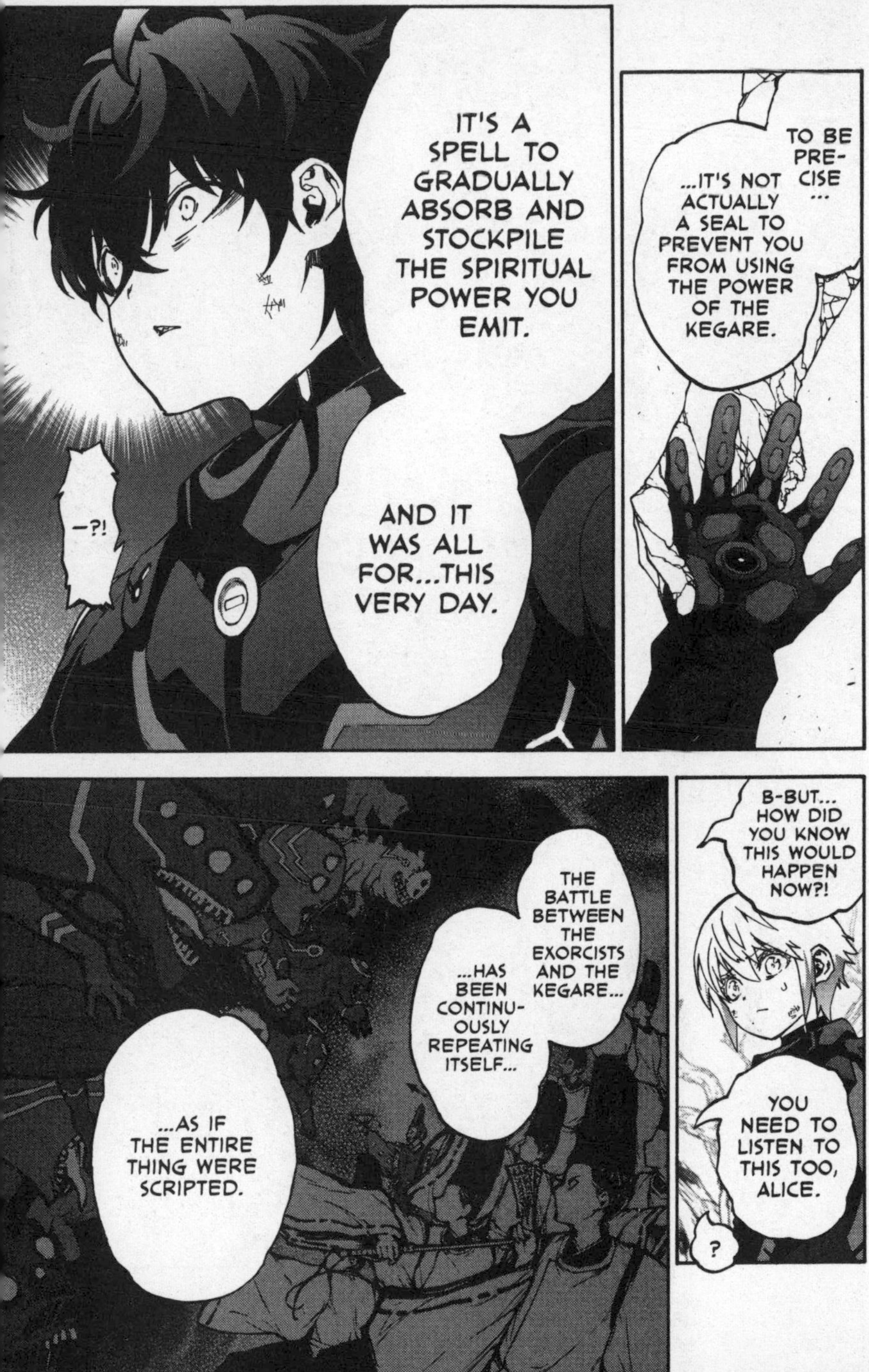
TO BE PRECISE...
...IT'S NOT ACTUALLY A SEAL TO PREVENT YOU FROM USING THE POWER OF THE KEGARE.
IT'S A SPELL TO GRADUALLY ABSORB AND STOCKPILE THE SPIRITUAL POWER YOU EMIT.
AND IT WAS ALL FOR...THIS VERY DAY.
—?!
B-BUT... HOW DID YOU KNOW THIS WOULD HAPPEN NOW?!
YOU NEED TO LISTEN TO THIS TOO, ALICE.
?
THE BATTLE BETWEEN THE EXORCISTS AND THE KEGARE...
...HAS BEEN CONTINUOUSLY REPEATING ITSELF...
...AS IF THE ENTIRE THING WERE SCRIPTED.

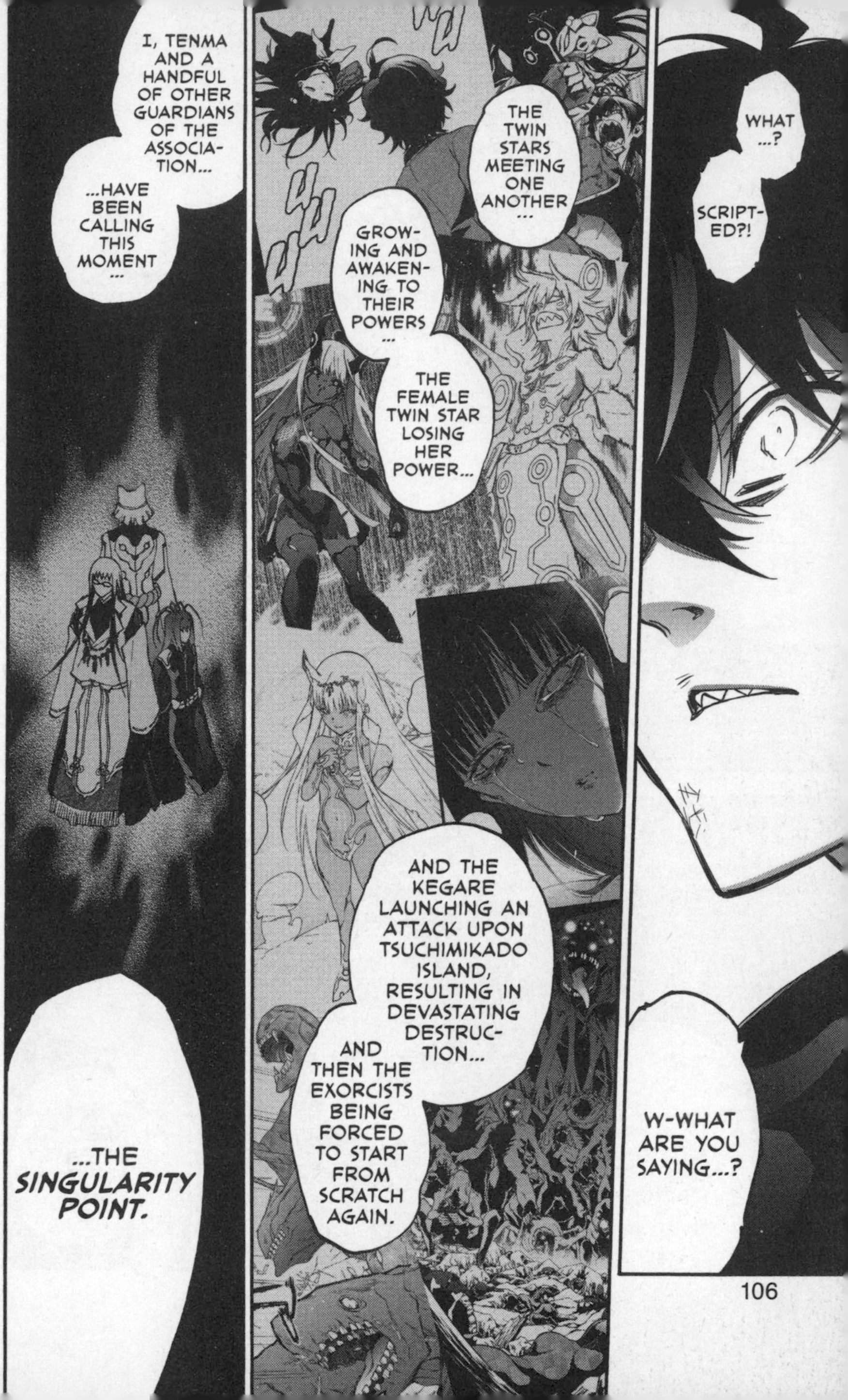
WHAT ...?
SCRIPTED?!
W-WHAT ARE YOU SAYING...?
THE TWIN STARS MEETING ONE ANOTHER ...
GROWING AND AWAKENING TO THEIR POWERS ...
THE FEMALE TWIN STAR LOSING HER POWER...
AND THE KEGARE LAUNCHING AN ATTACK UPON TSUCHIMIKADO ISLAND, RESULTING IN DEVASTATING DESTRUCTION...
AND THEN THE EXORCISTS BEING FORCED TO START FROM SCRATCH AGAIN.
I, TENMA AND A HANDFUL OF OTHER GUARDIANS OF THE ASSOCIATION...
...HAVE BEEN CALLING THIS MOMENT ...
...THE *SINGULARITY POINT.*

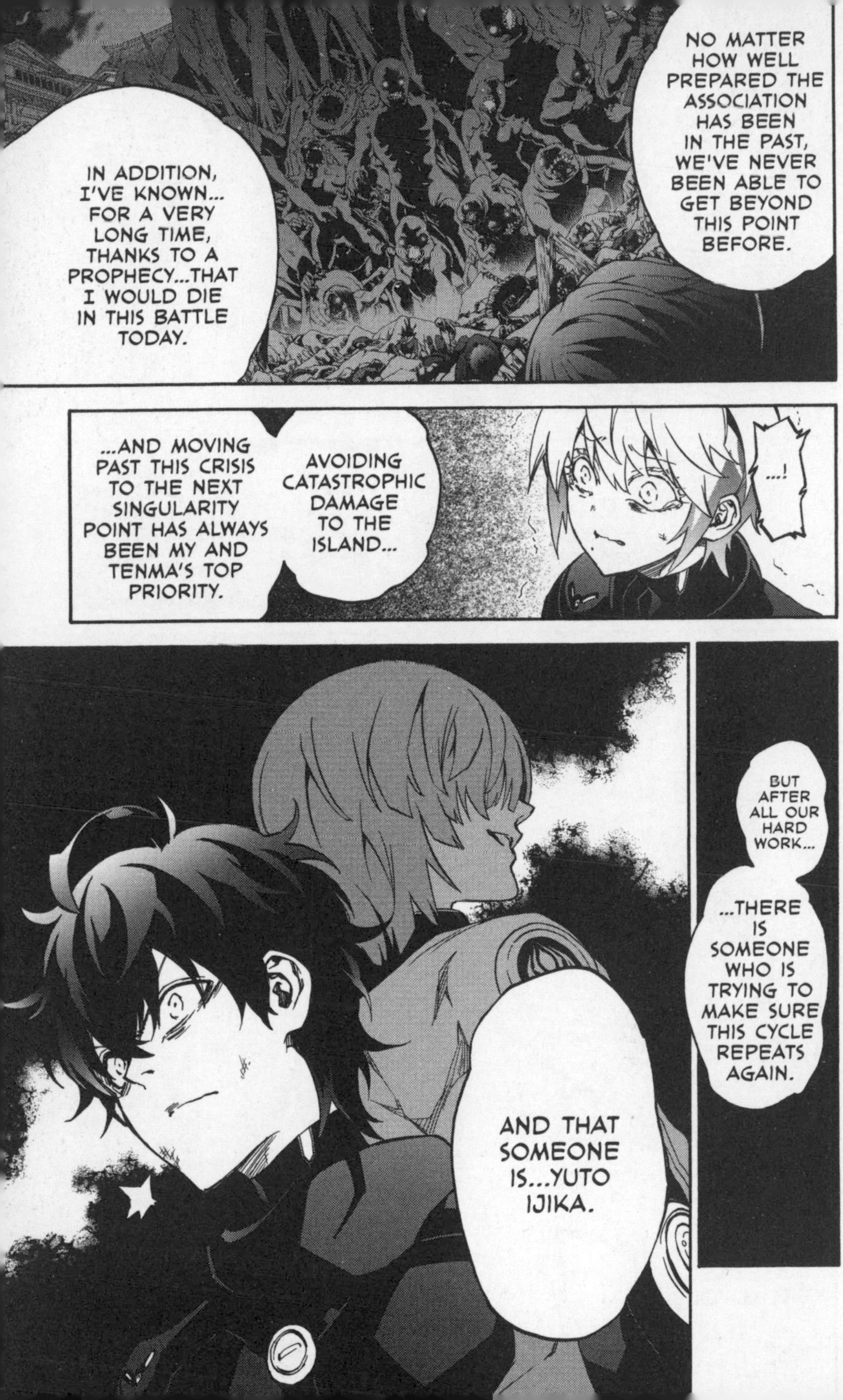
NO MATTER HOW WELL PREPARED THE ASSOCIATION HAS BEEN IN THE PAST, WE'VE NEVER BEEN ABLE TO GET BEYOND THIS POINT BEFORE.
IN ADDITION, I'VE KNOWN... FOR A VERY LONG TIME, THANKS TO A PROPHECY...THAT I WOULD DIE IN THIS BATTLE TODAY.
...!
AVOIDING CATASTROPHIC DAMAGE TO THE ISLAND...
...AND MOVING PAST THIS CRISIS TO THE NEXT SINGULARITY POINT HAS ALWAYS BEEN MY AND TENMA'S TOP PRIORITY.
BUT AFTER ALL OUR HARD WORK...
...THERE IS SOMEONE WHO IS TRYING TO MAKE SURE THIS CYCLE REPEATS AGAIN.
AND THAT SOMEONE IS...YUTO IJIKA.

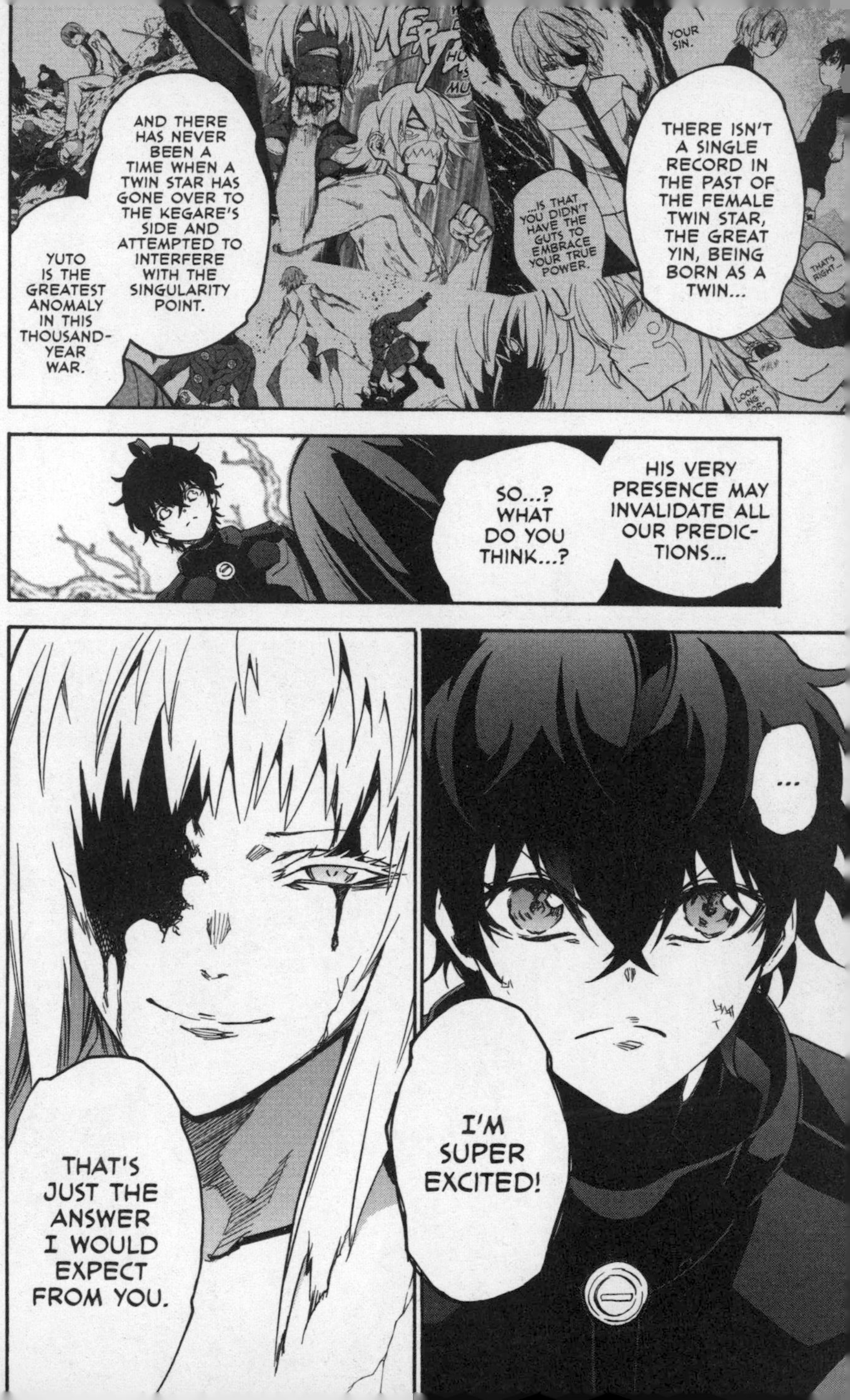

YOUR SIN.
THERE ISN'T A SINGLE RECORD IN THE PAST OF THE FEMALE TWIN STAR, THE GREAT YIN, BEING BORN AS A TWIN...
THAT'S RIGHT...
...IS THAT YOU DIDN'T HAVE THE GUTS TO EMBRACE YOUR TRUE POWER.
AND THERE HAS NEVER BEEN A TIME WHEN A TWIN STAR HAS GONE OVER TO THE KEGARE'S SIDE AND ATTEMPTED TO INTERFERE WITH THE SINGULARITY POINT.
YUTO IS THE GREATEST ANOMALY IN THIS THOUSAND-YEAR WAR.
HIS VERY PRESENCE MAY INVALIDATE ALL OUR PREDICTIONS...
SO...? WHAT DO YOU THINK...?
...
I'M SUPER EXCITED!
THAT'S JUST THE ANSWER I WOULD EXPECT FROM YOU.

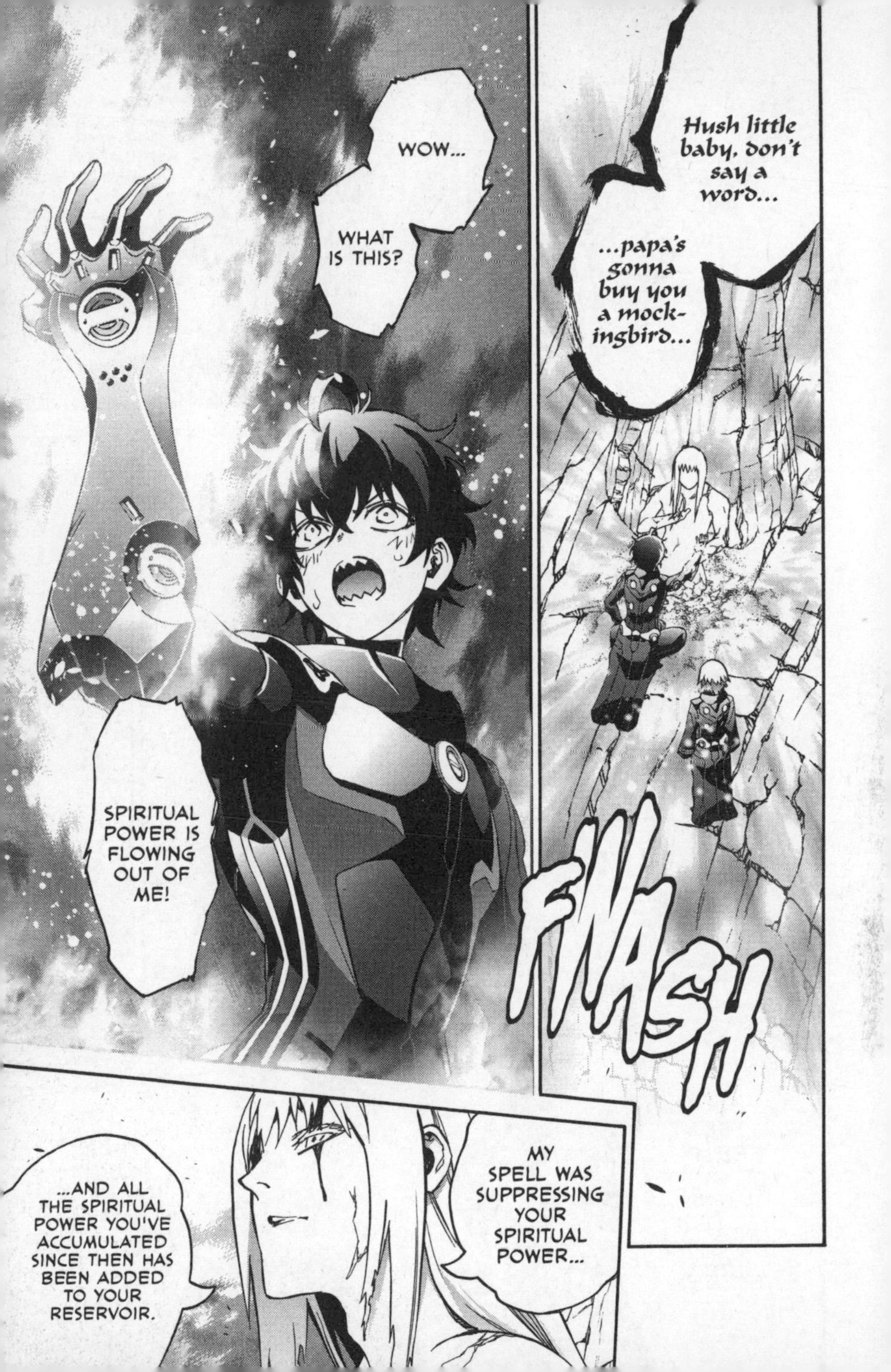
Hush little baby, don't say a word...
...papa's gonna buy you a mock-ingbird...
FNASH
WOW...
WHAT IS THIS?
SPIRITUAL POWER IS FLOWING OUT OF ME!
MY SPELL WAS SUPPRESSING YOUR SPIRITUAL POWER...
...AND ALL THE SPIRITUAL POWER YOU'VE ACCUMULATED SINCE THEN HAS BEEN ADDED TO YOUR RESERVOIR.

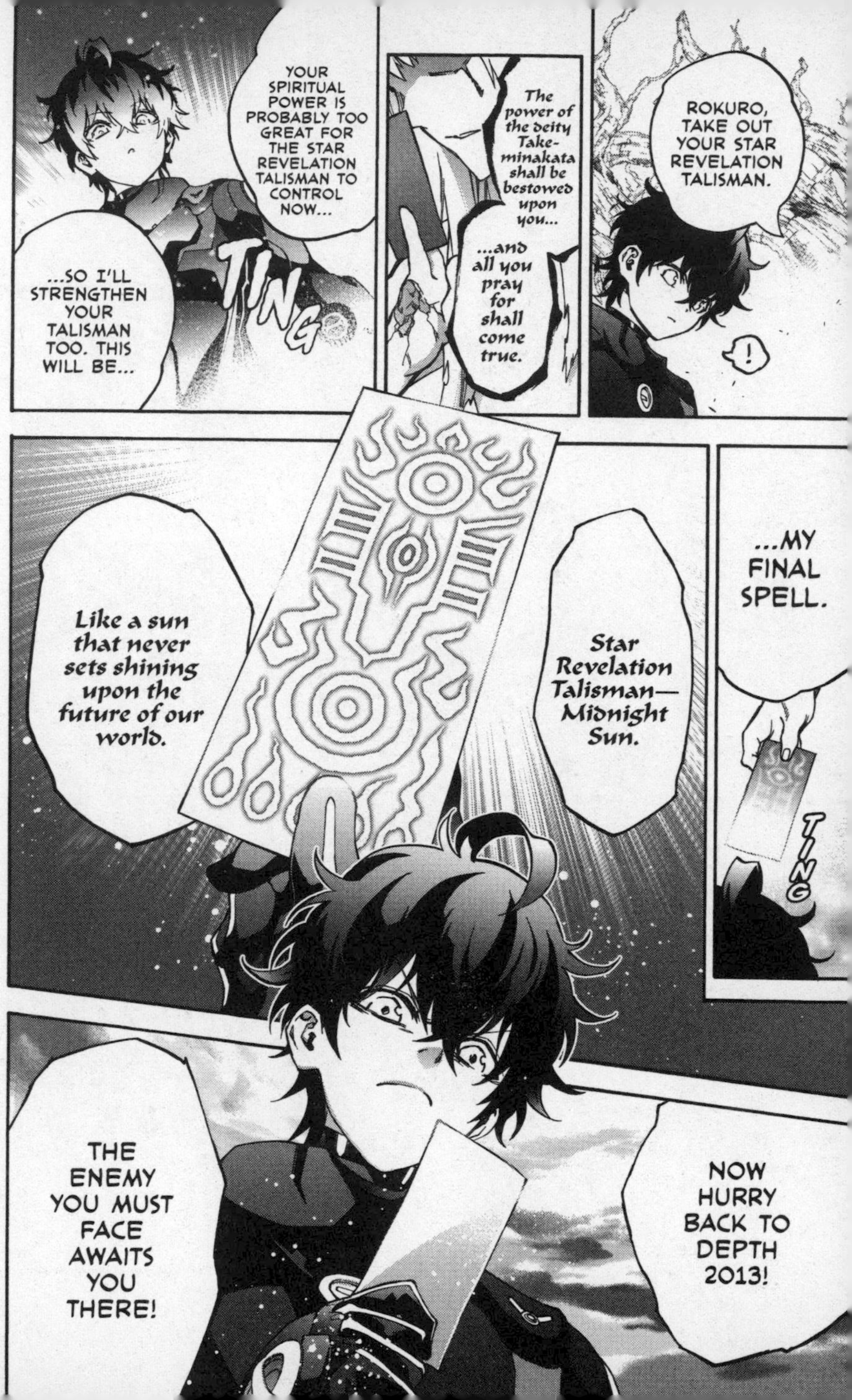
ROKURO, TAKE OUT YOUR STAR REVELATION TALISMAN.
!
The power of the deity Take-minakata shall be bestowed upon you...
...and all you pray for shall come true.
YOUR SPIRITUAL POWER IS PROBABLY TOO GREAT FOR THE STAR REVELATION TALISMAN TO CONTROL NOW...
TING
...SO I'LL STRENGTHEN YOUR TALISMAN TOO. THIS WILL BE...
...MY FINAL SPELL.
TING
Star Revelation Talisman— Midnight Sun.
Like a sun that never sets shining upon the future of our world.
NOW HURRY BACK TO DEPTH 2013!
THE ENEMY YOU MUST FACE AWAITS YOU THERE!

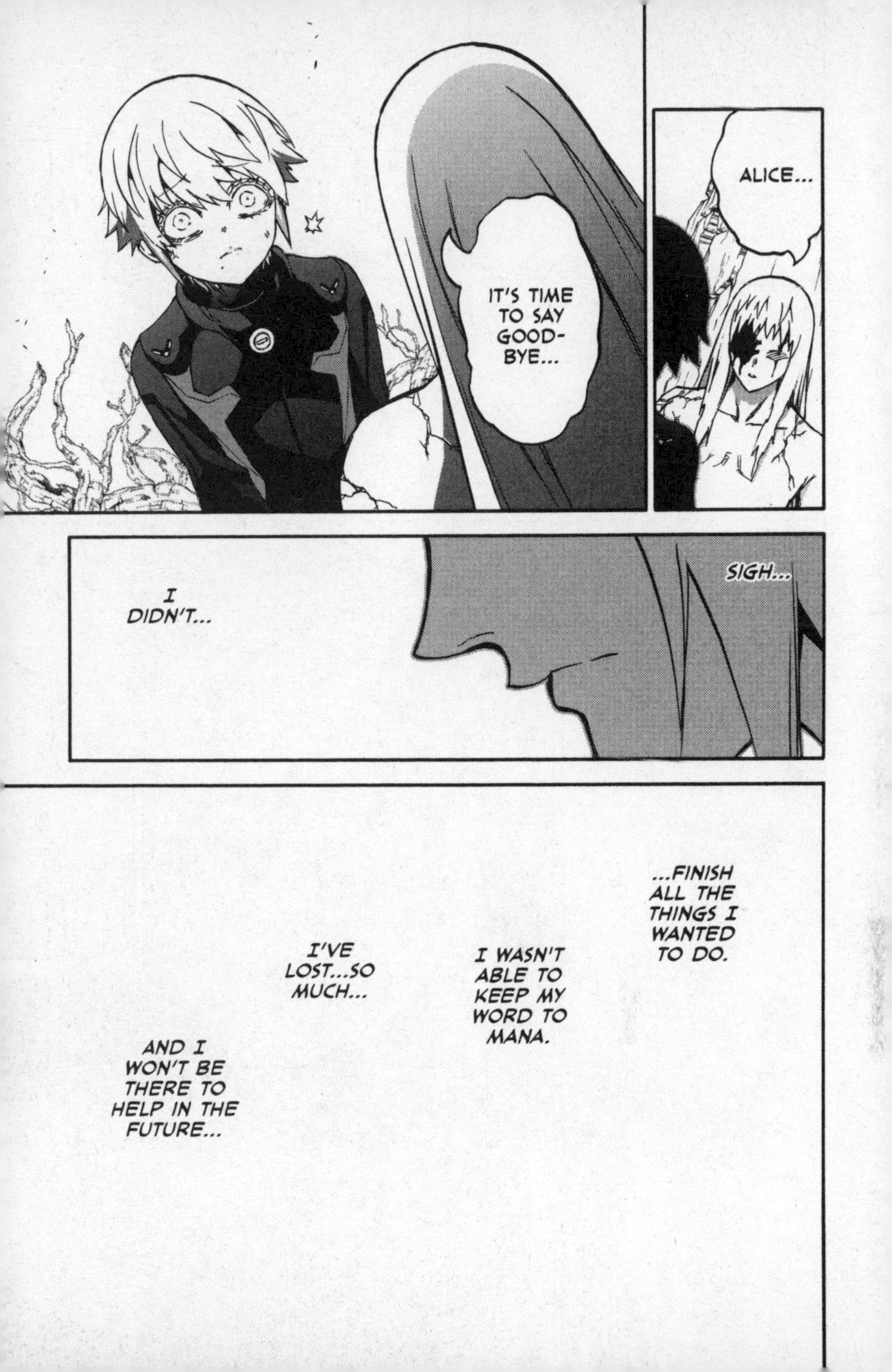
ALICE...
IT'S TIME TO SAY GOOD-BYE...
SIGH...
I DIDN'T...
...FINISH ALL THE THINGS I WANTED TO DO.
I WASN'T ABLE TO KEEP MY WORD TO MANA.
I'VE LOST...SO MUCH...
AND I WON'T BE THERE TO HELP IN THE FUTURE...

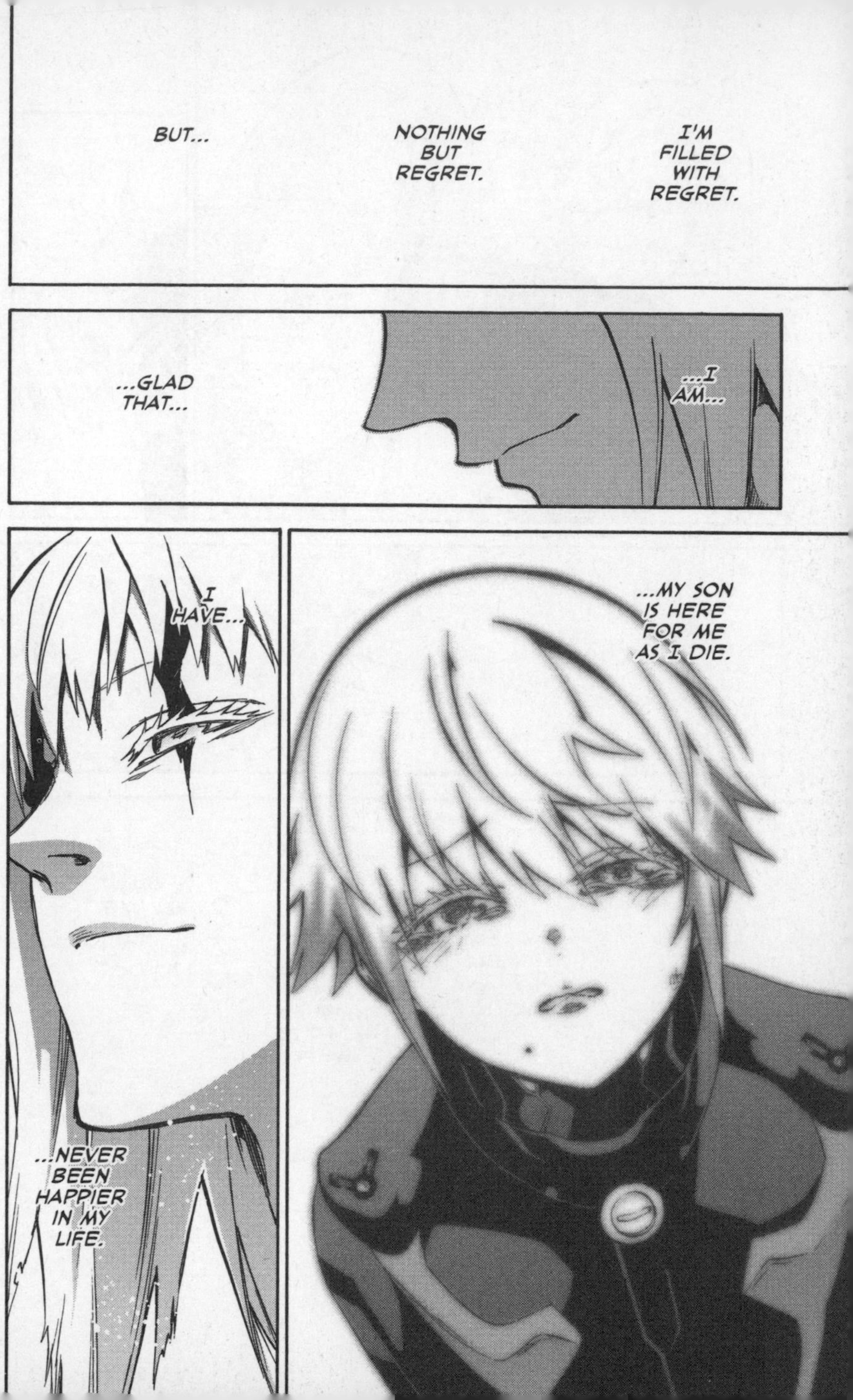
I'M FILLED WITH REGRET.
NOTHING BUT REGRET.
BUT...
...I AM...
...GLAD THAT...
...MY SON IS HERE FOR ME AS I DIE.
I HAVE...
...NEVER BEEN HAPPIER IN MY LIFE.

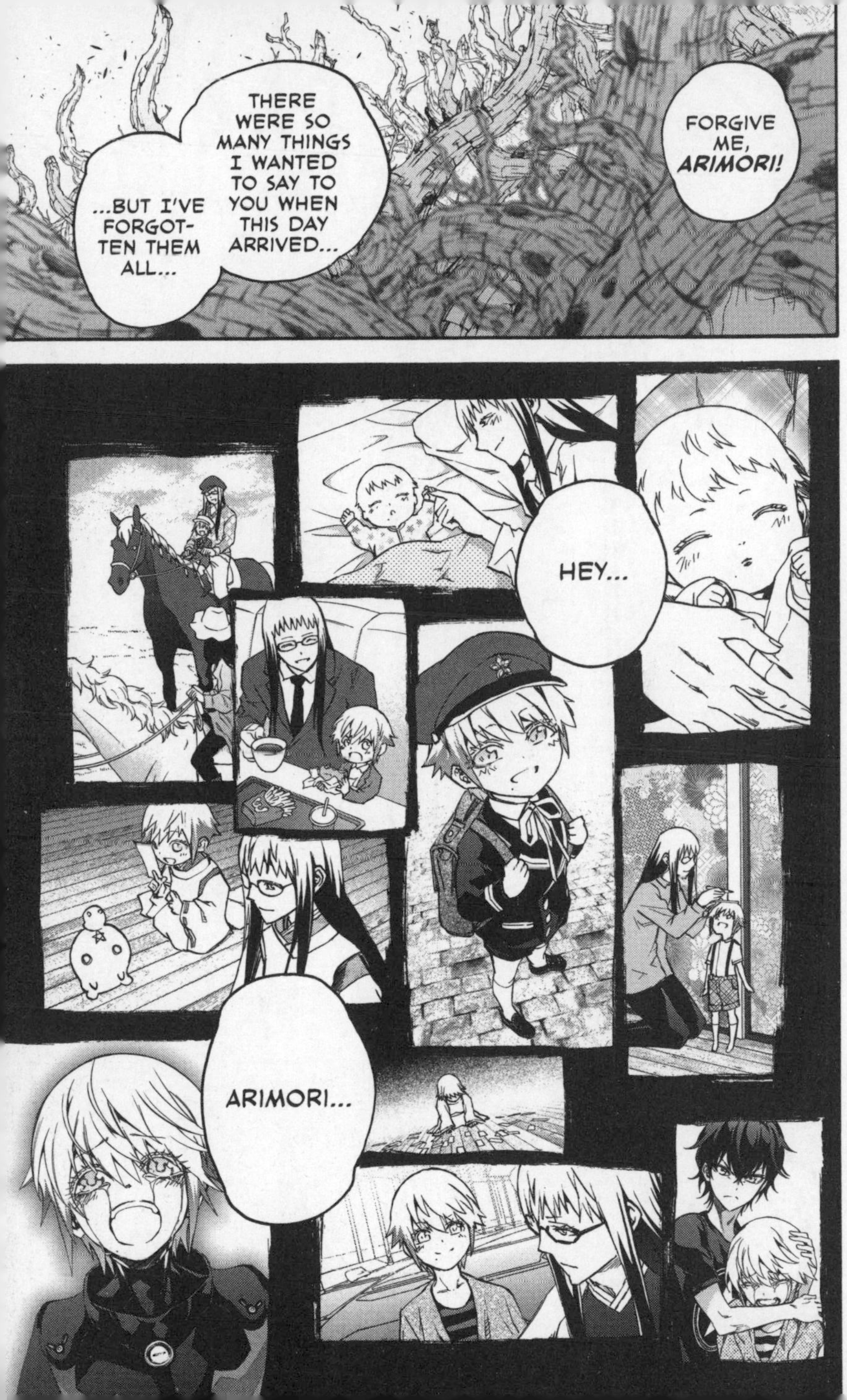
FORGIVE ME, ARIMORI!
THERE WERE SO MANY THINGS I WANTED TO SAY TO YOU WHEN THIS DAY ARRIVED...
...BUT I'VE FORGOT-TEN THEM ALL...
HEY...
ARIMORI...

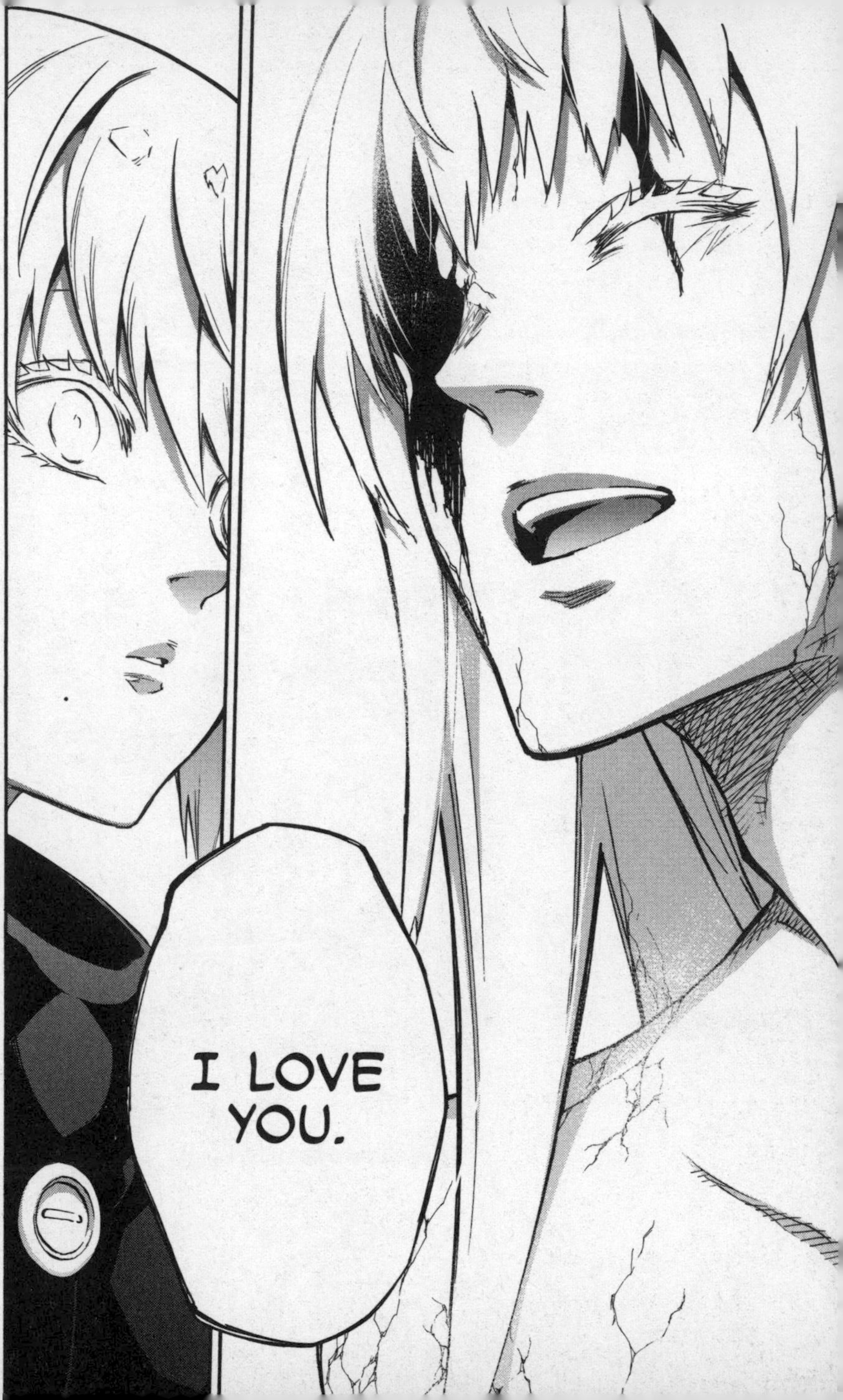
I LOVE YOU.

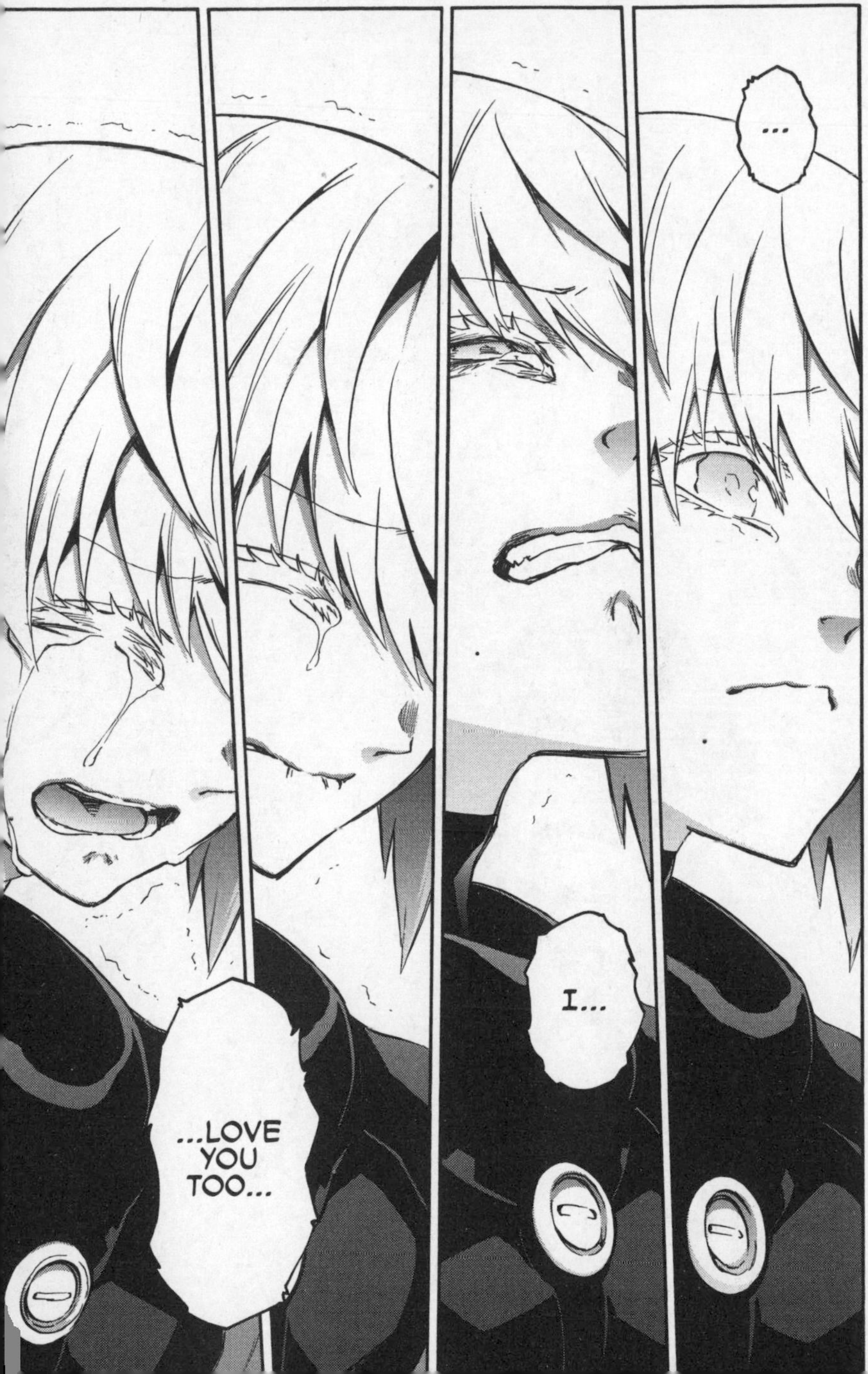
...
I...
...LOVE YOU TOO...

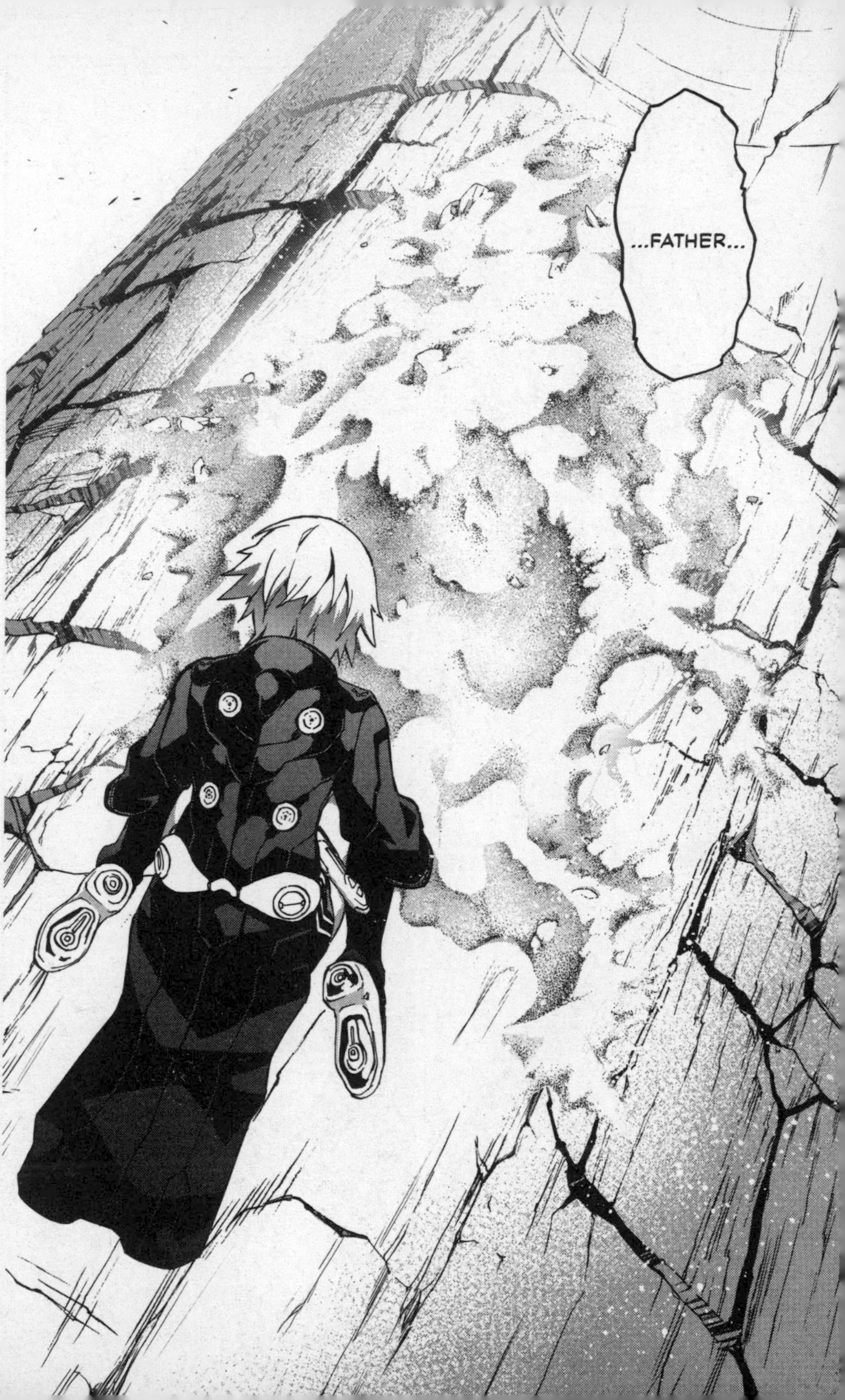
...FATHER...

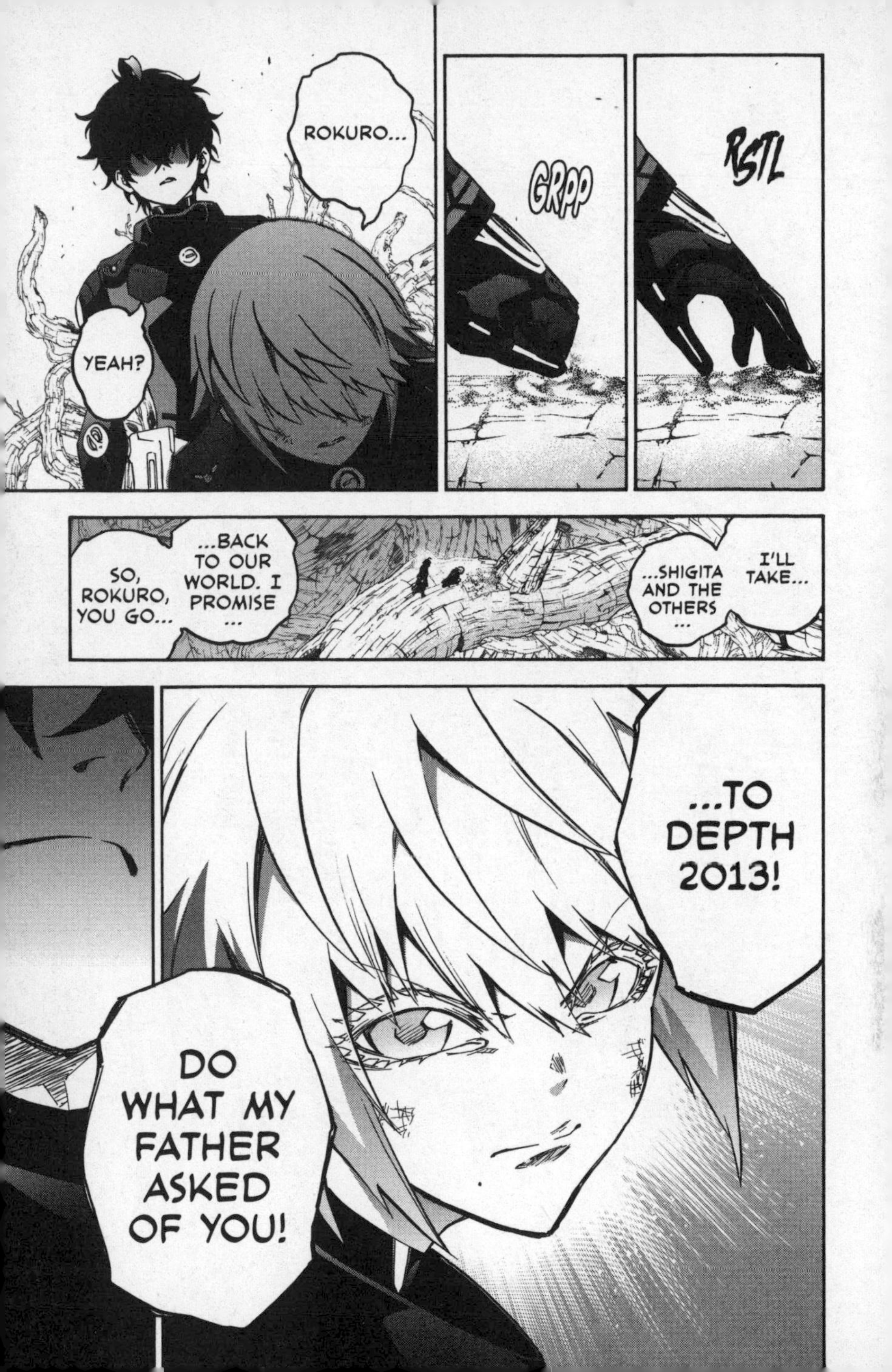

RSTL
GRPP
ROKURO...
YEAH?
I'LL TAKE...
...SHIGITA AND THE OTHERS...
...BACK TO OUR WORLD. I PROMISE...
SO, ROKURO, YOU GO...
...TO DEPTH 2013!
DO WHAT MY FATHER ASKED OF YOU!

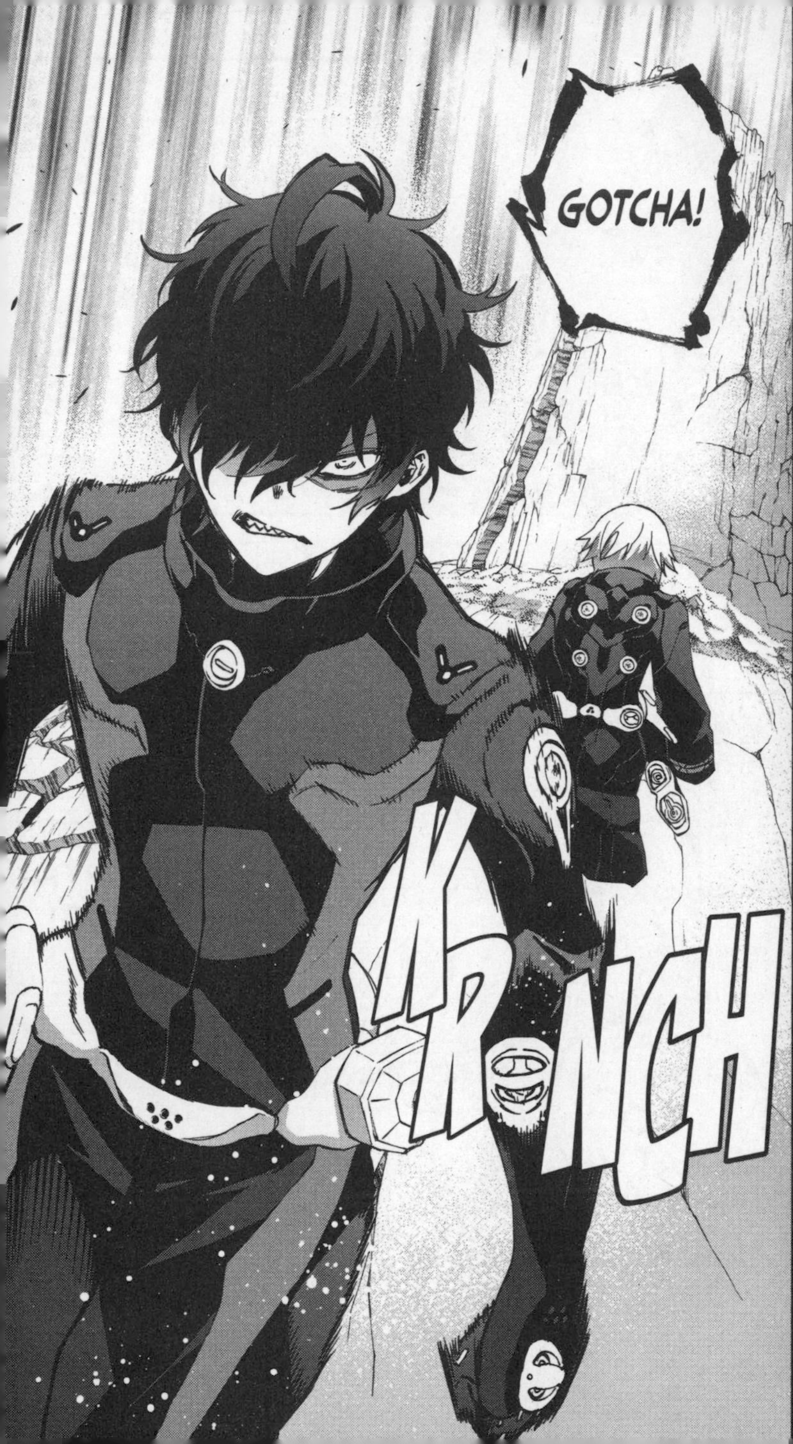
GOTCHA!
KRNCH

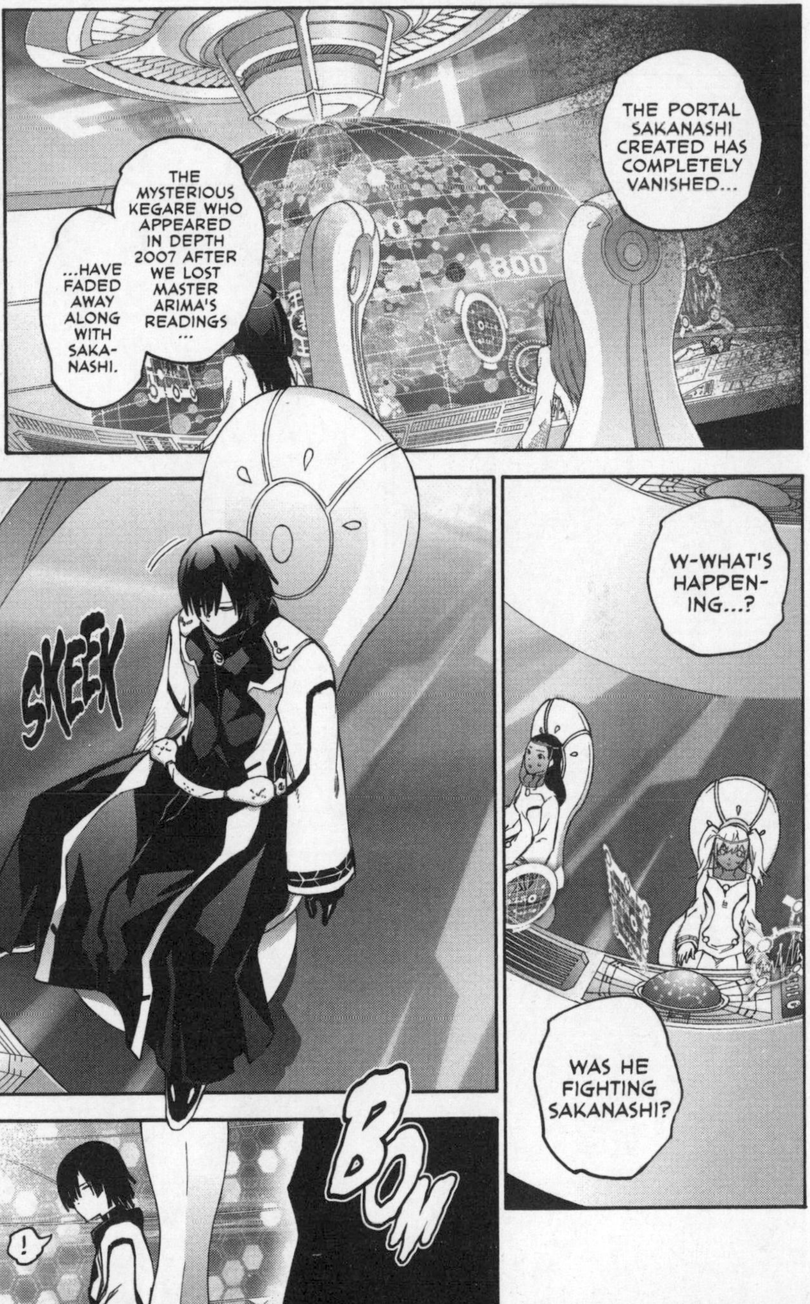
THE PORTAL SAKANASHI CREATED HAS COMPLETELY VANISHED...
THE MYSTERIOUS KEGARE WHO APPEARED IN DEPTH 2007 AFTER WE LOST MASTER ARIMA'S READINGS...
...HAVE FADED AWAY ALONG WITH SAKA-NASHI.
1800
W-WHAT'S HAPPEN-ING...?
WAS HE FIGHTING SAKANASHI?
SKEEK
BOM
!

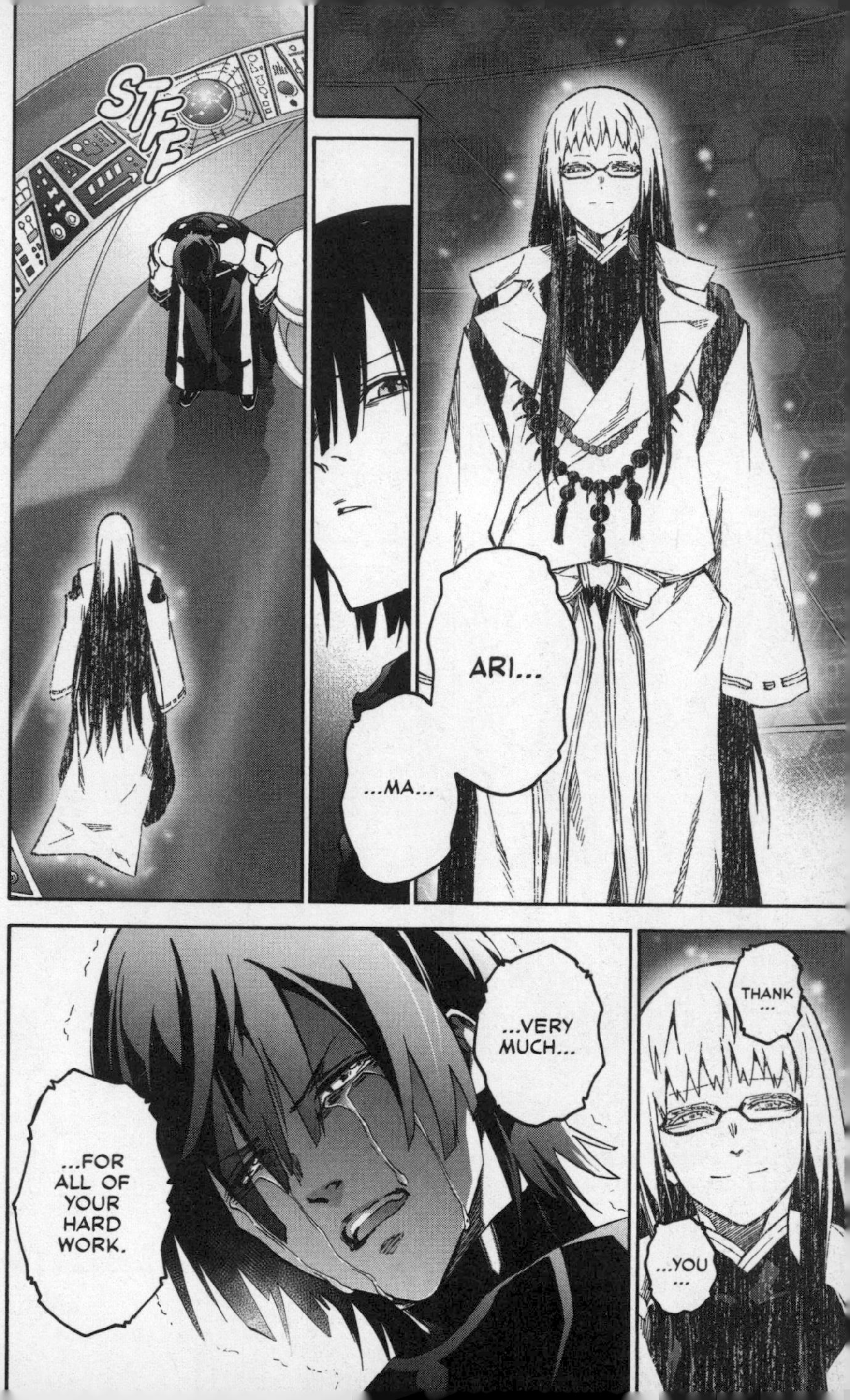
ARI...
...MA...
STFF
THANK...
...YOU...
...VERY MUCH...
...FOR ALL OF YOUR HARD WORK.

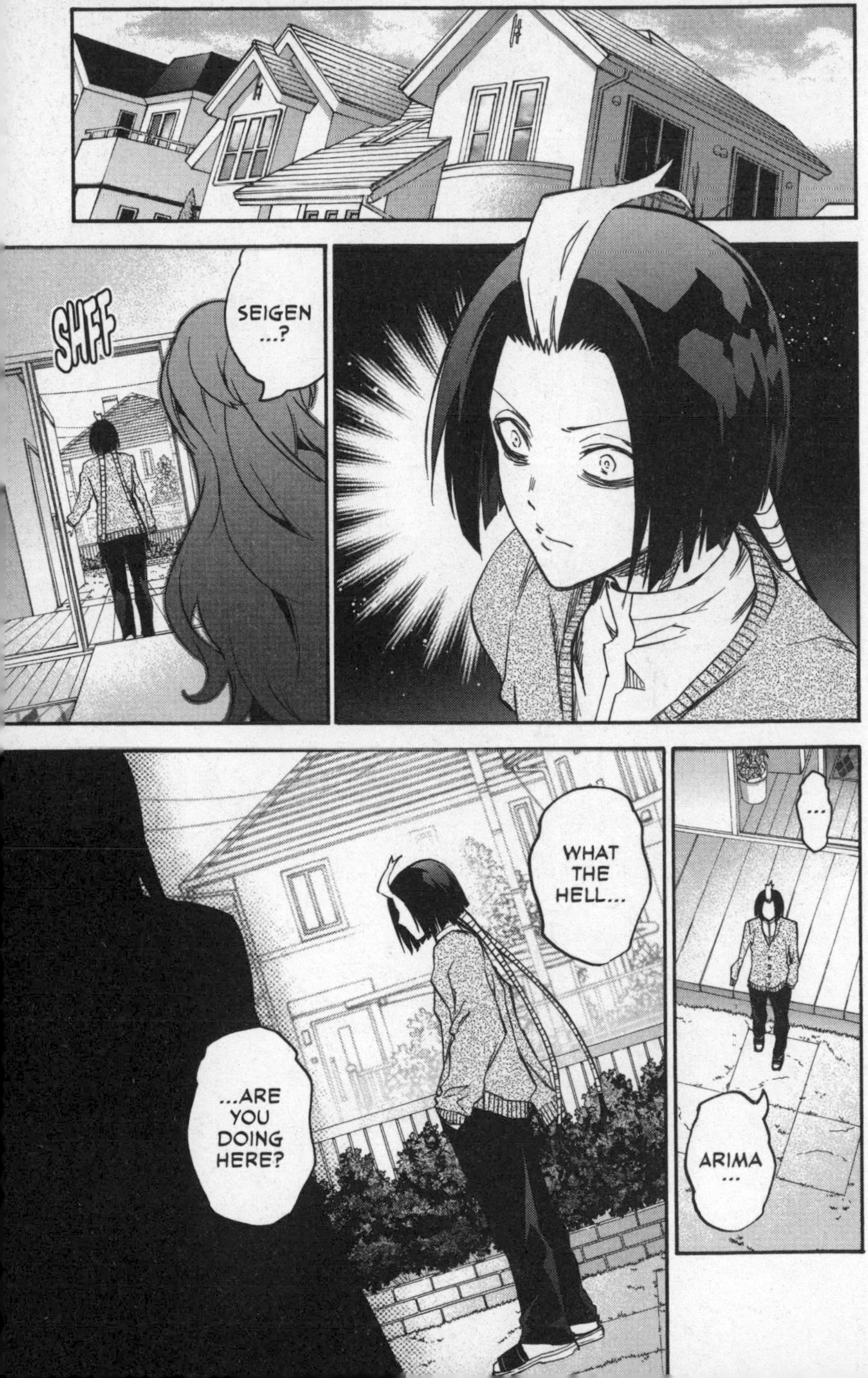
SHFF
SEIGEN ...?
...
ARIMA ...
WHAT THE HELL...
...ARE YOU DOING HERE?

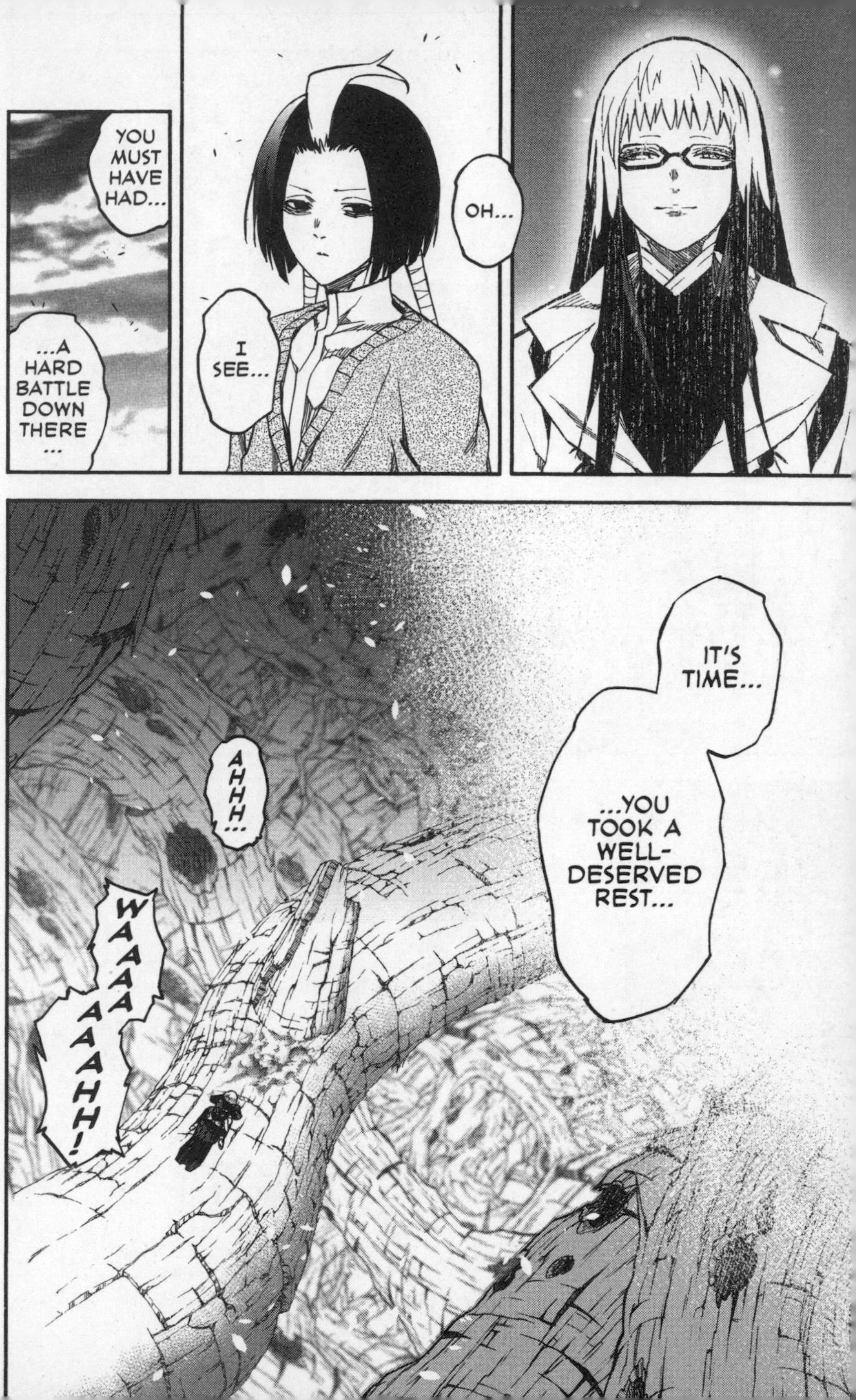
OH...
I SEE...
YOU MUST HAVE HAD...
...A HARD BATTLE DOWN THERE...
IT'S TIME...
...YOU TOOK A WELL-DESERVED REST...
AHHH...
WAAAAAAAHH!

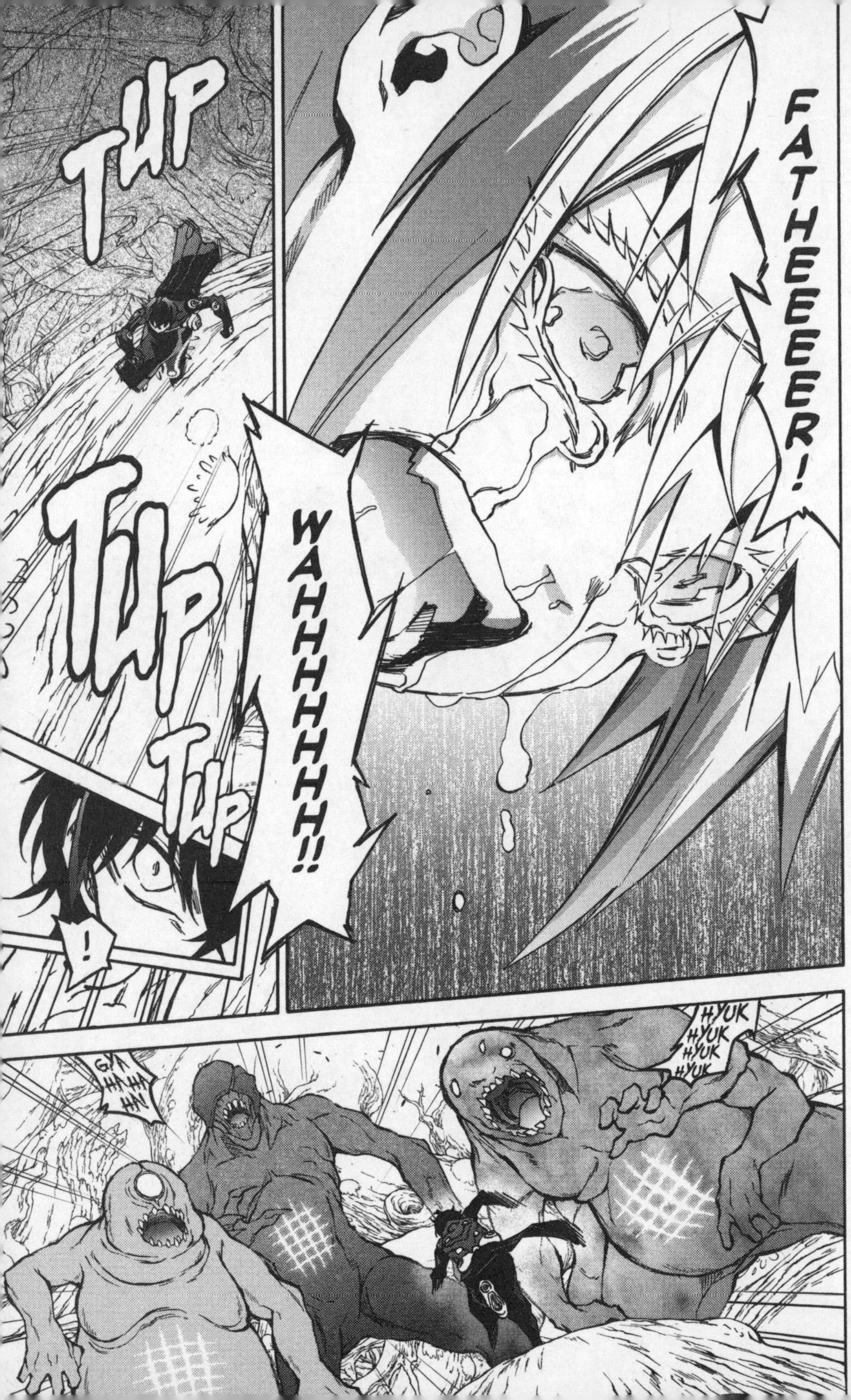
FATHEEEER!
WAHHHHHHH!!
TUP
TUP
TUP
!
HYUK HYUK HYUK HYUK
GAHAHAHA!

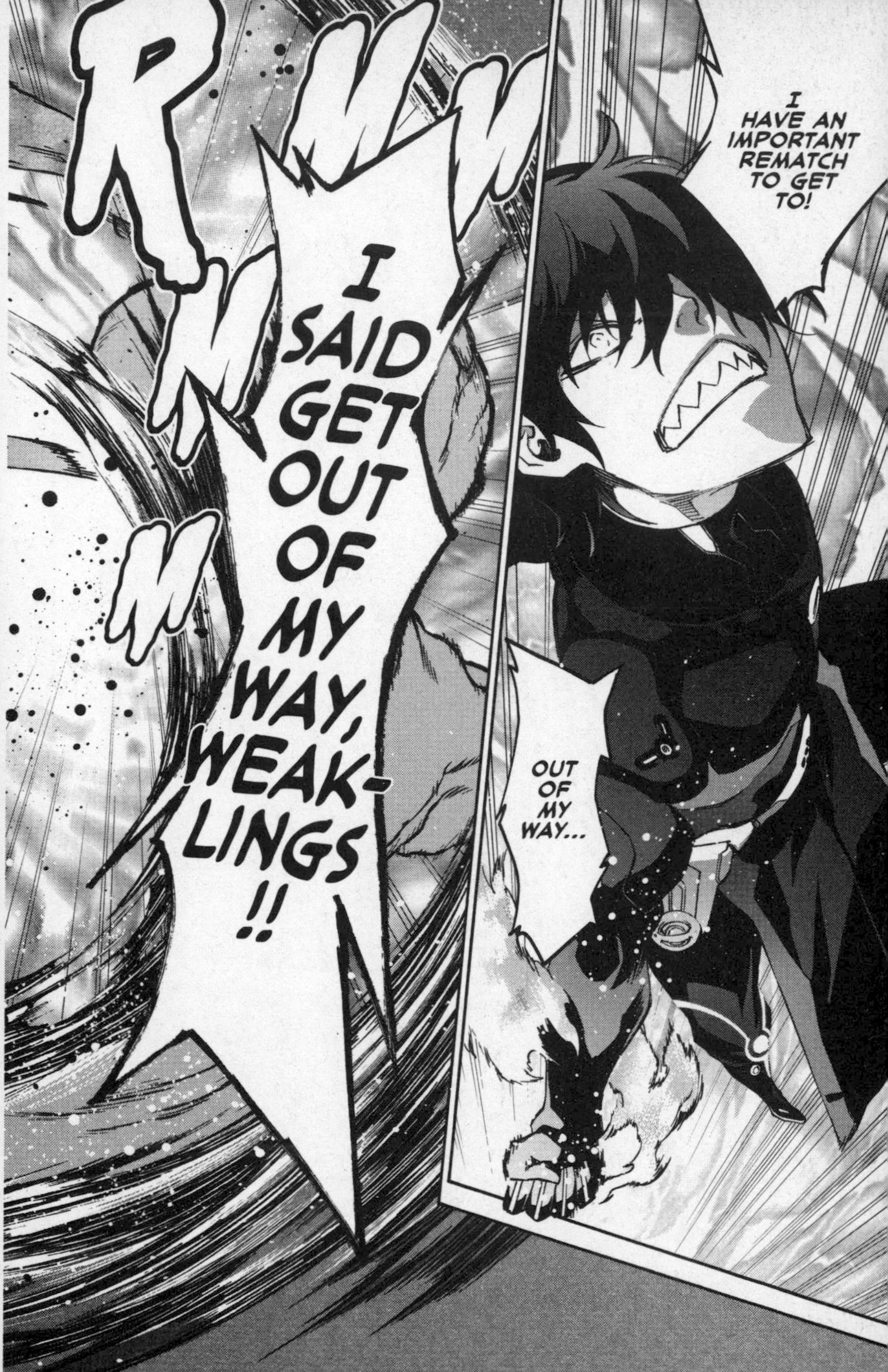
I HAVE AN IMPORTANT REMATCH TO GET TO!
OUT OF MY WAY...
I SAID GET OUT OF MY WAY, WEAK-LINGS!!

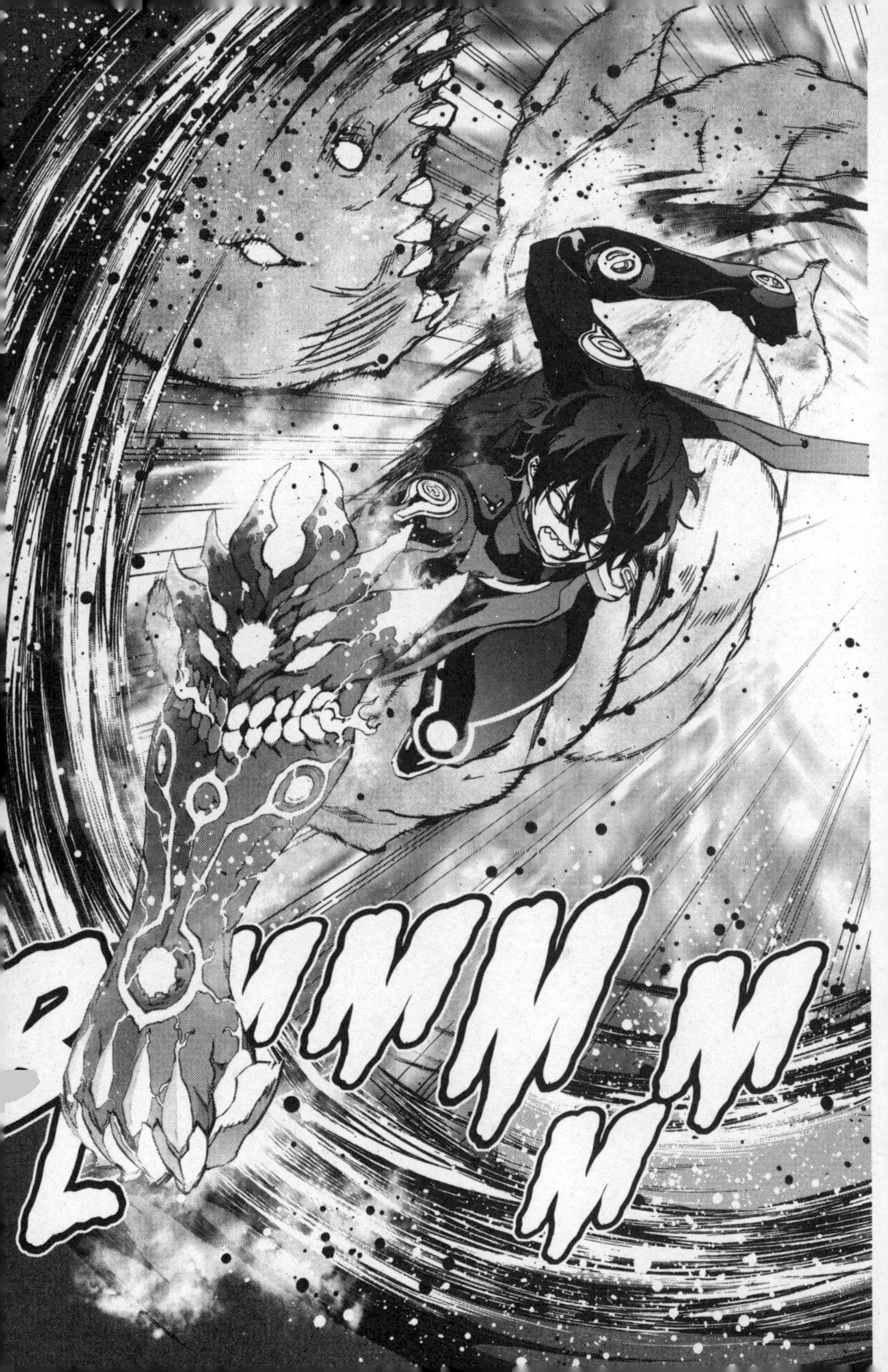

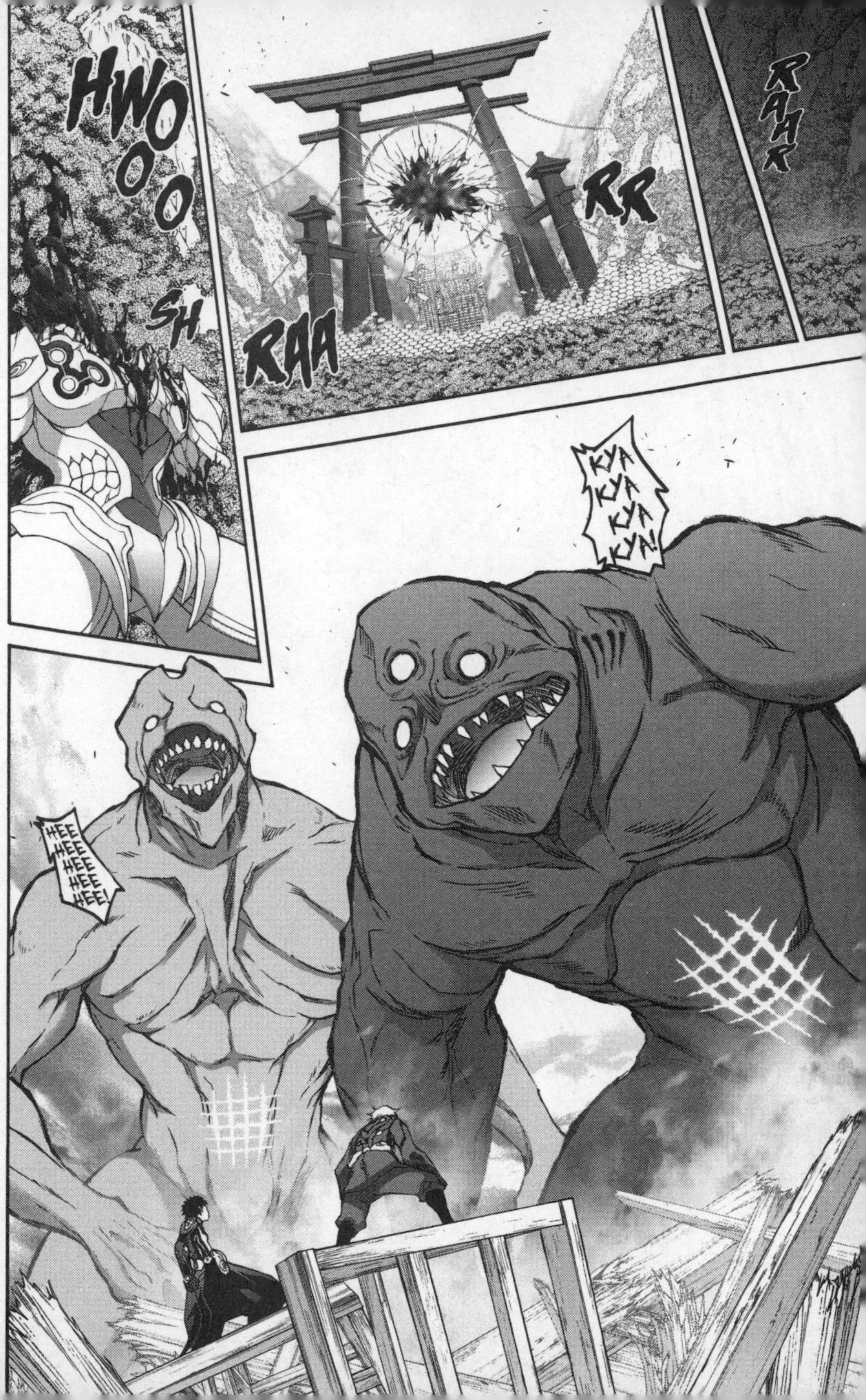
RAAHR
RR
RAA
HWOOOO
SH
KYA KYA KYA KYA!
HEE HEE HEE HEE HEE!

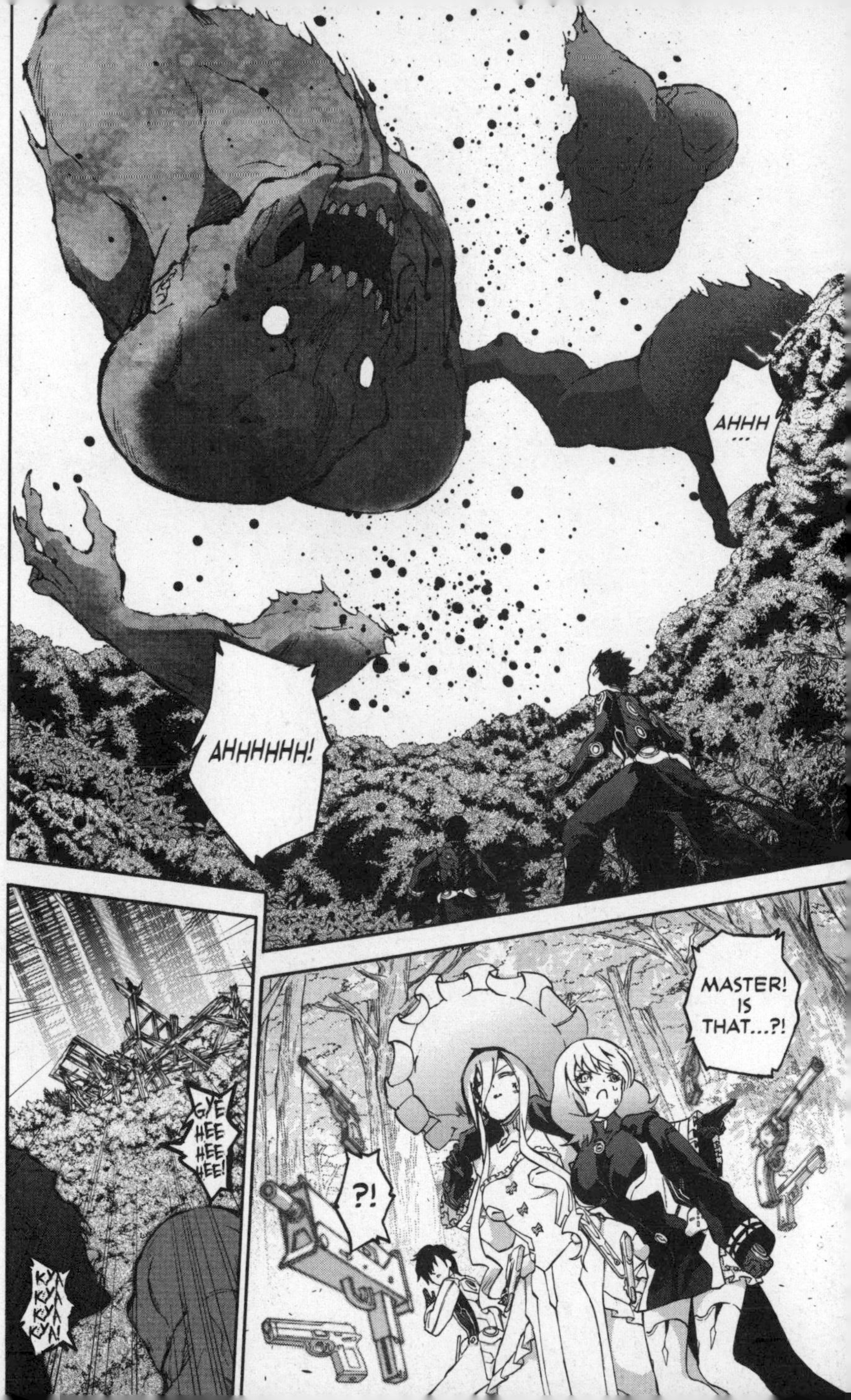
AHHH...
AHHHHHH!
MASTER! IS THAT...?!
?!
GYEHEE HEE HEE!
KYAKYAKYAKYA!

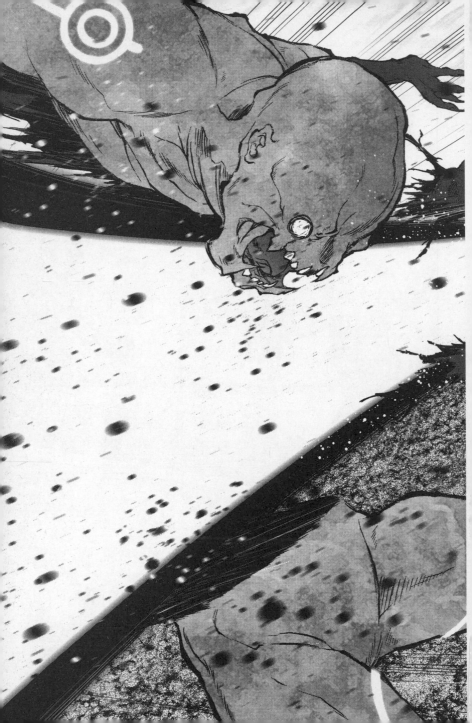

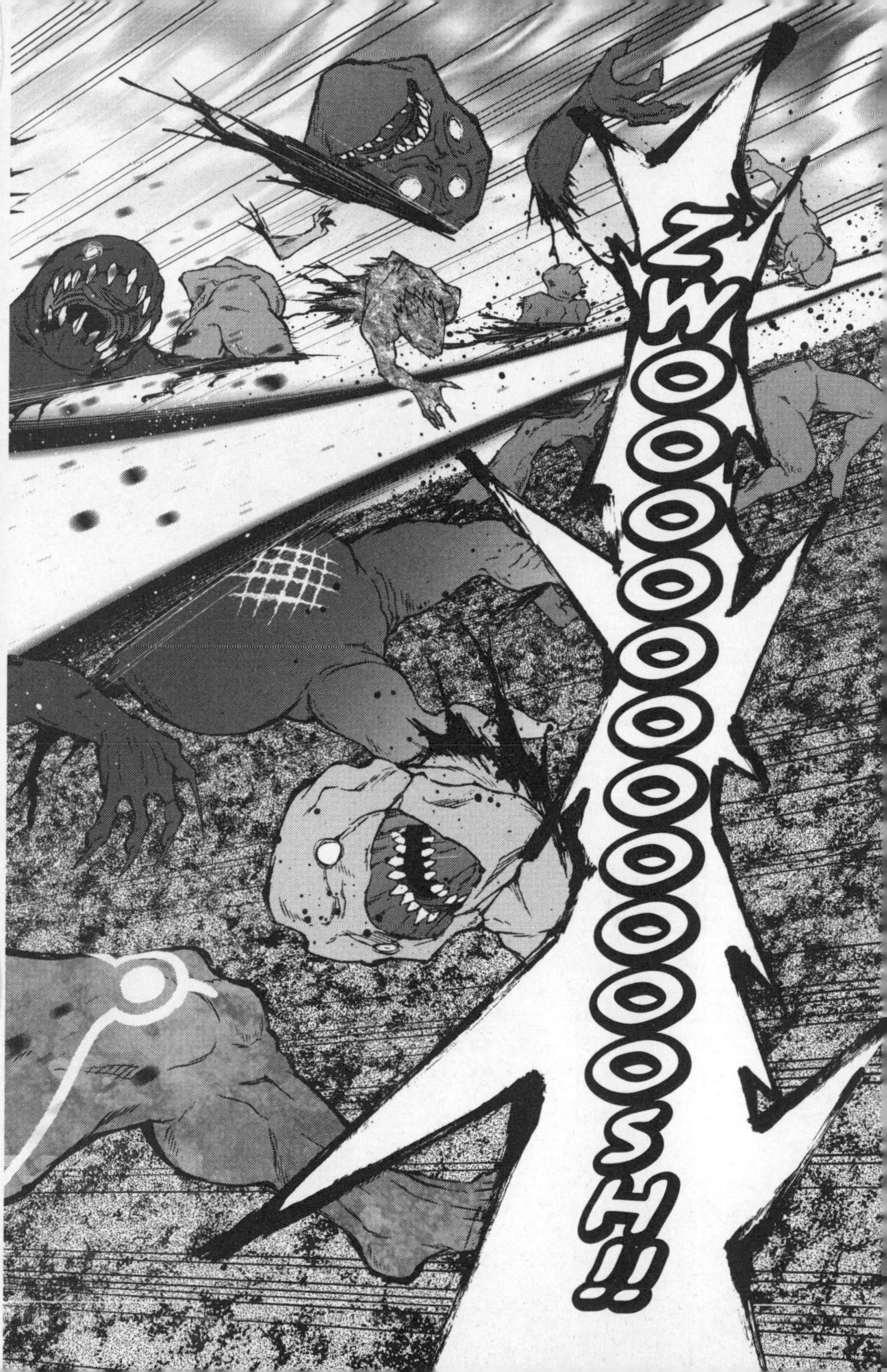
ZWOOOOOOOOOOOOOSH!!

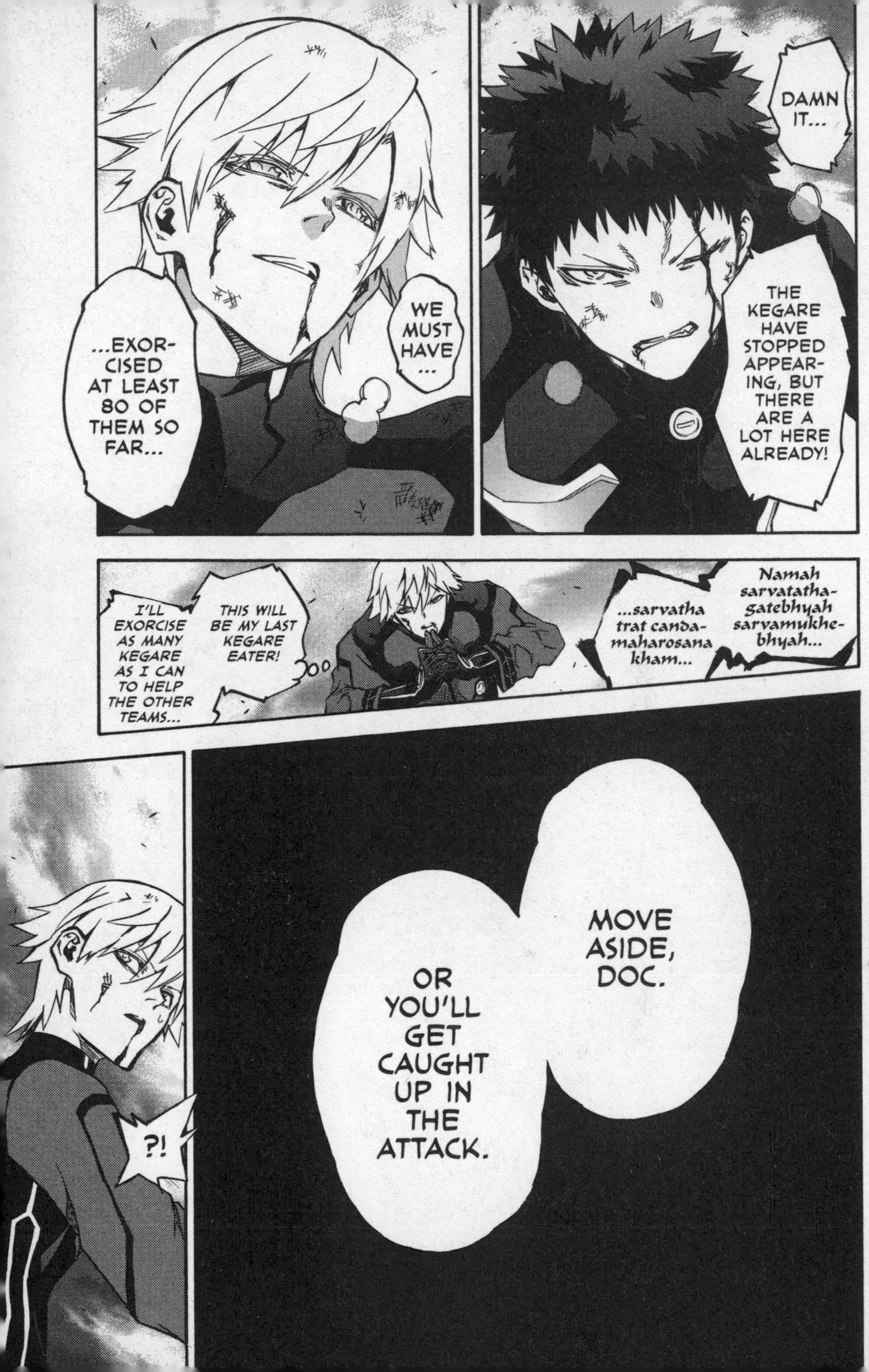
DAMN IT...
THE KEGARE HAVE STOPPED APPEAR-ING, BUT THERE ARE A LOT HERE ALREADY!
WE MUST HAVE...
...EXOR-CISED AT LEAST 80 OF THEM SO FAR...
Namah sarvatatha-gatebhyah sarvamukhe-bhyah...
...sarvatha trat canda-maharosana kham...
THIS WILL BE MY LAST KEGARE EATER!
I'LL EXORCISE AS MANY KEGARE AS I CAN TO HELP THE OTHER TEAMS...
MOVE ASIDE, DOC.
OR YOU'LL GET CAUGHT UP IN THE ATTACK.
?!

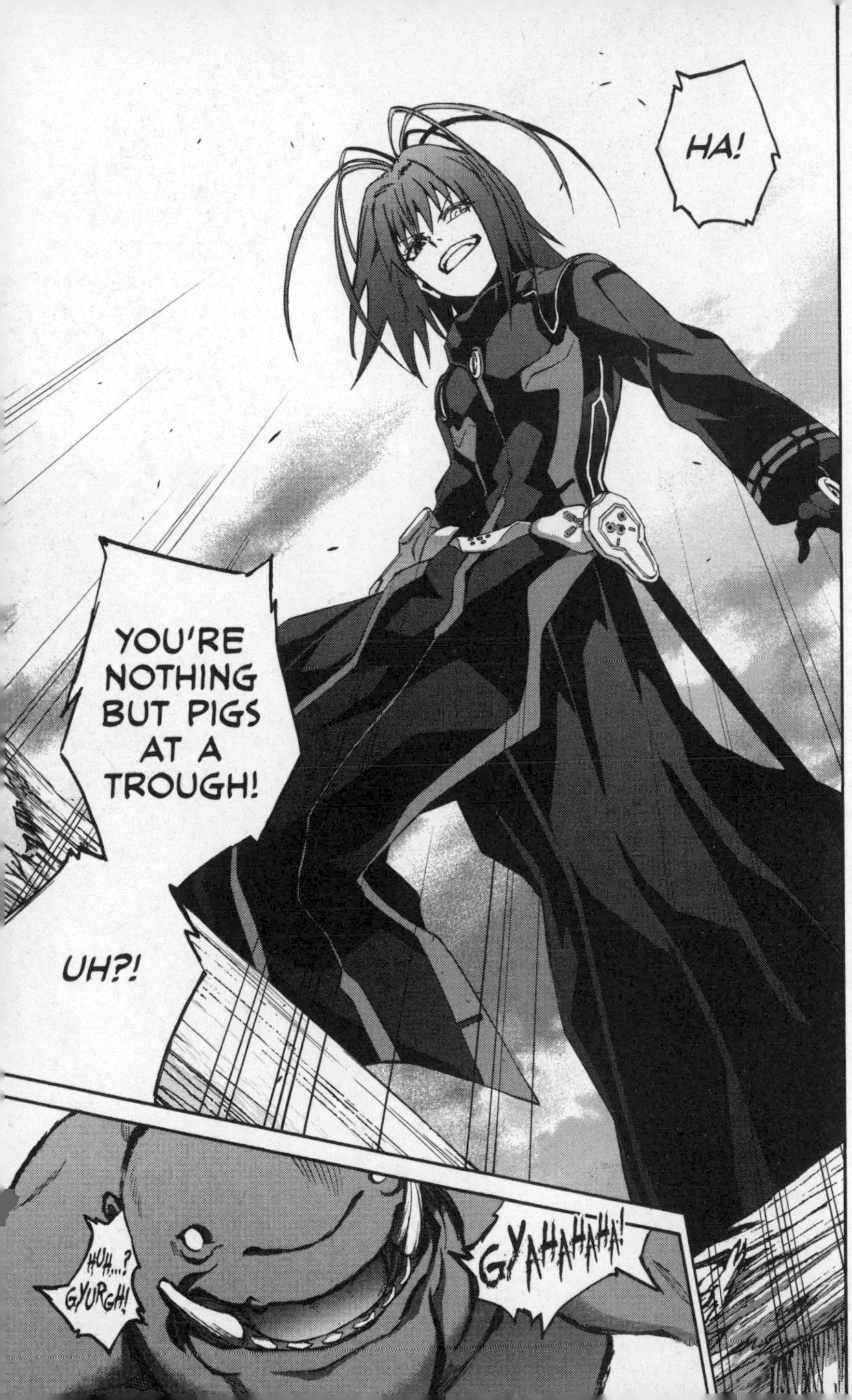
HA!
YOU'RE NOTHING BUT PIGS AT A TROUGH!
UH?!
GYAHAHAHA!
HUH...? GYURGH!

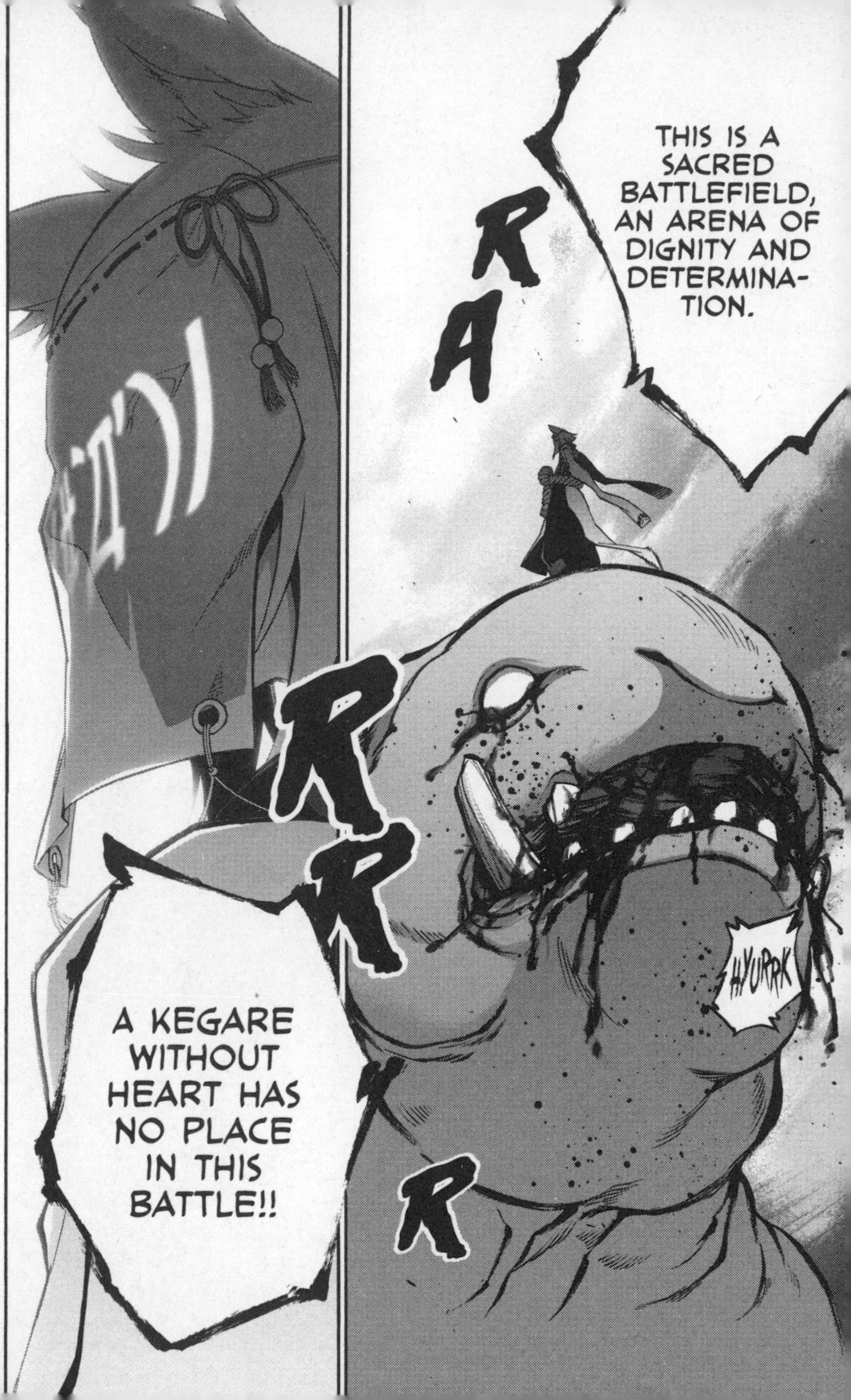

THIS IS A SACRED BATTLEFIELD, AN ARENA OF DIGNITY AND DETERMINATION.
RA
RRR
HYURRK
A KEGARE WITHOUT HEART HAS NO PLACE IN THIS BATTLE!!

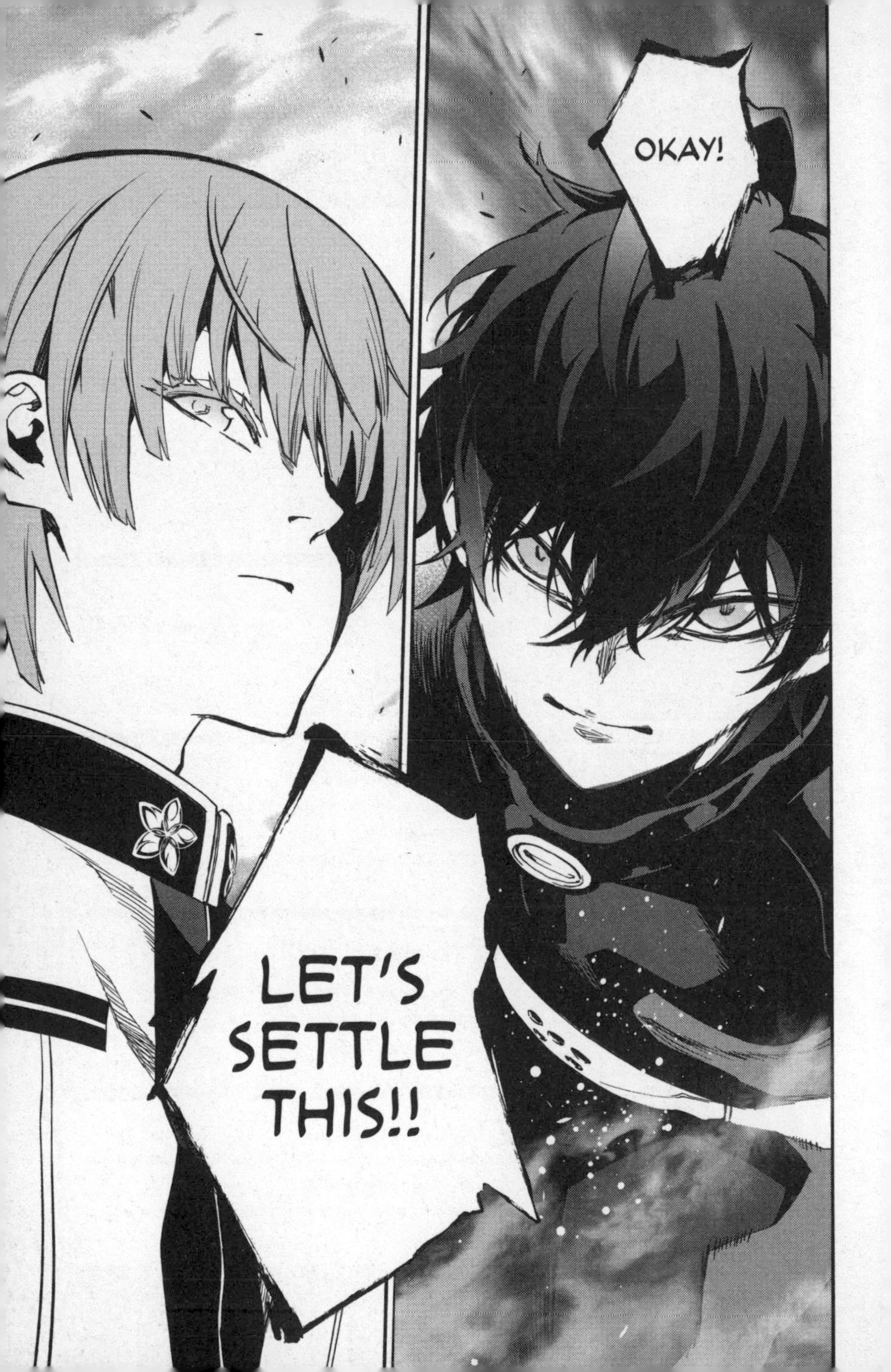
OKAY!
LET'S SETTLE THIS!!

CHARACTER PROFILE 5

The fifth character profile in this series, continued from pages 38 and 39, focuses on the Basara. I'll also be introducing the rare Basara who appeared in the novels as well.

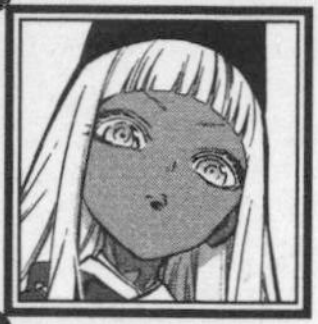

Chinu (? years old)

Birthday: ? Blood type: ? Height: 4'8" Weight: 77.2 lbs.

Likes: Human culture, small talk

Dislikes: Fighting, Sakanashi

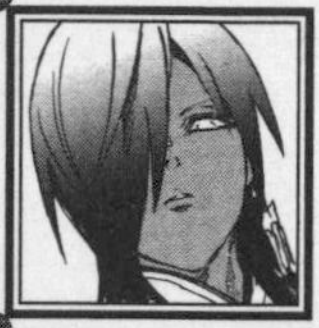

Sakanashi (? years old)

Birthday: June 4 Blood type: ? Height: 6'3" Weight: 174.2 lbs.

Likes: Nothing in particular

Dislikes: Nothing in particular

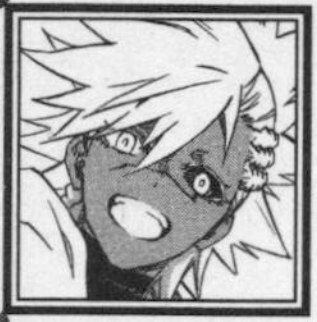

Gabura (? years old)

Birthday: December 20 Blood type: ? Height: 6'2" Weight: 165.4 lbs.

Likes: Thrills, violence

Dislikes: Boredom, weaklings

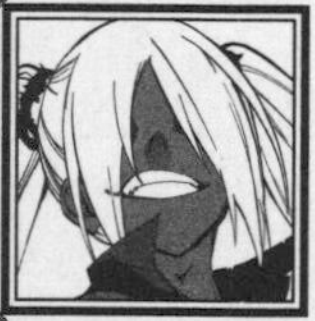

Hijirimaru (? years old)

Birthday: May 4 Blood type: ? Height: 6'1" Weight: 158.7 lbs.

Likes: The real world, hunting humans

Dislikes: Sakanashi, Gabura, begin looked down upon

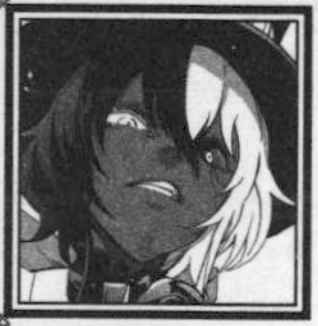

Shiromi (? years old)

Birthday: May 17 Blood type: ? Height: 6'0" Weight: 152.1 lbs.

Likes: Experiments, butchering humans

Dislikes: Higano, Hijirimaru(?)

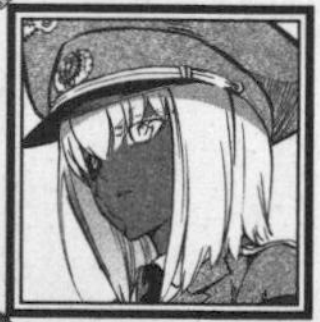

Kaguya (? years old)

Birthday: December 21 Blood type: ? Height: 5'6" Weight: 130 lbs.

Likes: Her beloved, beauty treatments

Dislikes: Anyone who interferes with her "romantic relationship"

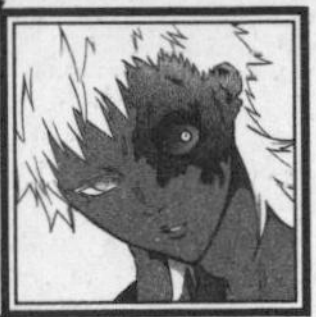

Gaja (? years old)

Birthday: July 25 Blood type: ? Height: 6'6" Weight: 183 lbs

Likes: Peace, the child from long ago

Dislikes: Fighting, the exorcist from long ago

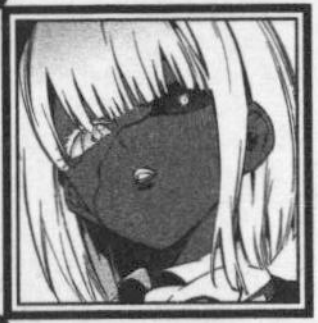

Shioji (? years old)

Birthday: June 21 Blood type: ? Height: 4'11" Weight: 90.4 lbs.

Likes: Books, tragedies, coffee (or coffee substitutes)

Dislikes: Happy endings

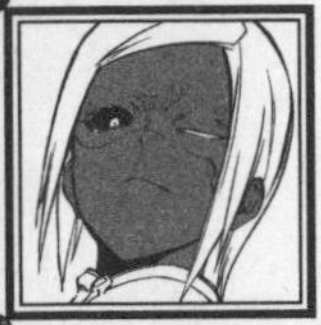

Higano (? years old)

Birthday: March 9 Blood type: ? Height: 6'2" Weight: 163.1 lbs.

Likes: The real world, Hijirimaru enjoying himself

Dislikes: Weak humans, those who get in Hijirimaru's way

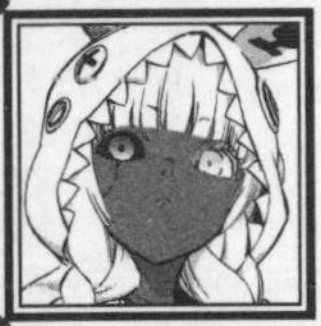

Yuzuriha (? years old)

Birthday: April 14 Blood type: ? Height: 5'3" Weight: 103.6 lbs.

Likes: Sakanashi, pain

Dislikes: Volunteering for anything

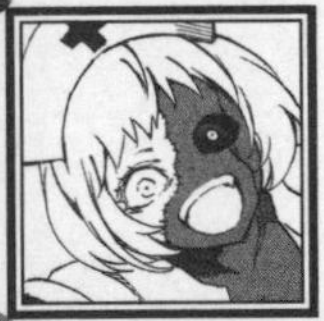

Chikura (? years old)

Birthday: ? Blood type: ? Height: 5'4" Weight: 119 lbs.

Likes: Suffering humans, injections

Dislikes: Pretty things

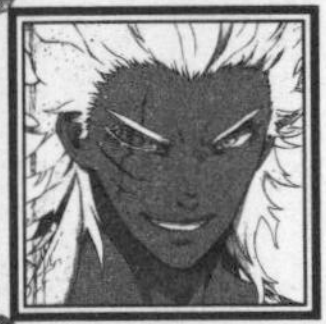

Onogoro (Deceased: ? years old)

Birthday: ? Blood type: ? Height: 6'6" Weight: 200.6 lbs.

Likes: Fear, himself

Dislikes: Sakanashi, stupid humans

Twin Star Exorcists

ONMYOJI

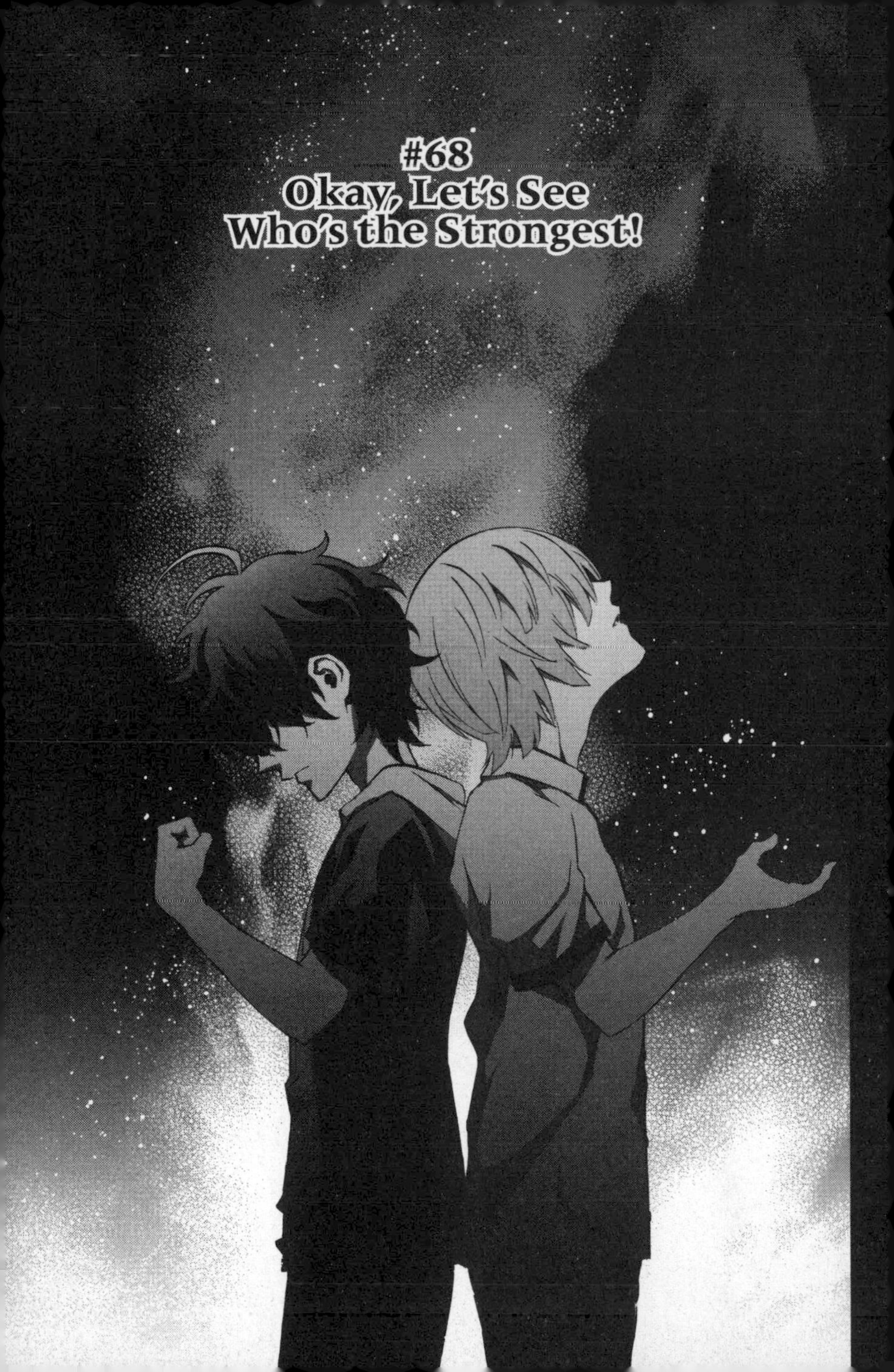
#68
Okay, Let's See
Who's the Strongest!

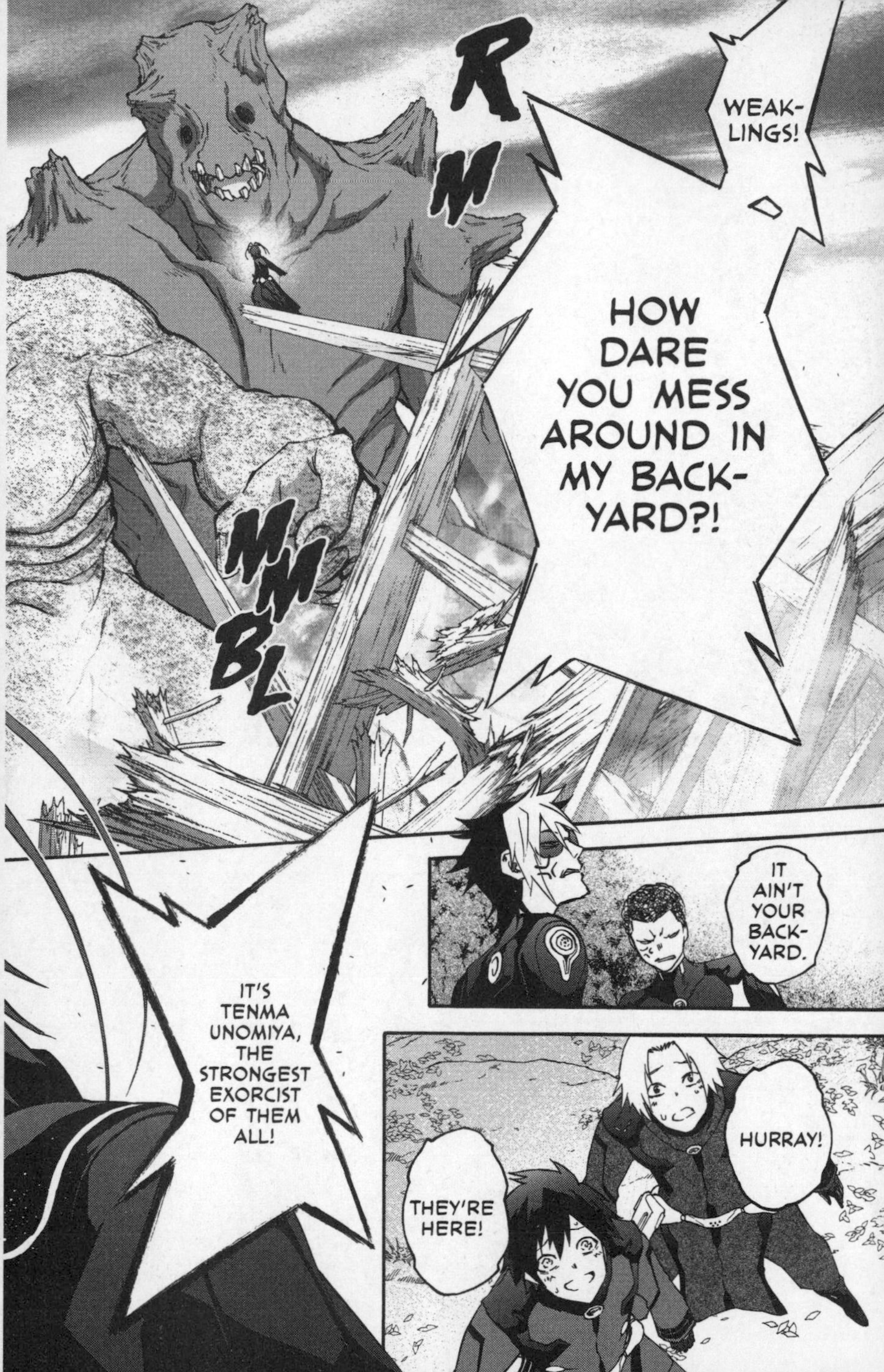
WEAK-LINGS!
HOW DARE YOU MESS AROUND IN MY BACK-YARD?!
RM
MMMBL
IT AIN'T YOUR BACK-YARD.
HURRAY!
THEY'RE HERE!
IT'S TENMA UNOMIYA, THE STRONGEST EXORCIST OF THEM ALL!

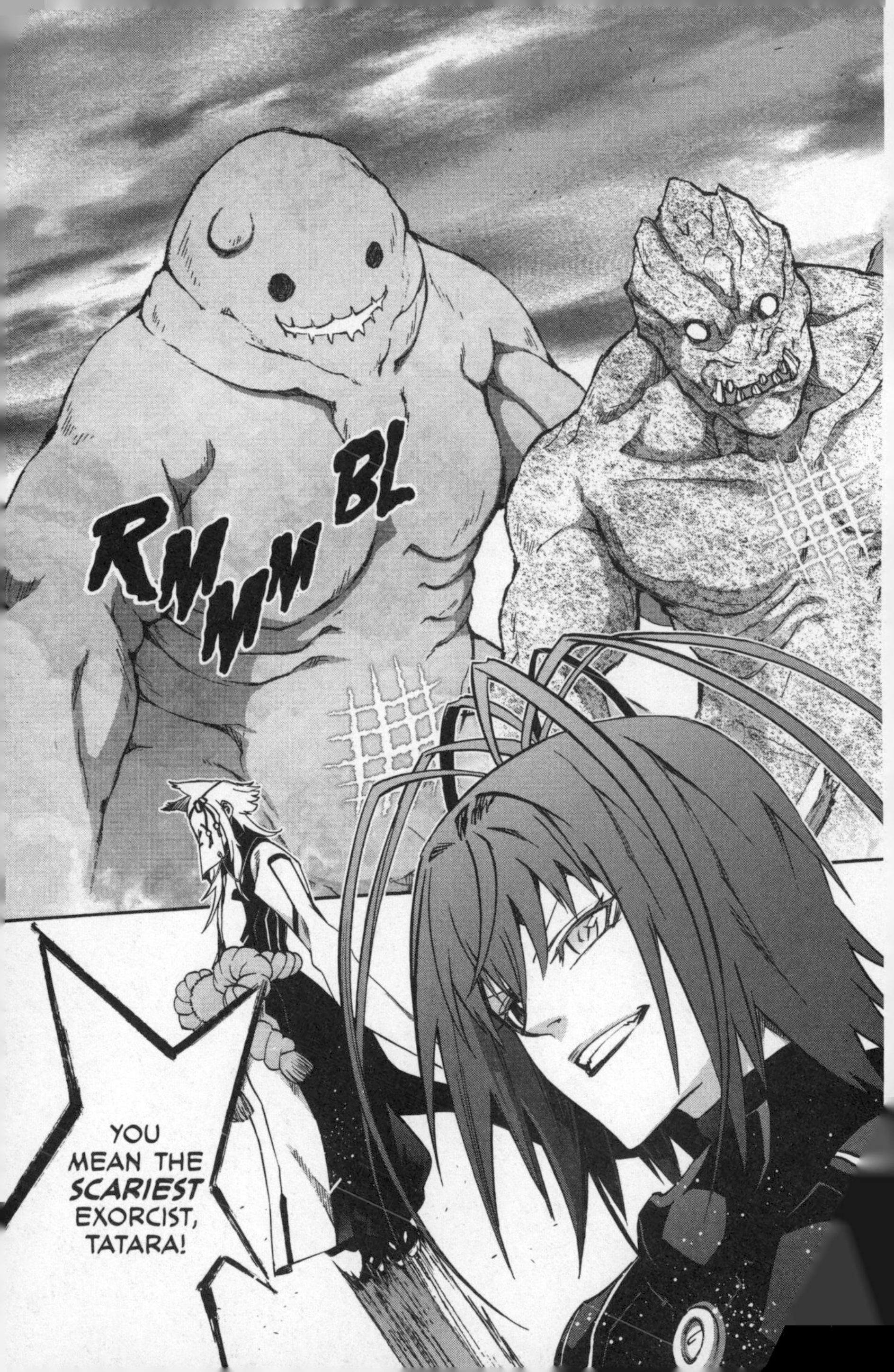
RMMMM BL
YOU MEAN THE SCARIEST EXORCIST, TATARA!

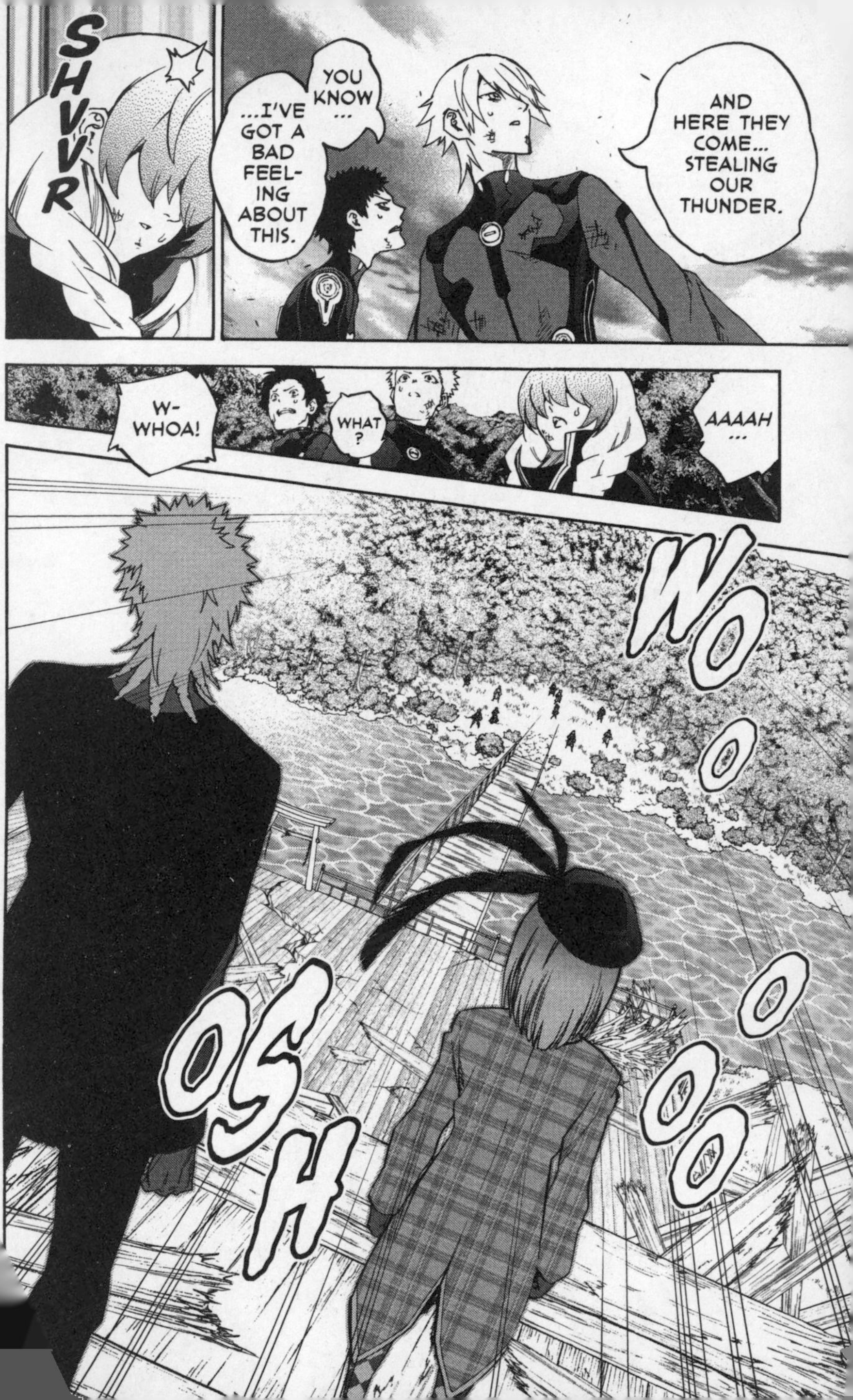

AND HERE THEY COME... STEALING OUR THUNDER.
YOU KNOW...
...I'VE GOT A BAD FEEL-ING ABOUT THIS.
SHVVR
AAAAH...
WHAT?
W-WHOA!
WOOOOOOO
OSH

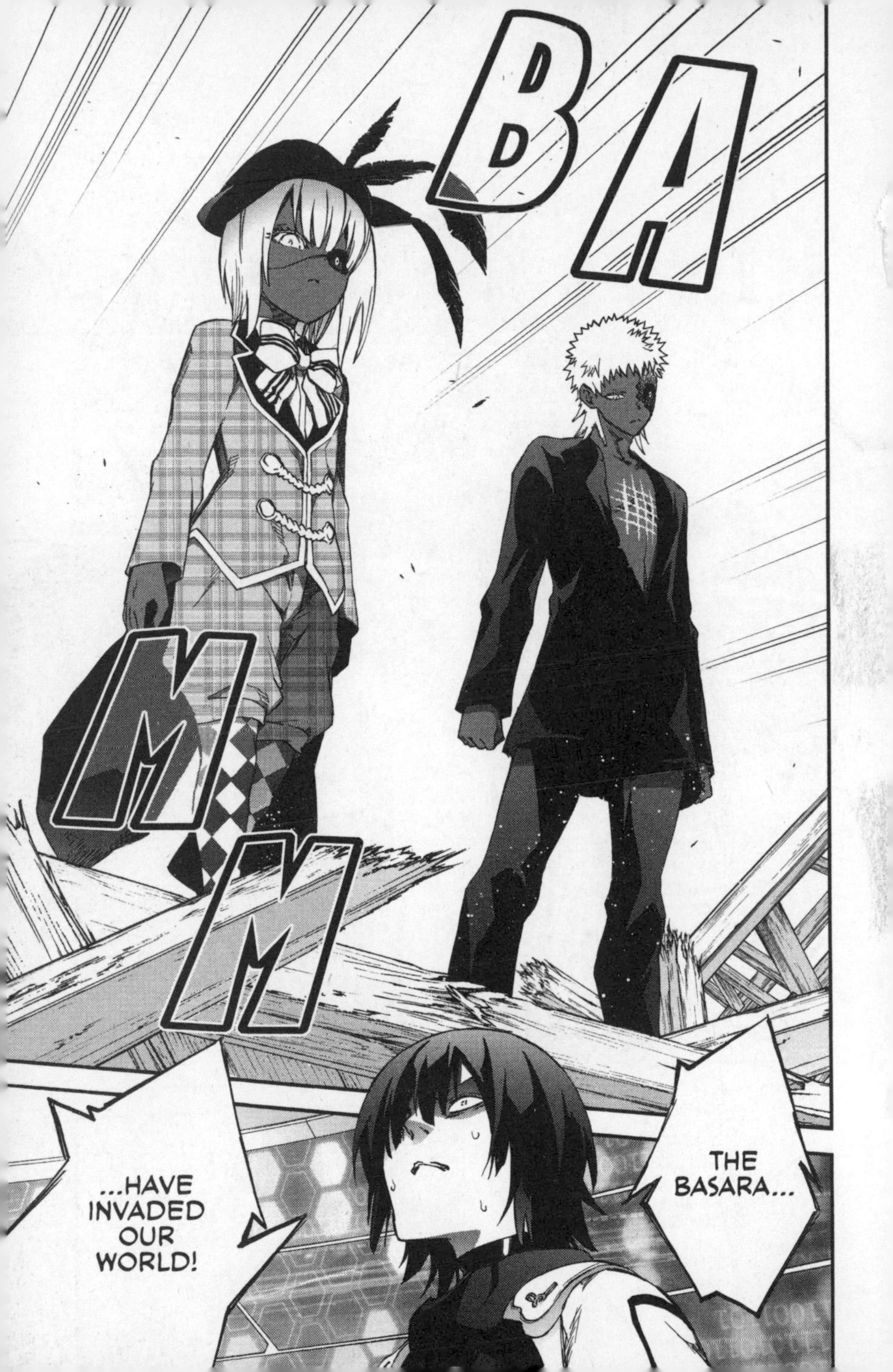
BAMM
THE BASARA...
...HAVE INVADED OUR WORLD!

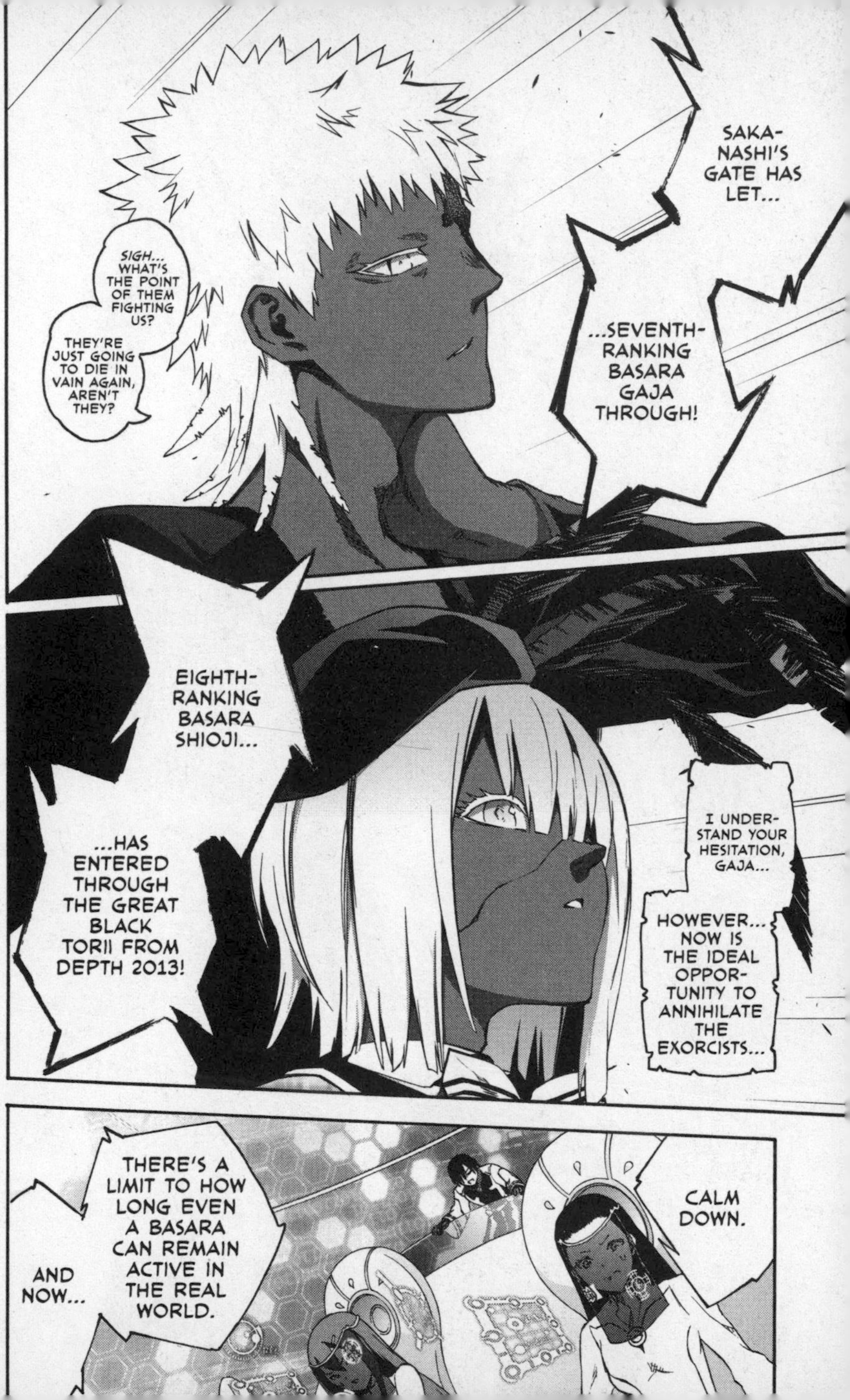
SAKA-NASHI'S GATE HAS LET...
...SEVENTH-RANKING BASARA GAJA THROUGH!
SIGH... WHAT'S THE POINT OF THEM FIGHTING US?
THEY'RE JUST GOING TO DIE IN VAIN AGAIN, AREN'T THEY?
EIGHTH-RANKING BASARA SHIOJI...
...HAS ENTERED THROUGH THE GREAT BLACK TORII FROM DEPTH 2013!
I UNDER-STAND YOUR HESITATION, GAJA...
HOWEVER... NOW IS THE IDEAL OPPOR-TUNITY TO ANNIHILATE THE EXORCISTS...
CALM DOWN.
THERE'S A LIMIT TO HOW LONG EVEN A BASARA CAN REMAIN ACTIVE IN THE REAL WORLD.
AND NOW...

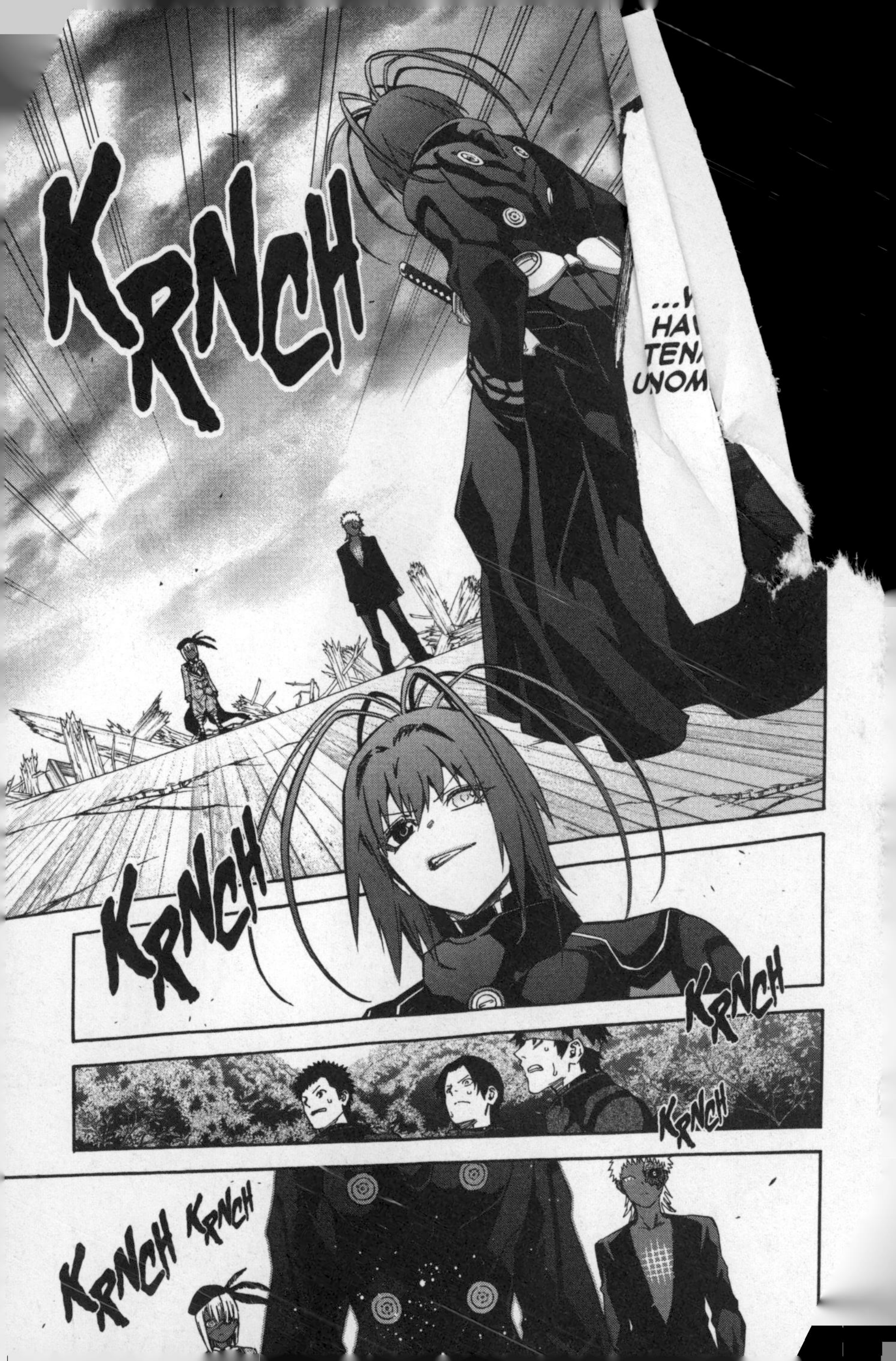

...W
HAV
TENA
UNOM
KRNCH
KRNCH
KRNCH
KRNCH
KRNCH
KRNCH

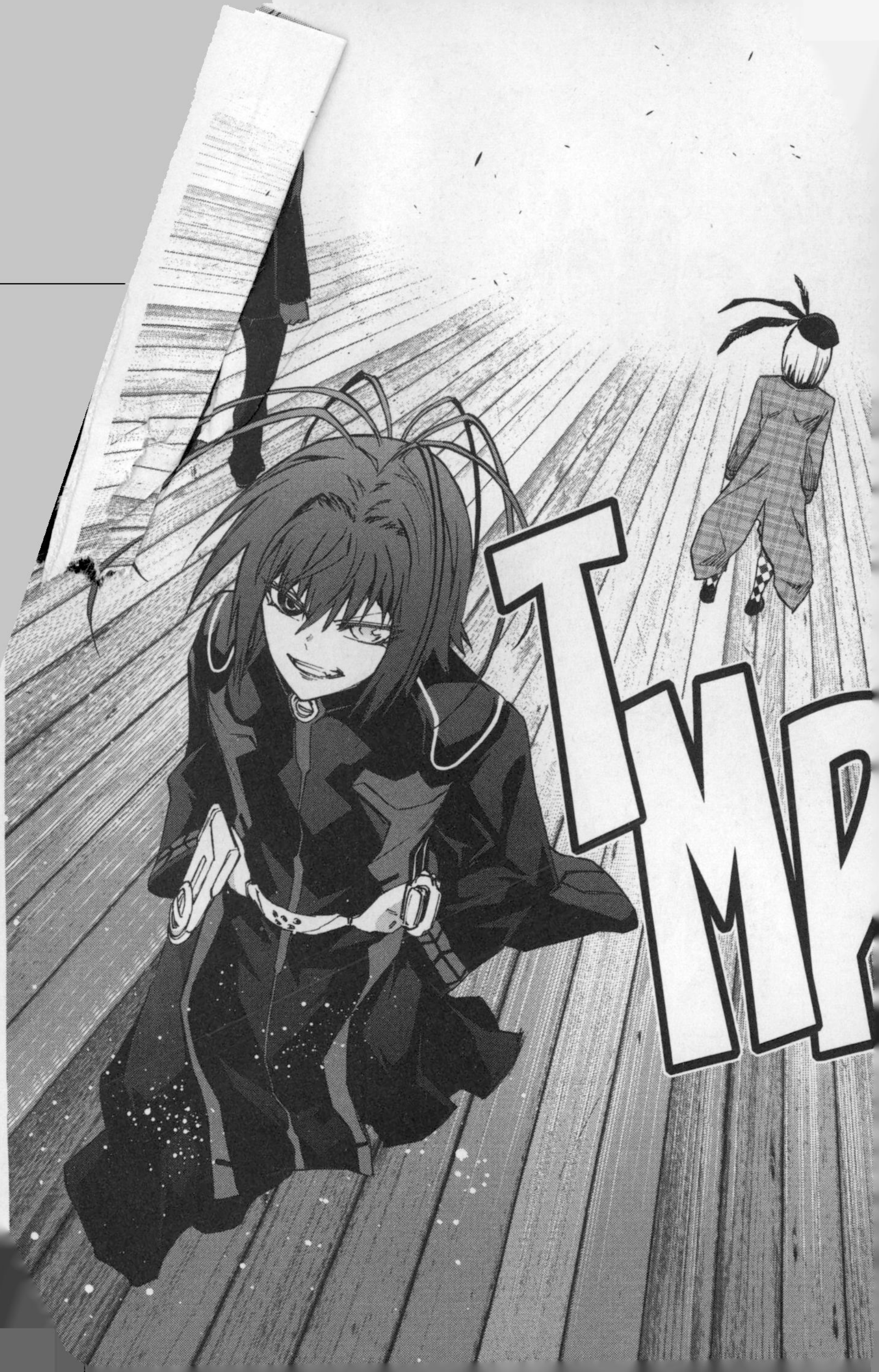
TMP

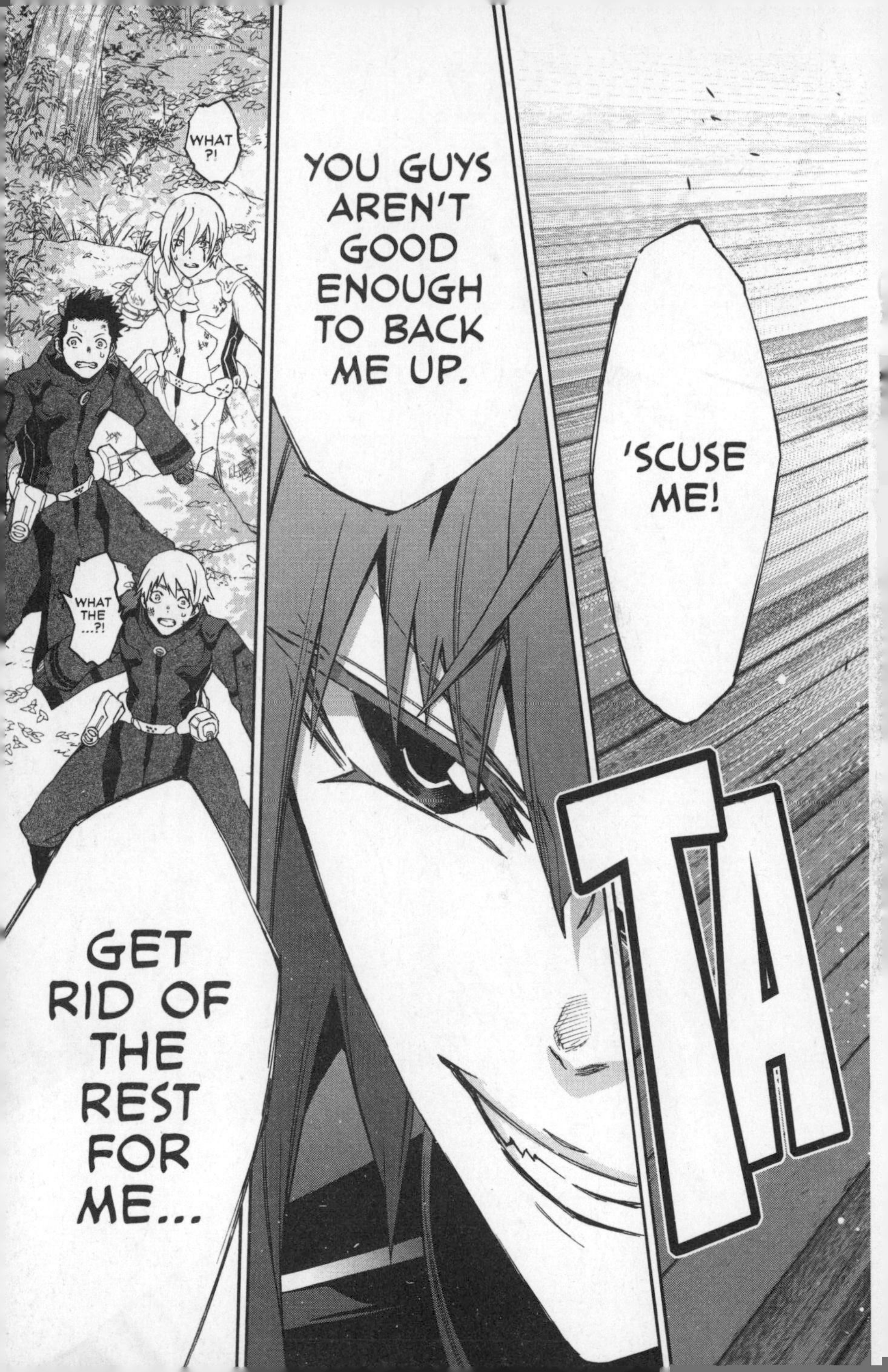
'SCUSE ME!
TA
YOU GUYS AREN'T GOOD ENOUGH TO BACK ME UP.
GET RID OF THE REST FOR ME...
WHAT ?!
WHAT THE ...?!

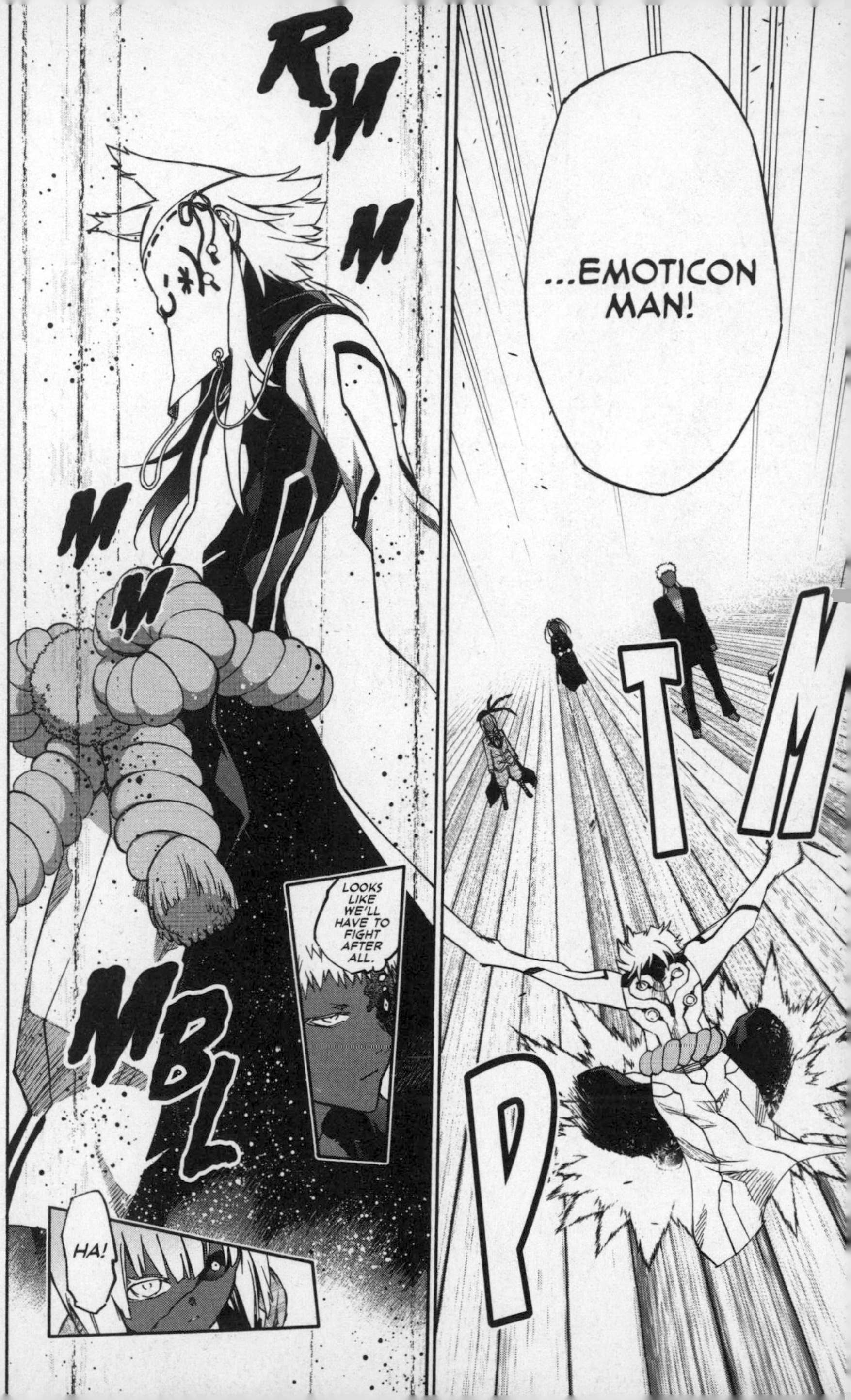
...EMOTICON MAN!
TMP
RMMMMMBL
LOOKS LIKE WE'LL HAVE TO FIGHT AFTER ALL.
HA!

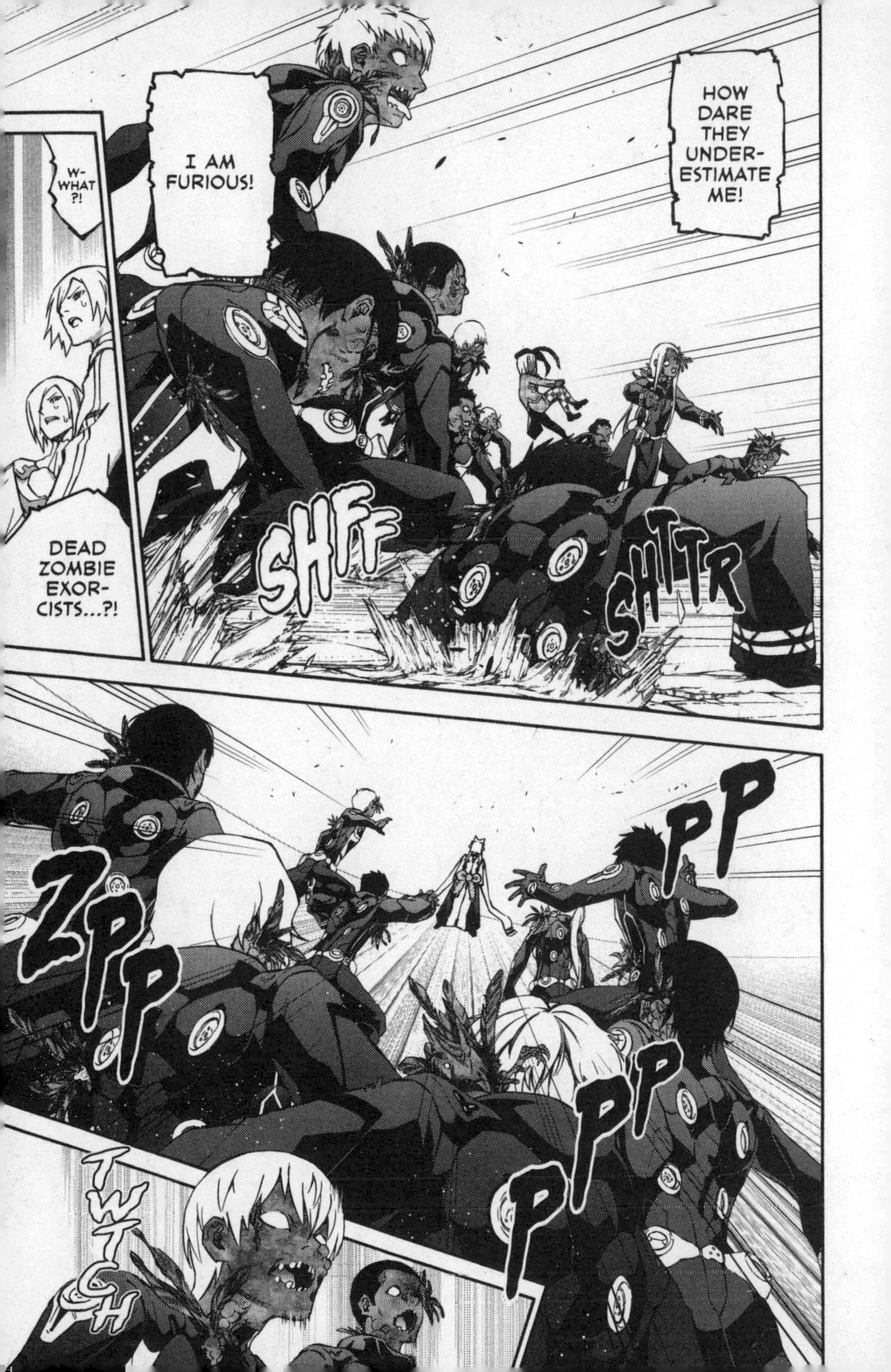
HOW DARE THEY UNDER-ESTIMATE ME!
I AM FURIOUS!
SHTTR
SHFF
W-WHAT?!
DEAD ZOMBIE EXORCISTS...?!
PP
ZPPP
PPPP
TWITCH

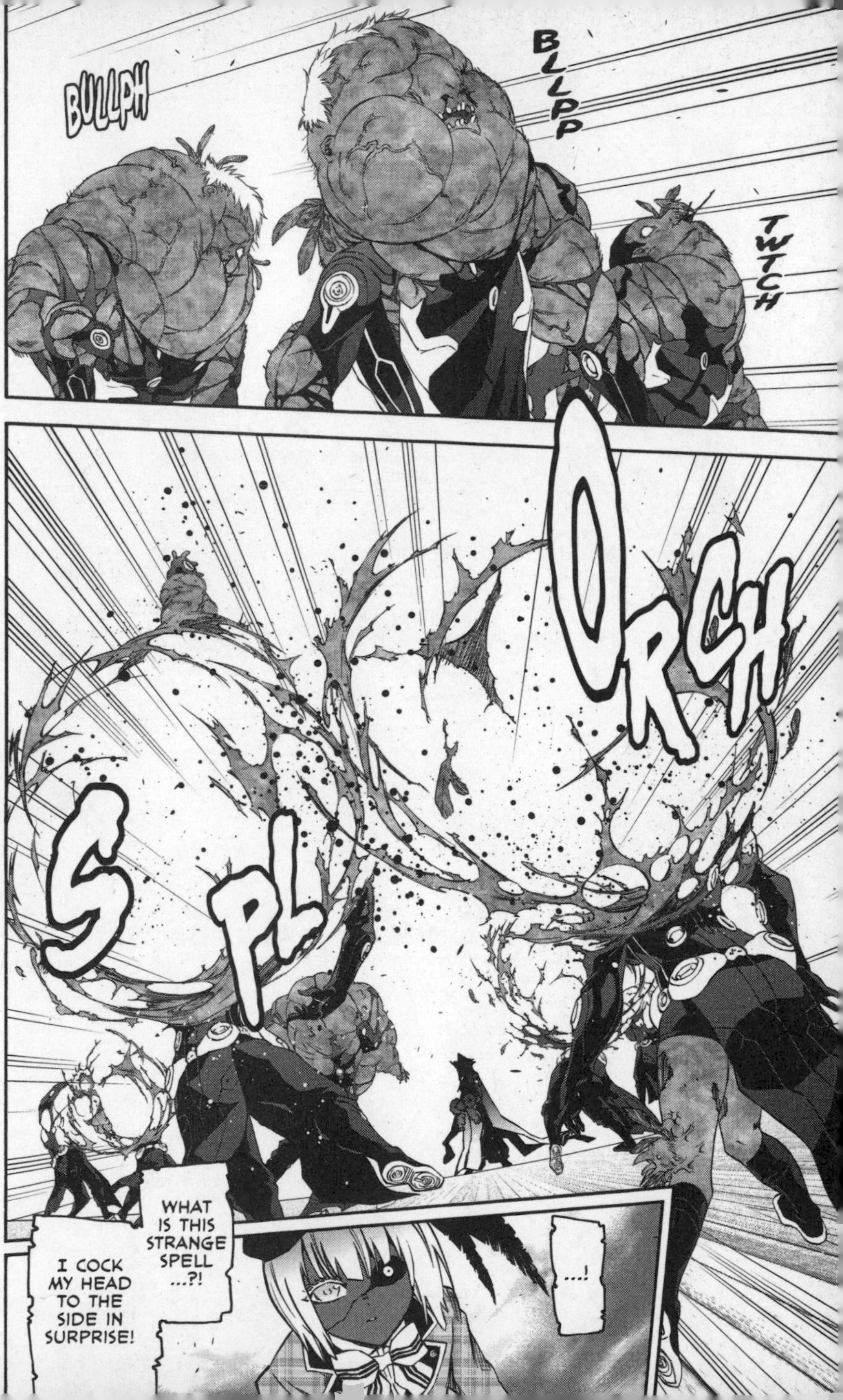
TWTCH
BLLPP
BULLPH
S PL ORCH
...!
WHAT IS THIS STRANGE SPELL ...?!
I COCK MY HEAD TO THE SIDE IN SURPRISE!

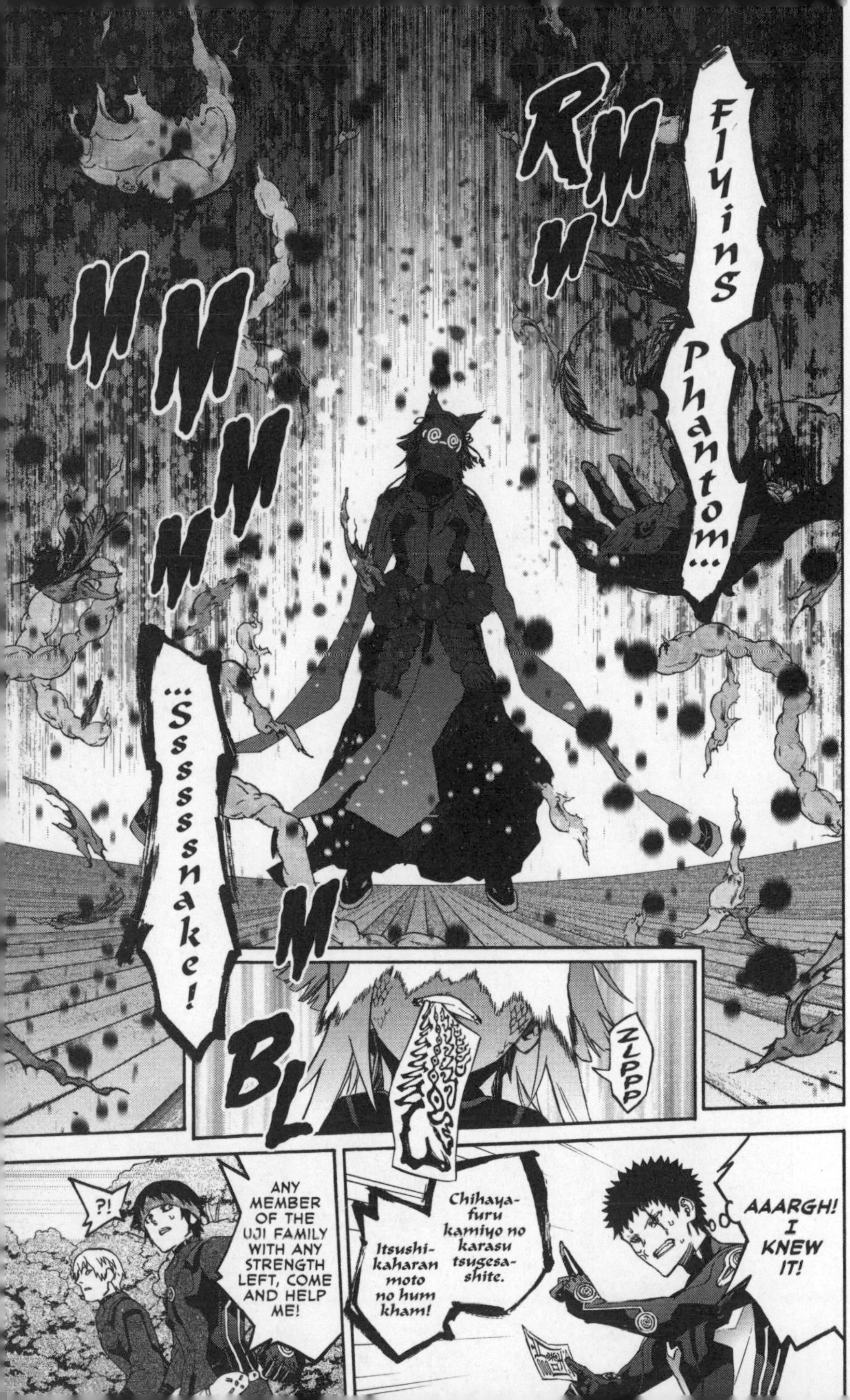
RMMM
Flying Phantom...
MMMMMMM
...Sssssnake!
ZLPPP
BL
AAARGH! I KNEW IT!
Chihaya-furu kamiyo no karasu tsugesa-shite.
Itsushi-kaharan moto no hum kham!
ANY MEMBER OF THE UJI FAMILY WITH ANY STRENGTH LEFT, COME AND HELP ME!
?!

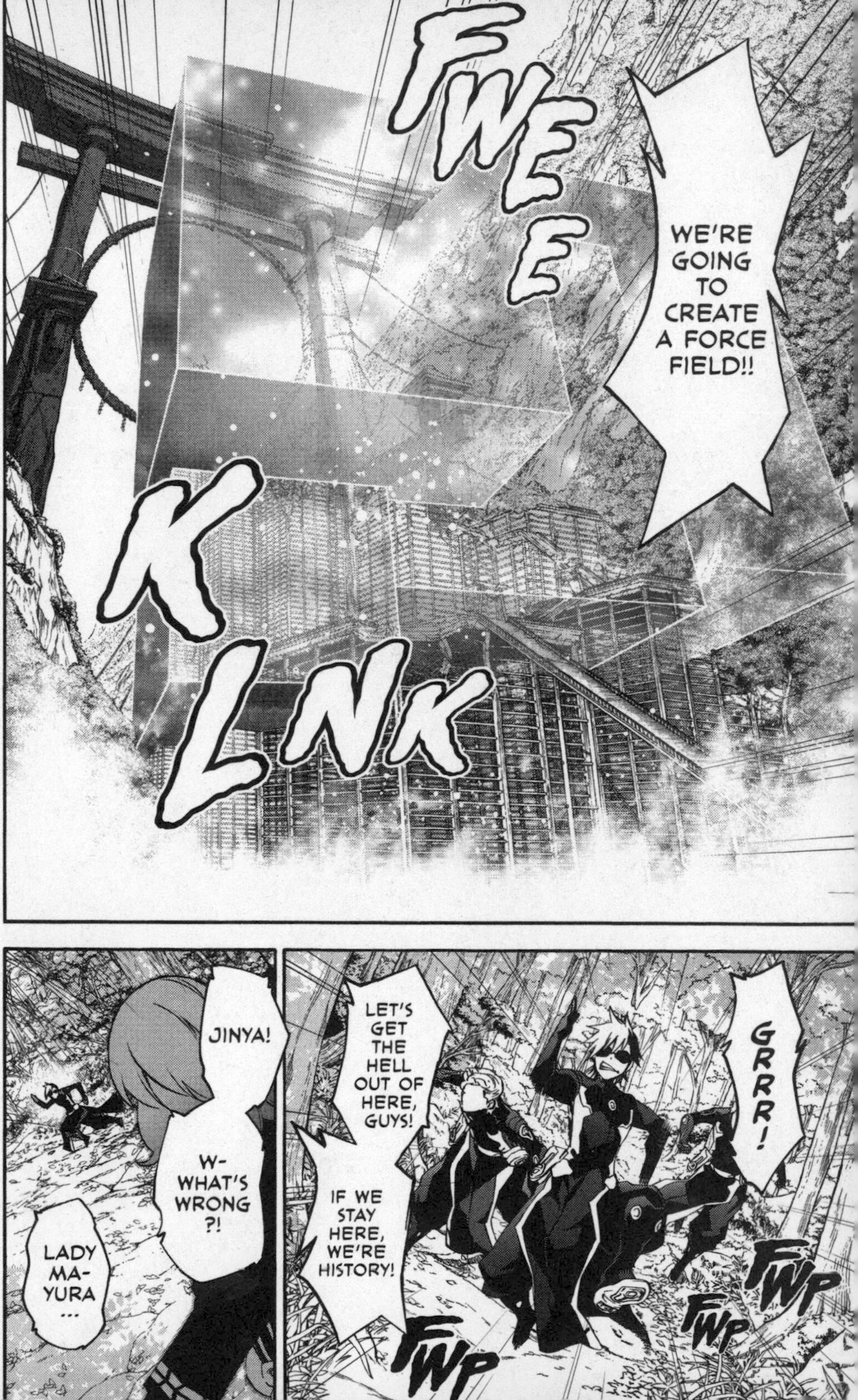
WE'RE GOING TO CREATE A FORCE FIELD!!
FWEE
KLNK
GRRR!
LET'S GET THE HELL OUT OF HERE, GUYS!
IF WE STAY HERE, WE'RE HISTORY!
FWP
FWP
FWP
JINYA!
W-WHAT'S WRONG?!
LADY MA-YURA...

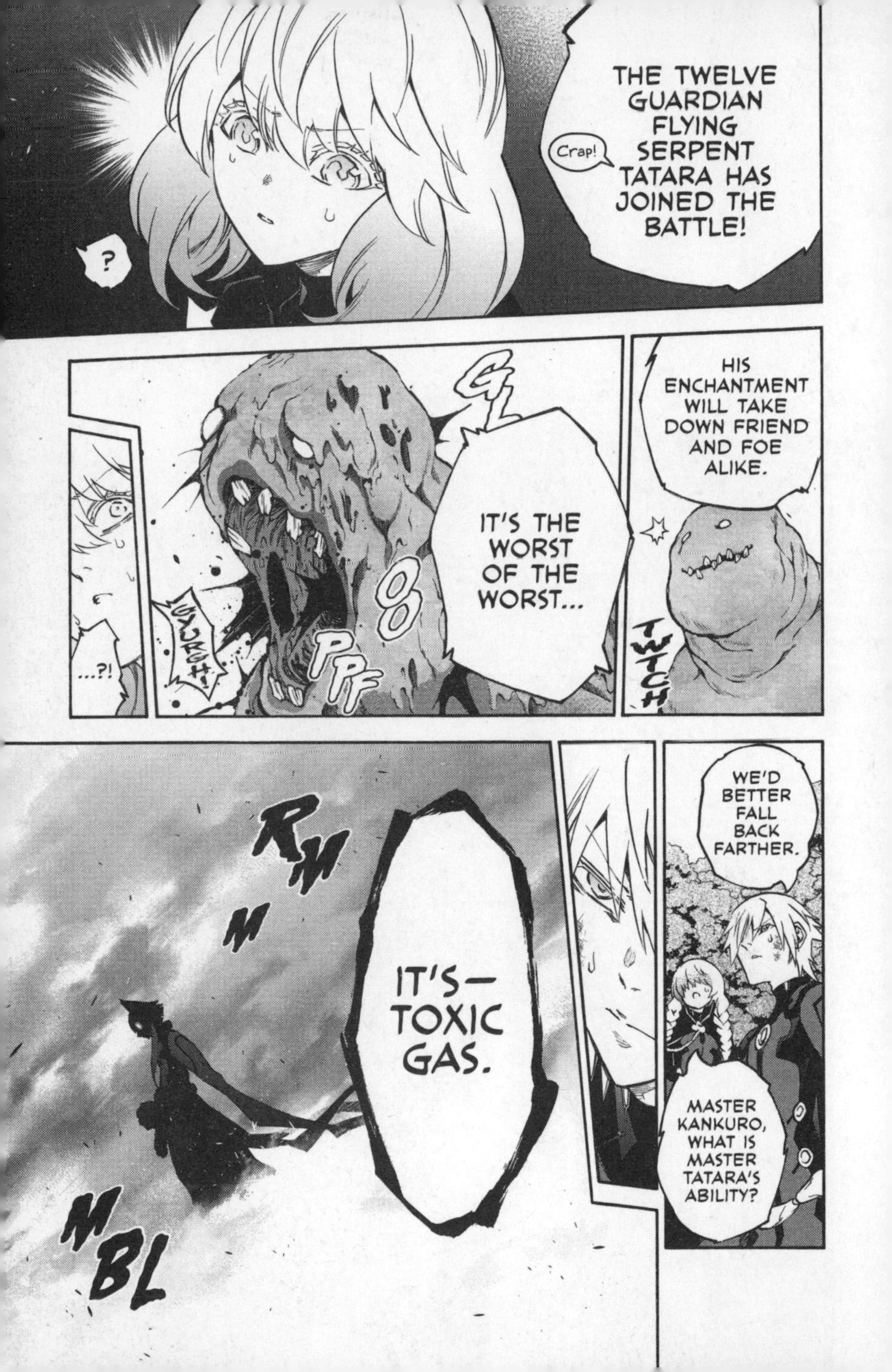
THE TWELVE GUARDIAN FLYING SERPENT TATARA HAS JOINED THE BATTLE!
Crap!
?
HIS ENCHANTMENT WILL TAKE DOWN FRIEND AND FOE ALIKE.
TWTCH
GL
IT'S THE WORST OF THE WORST...
O
PPF
GYURGH!
...?!
WE'D BETTER FALL BACK FARTHER.
MASTER KANKURO, WHAT IS MASTER TATARA'S ABILITY?
IT'S— TOXIC GAS.
RMM
MBL

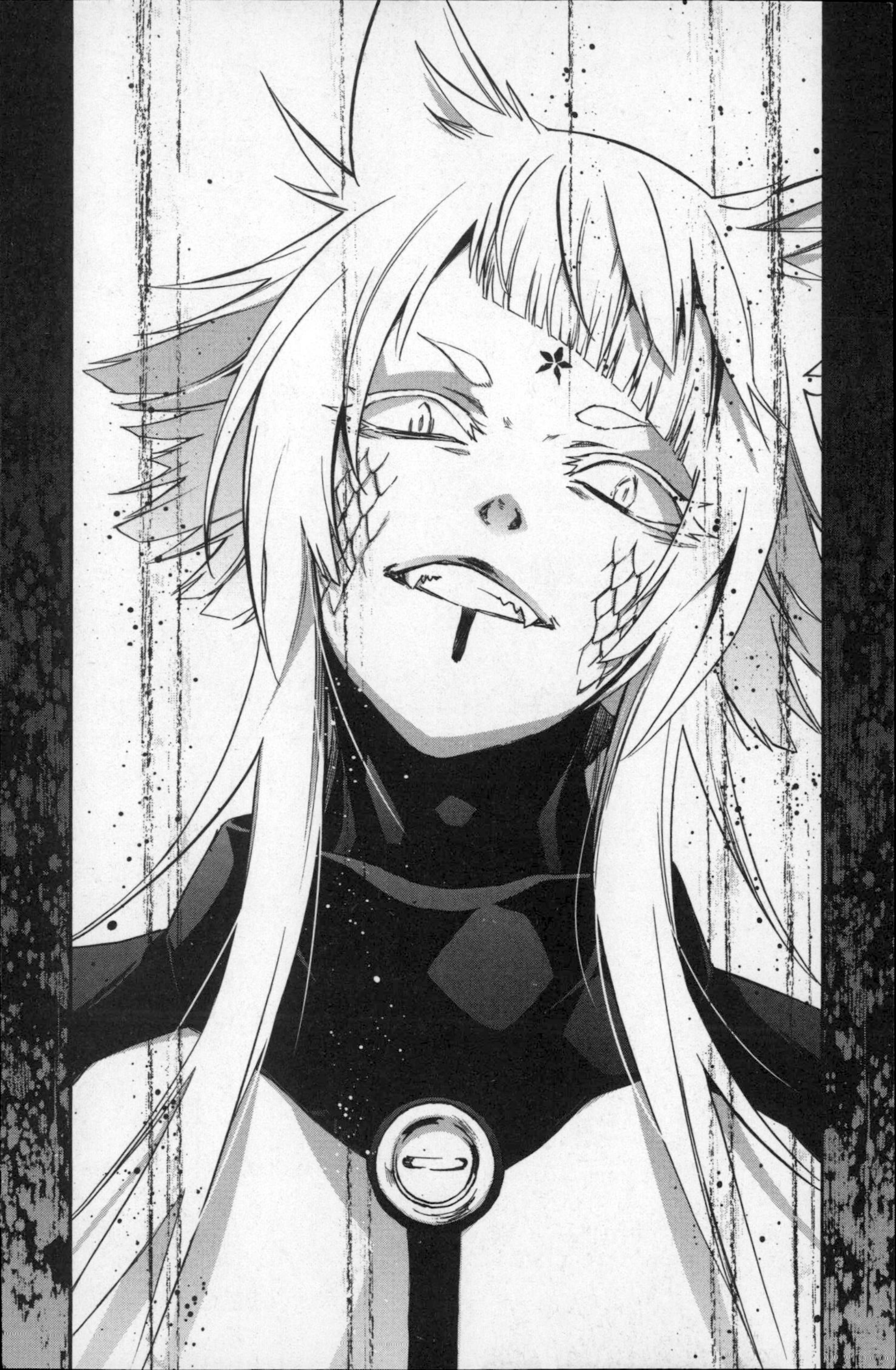

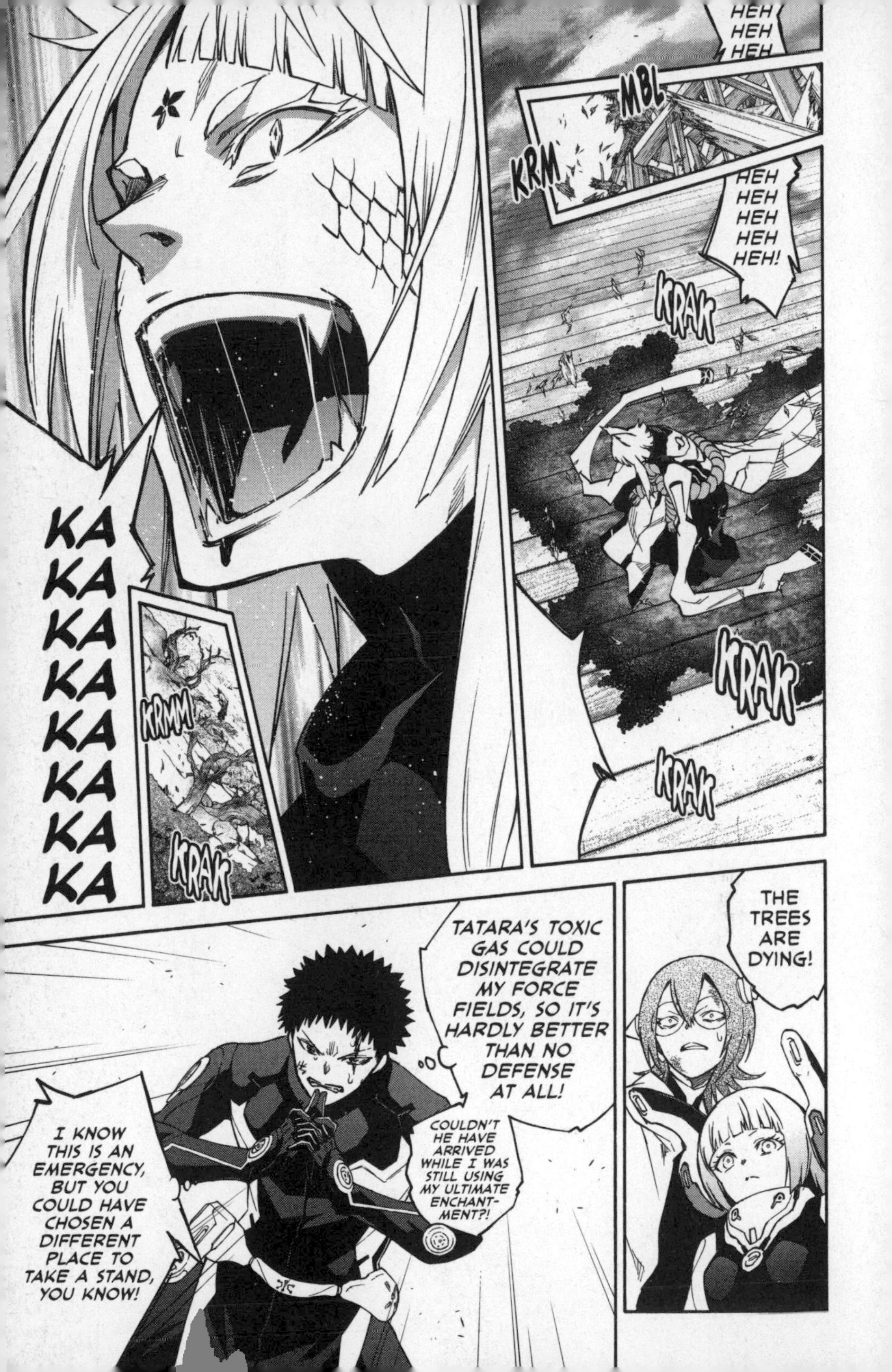

HEH HEH HEH
MBL
KRM
HEH HEH HEH HEH HEH!
KRAK
KRAK
KRAK
KA KA KA KA KA KA KA KA KA KA
KRMM
KRAK
THE TREES ARE DYING!
TATARA'S TOXIC GAS COULD DISINTEGRATE MY FORCE FIELDS, SO IT'S HARDLY BETTER THAN NO DEFENSE AT ALL!
COULDN'T HE HAVE ARRIVED WHILE I WAS STILL USING MY ULTIMATE ENCHANT-MENT?!
I KNOW THIS IS AN EMERGENCY, BUT YOU COULD HAVE CHOSEN A DIFFERENT PLACE TO TAKE A STAND, YOU KNOW!

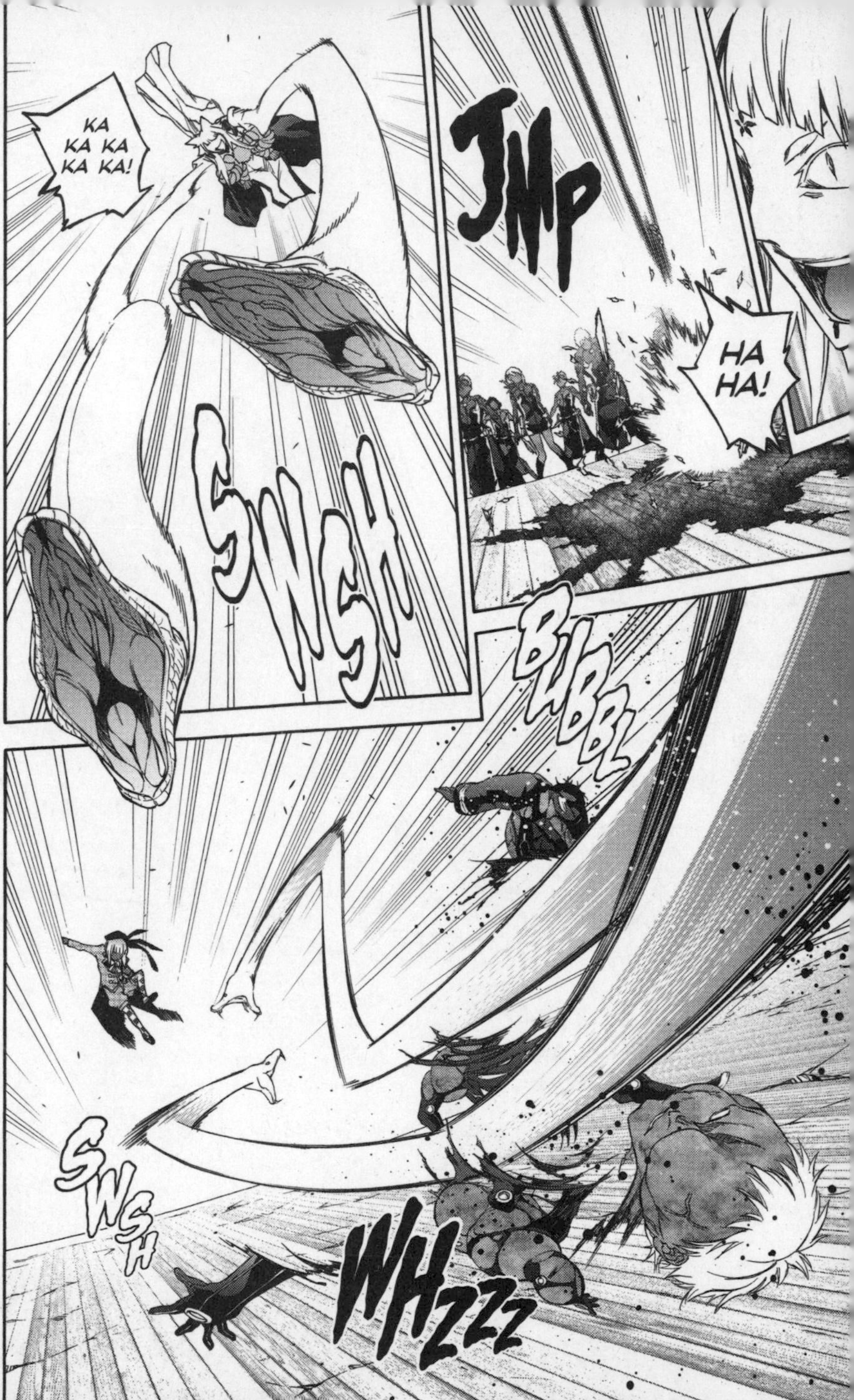
JMP
HA HA!
KA KA KA KA KA!
SWNGH
BUBBL
WHZZZ
SWSH

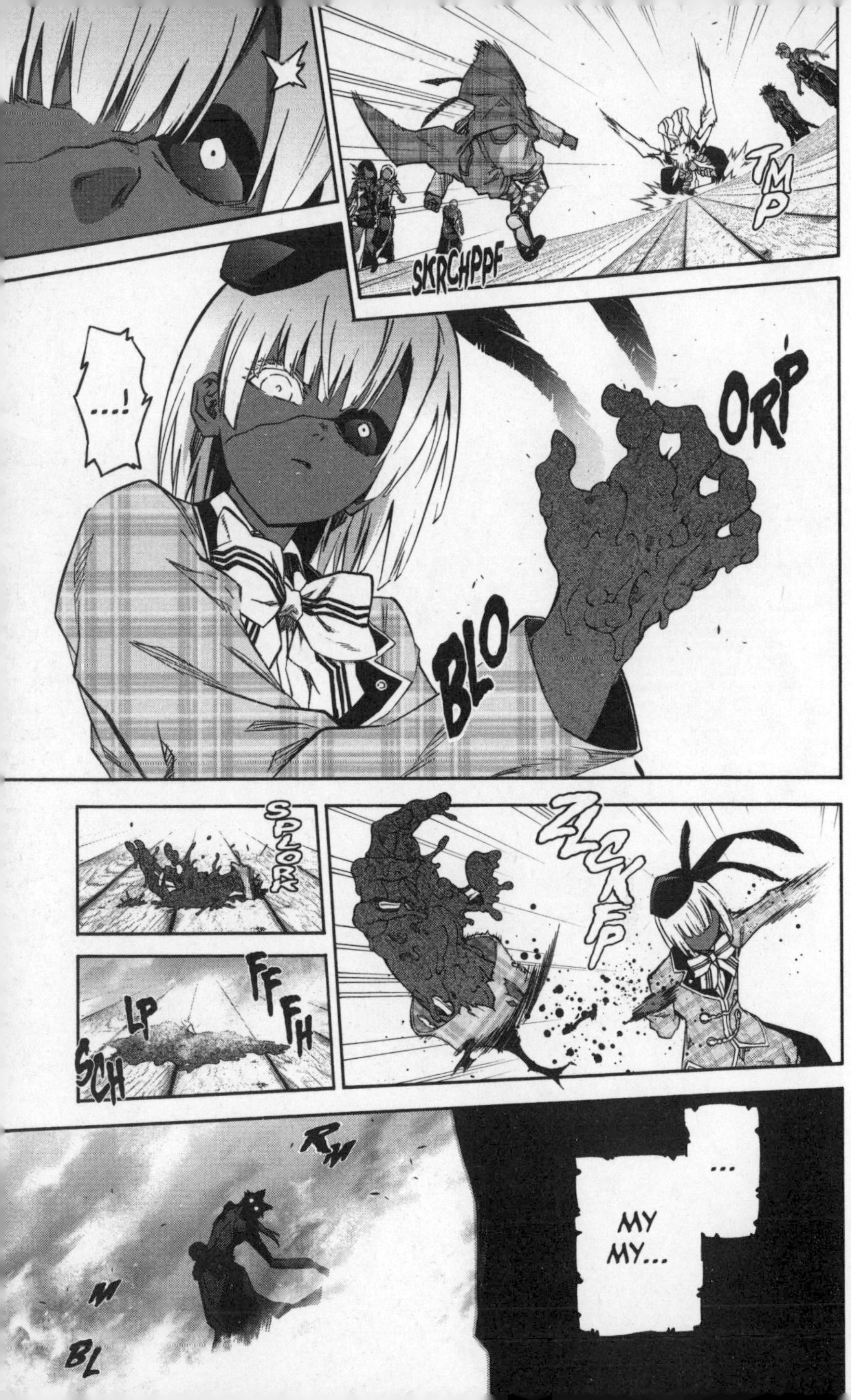
TMP
SKRCHPPF
ORP
BLO
...!
ZLCKFP
SPLORK
FFFH
SCHLP
...
MY MY...
RM
MBL

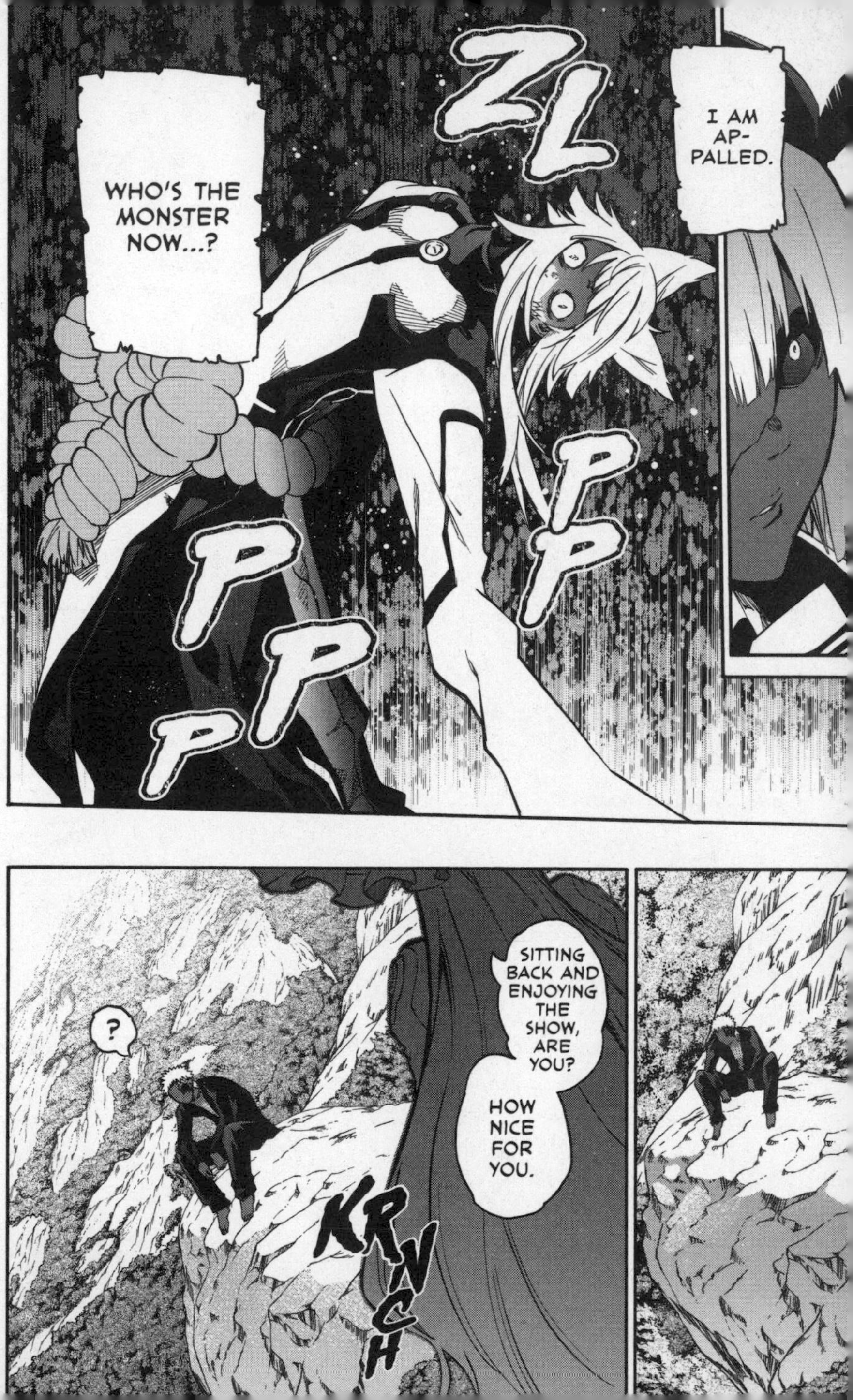
I AM AP-PALLED.
ZL
WHO'S THE MONSTER NOW...?
PP
PPP
SITTING BACK AND ENJOYING THE SHOW, ARE YOU?
HOW NICE FOR YOU.
?
KRNCH

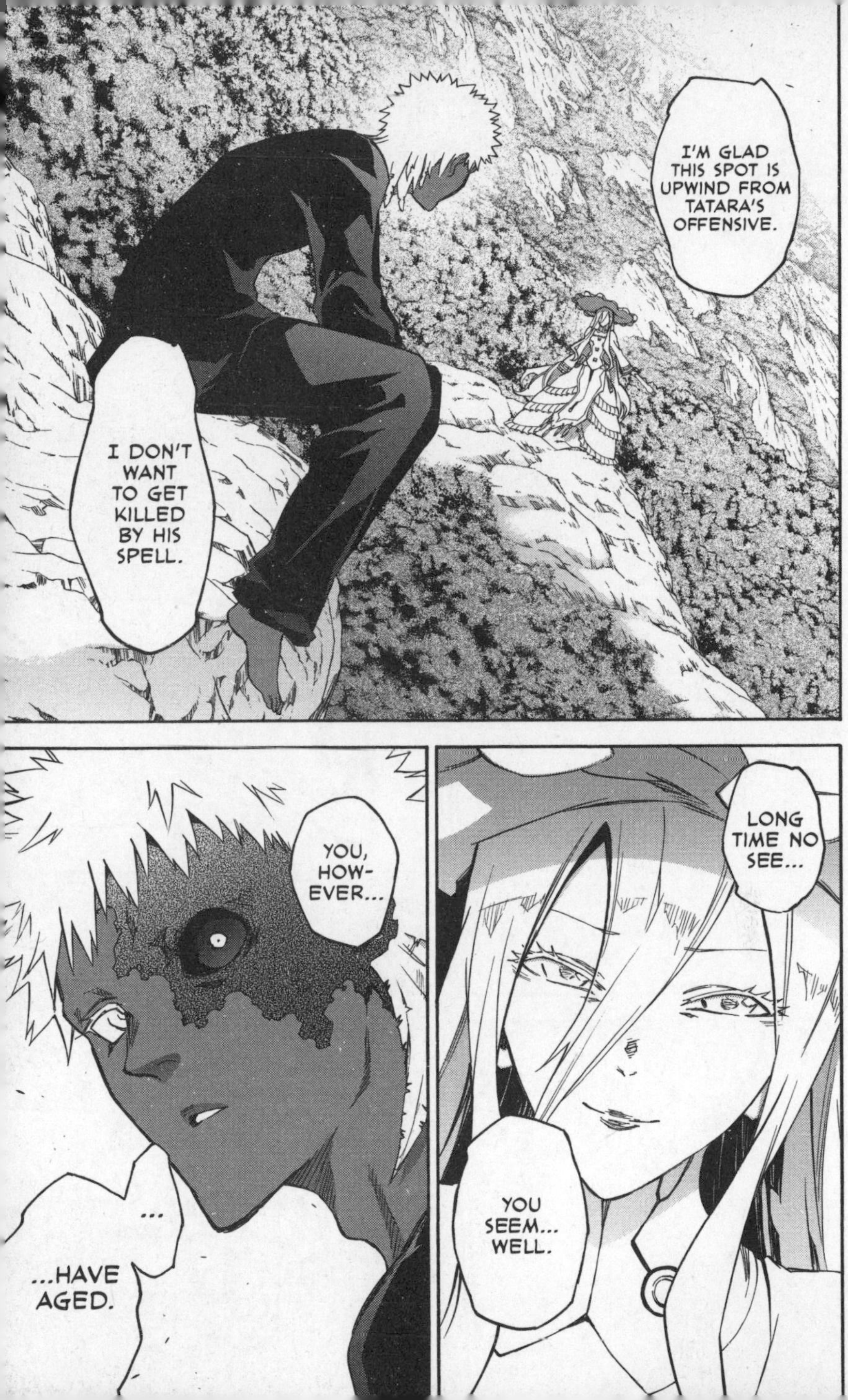
I'M GLAD THIS SPOT IS UPWIND FROM TATARA'S OFFENSIVE.
I DON'T WANT TO GET KILLED BY HIS SPELL.
LONG TIME NO SEE...
YOU SEEM... WELL.
YOU, HOW-EVER...
...
...HAVE AGED.

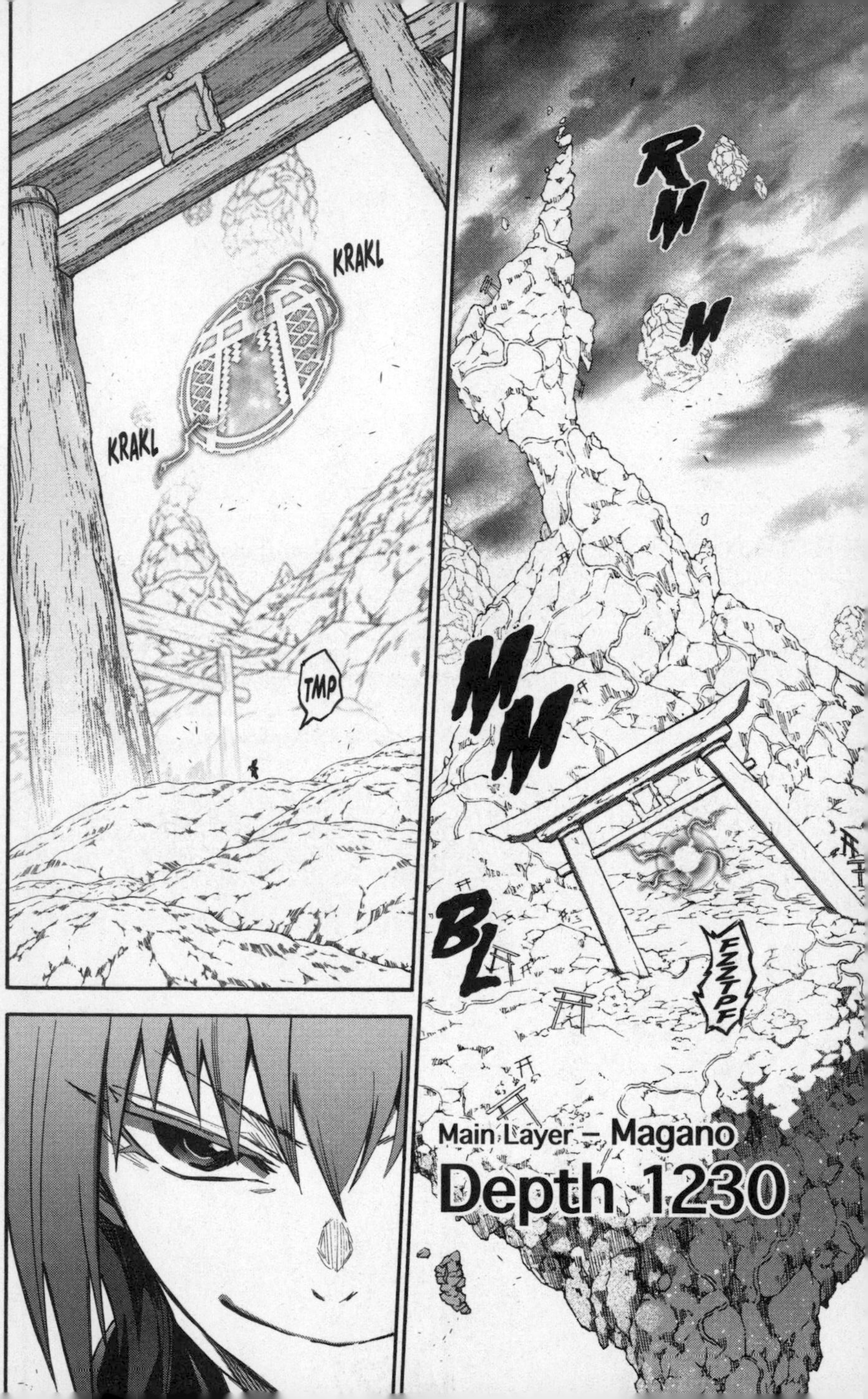
RM
M
MM
BL
FZZTPF
Main Layer – Magano
Depth 1230
KRAKL
KRAKL
TMP

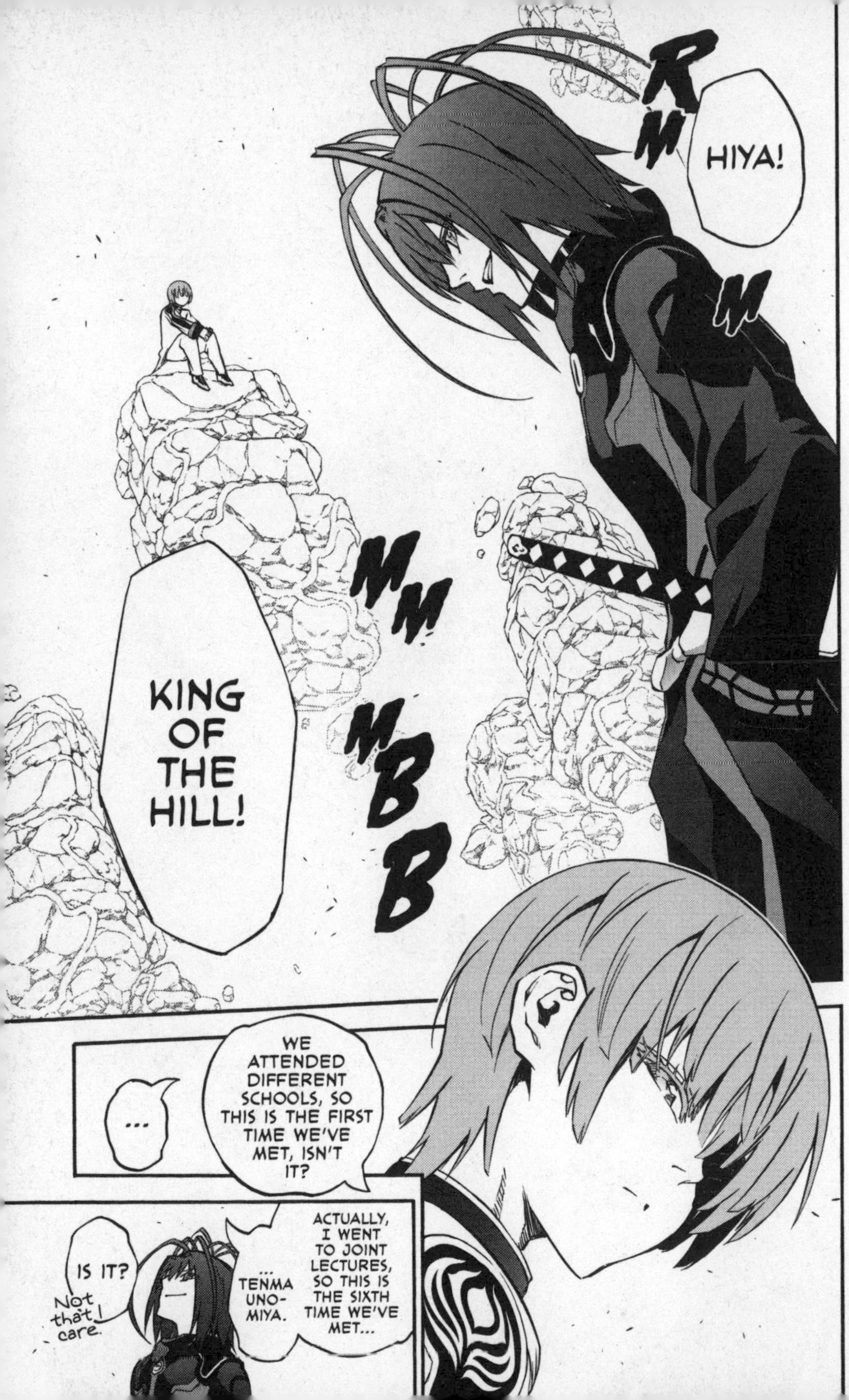
HIYA!
RMM
M
MM
MBB
KING OF THE HILL!
WE ATTENDED DIFFERENT SCHOOLS, SO THIS IS THE FIRST TIME WE'VE MET, ISN'T IT?
...
ACTUALLY, I WENT TO JOINT LECTURES, SO THIS IS THE SIXTH TIME WE'VE MET...
... TENMA UNO-MIYA.
IS IT?
Not that I care.

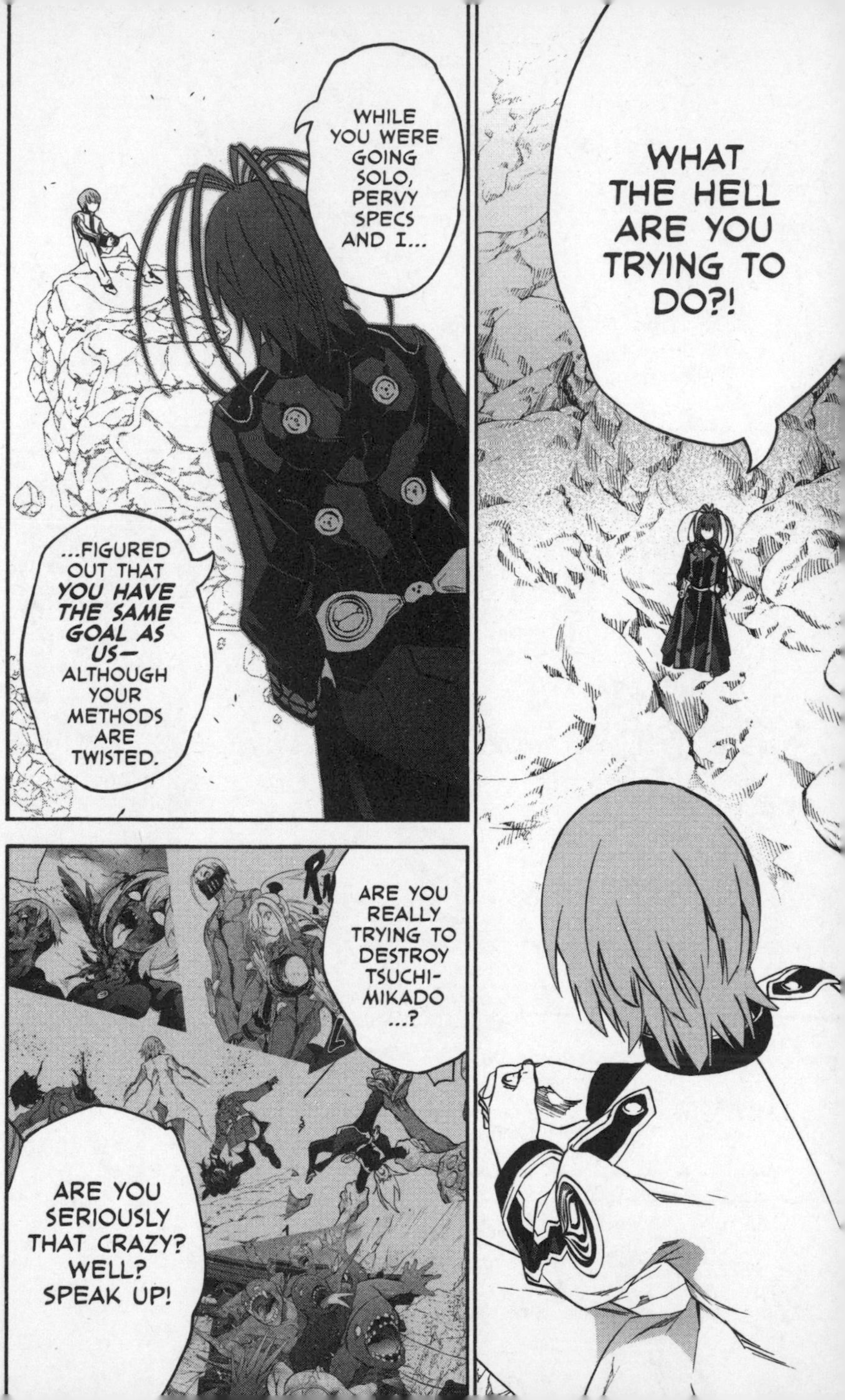
WHAT THE HELL ARE YOU TRYING TO DO?!
WHILE YOU WERE GOING SOLO, PERVY SPECS AND I...
...FIGURED OUT THAT *YOU HAVE THE SAME GOAL AS US*— ALTHOUGH YOUR METHODS ARE TWISTED.
ARE YOU REALLY TRYING TO DESTROY TSUCHI-MIKADO ...?
ARE YOU SERIOUSLY THAT CRAZY? WELL? SPEAK UP!

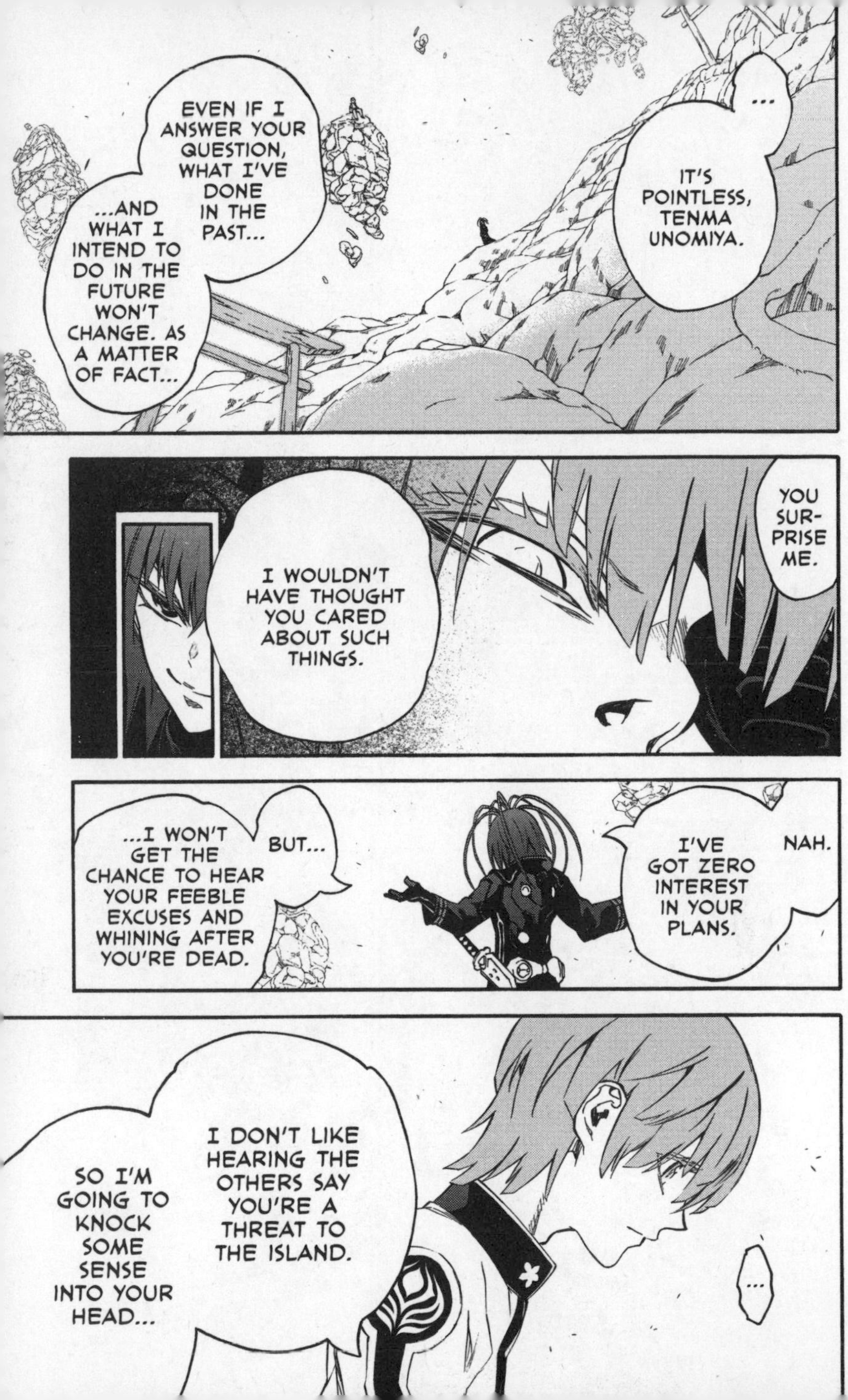
...
IT'S POINTLESS, TENMA UNOMIYA.
EVEN IF I ANSWER YOUR QUESTION, WHAT I'VE DONE IN THE PAST...
...AND WHAT I INTEND TO DO IN THE FUTURE WON'T CHANGE. AS A MATTER OF FACT...
YOU SURPRISE ME.
I WOULDN'T HAVE THOUGHT YOU CARED ABOUT SUCH THINGS.
NAH.
I'VE GOT ZERO INTEREST IN YOUR PLANS.
BUT...
...I WON'T GET THE CHANCE TO HEAR YOUR FEEBLE EXCUSES AND WHINING AFTER YOU'RE DEAD.
...
I DON'T LIKE HEARING THE OTHERS SAY YOU'RE A THREAT TO THE ISLAND.
SO I'M GOING TO KNOCK SOME SENSE INTO YOUR HEAD...

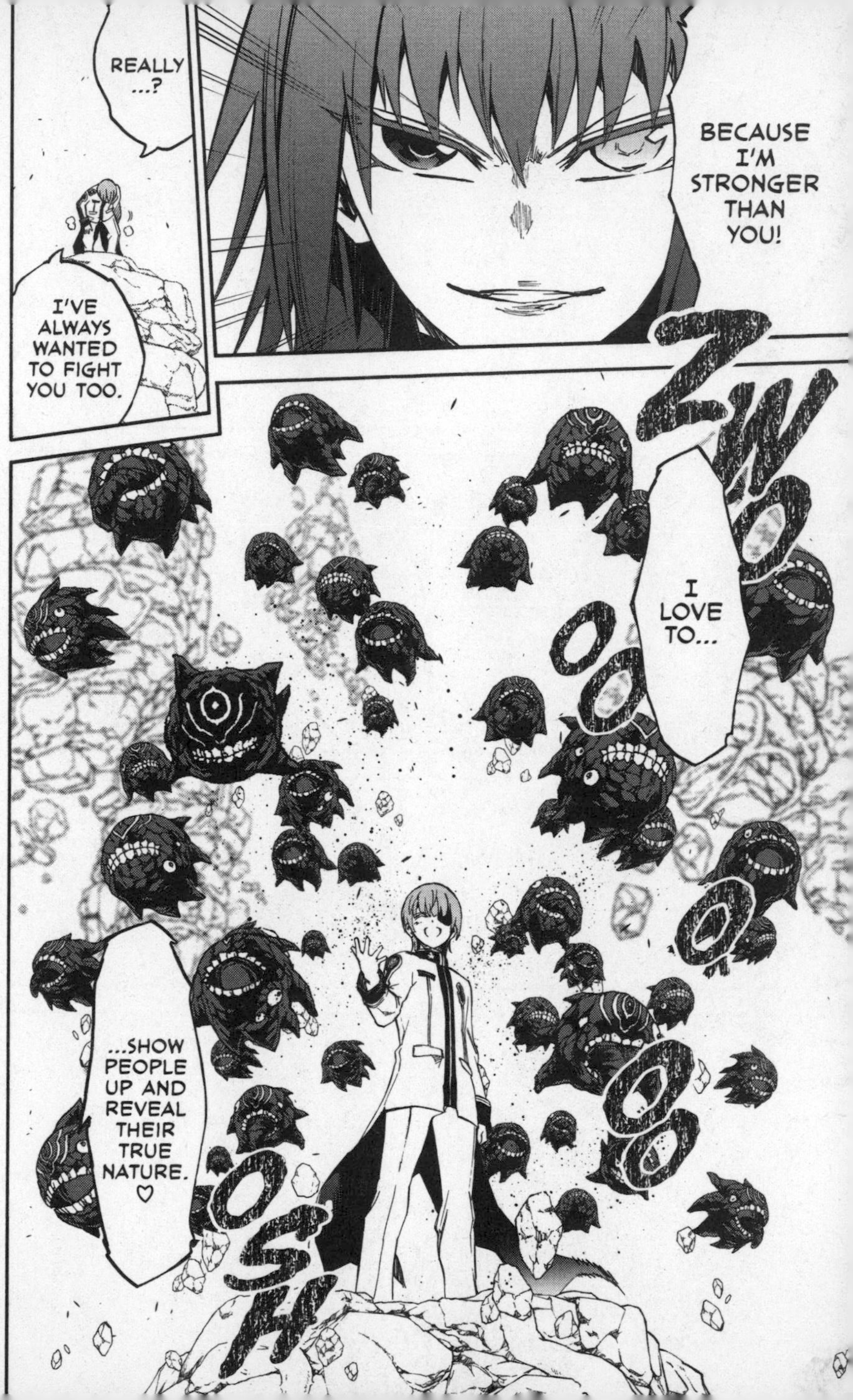
BECAUSE I'M STRONGER THAN YOU!
REALLY ...?
I'VE ALWAYS WANTED TO FIGHT YOU TOO.
ZWOOOOOSH
I LOVE TO...
...SHOW PEOPLE UP AND REVEAL THEIR TRUE NATURE. ♡

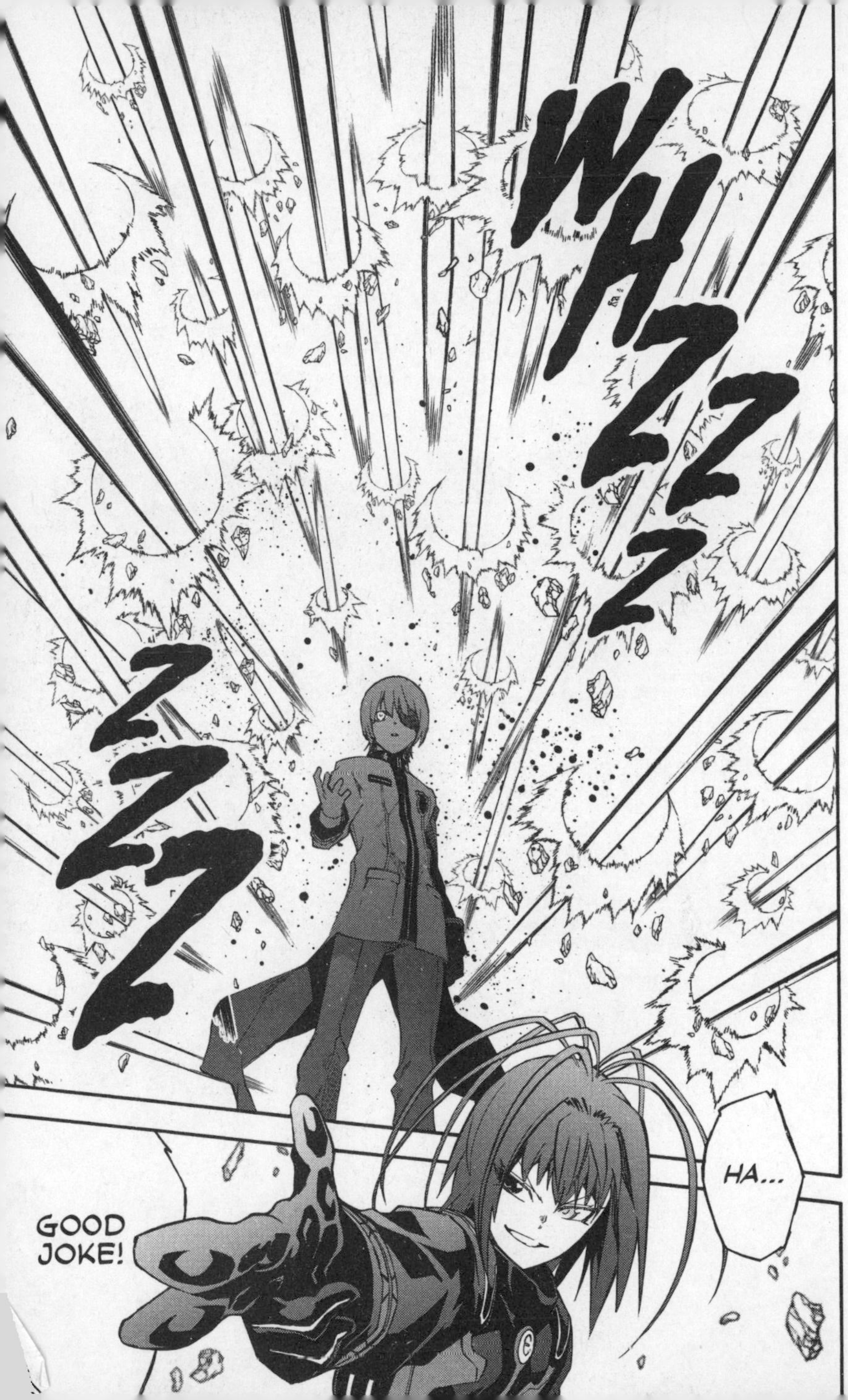
WHZZZZ
ZZZZ
HA...
GOOD JOKE!

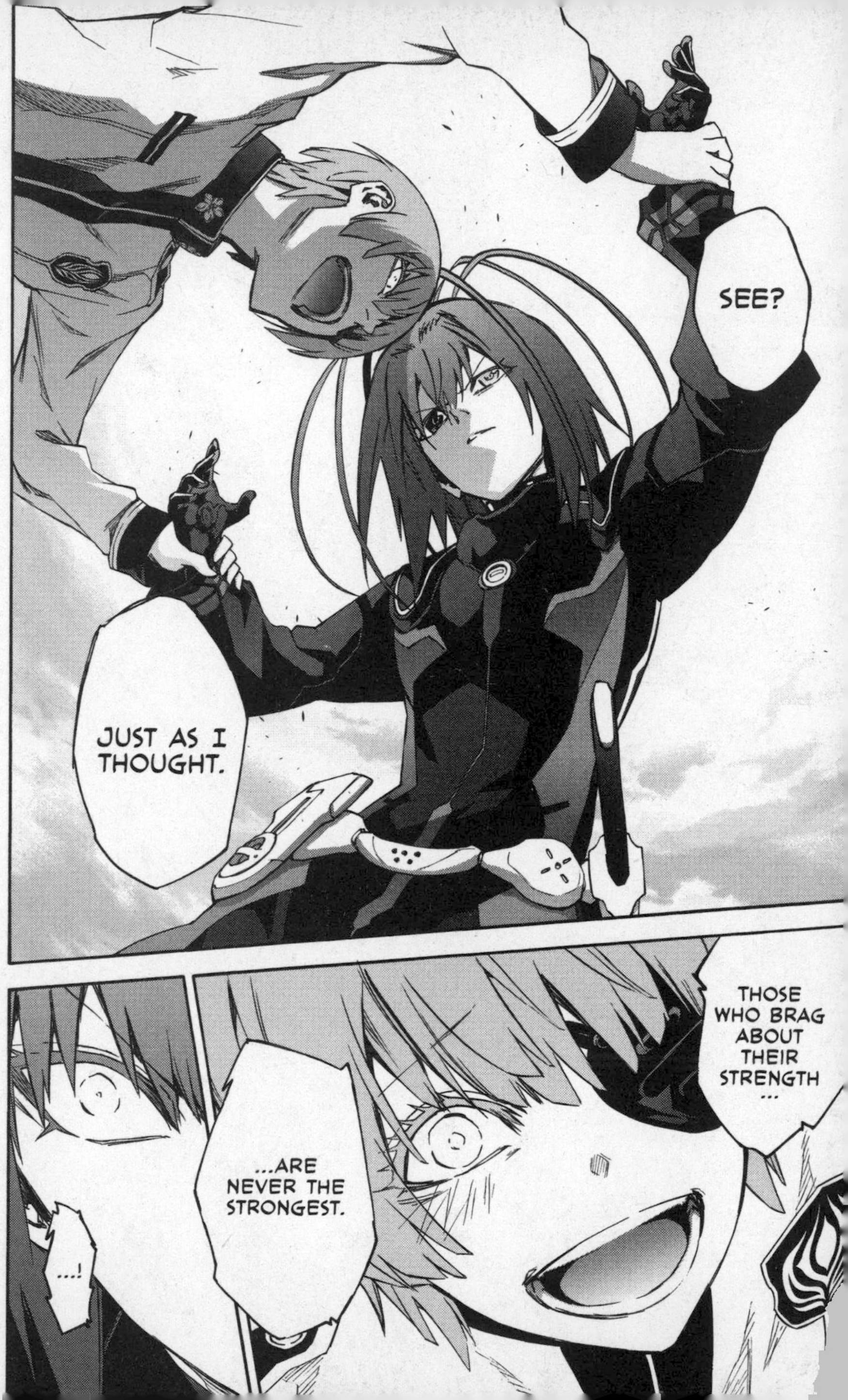
SEE?
JUST AS I THOUGHT.
THOSE WHO BRAG ABOUT THEIR STRENGTH ...
...ARE NEVER THE STRONGEST.
...!

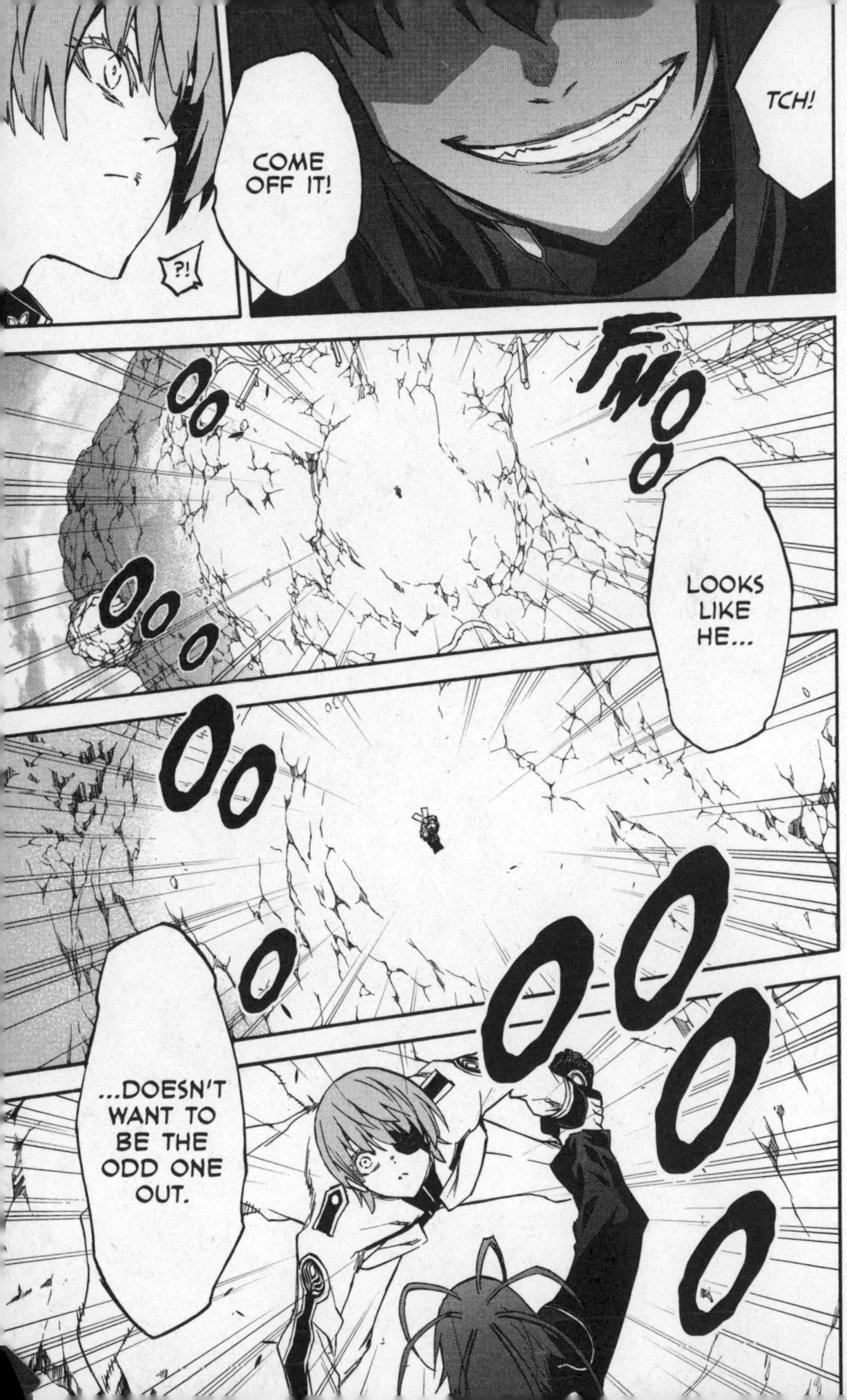

TCH!
COME OFF IT!
?!
FWOOOOOOOOOOOOOOOOO
LOOKS LIKE HE...
...DOESN'T WANT TO BE THE ODD ONE OUT.

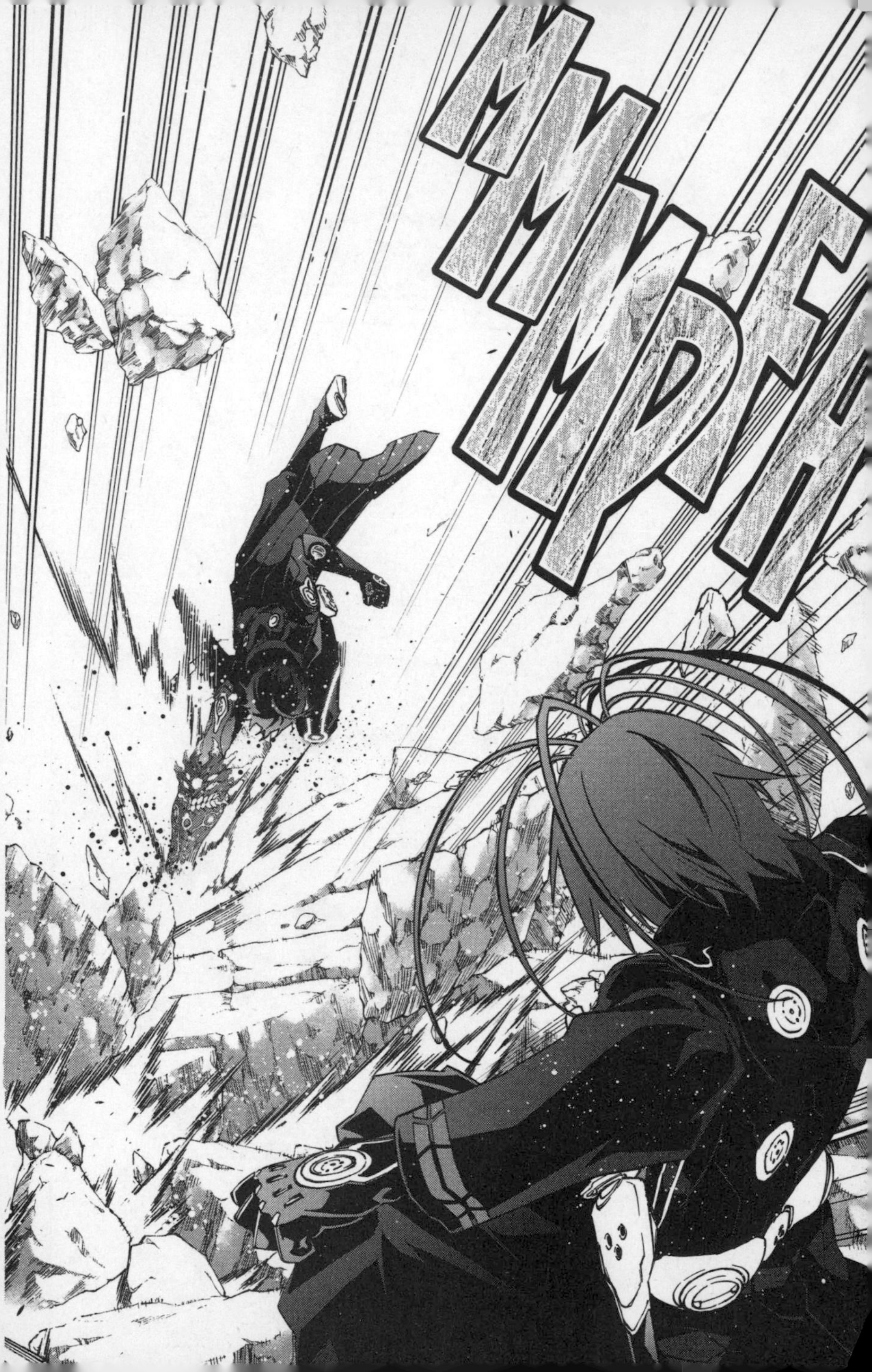

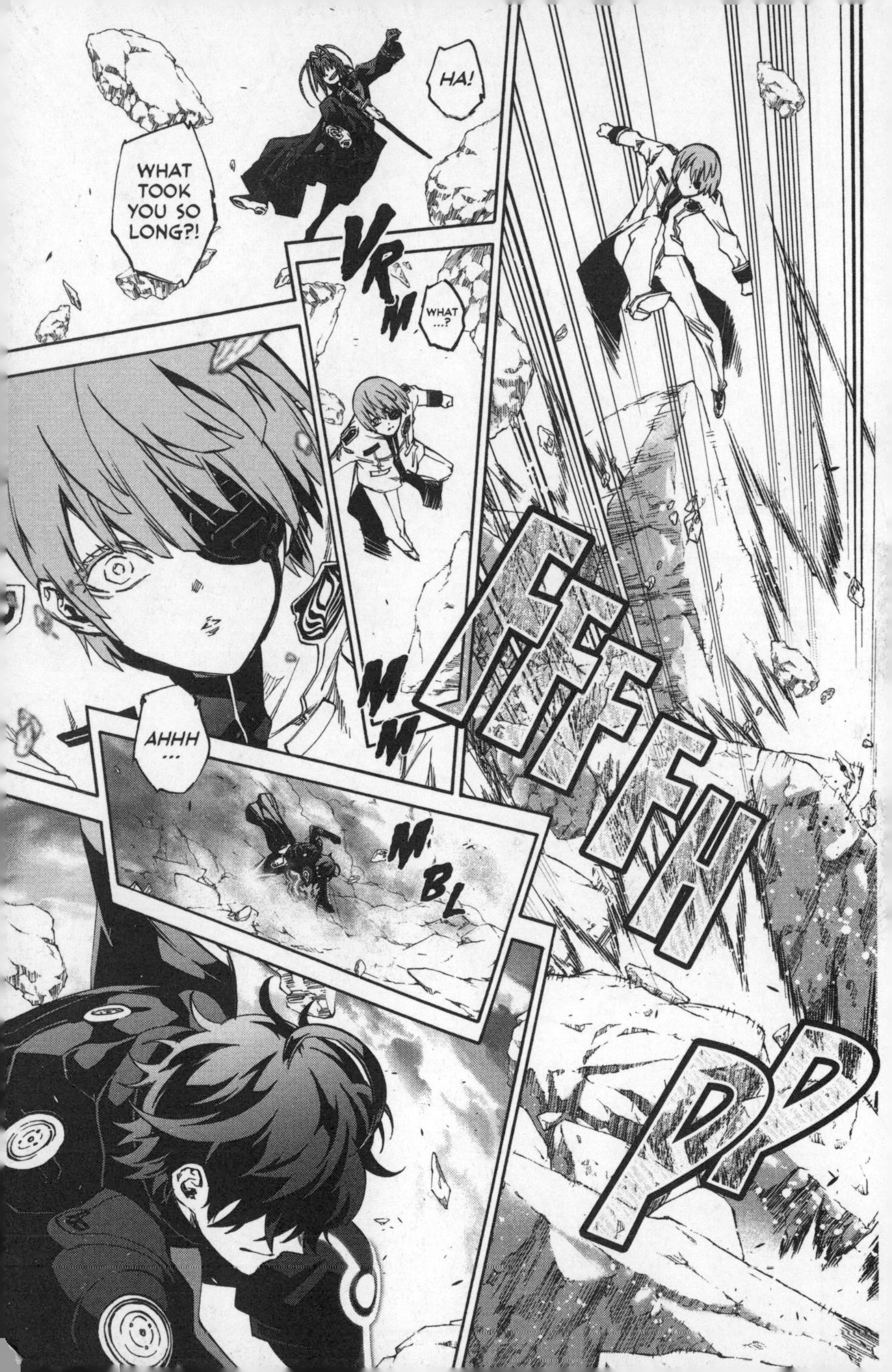
HA!
WHAT TOOK YOU SO LONG?!
VRM
WHAT ...?
MMM
AHHH ...
MBL

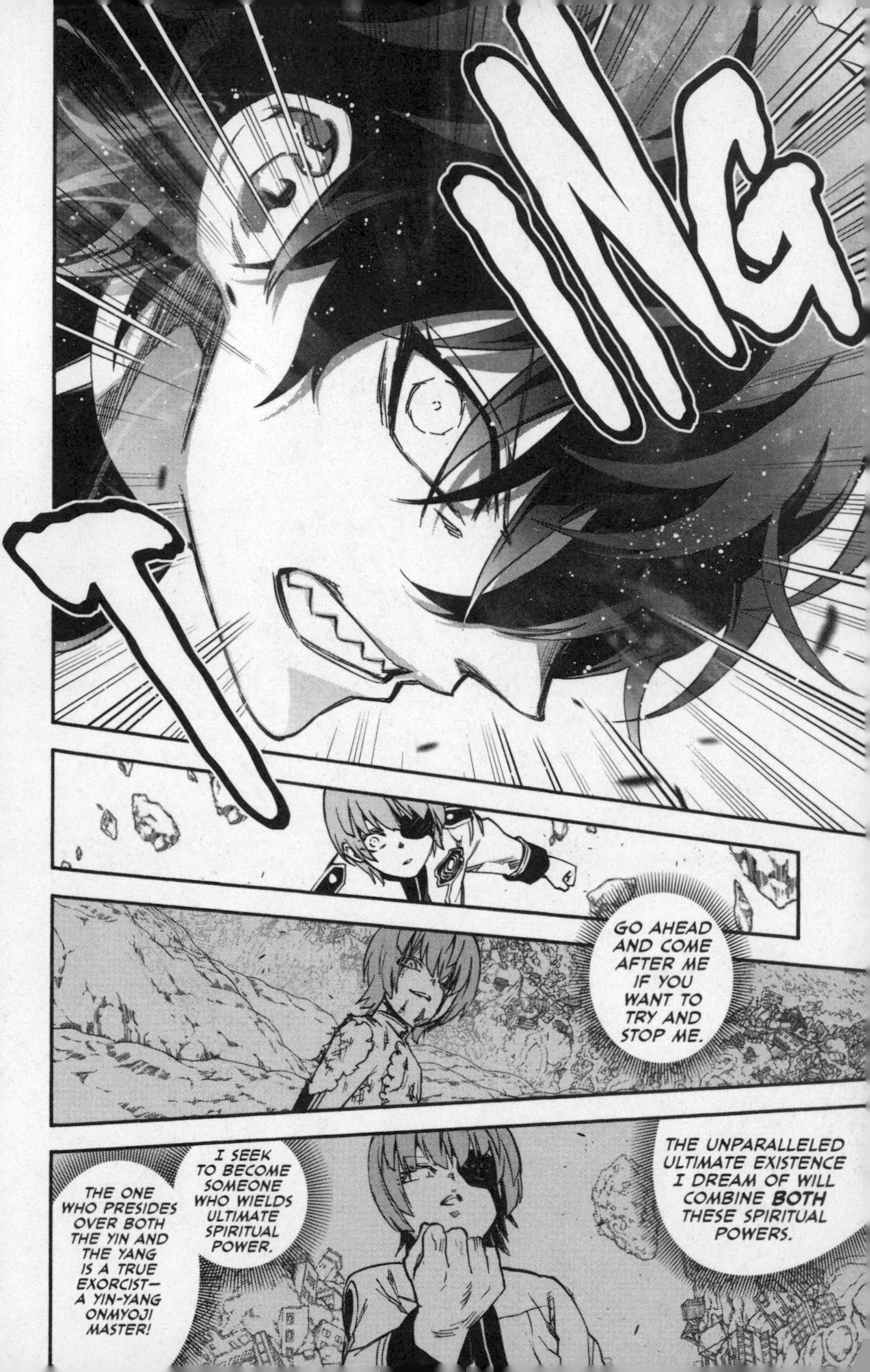
NG
GO AHEAD AND COME AFTER ME IF YOU WANT TO TRY AND STOP ME.
THE UNPARALLELED ULTIMATE EXISTENCE I DREAM OF WILL COMBINE **BOTH** THESE SPIRITUAL POWERS.
I SEEK TO BECOME SOMEONE WHO WIELDS ULTIMATE SPIRITUAL POWER.
THE ONE WHO PRESIDES OVER BOTH THE YIN AND THE YANG IS A TRUE EXORCIST— A YIN-YANG ONMYOJI MASTER!

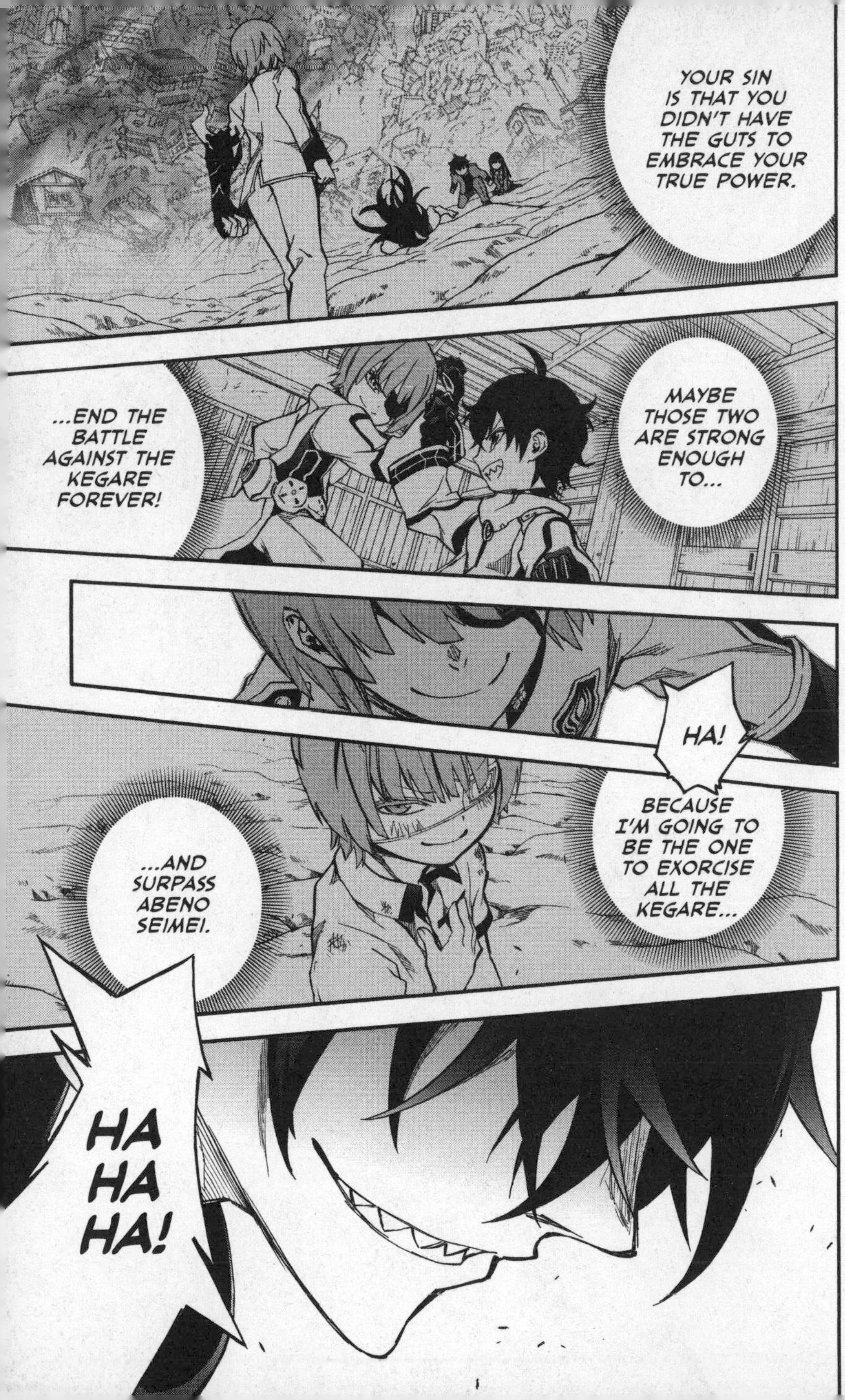
YOUR SIN IS THAT YOU DIDN'T HAVE THE GUTS TO EMBRACE YOUR TRUE POWER.
MAYBE THOSE TWO ARE STRONG ENOUGH TO...
...END THE BATTLE AGAINST THE KEGARE FOREVER!
HA!
BECAUSE I'M GOING TO BE THE ONE TO EXORCISE ALL THE KEGARE...
...AND SURPASS ABENO SEIMEI.
HA HA HA HA!

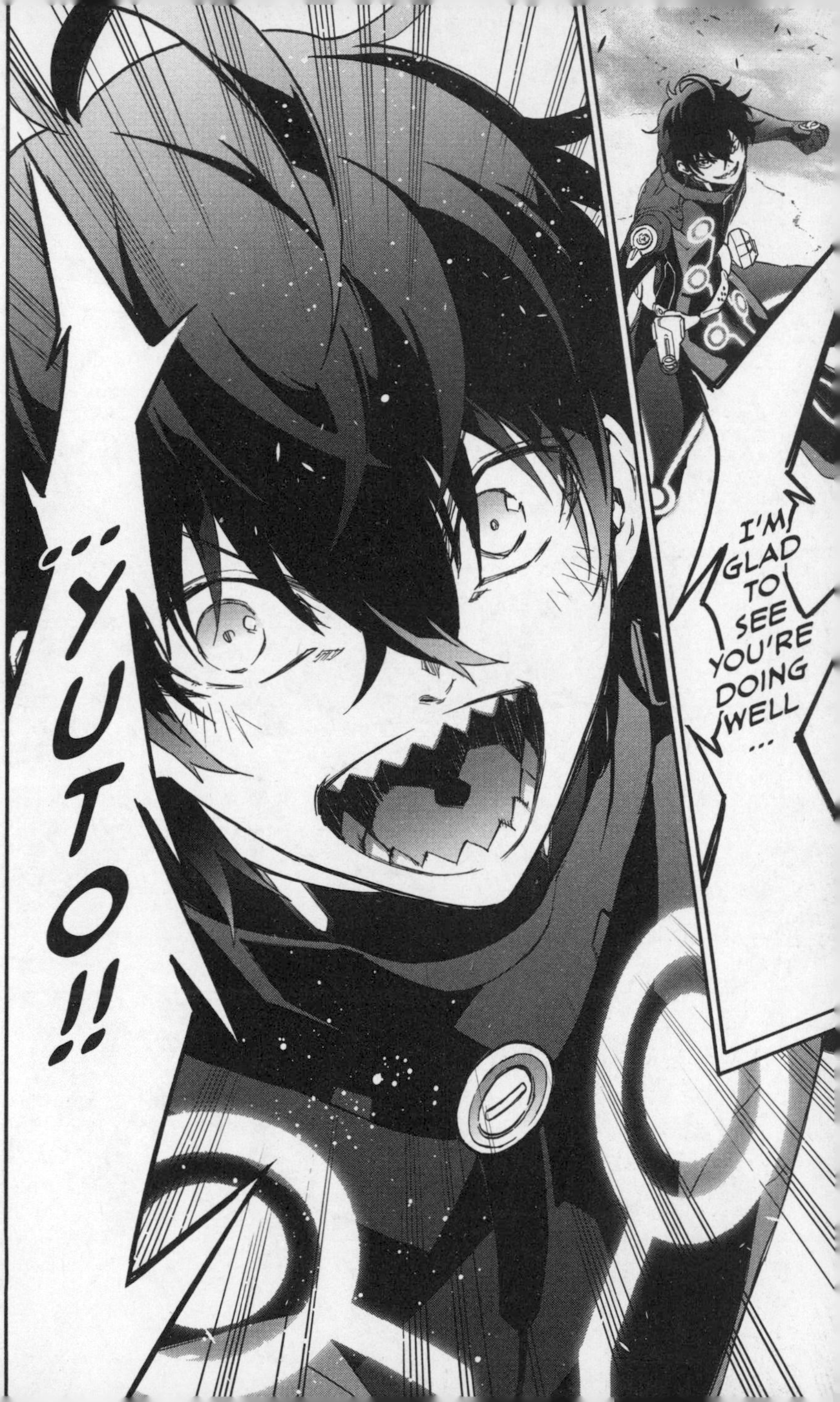
I'M GLAD TO SEE YOU'RE DOING WELL...
...YUTO!!

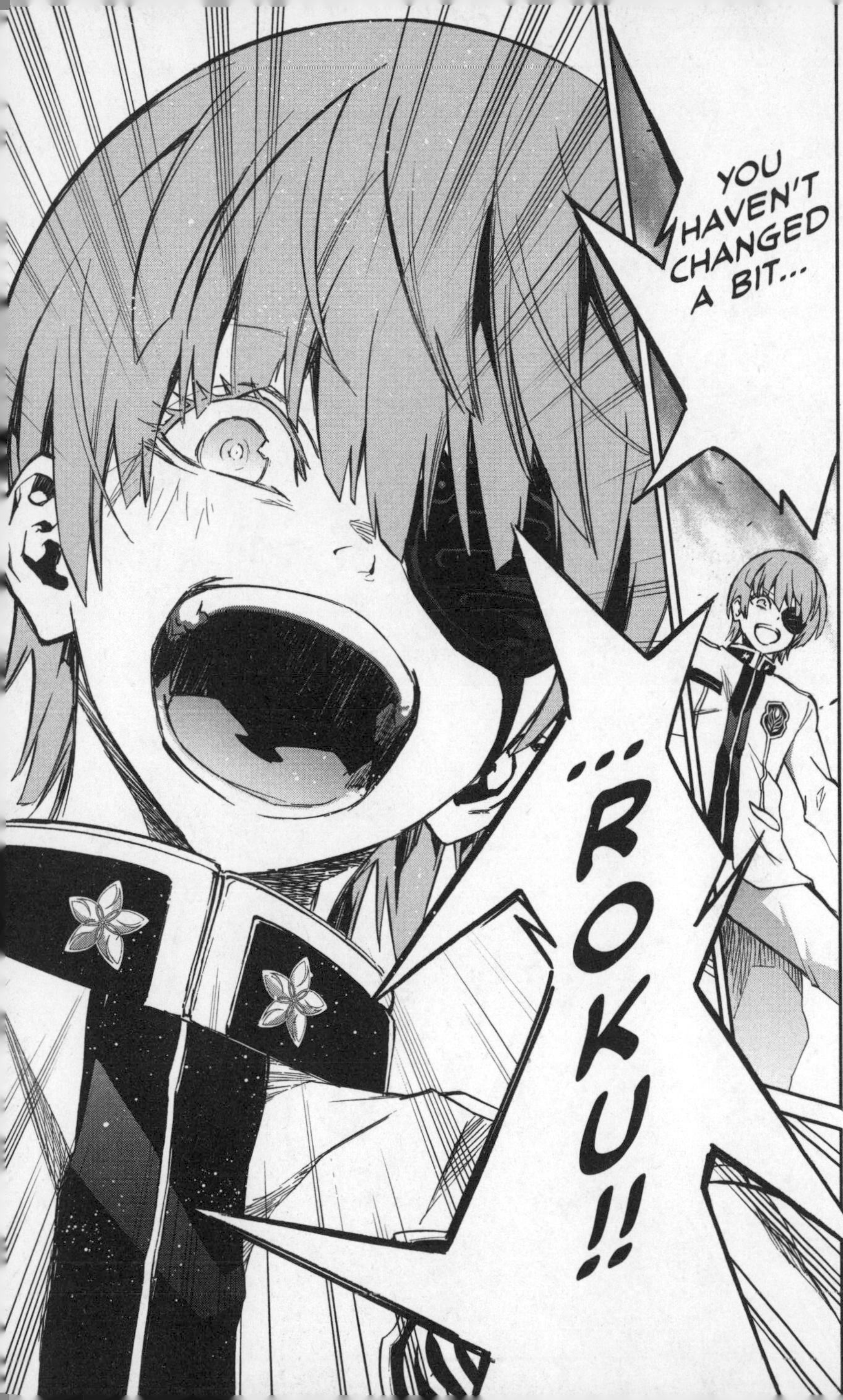
YOU HAVEN'T CHANGED A BIT...
...ROKU!!

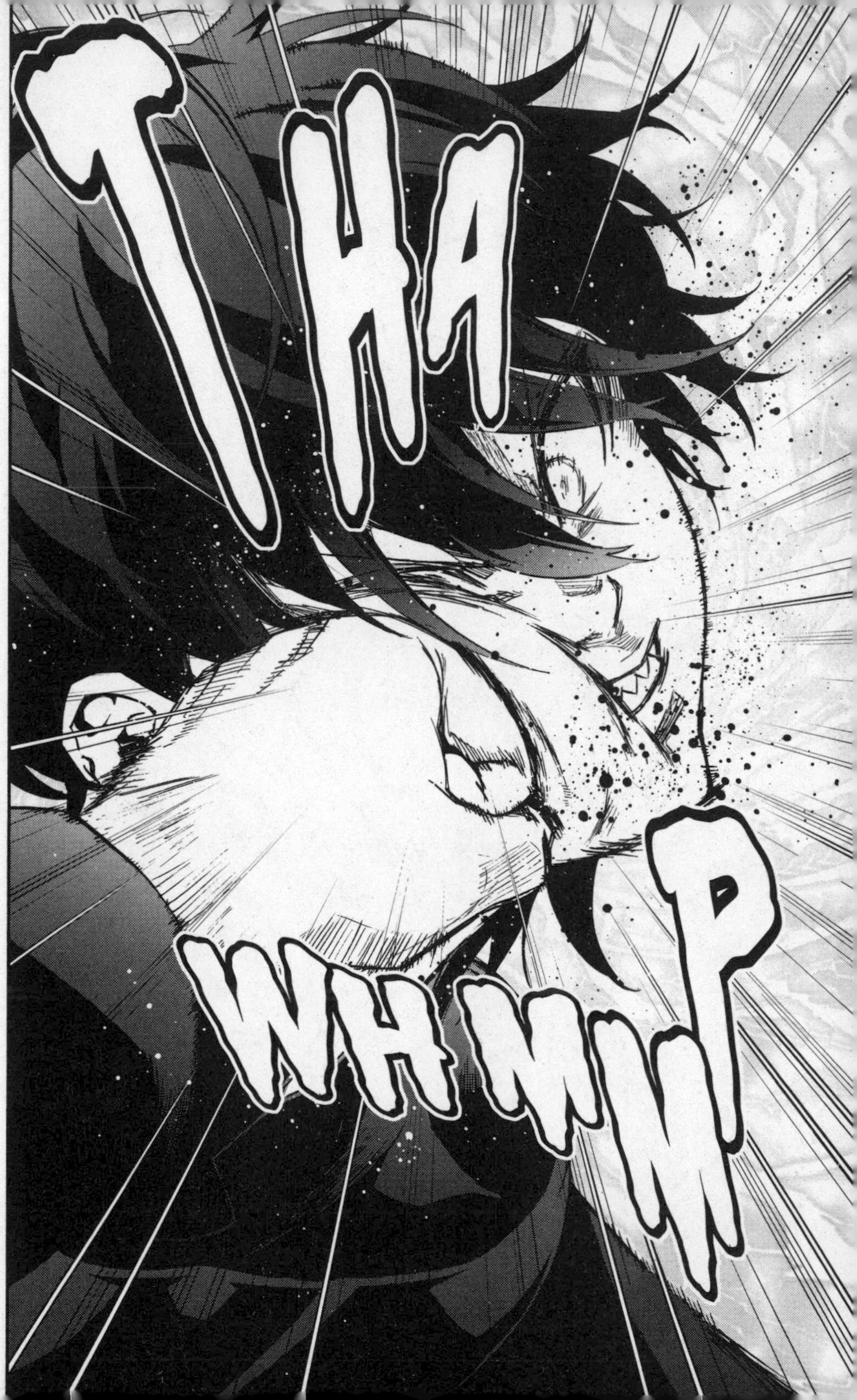
THWHAMP

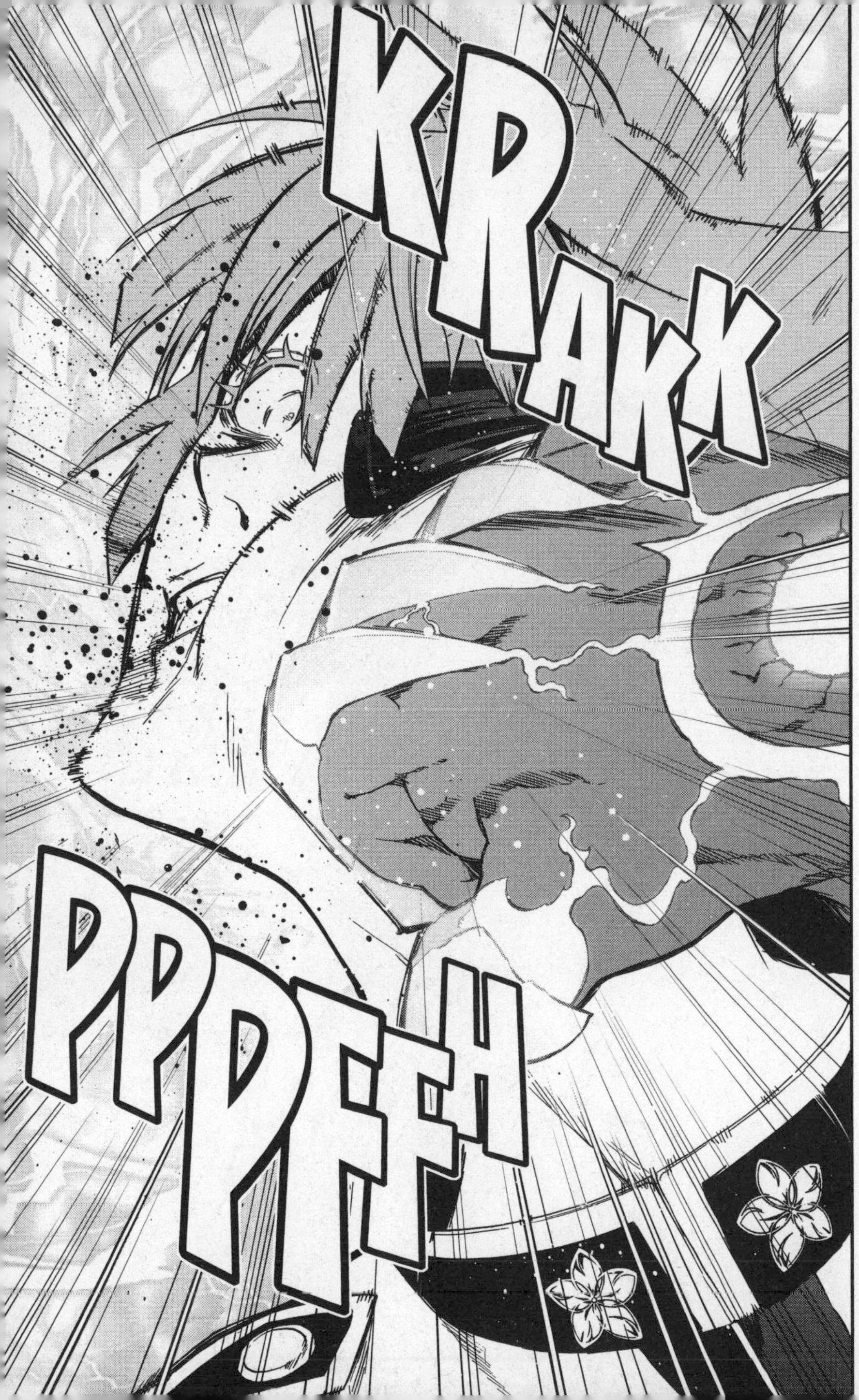
KRAKK
PPFFH

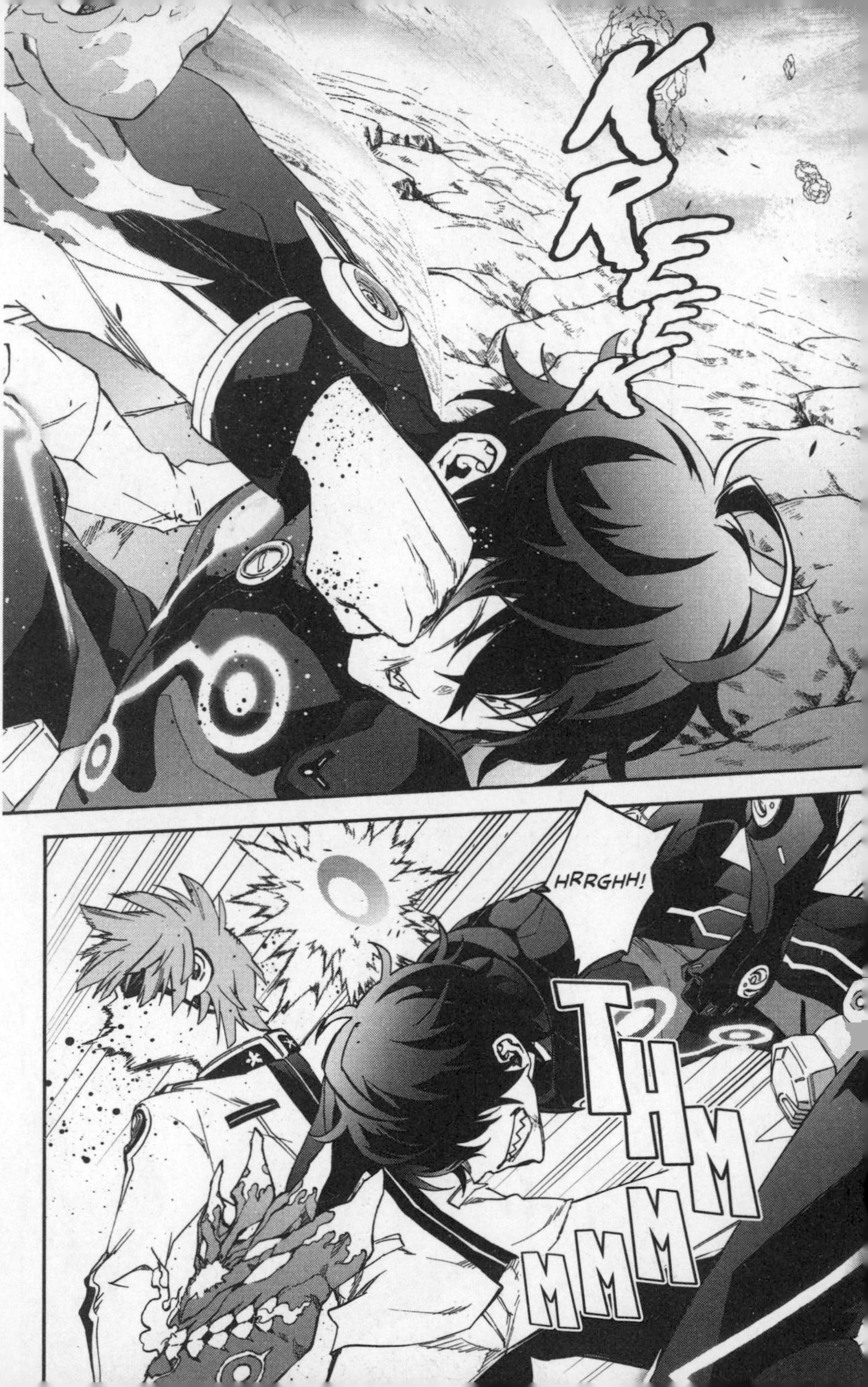
KREEK
HRRGHH!
THMMMMM

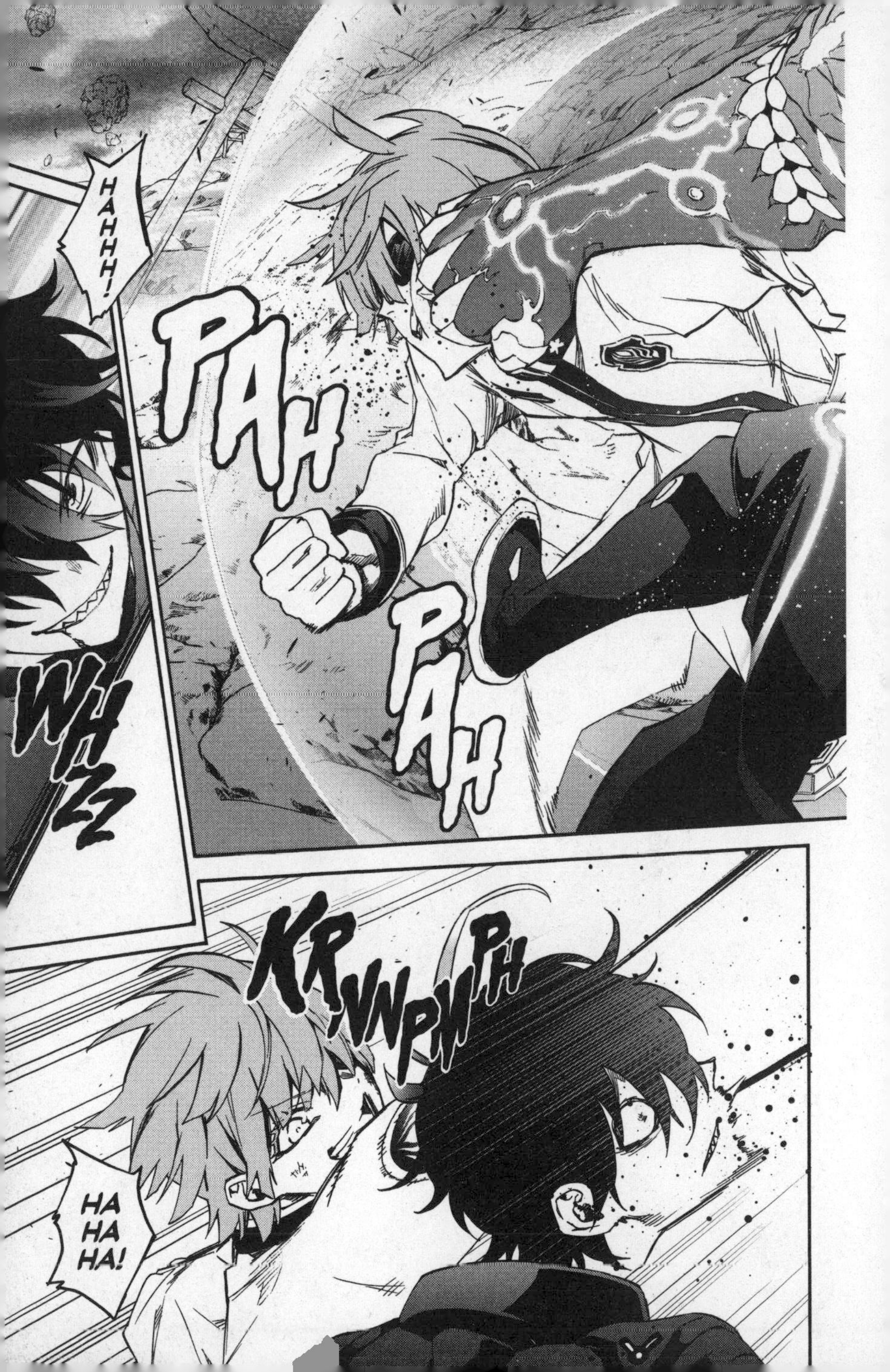
PAH
PAH
HAHHH!
WHZZ
KRNNPWPH
HA HA HA!

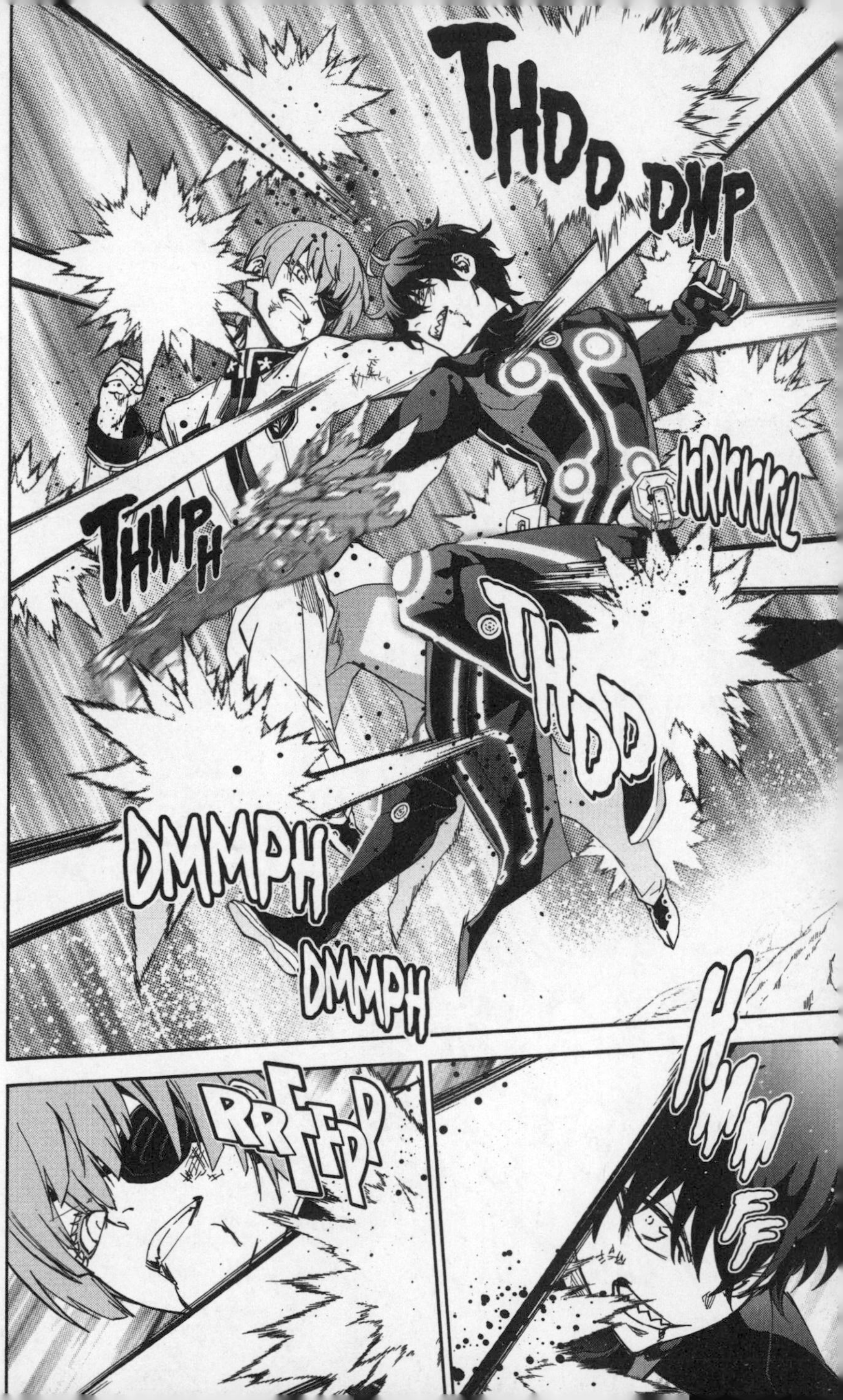
THDD DMP
KRKKKL
THMPH
THDD
DMMPH
DMMPH
HMMMFF
RRFEDP

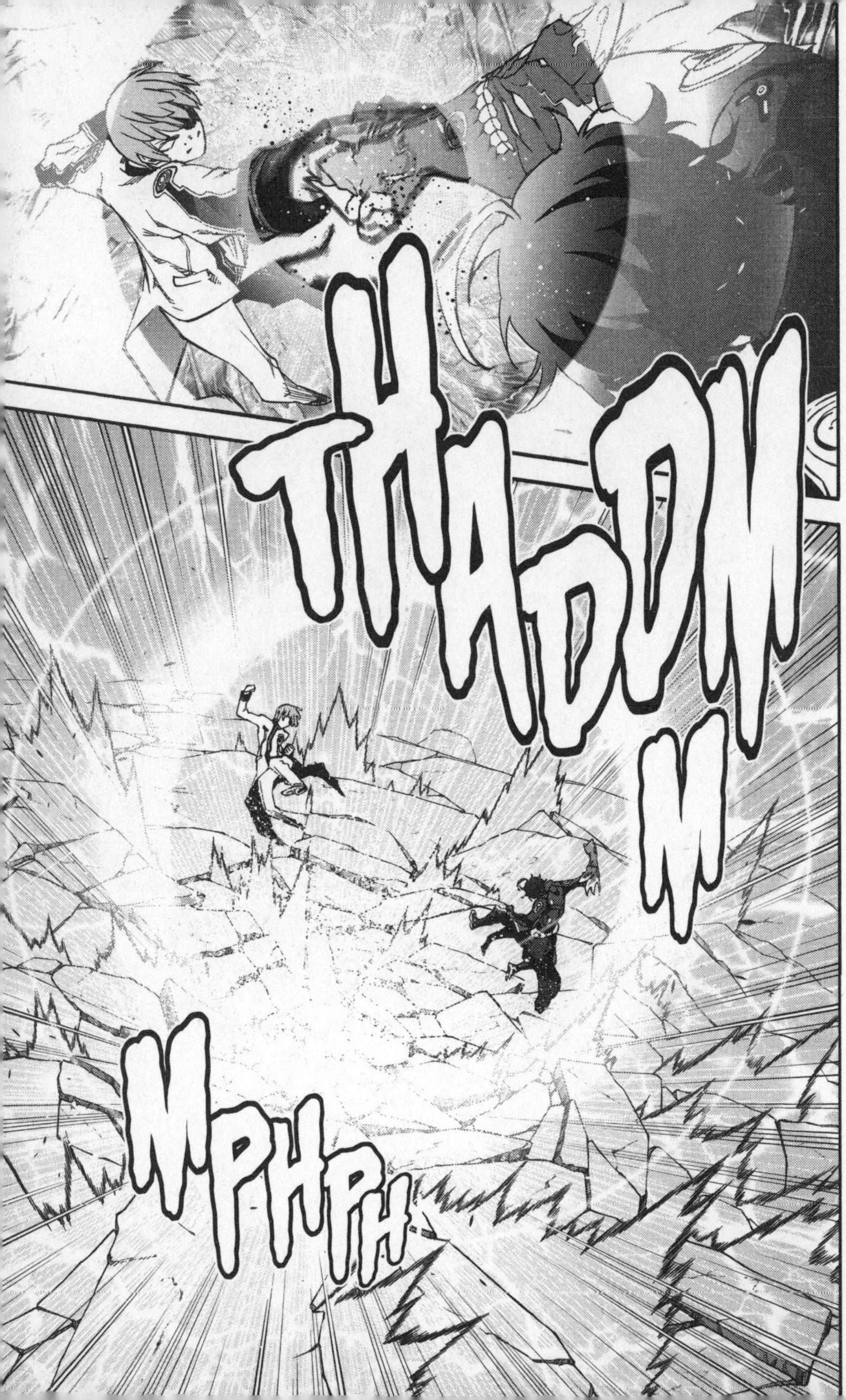
THADOMM
MPHPH

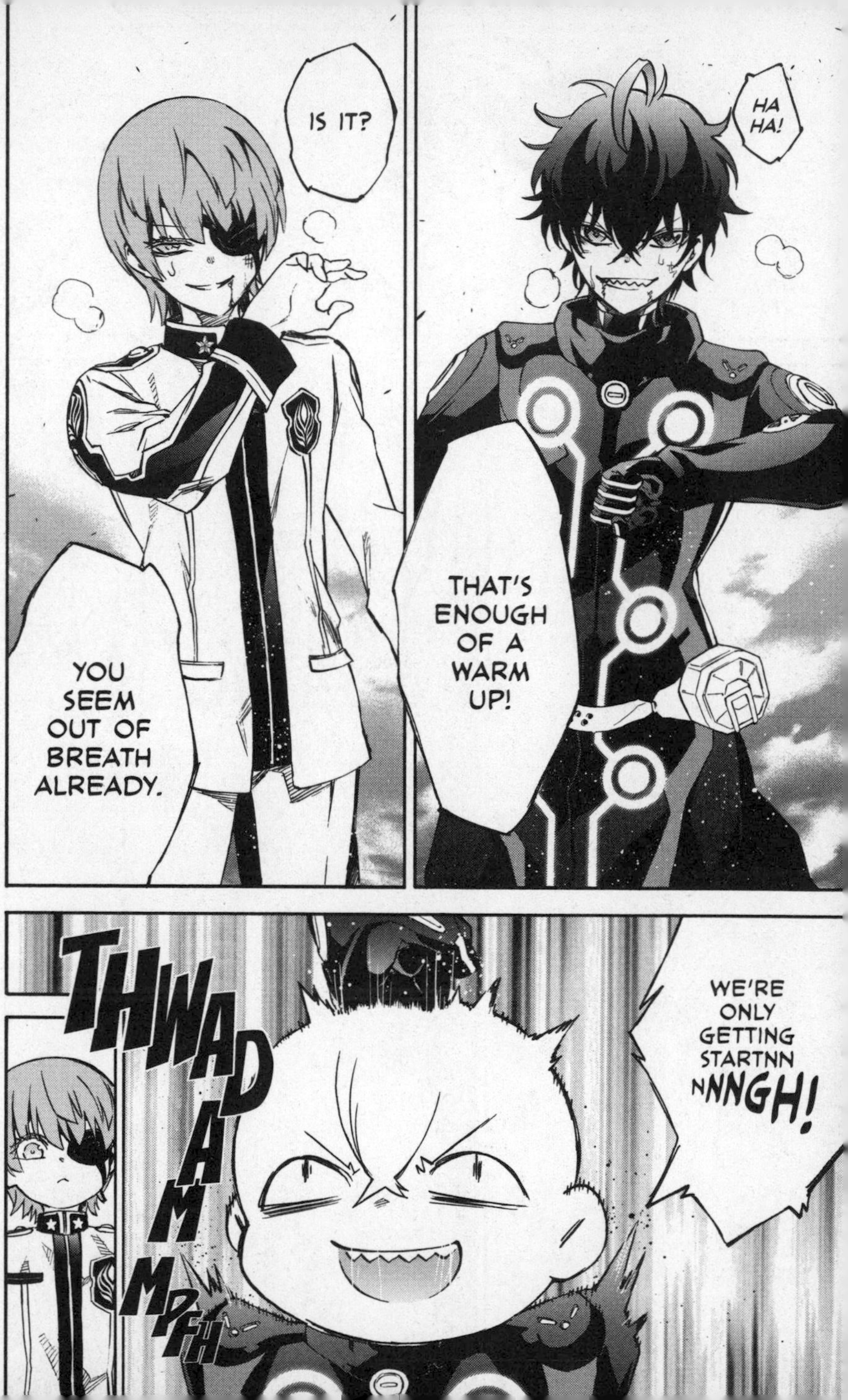
HA HA!
THAT'S ENOUGH OF A WARM UP!
IS IT?
YOU SEEM OUT OF BREATH ALREADY.
WE'RE ONLY GETTING STARTNN NNNGH!
THWADAMMMPFH

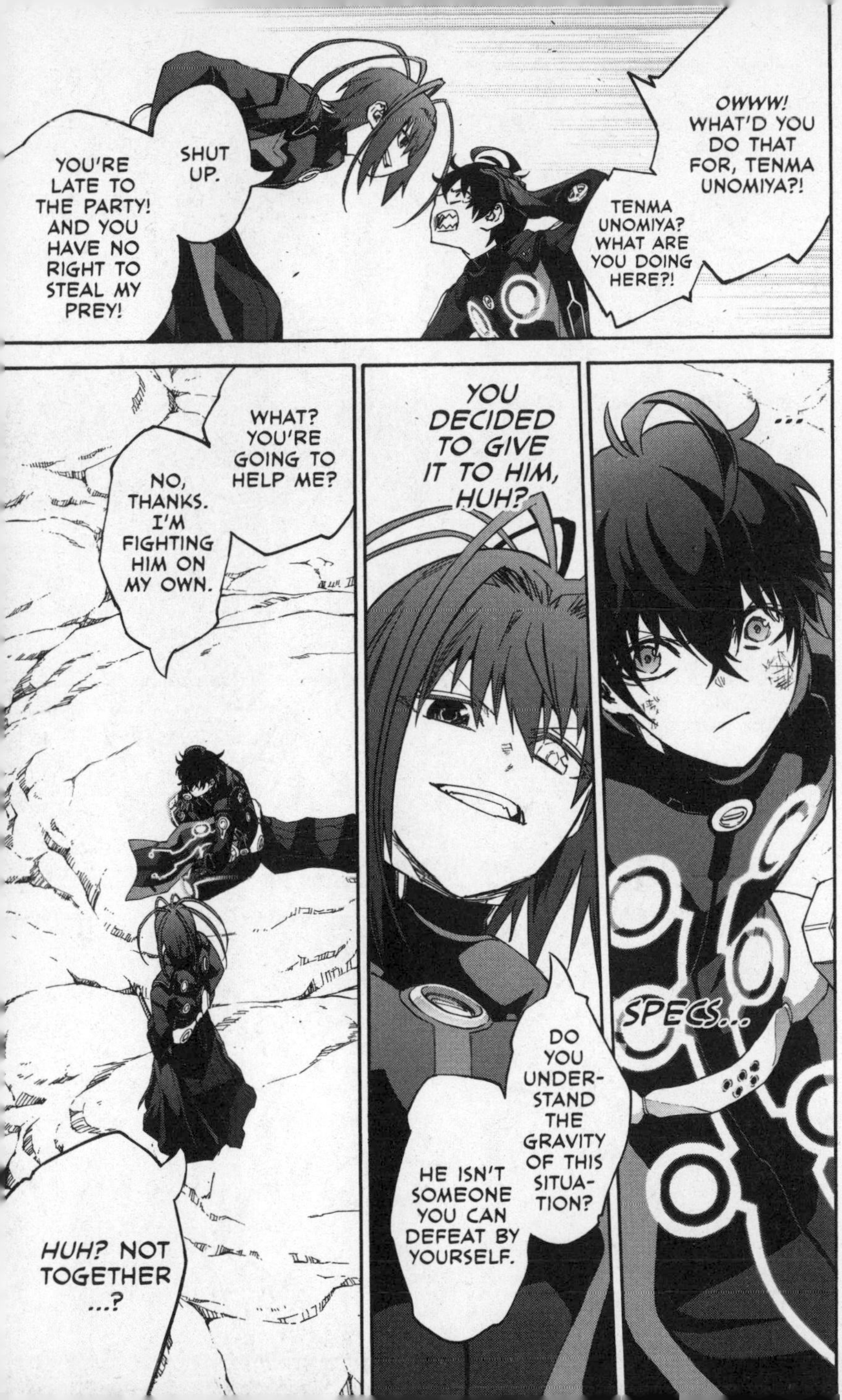

OWWW! WHAT'D YOU DO THAT FOR, TENMA UNOMIYA?!
TENMA UNOMIYA? WHAT ARE YOU DOING HERE?!
SHUT UP.
YOU'RE LATE TO THE PARTY! AND YOU HAVE NO RIGHT TO STEAL MY PREY!
...
SPECS...
YOU DECIDED TO GIVE IT TO HIM, HUH?
DO YOU UNDER-STAND THE GRAVITY OF THIS SITUA-TION?
HE ISN'T SOMEONE YOU CAN DEFEAT BY YOURSELF.
WHAT? YOU'RE GOING TO HELP ME?
NO, THANKS. I'M FIGHTING HIM ON MY OWN.
HUH? NOT TOGETHER ...?

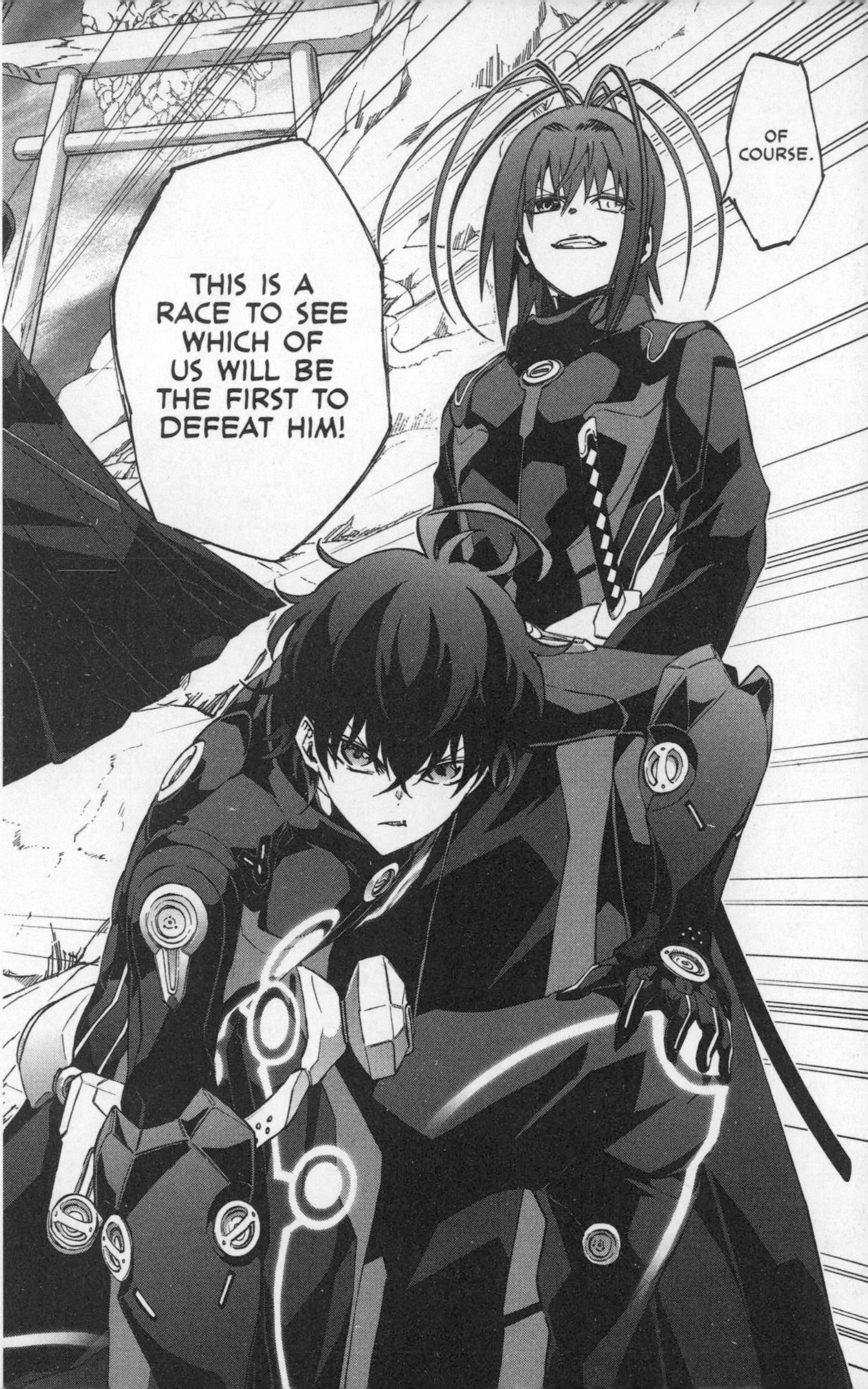
OF COURSE.
THIS IS A RACE TO SEE WHICH OF US WILL BE THE FIRST TO DEFEAT HIM!

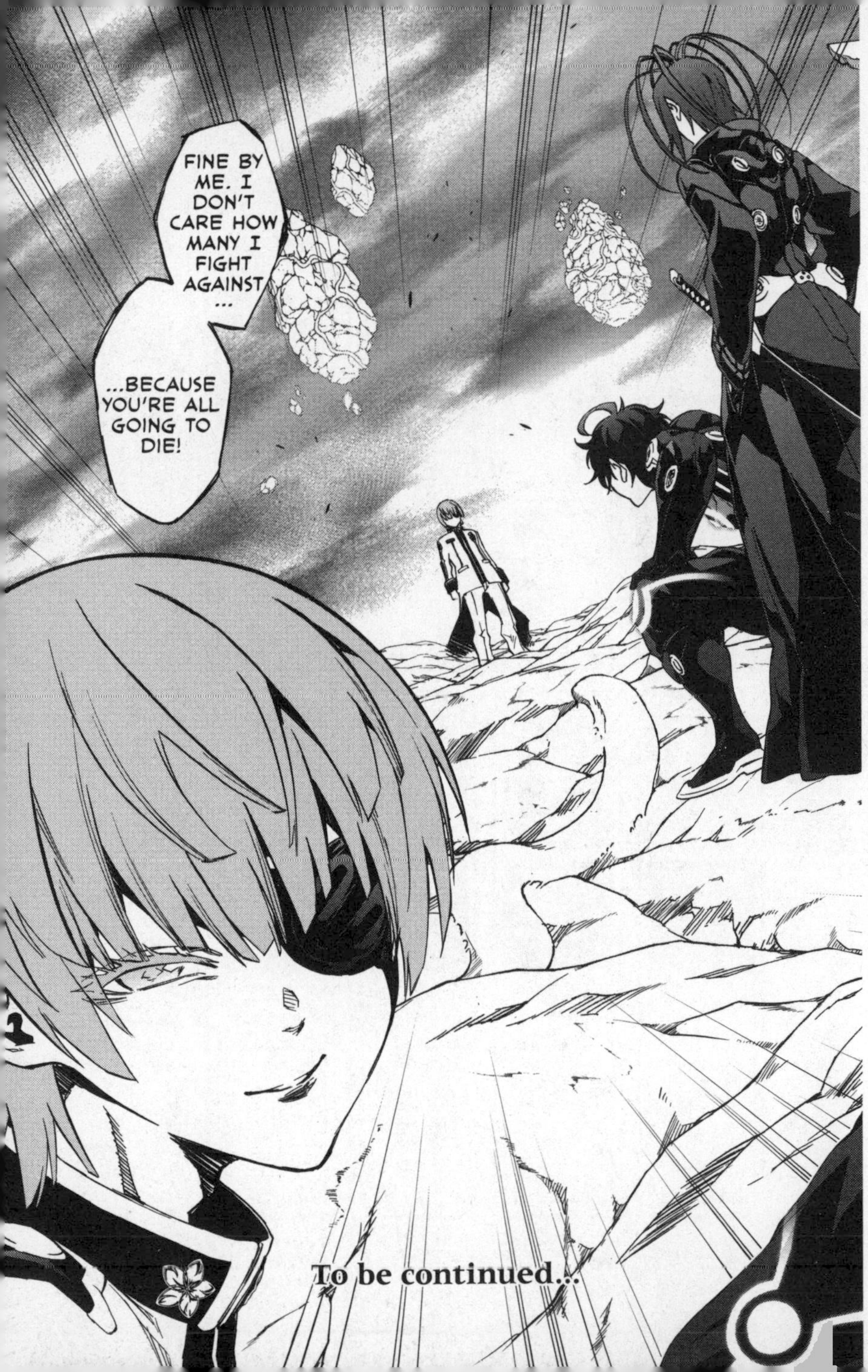
FINE BY ME. I DON'T CARE HOW MANY I FIGHT AGAINST...
...BECAUSE YOU'RE ALL GOING TO DIE!
To be continued...

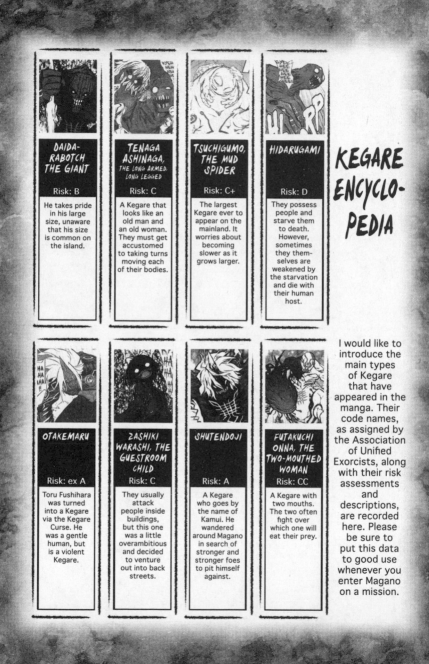

KEGARE ENCYCLOPEDIA

I would like to introduce the main types of Kegare that have appeared in the manga. Their code names, as assigned by the Association of Unified Exorcists, along with their risk assessments and descriptions, are recorded here. Please be sure to put this data to good use whenever you enter Magano on a mission.

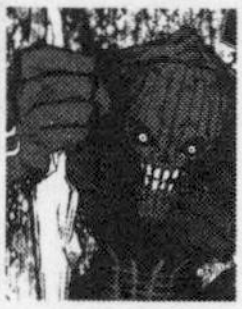

DAIDARABOTCH THE GIANT

Risk: B

He takes pride in his large size, unaware that his size is common on the island.

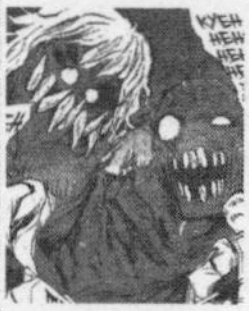

TENAGA ASHINAGA, THE LONG ARMED, LONG LEGGED

Risk: C

A Kegare that looks like an old man and an old woman. They must get accustomed to taking turns moving each of their bodies.

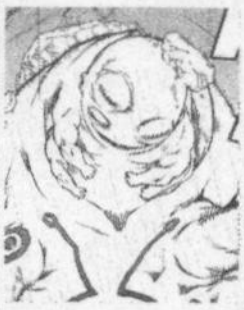

TSUCHIGUMO, THE MUD SPIDER

Risk: C+

The largest Kegare ever to appear on the mainland. It worries about becoming slower as it grows larger.

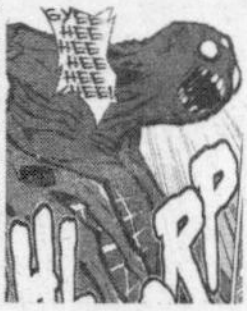

HIDARUGAMI

Risk: D

They possess people and starve them to death. However, sometimes they themselves are weakened by the starvation and die with their human host.

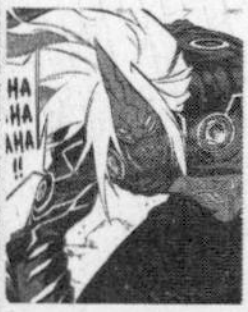

OTAKEMARU

Risk: ex A

Toru Fushihara was turned into a Kegare via the Kegare Curse. He was a gentle human, but is a violent Kegare.

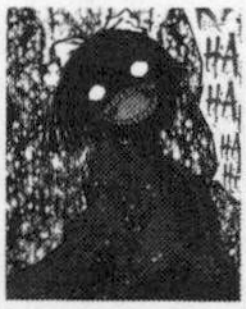

ZASHIKI WARASHI, THE GUESTROOM CHILD

Risk: C

They usually attack people inside buildings, but this one was a little overambitious and decided to venture out into back streets.

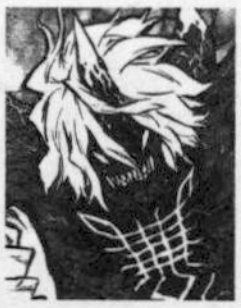

SHUTENDOJI

Risk: A

A Kegare who goes by the name of Kamui. He wandered around Magano in search of stronger and stronger foes to pit himself against.

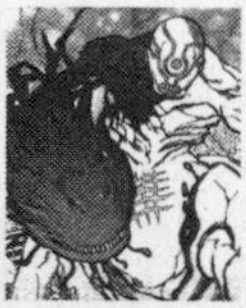

FUTAKUCHI ONNA, THE TWO-MOUTHED WOMAN

Risk: CC

A Kegare with two mouths. The two often fight over which one will eat their prey.

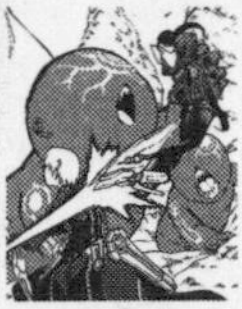

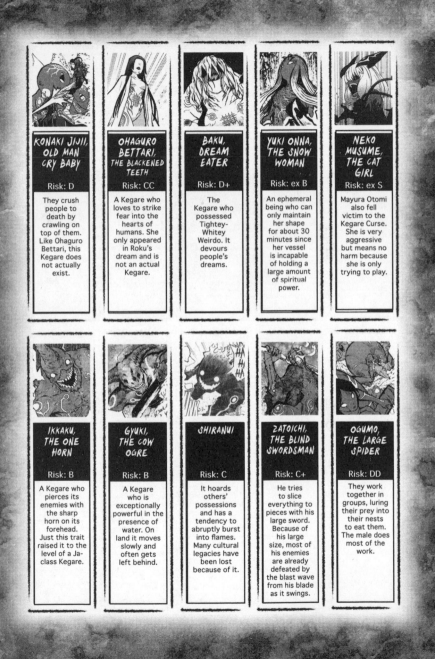

KONAKI JIJII, OLD MAN CRY BABY

Risk: D

They crush people to death by crawling on top of them. Like Ohaguro Bettari, this Kegare does not actually exist.

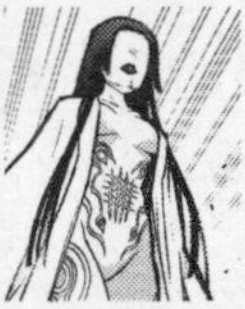

OHAGURO BETTARI, THE BLACKENED TEETH

Risk: CC

A Kegare who loves to strike fear into the hearts of humans. She only appeared in Roku's dream and is not an actual Kegare.

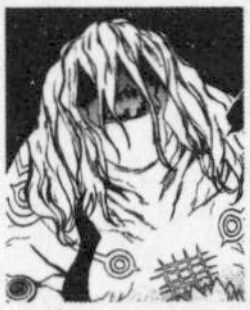

BAKU, DREAM EATER

Risk: D+

The Kegare who possessed Tightey-Whitey Weirdo. It devours people's dreams.

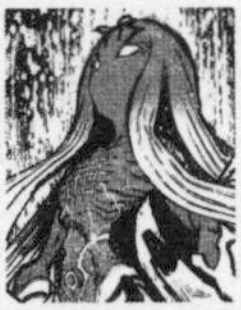

YUKI ONNA, THE SNOW WOMAN

Risk: ex B

An ephemeral being who can only maintain her shape for about 30 minutes since her vessel is incapable of holding a large amount of spiritual power.

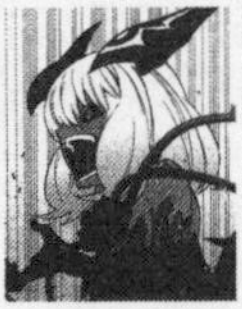

NEKO MUSUME, THE CAT GIRL

Risk: ex S

Mayura Otomi also fell victim to the Kegare Curse. She is very aggressive but means no harm because she is only trying to play.

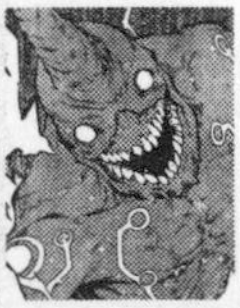

IKKAKU, THE ONE HORN

Risk: B

A Kegare who pierces its enemies with the sharp horn on its forehead. Just this trait raised it to the level of a Ja-class Kegare.

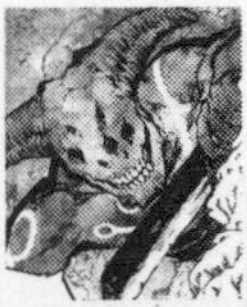

GYUKI, THE COW OGRE

Risk: B

A Kegare who is exceptionally powerful in the presence of water. On land it moves slowly and often gets left behind.

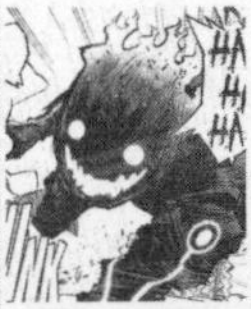
HA
HA
HA
HA

SHIRANUI

Risk: C

It hoards others' possessions and has a tendency to abruptly burst into flames. Many cultural legacies have been lost because of it.

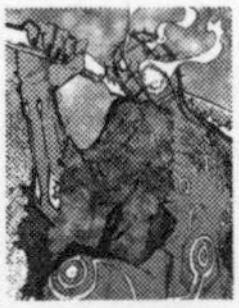

ZATOICHI, THE BLIND SWORDSMAN

Risk: C+

He tries to slice everything to pieces with his large sword. Because of his large size, most of his enemies are already defeated by the blast wave from his blade as it swings.

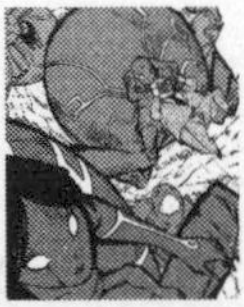

OGUMO, THE LARGE SPIDER

Risk: DD

They work together in groups, luring their prey into their nests to eat them. The male does most of the work.

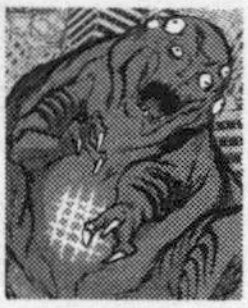

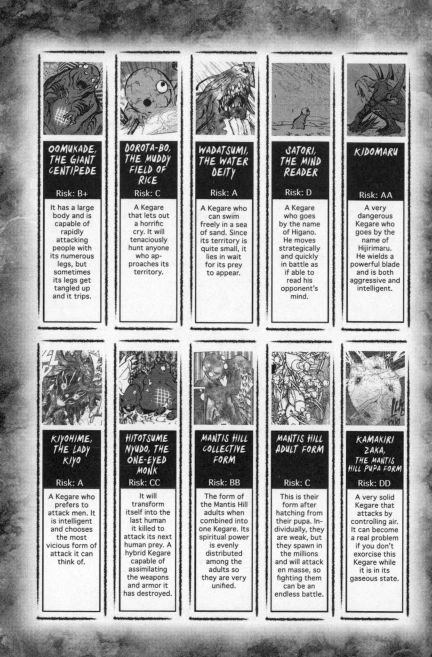

OOMUKADE, THE GIANT CENTIPEDE

Risk: B+

It has a large body and is capable of rapidly attacking people with its numerous legs, but sometimes its legs get tangled up and it trips.

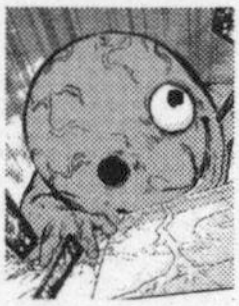

DOROTA-BO, THE MUDDY FIELD OF RICE

Risk: C

A Kegare that lets out a horrific cry. It will tenaciously hunt anyone who approaches its territory.

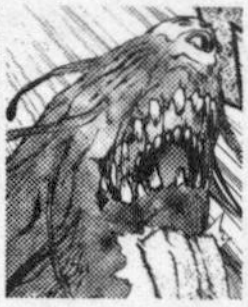

WADATSUMI, THE WATER DEITY

Risk: A

A Kegare who can swim freely in a sea of sand. Since its territory is quite small, it lies in wait for its prey to appear.

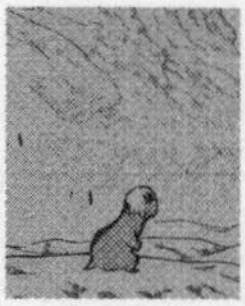

SATORI, THE MIND READER

Risk: D

A Kegare who goes by the name of Higano. He moves strategically and quickly in battle as if able to read his opponent's mind.

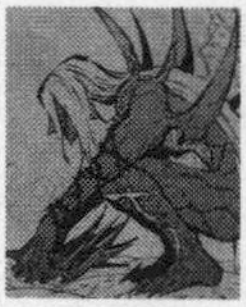

KIDOMARU

Risk: AA

A very dangerous Kegare who goes by the name of Hijirimaru. He wields a powerful blade and is both aggressive and intelligent.

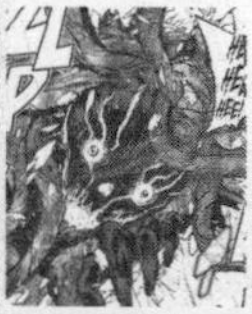

KIYOHIME, THE LADY KIYO

Risk: A

A Kegare who prefers to attack men. It is intelligent and chooses the most vicious form of attack it can think of.

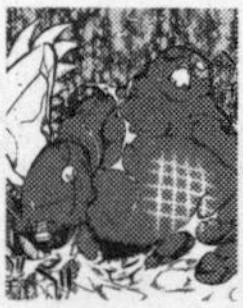

HITOTSUME NYUDO, THE ONE-EYED MONK

Risk: CC

It will transform itself into the last human it killed to attack its next human prey. A hybrid Kegare capable of assimilating the weapons and armor it has destroyed.

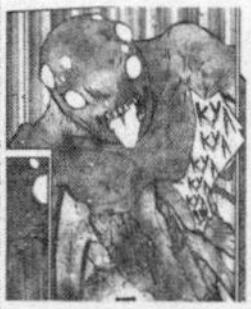

MANTIS HILL COLLECTIVE FORM

Risk: BB

The form of the Mantis Hill adults when combined into one Kegare. Its spiritual power is evenly distributed among the adults so they are very unified.

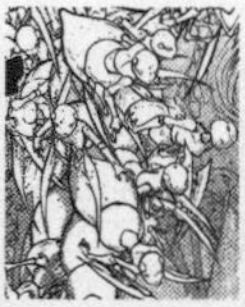

MANTIS HILL ADULT FORM

Risk: C

This is their form after hatching from their pupa. Individually, they are weak, but they spawn in the millions and will attack en masse, so fighting them can be an endless battle.

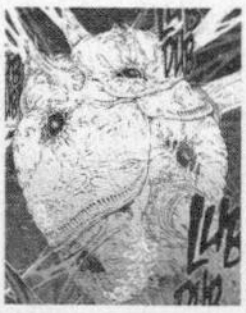

KAMAKIRI ZAKA, THE MANTIS HILL PUPA FORM

Risk: DD

A very solid Kegare that attacks by controlling air. It can become a real problem if you don't exorcise this Kegare while it is in its gaseous state.

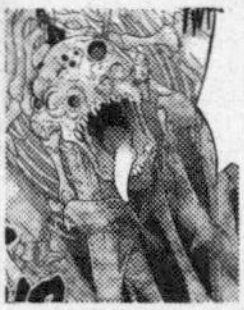

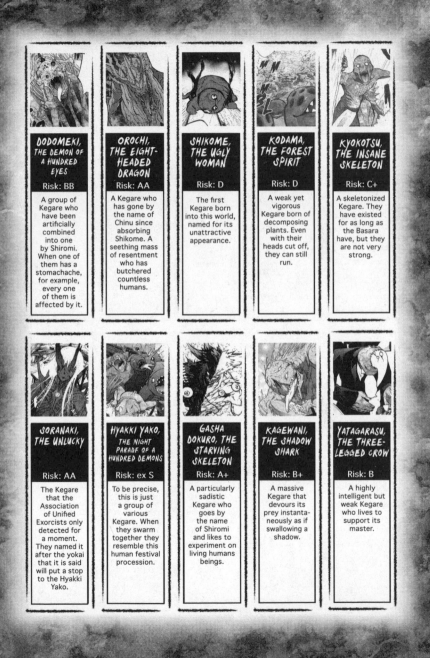

DODOMEKI, THE DEMON OF A HUNDRED EYES

Risk: BB

A group of Kegare who have been artificially combined into one by Shiromi. When one of them has a stomachache, for example, every one of them is affected by it.

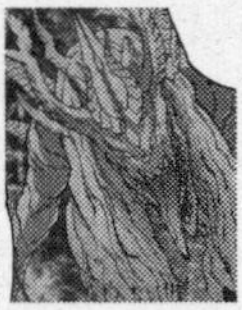

OROCHI, THE EIGHT-HEADED DRAGON

Risk: AA

A Kegare who has gone by the name of Chinu since absorbing Shikome. A seething mass of resentment who has butchered countless humans.

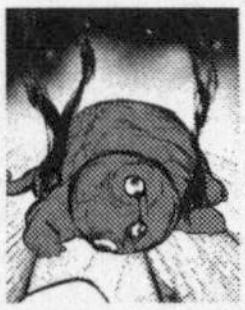

SHIKOME, THE UGLY WOMAN

Risk: D

The first Kegare born into this world, named for its unattractive appearance.

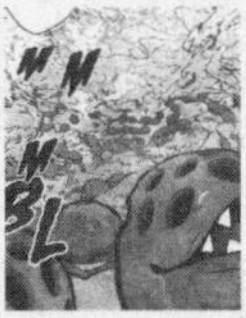

KODAMA, THE FOREST SPIRIT

Risk: D

A weak yet vigorous Kegare born of decomposing plants. Even with their heads cut off, they can still run.

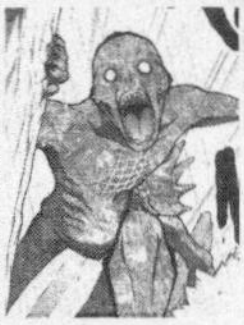

KYOKOTSU, THE INSANE SKELETON

Risk: C+

A skeletonized Kegare. They have existed for as long as the Basara have, but they are not very strong.

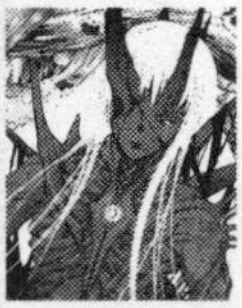

SORANAKI, THE UNLUCKY

Risk: AA

The Kegare that the Association of Unified Exorcists only detected for a moment. They named it after the yokai that it is said will put a stop to the Hyakki Yako.

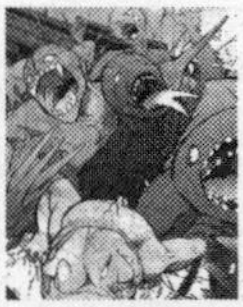

HYAKKI YAKO, THE NIGHT PARADE OF A HUNDRED DEMONS

Risk: ex S

To be precise, this is just a group of various Kegare. When they swarm together they resemble this human festival procession.

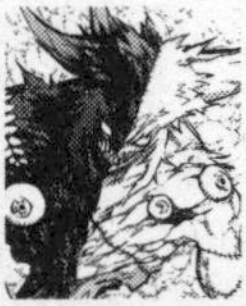

GASHA DOKURO, THE STARVING SKELETON

Risk: A+

A particularly sadistic Kegare who goes by the name of Shiromi and likes to experiment on living humans beings.

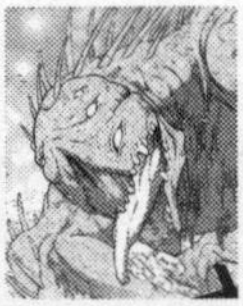

KAGEWANI, THE SHADOW SHARK

Risk: B+

A massive Kegare that devours its prey instantaneously as if swallowing a shadow.

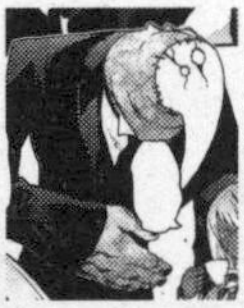

YATAGARASU, THE THREE-LEGGED CROW

Risk: B

A highly intelligent but weak Kegare who lives to support its master.

Hm...

I've moved out of the space I've been using
as my studio for the past six years. It was the
place where I completed *Binbougami ga!* and
began working on *Twin Star Exorcists*, so it's been
a very emotional experience for me... Now I'm
excited to see what new work will be created
in my new studio! However, it's on the fifth floor
of a five-story building with no elevator...!

...Arima. Well done...

YOSHIAKI SUKENO was born July 23, 1981, in Wakayama, Japan.
He graduated from Kyoto Seika University, where he studied manga.
In 2006, he won the Tezuka Award for Best Newcomer Shonen Manga
Artist. In 2008, he began his previous work, the supernatural comedy
Binbougami ga!, which was adapted into the anime *Good Luck Girl!* in 2012.

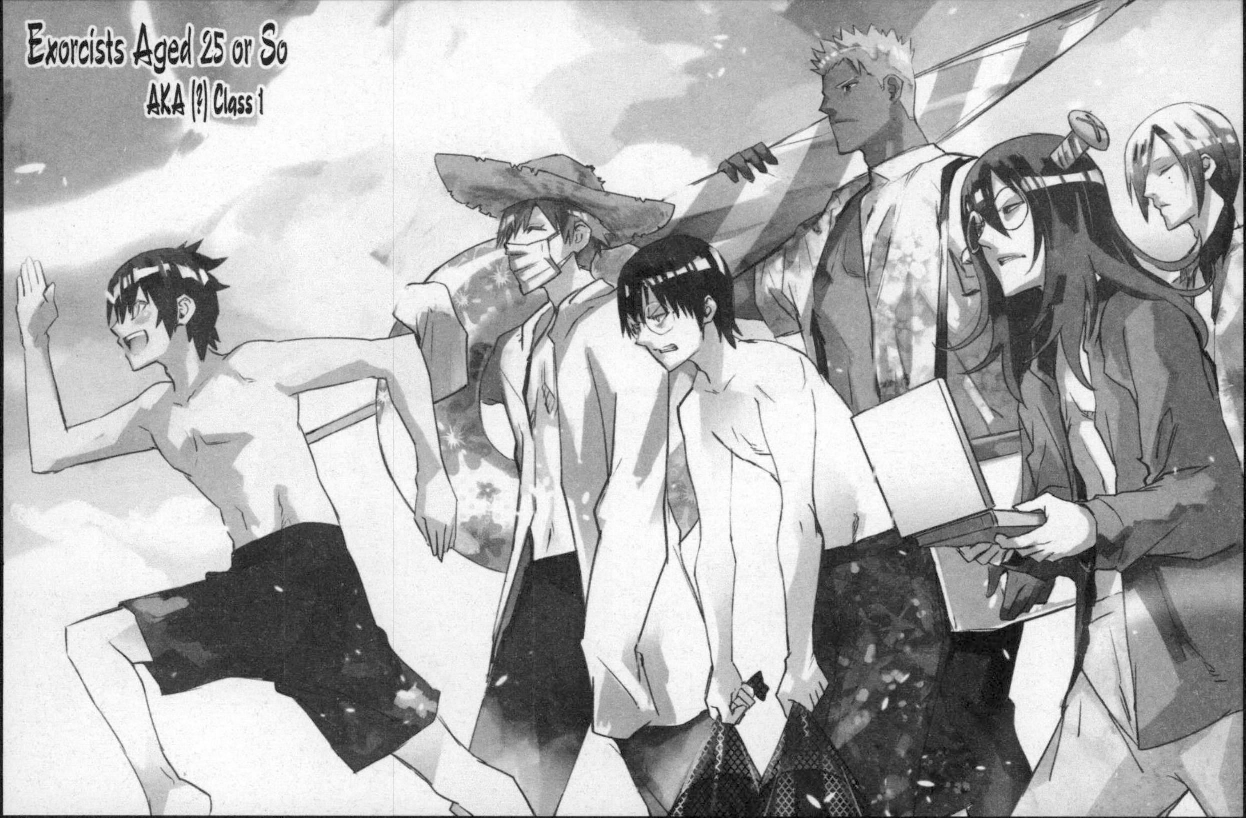
Exorcists Aged 25 or So
AKA [?] Class 1

Hall of Eternity
Operators

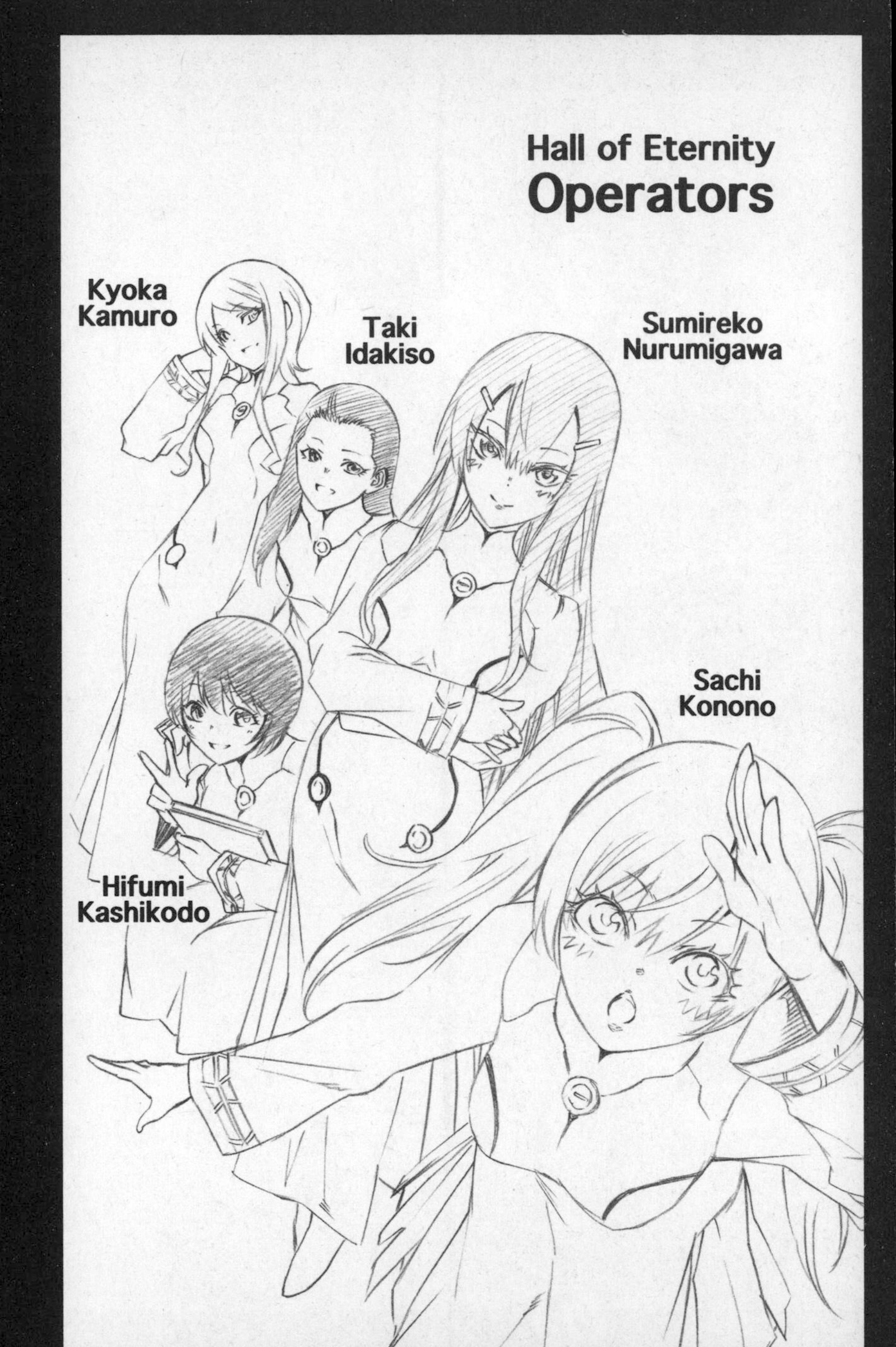

Kyoka Kamuro
Taki Idakiso
Sumireko Nurumigawa
Sachi Konono
Hifumi Kashikodo

Twin Star Exorcists
ONMYOJI

—SHONEN JUMP Manga Edition—

STORY & ART **Yoshiaki Sukeno**

TRANSLATION **Tetsuichiro Miyaki**
ENGLISH ADAPTATION **Bryant Turnage**
TOUCH-UP ART & LETTERING **Stephen Dutro**
DESIGN **Shawn Carrico**
EDITOR **Annette Roman**

SOUSEI NO ONMYOJI © 2013 by Yoshiaki Sukeno
All rights reserved.
First published in Japan in 2013 by SHUEISHA Inc., Tokyo.
English translation rights arranged by SHUEISHA Inc.

Printed in the U.S.A.

Published by VIZ Media, LLC
P.O. Box 77010
San Francisco, CA 94107

10 9 8 7 6 5 4 3 2 1
First printing, May 2020

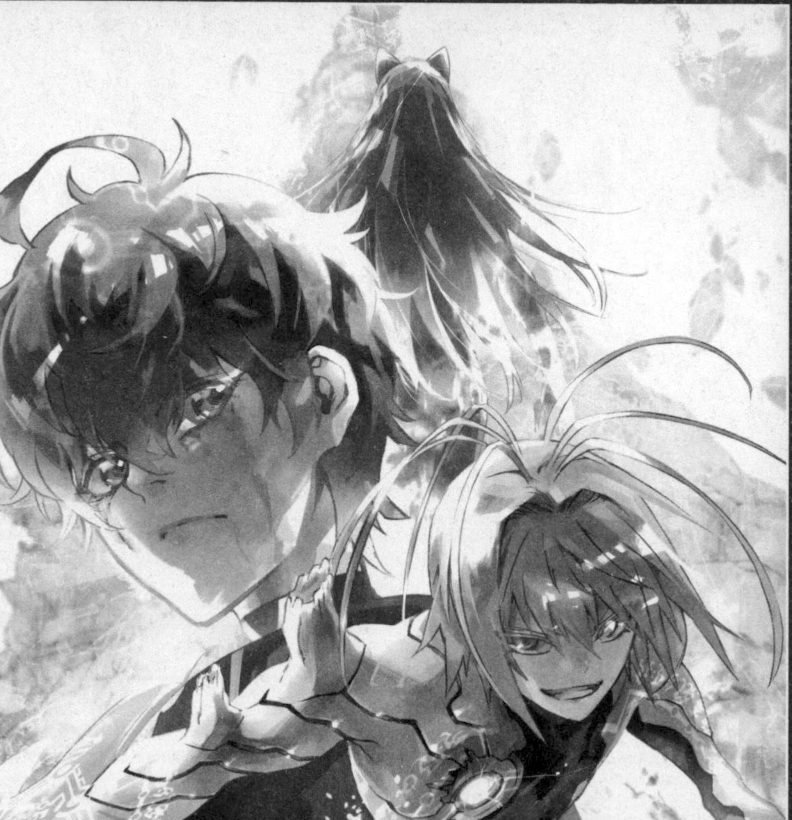
The battle against Yuto rages on, but without Benio, Rokuro can't access the power of the Twin Stars. Or can someone replace her...? Then, the ominous reason Yuto became a Kegare is revealed...
VOLUME 19

Twin Star Exorcists
ONMYOJI

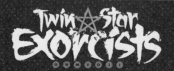

DEMON SLAYER
KIMETSU NO YAIBA

Story and Art by
KOYOHARU GOTOUGE

In Taisho-era Japan, kindhearted Tanjiro Kamado makes a living selling charcoal. But his peaceful life is shattered when a demon slaughters his entire family. His little sister Nezuko is the only survivor, but she has been transformed into a demon herself! Tanjiro sets out on a dangerous journey to find a way to return his sister to normal and destroy the demon who ruined his life.

YOU'RE READING THE **WRONG WAY!**

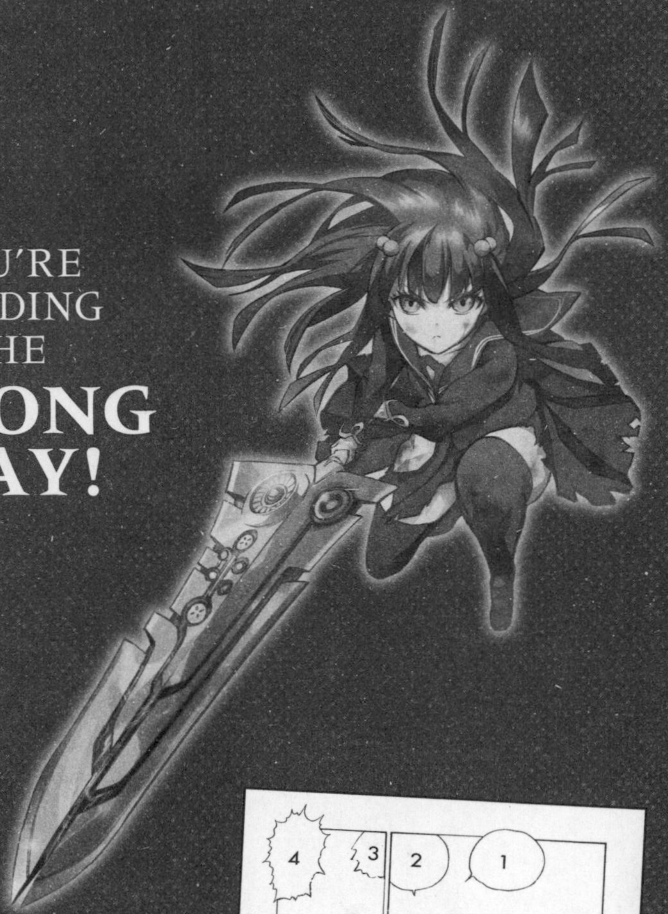

Twin Star Exorcists reads from right to left, starting in the upper-right corner. Japanese is read from right to left, meaning that action, sound effects and word-balloon order are completely reversed from English order.

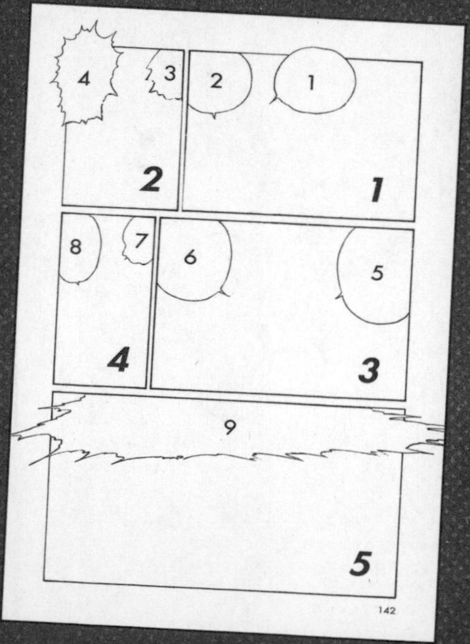

1
2
3
4
1
2
5
6
7
8
3
4
9
5
142